MEMORY, MUSIC,
AND RELIGION

MEMORY, MUSIC, AND RELIGION

MOROCCO'S MYSTICAL CHANTERS

EARLE H. WAUGH

University of South Carolina Press

Published in Columbia, South Carolina, by the
University of South Carolina Press

Manufactured in the United States of America

09 08 07 06 05   5 4 3 2 1

Library of Congress Cataloging-in-Publication Data

Waugh, Earle H., 1936–
    Memory, music, and religion : Morocco's mystical chanters / Earle H. Waugh.
        p. cm. — (Studies in comparative religion)
    Includes bibliographical references and index.
    ISBN 1-57003-567-9 (cloth : alk. paper)
    1. Music—Religious aspects—Islam. 2. Singing—Religious aspects—Islam.
3. Memory—Religious aspects—Islam. 4. Sufism—Morocco. 5. Dervishes—Morocco.
6. Sufism—Rituals. I. Title. II. Studies in comparative religion (Columbia, S.C.)
    BP189.65.M87W38 2005
    297.4'0964—dc22
                                                                2004027073

For Richard, Kimberly, Jane,
Erin, and Rhiannon

The night of the world may be dark . . . yet in this darkness, for your sake, He created the moon to shine.

Hamid ad-din Suwali (d. 1276)

CONTENTS

ILLUSTRATIONS

SERIES EDITOR'S PREFACE

Sufism, Islam's mystical tradition, flourishes in many varieties across the world of Islam and Muslim peoples. And although strongly anti-Sufi sentiments from puritanical Muslim interests have arisen over the past century or so, the Sufi Path, which many Muslims characterize as the "heartbeat" of Islam, persists and provides ways for people to discover and embody profoundly satisfying and enduring spiritual guidance and fulfillment in relation to God and to their ancient, hallowed, and ongoing traditions.

Earle H. Waugh is a leading pioneer in the Western study of Sufi practices of chanting and meditation. His first book on the subject, *The Munshidīn of Egypt: Their World and Their Song,* was published in this series in 1989 and has been a benchmark ever since. The long-awaited subject of this preface provides the results of Waugh's distinctive and distinguished combination of groundbreaking field research and original theoretical discourse in the opposite end of North Africa from Egypt: Morocco.

This book will be of interest not only to scholars of Islam and their students, but to all readers interested in the academic study of religion. That is because Waugh sets forth a theory of religion as remembrance. Branching out from some of the thinking of Mircea Eliade on ritual returns to origins, Waugh writes: "Memory is seen to carry the freight of religious meaning" (186). Unlike Eliade's discourse, Waugh's considers ritual remembrance—in the case of Moroccan mystical chanters in the present day—to be an ongoing, potent system of spiritual awareness, where "the munshid [the chanter] works within a religious ecology with its own coding system" (187). There is something akin to "sacramental" meaning and power in memory, because it makes possible the experiencing of something like a "Real Presence," to borrow from Anglican eucharistic theology. I do not intend to suggest that Christian sacramentalism is privileged to teach us what Moroccan Sufi chanting is really about—far from it. Rather, Waugh's discourse on religious memory and acts of remembrance can help us understand both the Sufi ritual coding system underlying performance of *dhikr* (which means "remembering," after all) and, as master of the kitchen Brother Lawrence declared, "a sense of the Presence of God" wherever such is experienced.

FREDERICK MATHEWSON DENNY

PREFACE

I shudder at the idea of ancient Egyptians. It was in these pyramids that was conceived the idea of Jehovah. Terrible mixture of the cunning and the awful.

Herman Melville, Journals

I remember her as she was lying under the dust,
Yet she came to me just as I used to know her before!
And we became as we used to be, and our time came back to us,
Just as we used to know each other before, and the return is sweeter!

Ibn Ḥazm, Ṭawq (d. 1064)

We are condemned to remember. Even when we wish to forget, or discover that we have forgotten, memory shapes our being. After a career in religious studies, I am now convinced we need other bases for understanding what has been identified as religion, and memory has a particular attraction. This conviction arises both out of my career and out of this study, with its focus on people for whom memory is the means of engaging reality.

This book is about a group of people for whom remembering is *the* ritual of life. They express the view that conscious activating of memory's powers engages us with a reality that is quite beyond our abilities to articulate otherwise. It is the style and content of memory that betrays us, limits us, and finally provides us with meaning, shaping our perceptions of time.

The last century was, in a way, the moment when we lost faith in history, at least public history. Grand schemes purporting to tell us of the world's history have expired, because wars and atrocities happened that bore no relationship to our perceived, public history. Quite simply, we could not account for the diversity by positing a grand history.

For a history is never content with the obvious connections and mundane reasons; it pushes increasingly to the exotic and unknown as the taproot of what has occurred. In a certain sense, the incorporation of archaic peoples and so-called primitive civilizations into the Western mode of writing history ended the ability to control the data and, therefore, the outcome in depicting human development, for those peoples lived in such different circumstances and responded to such variegated stimuli that we could scarcely imagine the worlds they inhabited. The effort to universalize human history has ended with the pursuit of the spectacular to enliven understanding.

That urge began far earlier than the destruction of essentialist ideas by the post-modernists. Consider Herman Melville. He made his name by publishing adventure books about foreign travels and life on the sea, and he cut his public teeth by bringing Polynesia and Tahiti into the world's parlors. In 1892, only a year after his triumphant *Moby Dick*, he wiped out his reputation with a thinly veiled attack on Christianity, and the book bombed. He fled to the Middle East for religious renewal, and his tryst with the pyramids. The search failed.

Surely it is not just that Melville both found and lost himself abroad. Among the things his South Seas adventures gave him was distance from his own culture, sufficient that he could find a place within himself to critique his society. It led him to critically assess his own religious foundations. His trip to the Middle East was an effort to reestablish their validity. It did not; one cannot establish one's own history by plotting it against another's. A worthy lesson here . . . encountering another religious culture provides cognitive distance, but that will not necessarily solve religious problems at home. Why pursue the ever more exotic in order to understand what lives within your dwelling?

It was halfway through this study that a friend asked, in actual innocence: "Why are you attracted by the exotic?" It was not meant as a profound question, for I had scarcely thought of the Moroccans as exotic, and thought not at all that coming to understand the munshidūn was out of the ordinary. Nevertheless, the question changed the direction of my work. I had to ask just why I was doing this research, and what it said about me and the Western culture that was part of my modus operandi.

Certainly I knew that one must be careful about the extraordinary when studying abroad—it is very much like a siren luring one aside. Yet the armchair scholars who rummage through ancient texts offer no solution to the problem. They are victims of the same disease. One need only recall one of the greats in the discipline, Sir James Frazer. His *Golden Bough* can be seen as a collection of exotica, a signal that religious "facts" have a selectivity and inalienable distortion about them to those struggling with global culture. Not surprisingly, Wittgenstein (among others) was troubled by this classic of the history of religions. As he noted: "We might say 'every view has its charm,' but this would be wrong. What is true is that every view is significant for him who sees it so (but that does not mean 'sees it as something other than it is'). And in this sense every view is equally valid."[1] In effect, there is a charm to seeing the exotica of the religious life as crucial.

Yet all collections of "facts" cannot be equally valid. Some excellent scholars have written of Morocco and its religion over the last century and a half, and even if a case could be made that they had not quite caught the nuances of Islam as practiced there, I do not think that all scholarship on Morocco is equally valid, as one reading of Wittgenstein would seem to suggest. Nor are all postmodernist critiques equally valid. The hard issues of scholarship are just as intransigent.

Nor was the Frazerian exotic quality the attraction at the heart of this study. Rather, Morocco's distinctive history and culture within Islam, along with the special place given to memory, recommends it as the basis for exploring religious memory. Furthermore, it is precisely because Morocco is such a cultural mix, with a variety of Islamic visions within it, that it encourages s to move in a new direction in religious studies, for surely the notion of an amalgam of cultures united by a religion holds in the Moroccan case.

Still, our Western categories for designating religious data may be too inflexible and too essentialist to encompass what is holding all these features together, if for no other reason than that the "official" depiction of what is religious will not release sufficient hold to allow it. We have spent much of our time in the West trying to say what religion is, to provide an intellectual scaffold so to speak, whereas it would appear to be that religion operates best as a series of processes, including one for the constructing of a collective memory. This seems to be what is going on in Morocco.

The inspiration for studying Morocco from this perspective came from the peculiar experience offered by my own country of Canada. For most academics such a motivation would be much too provincial. Yet as anyone who has followed Canadian developments over the past decade knows, the country has confronted the trauma of a potential breakup not once but twice. Detecting the glue that keeps Canadians together is not an easy task, but one that has become a kind of national pastime for intellectuals. For me, it is on a par with trying to detect the ingredients that give Morocco its stability. How do you identify the glue that holds a people and a civilization together?

A few years ago many people would have said that hockey, the ice kind, held Canada together, because hockey in Canada constitutes something with national and cultural significance. It goes beyond its sporting origins. It functions as an important public integrator in a country that is massive, disjointed, and socially and politically fragmented. Most of us firmly hold that, even if Quebec were to separate from the rest of the country, we still would have a mythic connection to Quebecers at least on one level, since playing hockey unites the people across the northern part of America in a way far more significant than that which rises from political antagonism. Nor is this just an old boys' game. Women and girls have taken over the arena as well. In short, hockey functions as a quasi-transcendent integrator, overriding ethnic and political segmentation. But hockey is only one of a whole range of possible connectors: the concept of geo-piety, the attraction of pristine natural beauty, a set of common social goals, and the memory of ancestors are others.

For sake of argument, let us allow hockey to stand for this range of possible connectors. At certain moments, hockey makes a claim upon Canadians, even if they are indifferent to the game, or even hate it. This is so because the interpreted past in Canada always includes references to Canada's national sport and its heroes. It has a solid place in Canada's community construction. Thus hockey helps create a certain kind of collective memory. Upon analysis though, we find that there are considerable variations in what Canadians remember about this sport's past, and also just how much engagement people have had with it. Despite that, it continues to play a significant role in defining Canadian identity, even as it is very evasive as to its nature.

It is this inchoate yet meaningful character that inspired me to go beyond the diversity within Morocco's ethnic makeup (Arab, Berber, African) to examine the nature of the Islamic glue behind the national identity and to explore the long and complicated memory of Sufism and the saints. Even today, when modernity and secularism seem present on every side, the nation is replete with references to the powerful past of Sufism and its contemporary offspring, and just as in Canada's case, the symbols of unity are very difficult to unpack. Also like hockey, commitment to this connector system lies outside the usual parameters of definitions of either nationhood or orthodox religion. That is why I have looked to memory and the munshid phenomenon as a way to unravel Morocco's identity. Along the way, they also teach us important lessons about the way religion operates.

So why should it be important for this study to go ahead? For one, for scientific purposes, because many have seen the Sufi tradition as a transcending, unifying element in the Moroccan national consciousness, analogous to the integrators I have been talking about, and having the same kind of diverse cultural connectors. I have deliberately tried to see Sufism as having a broader dimension than the exclusively religious, functioning in the religious culture of Morocco as hockey does in the supposed secular culture of Canada. This study is also important because I change the basic way of looking at the religious expression that molds the mystical singer in Morocco. For scientific purposes, too, this study has relevance, because the constructing ability of memory allows science to exist and develop—had we no confidence in memory, our notion of science could not exist. Here was the wedding of science and religion in an important trajectory of consciousness. Thus, though I have tried to encompass as much detail as possible, there are lacunae, and the reader will want to contend with those. But there may be sufficient detail to sketch how memory defines religion for these Muslims. Thus, without doubt, this is a tentative exploration, through a viable and dynamic religious culture, of another way of conceiving religious meaning.

One more note of a technical nature is necessary, and that concerns the transliteration of Arabic and Berber words. I have opted to use a transliterated form most common in Moroccan discourse, even while trying to keep some relationship of words to the classical or standard form of Arabic. Thus the classical word *burda* for cloak is rendered *bourda* here, as is customary in most written samples. Otherwise I have used transliterated standard Arabic. Readers will recognize that it is difficult to always be consistent with such diverse sources and forms of expression available. Where possible, I have tried to be gender inclusive by the use of s/he for the singular form, even though my sources may lean to the use of the masculine form, precisely because women have made an important contribution to this form of religion. Yet I could not always be consistent in this, and I hope the reader will accept that one has sometimes to struggle with English over the issue.

One cannot research a subject like this without acknowledging that it is the people with whom you have related that contributes most to your understanding. Morocco constitutes an exceptionally distinctive and lively Muslim society, and I have appreciated the hospitality offered to a religion specialist who is curious about the relationship between sacred matters and culture in that society. I visited there four times between 1992 and 1996, in varying times ranging from three weeks to several months. Both the beauty and the variety of Morocco's land and people are delightful, and one can almost be guaranteed some new and fascinating experience every day. Among those who were of immense assistance to me is Sayyid al-Takkifī. A graduate student at Muhammad V University in Rabat, Sayyid suffered my ignorance with grace and benevolence. He took me all over Morocco, introduced me to important people, and aided in recording munshidūn, their shaikhs, and muqaddams and the ordinary adepts of dhikr. He also aided me greatly in gaining access to library resources and facilitating the collection of articles. My initial contact was ʿAbdullāh Ṣāliḥ al-Soufyān, who kindly set up my first contacts and introduced me to Sayyid. He also utilized his extensive network to help me interview critical individuals in this study.

So far as I know, none of my immediate researchers were practicing Sufis, so neither ʿAbdullāh nor Sayyid was committed to this way themselves. Yet they went far beyond what they had to do to make me aware of people, trends, and insights. They were convincing scholars in their own right who were genuinely interested in such an academic enterprise.

As for the munshidūn, they were quite blatant: "We think we contribute and have contributed a great deal to Morocco, its religion, and its culture, yet no one pays much attention to us. . . . At least you want to study what we do and why. That's important to us, and we will help as much as we can." Even the work of the munshidūn has various interpretations by those who count themselves among the category, and there are controversies within the ranks, some of which are examined here. But beyond that is the clear implication that the munshid is a master of a memory complex that is crucial for religion, and we should study it for what it tells us, not just for Morocco, but for all human spiritual pursuits.

Ḥajj Muḥammad Bennīs, Ḥasan Amr Ṭayyib, Dr. Fouzī Skalī, and Dr. Khalid Berkāwī, Aḥmad Ṭawfīq, and Shaikh Sayyid Barrāda of Fez, Shaikh Idris al-Mahjūb, muqaddam of the ʾAissawiyya ṭarīqa, and the Sahara-born chanter extraordinaire Ḥusain al-Toulālī in Meknes—all were generous in granting me interviews. I also received important information from Abū al-Faṣl Abū al-Laṭīf ibn Manṣour, a Sufi singer in Marrakech, as well as from Shaikh Sīdī Ghali al-Darqāwiyya, Dr. ʿAbd'l Majīd al-Saghīr, *baḥḥathah* in the Ṭarīqa al-Darqāwiyya al-Ḥarrāqiyya in Tetouan, and from Abū Ayoub Moḥammed Ḥamid Trikī in Marrakech and

Aḥmed Nājmi in Taroudant. To Moulāy Aḥmad Boukouli of Essaouira, and Muḥammad Badjdūb of Salé, my thanks and appreciation. To several munshidūn I owe a special word of gratitude: Ibrahīm al-Ashhab and Nabīl al-Jaiy of Rabat and Zākī ʿAlī of Agadir, as well as Muḥammad al-Timsimānī of Tangier. I am also grateful to Dr. Muḥammad Abū Ṭālib and Dr. ʿAlī Maḥmoud al-Makkī of Marrakech for their willingness to talk to me about my research topic. Dr. Aḥmad Abū Ṭālib, professor of English at Muhammad V University in Rabat, Dr. Muḥammad Bin Cherīfa, Dr. Abbās al-Jirārī, now retired professor of Andalusian culture in Morocco, and Dr. Ṭāhā ʿAbduʾl-Raḥman, professor of philosophy and head of the department, as well as a muqaddam of the Bu Dshishiyya, all provided me with valuable insights on taṣawwuf (Sufism) in Morocco. I was also able to discuss my research with Dr. Aḥmad Baḥrī, professor of Maghribian Sufi history, in Marrakech. Dr. Muḥammad Isṭātū, professor of Islamic philosophy in Rabat and well-known Sufi poet, Dr. Muḥammad Essourira of Muhammad V University, and Dr. Evelyn Early, then officer in the American embassy in Rabat, were also very helpful.

Important comments about the Ginawa were made by Bilāl al-Ḥidān, originally from Boufrikrane but, at the time of this research, studying in Rabat. Prof. Muḥammed al-Nouhī of Agadir and Ph.D. student at the University of Alberta was of immense assistance in weighing the data presented here, and Dr. Muḥammad Deeb did a preliminary analysis of Dr. Jirārī's important book on the malḥūn for this study. My son Erin and his associate Andrej Golinas, both in the Department of Music, provided help in transforming music on tapes into the written form used here; I am deeply indebted to them. By the final stage of vetting and editing the text, many changes had been made, and I am grateful to the two anonymous reviewers for the Press and to Barry Blose, editor, Scott Evan Burgess, project editor, and Carolyn Russ, copy editor, who provided assistance beyond the normal; I am particularly appreciative for the suggestion for the current title, which comes from one of the reviewers.

The early inspiration for this work came after an invitation from His Excellency Muhammad Ben ʿAīsa, then minister of culture, to attend the annual conference on arts and letters at Asilah. The camaraderie of that conference and the subsequent contact with Sufi chanters in Morocco inspired a return trip, sponsored by a three-year Social Sciences and Humanities Research Council (SSHRC) grant. I am deeply indebted to Dr. Ben ʿAīsa and to the SSHRC for their support, since none of this could have been achieved without them.

The University of Alberta granted me sabbaticals both in 1991–92 and 1998–99. Without the freedom to work in a concentrated manner I have grave doubts whether this writing could have been concluded. As it is, administrative activities have delayed the volume more than I would have wished. Despite that, I wish to thank the university for its fine support.

It is axiomatic that families always are loyal supporters of projects. Early on that was true of my wife Mary-Ellen, but her enthusiasm dipped when it necessitated research trips back to Morocco without her. Nevertheless, she and Rhiannon were gratified when this study was completed, for they were finally able to participate in the conclusion of a long and difficult project, a tangible payback for their early confidence and later patience. I am thankful to them for their encouragement; I trust the absences have proven worthwhile.

Finally, to all the many people I talked with in Morocco, in shops and streets, mosques and zāwiyas, who passed on valuable insights and conceptions that may have played a role in this book but whose names were never learned or whose comments were collected but retained subliminally, much heartfelt thanks. I hope this book will transfer to its reader some of their generosity of spirit. With the same kind of appreciation, I offer my grateful hand to Morocco, the land itself, whose wonders, if it did not provide the solution to any problems, at least did deliver a different, deeper inspiration. It will be to the readers to determine whether they find that inspiration sufficient to open for them another window on a delightful people as well as another point of view on the age-old problem of understanding religion.

1

EXAMINING FOUNDATIONS

The Formation of the Islamic Chanter Tradition

At that time I realized that God—for me, at least—was one of the most immediate of experiences.

Carl G. Jung, Memories, Dreams, Reflections

We want to work with you because, at the very least, you recognize how important our chanting is.

Moroccan munshid Ashḥab

Scholarship makes its own demands, and the desire to expand a certain area of understanding has its own irresistible pull. I had gone to Morocco to continue a project begun several years earlier with the publishing of *The Munshidīn of Egypt: Their World and Their Song*[1] . . . to map the way in which a distinctive group within Islamic mysticism gives us insight into religion itself. I had hoped it would be an easy study, perhaps something like Egypt, with Berber ancillaries. I was wrong.

For starters, I had hoped to find the mystical orders (groups of Sufis following specific Sufi saints called *ṭarīqa*, pl. *ṭuruq*) and their network functioning the same way in Morocco as in Egypt, that is, I had hoped to move easily into understanding the Islamic character of Morocco through the widespread allegiance to the saint, a figure associated with great piety who became the head of a group of devotees. Everything I had read had led me to think that the saints and their zāwiyas (institutional home of the order) unified the country in a deep, perhaps subconscious manner.[2] When I arrived in Morocco, I did not find that to be so. It is true that people have a local relationship with a ṭarīqa, with attendant loyalties and hopes, but local loyalties do not guarantee larger allegiances. There are many who would have no connection to them, just as thousands in the West have no interest in church but are nominally Christian. Rather, the zāwiyas exist in Morocco in much the same way as powerful congregations do in North America. They have a core of adherents and attendees, and their influence spreads out into the community, in ever-widening, ever-diminishing ripples. Clearly the zāwiyas have tapped into a significant religious structure. But they themselves are not the institutional glue, nor are the saints, any more than some kind of ephemeral commitment to Christianity marks the glue for society in Canada or the United States.

Past scholarship singled out saint worship or some modification of saint worship as the crucial element linking people together. After all, Geertz crafted a popular definition of religion, the symbol system, based on Moroccan data.[3] The land of Morocco was certainly holy, considering the many tombs of saints found within it, but I looked in vain for an overriding symbol system and did not find adherence to a mythological saint who was the glue that held the whole. Indeed, I found today some resistance to the saint as the center of religious life. There was and is no commitment to a unitary marabout culture in itself. "Marabout" is the French translation of "Murābiṭ," saintly families reflecting connection to descendants to Sufi saints and to descendants of ʿAli and Fatimah.

So I concluded that if the marabout tradition had ever rooted all Moroccans directly to the realities of Islam and Allah, then Morocco was clearly in a post-Islamic situation. And since that hardly was the case, other perspectives had to be sought. While many saints' tombs could be found in Morocco, there were major differences from area to area and between urban and rural areas. As well, there were major differences between the way traditional maraboutic religion functioned and the way the newer, ṭarīqa-defined groups saw themselves. Then there were hints of a newer, spiritual interpretation of ṭarīqa life, based on personal religious commitments. It was not, then, the ṭarīqa structure itself that provided an entree into Moroccan religious identity since the Moroccans themselves did not hold it to be foundational.

Nor did all groups participate in the munshidūn tradition. Clearly I could not argue that the munshidūn tradition was universally acknowledged and adhered to. This meant that my study of the munshid complex could only be held to be a cipher, a pointer toward a theme. I came to the conclusion that no segment that one could study encompassed the whole range of what was experienced as religion, and my work therefore had to be a kind of case study. This book attempts to grasp some basic religio-cultural components of Morocco in and through the chanter tradition, and by that means to enlist some insight into the construction of religion in a more universal sense.

What I had to determine was how the realities experienced by the munshidūn delivered cohesion not only with zāwiya truths but also with the Moroccan sense of well-being. What did they both articulate that was a deeper, more common structure? According to my study, what seemed to predominate is a lively loyalty to a remembered reality.

The constitution of this past transcendence varies widely, but it is all integrated either personally or socially into an ecology of religious consciousness for Moroccans. This understanding forms the backbone of my study: an articulation of how this remembered reality is rendered into a viable religious system.

Yet the more I struggled with the material I collected, the more my approach seemed to have a basic problem at its heart: Western religious scholarship really has limited resources to plumb the depth of some religious data. It did not seem to have the ability to shape an understanding of Moroccan Islamic culture. What was even more obvious was that the discipline of the history of religions (or comparative religions, or whatever label is convenient) had been formulated in such a way as to minimize comprehension of another way of thinking about religious verities. That is, theoreticians in religion appeared to have missed a central factor in understanding religion because Moroccan religion just did not fit the categories designed by Western scholarship to articulate religion.

Memory and the History of Religions

A central problem to be confronted was the role of a "public" history in the existential awareness of being Moroccan and being Muslim. I returned to Mircea Eliade's formulation of the mythological situation, since religious scholarship had indicated that the most atomic element of religion is its mythic structure. He argued that the primordial, sacred history was crucial because "it explains, and by the same token justifies, the existence of the world, of man and of society."[4] Eliade's characterization of sacred history as having an explanatory function is based upon the notion that human religious requirements are exhausted through rational structures; the impulse to know and comprehend is a cognitive practice satisfying the basic understanding of existence in the world. It follows that if one knows one's history then one should comprehend both personal and corporate identity.

Eliade went on from there to draw upon the extensive work of Hans Schärer among the Dayak, that is, an African people, to develop a basic metaphor for understanding the formation of sacred history and how it shapes a people's consciousness. Schärer wrote, "Through the cosmogonic myth and its sequel, the Dayak progressively unveils the structures of reality and of his own proper mode of being. What happened in the beginning describes at once both the original perfection and the destiny of each individual."[5]

Now the real question is how the average Dayak engages this sacred history. Are they even aware that this is sacred history, or is it just history? Eliade's contention was that the various ingredients of the myth were apprehended in the narrative's manifold personages and their doings, which then gave shape to the individual, for by knowing the myth, one knew one's person.

The perspective left out of this theoretical construction is memory.[6] Eliade clearly thought that Schärer knew all the details of the Dayak system and presented all the myths in a comprehensive package. But the "facts" from the Dayak are not like tools lying about. They are constructions built by past experience and transmitted to Schärer in an explanatory language by knowledgeable people, usually elders. Their explanations arose out of constructed memories, validated by ritual experiences and pieced together through learned situations. In fact, Eliade's notion of humans in archaic times stresses the role of remembering what happened *in illo tempore,* that is, before historical time began. This mandatory and exemplary moment stands as the most important time, for all meaningful events flow from that era. Clearly Eliade believed that the critical aspect of this scenario was the religious efficacy of returning to the sacred moment, a returning that he saw objectified in ritual, myth, and religious beliefs. The formal recounting of what happened at the paradigmatic moment and its expression in an articulated system is usually what we call history.

But we now know that some people, perhaps all of us, do not connect with everything that is expressed as formal history. This includes not just the history of the tribe or the people but also the private formal histories by which we construct ourselves for others. Among Aboriginal peoples around the world, there are different formal histories for men and for women. Formal histories are very selective in what they present as "our" story. In addition, each national history is a professional amalgam crafted by experts and passed on in common understandings, speeches, books, and courses. We come to know this as our history.

Surely this process is less than it implies. It is only when we become conscious of history as a framework that we begin to see that history is always related back to something that engages it for ourselves . . . our personal experience. We remember something that connects us to a historical moment, enlivening it to make it ours. Thus, history can most clearly be said to be the creation of remembering, that is, of personalizing memory. For it is memory that makes the choices and brings the past into play in our existence.

Eliade apparently thought the process of going back worked the same way for all archaic people, who were motivated by similar returnings. He did not see that going back was a process of memory, and that the process of memory and its meaning might modify the going back and its contemporary content.

Moreover, he identified this procedure as characteristic of the so-called primitive people, whereas my material indicated that returnings through memory are central to all human life, whether secular or religious. Thus memory plays a key role in all understandings of identity and collective existence, and reliance on that property of human experience is crucial for the Dayak, the archaic humans, and, I would argue, religious practitioners of any sort.

American historian of religions Jonathan Z. Smith also stressed the importance of memory, pointing out its long association with re-presentation theories; he did not tarry there, however, but moved on to a consideration of space, seeing in it a way to elucidate how humans relate to and construct their world of meaning, specifically in ritual formulations.[7] Memory is essential for filling up space with enactments replicating religion's establishment stories.

I see the process of memory as a constituent part of how we envision and experience our world. Memory is an activity by which connected patterns become possible, and hence it lies behind any attempt to bring meaning to phenomena. It would thus seem to be a prerequisite for most conceptions of science, since some pattern established in the past becomes the focus of replication or of construction. We believe that we can access the scientific achievements of the past through the "facts" in an article or book or experiment, and these forms provide a memory bank. We seem never to doubt that we have instant connection to the elements of this past, and we seem to think the context can be replicated . . . that memory operates in an ahistorical environment. Yet even the grasping of significance is a creative act. Religion, too, uses a "past" in this same kind of creative manner. In effect, memory is necessary for any attempt to link elements together into larger meaning settings, for what has been established in that past must be held to affirm an important ingredient that can be placed within a schematic providing intellectual satisfaction. So memory is necessary both to identify and retain "facts" as well as to place them in a comprehendible system. We will see that this notion of memory is crucial here.

Memory Theory and Religion

Recent Western theory of memory has vigorously explored the precise nature of memory and its intellectual underpinnings. Since recent research has important bearings on this study, an overview of relevant work is in order. In his groundbreaking book *White Gloves: How We Create Ourselves through Memory,* John Kotre draws on recent psychological research to point out that memory is a continuing creative element in experience and it impacts on life at many levels, not just at the conscious level. He argues that memory is more than a minor element—rather, it is a critical element in the construction of our selves. Moreover, the ingredients in our memories often become the basis for reinterpretation in the light of changed experience. He also points out how autosuggestion and stories become "memories." He sees three ingredients in each memory: (1) an original perception or fact, (2) an interpretative frame afterward that sets up the significance of the fact, and (3) the blended result that is then retained as a single memory. He also notes the importance of implicit or hidden memory (cryptomnesia). His argument stresses the role of memory in myth making, and hence in any construction of significance for one's life.[8] Memory is a constitutive ingredient in the self-formulating process, a process that has religious implications.

Kotre's theories can also be tied directly to Daniel Goleman's *Emotional Intelligence.* Goleman argues that, from the time of the Greeks, intelligence has always been conceived as indifferent or neutral with regard to personal feelings, whereas the evidence is that people use a collective awareness, which he designates as *emotional intelligence,* to make many different kinds of choices and to construct ingredients of their self-identity. Research shows that learning and knowledge were later additions to the emotional base of the brainstem, and that memory and learning were two tools that came with the growth of the limbic system, that mass of cells that developed around the brainstem.[9] Once the neocortex had evolved to its current size, a wide range of experiences could be processed and analyzed, and with that development came the power of memory. For in that memory was the weighing and evaluating procedure whose processes are stored in the amygdala, that small center that activates emotional responses and quickly signals positive or negative emotional impulses to any given datum.[10] Memory is the tool that provides the analytic possibility of such a response. Thus the amygdala is a kind of neural hot-wiring that instantaneously gives a reading on a situation and provides a powerful response.

In the past, psychology's interest in cognition and neuroscience's concern with the brain's physical structures kept the two apart, but this is no longer the case. For example, it is now possible to argue that there are several kinds of memory, and they cannot be understood only as processes; it seems that the brain systems approach is much more likely to provide the best way of understanding memory as a whole.[11] Moreover, although I will not analyze this directly in what follows, implicit memory, or encoded elements, function below the level of consciousness. This is congruent with the fact that Sufism has constructed its entire liturgical process with dhikr (remembrance) as a category of ontological significance. Dhikr is regarded by Sufis as the primary means of engagement with the spiritual realm, and is fundamental to the religious life.

In fact, Sufis have long argued for hidden and subliminal patterns and have contended that physical entities can be directly influenced by forces quite beyond the normal range of empirical senses. One case in Morocco quite startled me, involving a so-called prisoner of the shaikh. Many people needing assistance of various sorts come into the zāwiya and the shaikh's care, and some remain in the shaikh's household for years. They are known as prisoners of the shaikh, although there is no compulsion for them to remain at the zāwiya near the shaikh. One such individual came into a shaikh's home after having terrible nervous traumas. So long as he remained within three hundred meters of the zāwiya, he could function quite well. He remained there even after the death of the shaikh. Yet when the government decreed that all citizens had to appear at the government office to sign for an identification card, and he entered a car for the drive to the office, he was no further than the end of the street when he went quite out of his mind. The driver had to turn back to the zāwiya, where the individual returned to his normal behavior immediately. In effect, the role of the shaikh's baraka in controlling the man's problems even outlived the physical presence of the shaikh, for he was still living in the zāwiya many years later. In line with this case, contemporary studies point out the significance of implicit memory research on affective states[12] and also the significance of affective intensity for the encoding process.[13]

Sufis often speak about specific events of an unusual or even supernatural sort that have occurred because of their spiritual exercises, and these recollections clearly remain part of the topography of their lives. These "memories" become the basis for remembering the beneficence of God, as well as important indicators of their self-understanding. Thus Sufis have insisted that their remembering is a very specific kind of systemic expression, quite distinct from other kinds of memory. The peak experiences that constitute the core of this remembering form a kind of personal myth within the memory bank.

Yet, as is obvious in Aboriginal myth making, there is no one authoritative version of a myth, not even a creation myth, for myth making is always dependent upon the context, the audience, and the teller.[14] One could even say, admittedly with some distortion, that the myth is rediscovered with each telling. We note that the ancient Greek poets focused on two words, *mnēmosunē*, remembering, and *lēthē*, forgetting. The former word is, in fact, the name of the goddess who gives birth to the Muses in Hesiod's *Theogony*. It is the Muses' role to inspire the poets so they can provide people with *lēsmosunē*, "forgetfulness," so they will no longer remember the difficulties and sadnesses of life.[15] Thus the ongoing conflict between the darkness of lēthē and the light of mnēmosunē is exemplified in the poet, who hears the Muses and no longer remembers the grim events of the past.

The Greek notion is, however, more complicated than that, for in the cult of Trophonios, the initiate in the ritual of incubation drank from the springs of both remembrance and forgetfulness . . . in effect, both were necessary. They are clearly related and interdependent, since the Greeks use the word *alētheia* (literally, non-forgetfulness). As Nagy suggests, this implies a different model:

> These relationships can be conceived as a larger circle of *mnēmosunē* that includes an inner area of *lēthē*. The area of forgetting is visualized as the ongoing erasure of things not worth remembering, erasure by way of *lēthē*; the smaller circle of remembering, within the larger circle, is highlighted by the area of darkness surrounding it, the area of forgetting. In fact, there is a special word in the diction of archaic Greek poetry that formalizes this specialized and exclusive kind of remembering: that word is *alētheia*, normally glossed in English as "truth." The *alētheia* of the poet is the non-erasure of the poetic glory that is his to confer. The same concept . . . conventionally reinforces injunctions to be *memnēmenos* "mindful, remembering."[16]

In Nagy's view, the alētheia or truth becomes a kind of ideology within Panhellenism that is adjudicated for all versions of tradition wherever it is performed.[17] For our purposes, it signals that remembering and forgetting are core ingredients in one's own repertoire of identity. It is also noteworthy that Paul de Man saw forgetting as "part of the core experience of modernity," so that the more radical the forgetting, the more pronounced is the historicism.[18] It is clear that the desire to erase what comes before has taken on a new and distinct form in the modern era. This notion relates directly to the content of the remembering and how it plays a role in personal history or, in contemporary parlance, autobiographical memory.

This kind of memory is usually termed autobiographical because it is not just an episode along with other episodes but is seen to be constitutive of one's person. It is implicit memory. Singer and Salovey argue that autobiographical memories "reveal repetitive affective patterns and themes that stamp an individual's most important concerns and unresolved issues," and they contend that these memories act as "nuclear scripts" or "organizing metaphors" for one's personality.[19] The idea of memories as nuclear scripts or as organizing metaphors is important for this study, since I consider an analogical model of an *implicit mythological "domain"* to best account for the munshid's perceptions. Consequently these ideas will be helpful as a means of understanding the munshid's life and career.

Autobiographical Memory and Munshidūn Theory

Zonis quotes Karl Weintraub as saying that "real autobiography . . . is a weave in which self-consciousness is delicately threaded throughout interrelated experience. It may have such varied functions as self-explication, self-discovery, self-clarification, self-formation, self-presentation, self-justification. All these functions interpenetrate easily, but all are centred upon a self aware of its relation to its experiences."[20]

Autobiographical memory thus has a social dimension, a dimension critical to the "remembering" in Sufi liturgical rites. In her work on the role played by this kind of memory, Nelson states:

> The claim here is that the initial functional significance of autobiographical memory is that of sharing memory with other people; a function that language makes possible. Memories become valued in their own right—not because they predict the future and guide present action, but because they are shareable with others and thus serve a social solidarity function. I suggest that this is a universal human function, although one with variable, culturally specific rules. In this respect, it is analogous to human language itself, uniquely and universally human but culturally—and individually—variable. I suggest further that this social function of memory underlies all of our storytelling, history-making narrative activities, and ultimately all of our accumulated knowledge systems.[21]

Other aspects of current research on autobiographical memory are also significant.[22] An important feature is time, because this kind of memory always talks about the past. That memories should be framed by time is a critical factor,[23] since both personal history or narrative and group tradition are connected by this notion.[24] At the same time, this kind of memory reflects what is called *nested* characteristics, that is, "canyons are nested within mountains, trees are nested within canyons, leaves are nested within trees; and cells are nested within leaves. There are forms within forms both up and down the scale of size. Units are nested within larger units. Things are components of other things. They would constitute a hierarchy except that this hierarchy is not categorical but full of transitions and overlaps. Hence, for the terrestrial environment, there is no proper unit in terms of which it can be analyzed once and for all."[25]

Nested structure is essential in comprehending Sufism, since memories of the saint and the remembered ingredients of the group's past always play a role in interpretation of experience and in the construction of the self. In addition, as Nelson suggests in the quote above, autobiographical memory implies an audience or shared group. Memory and remembering are also important for societies and groups. It is worth reviewing a few of the more prominent groups' ideas for our purposes here.

René Girard is one of those scholars who has explored the relation of memory to shared social and intellectual meanings.[26] Girard develops the concept of "triangular" or "mimetic" desire, by which he affirms that humans do not within themselves create autonomous desires but rather mimic or model their lives on or through a mediator. Thus a subject person does not carve out a goal or meaning for life through dint of his or her autonomous machinations; rather, the person selects a legendary or mythic model that mediates the goal. In Girard's study of Don Quixote, the goal of being a perfect knight is mediated by Amadis of Gaule, who, Quixote holds, is "the pole, the star, the sun for brave and amorous knights, and we others who fight under the banner of love and chivalry should imitate him. Thus, my friend Sancho, I reckon that whoever imitates him best will come closest to perfect chivalry." Thus meaning incorporates a transcendent dimension that interposes itself between the subject and the object, becoming part of the sum total of the individual.[27]

Following this line of reasoning, every tale told has elements of the mythic within it, for it involves the working out of the goal through the model; each person becomes a conglomerate of transcendents.[28] For a religious people, a plethora of figures from the past provide the models for this transcendent dimension, and in the restatement of these models in contemporary experience, the religious community continues the great purposes of the transcendent in one's existence.[29] Memory is the constituting facilitator and the provider of the data by which one engages with this transcendent reality, making it thereby autobiographical.

In his book *How Societies Remember*, Connerton argues that societies have emphasized habitual performances as a means to convey and sustain memory. Eschewing the claims of symbolic representation, quasi-textual representation, or historical contextualization as adequate explanations, he contends that commemorative ceremonies shape communal memory: "There exists a variety of ceremonies which share certain common features: they do not simply imply continuity with the past by virtue of their high degree of formality and fixity; rather they have as one of their defining features the explicit claim to be commemorating such a continuity."[30]

This view is certainly validated by considering Arabic poetry, for commemorative rituals are well known in Arabic poetic recitals. In her study of the Arab oral epic *Sīra Banī Hilāl*, Connelly points out how important these rituals are even when the oral tradition becomes a written text:

These references to a primary oral rhetorical scene function as a contract with the reader. They remind him again and again, by virtue of their repetitions, what the compiler-collector-scribe (*mu'allif*) expects of his audience. He wants the reader to *hear* and to *remember* in his mind's ear the ceremonial performance of the *Hilāliyya* by a rabab poet. The mu'allif's rendition of the *Hilāliyya* is but a recollection of a true performance; or, to use the scribe's own words, a dhikr—a mentioning and a retelling of the sira which commemorates the ceremonial, ritual telling before the assembled community.[31]

Connelly had earlier pointed out that these texts are regarded in the same way as the written text of the Qur'ān . . . the speech of God as inscribed in the book.[32] So folk Arab remembering is precisely to lift listeners out of the present and put them back at their ancestral roots, to the foundational performance of the poet at the beginning of the epic's tradition. The mu'allif is not repeating words; he is creating a displacement—he is collapsing time and shifting space. The performance of the most powerful of the Arabic arts is really carried out in a ritual form because that form alone has the ability to create the proper framework for the experience the mu'allif wishes to set in place (discussed further in chapter 3.)

Thus, Connerton's view suggests that religious or commemorative ritual has an abiding role in framing human understanding in Moroccans' lives; if we accept that view, we could say that learning is an experience rooted in a ritual form. By participating in that ritual, one engages in an educational activity, in the development of mind. As in every traditional religious society, those who have access to religious learning become part of an elite. This notion is significant in understanding the work of the Sufi chanter.

I turn now to a more specific examination of how religions contribute to the construction of memory and how that memory provides a viable way of knowing.

Memory and the Construction of a Religious Category

Given the extraordinarily rich role that memory plays in religion, it is a phenomenon that is remarkably understudied. The construction of religious memory touches a deep and crucial nerve within religious consciousness. It is, of course, possible to argue that each and every religious text, each and every statement of religious claim, is constituted in and through memory. While the claim would invalidate many statements of the traditions themselves, such as that of Muslims who view the Qur'ān as the original text of God's Word, nevertheless it certainly applies to the Ḥadīth. Memory is irrevocably linked to all foundational truths and constitutes what might be termed a special ontological category of experience for all religions.

Hindu psychology, at least as presented in Sankya and Yoga, holds that the Buddhi, the totality of our emotional and mental processes, has as one of its components *smṛti*, remembrance or memory. As Zimmer explains it,

> Because the subtle matter of the inner organ assumes all the forms presented to it by the senses, objects tend to give to the mind a shape or character and to leave on it an impression, or "memory," more or less permanent. Not only the shape of the object itself, but also the associated feelings and thoughts, as well as the will and determination to act that it aroused, remain as vestiges, and these may be reanimated at a later date by the impingement of something new. In this way memories are excited, images or recollection aroused, and continuities of life-desire, fear, and manners of conduct founded.[33]

This subtle inner organ survives death and carries the memory of its achievements into the next transmigration. It thus is the vehicle for karmic transferal. Memory, in this sense, is a corner piece of early Hinduism's construction of a spiritual reality that transcends each earthly existence.

Later, of course, in Advaita Vedanta and then in Buddhism, such beliefs in the phenomenal reality of a subtle organ and even of memory were abandoned. For them, once the true reality comes into one's awareness, one is liberated from all references to thought and memory and can comprehend how they are both devices of *maya*. Still, until that moment of liberation comes, one engages in meditation and the rehearsing of verses from those who know the Blissful One. So even if devalued in later Hinduism and Buddhism, earthly memory remains a necessary part of human devotion.

Among the ancient Israelites, the story of their deliverance is the story of God's intervention on behalf of His people and the working out of God's will through them. Through the Jews, history becomes a revelatory instrument; God uses history to convey God's plan of redemption. Once the Temple was destroyed and Torah had became the dominant focus leading to what is called Judaism today, remembrance became an even greater tool for religious sentiment, for then it became a means of connecting with the suffering that had been experienced before by the people of God. Thus we find this remarkable passage written by the prominent rabbi Yom Tob Lipmann Heller after the Polish pogroms of 1648:

> What has occurred now is similar to the persecutions of old, and all that happened to the forefathers has happened to their descendants. Upon the former already the earlier generations composed *selihot* and narrated the events. *It is all one.* Therefore I said to myself—I shall go and glean among them, "for the fingernail of the former generations is worth more than the belly of the later one" [*Yoma* 9b]. Also because by reciting their prayers it will help our own to be accepted, since one cannot compare the words uttered by the small to those of the great. And thus their lips will move in the grave, and their words shall be like a ladder upon which our prayer will mount to heaven.[34]

Yerushalmi points out the primacy of liturgy and ritual over historical narrative, since the commemorative observance really preserves the memory of the event and not the precise historical record of it. Moreover, the earlier occurrence becomes a template for the more recent, so that history plays little role in assigning defining differences between them; indeed, the view is "for it is all one."[35] Even today, faced with the searing experience of the Holocaust, many Jews have abandoned history as a way of understanding Jewish identity and have constructed an identity, as Yerushalmi says, from various elements: "Myth and memory condition action."[36] Still, whatever way the Chosen People see as proper to remember, memory is a key component of divine purpose.

"This do in remembrance of me" is Jesus' formula, given the night of the betrayal leading to his death. It is the liturgical structure through which the plan of redemption is made real and living within the believer's life. In Christian theology, this memory reaches back to the Fall in the Garden of Eden and defines the sacred historical relationship that God put in place for His people. In Christianity, Jewish memory was transformed into a historical plan to bring about the salvation of all people, not just the Chosen People, but a plan of God's grace and forgiveness for all. Memory is thus both the vehicle for participating in the life of Jesus and the foundational plan that turns a long story into a narrative of redemption.

The North African bishop St. Augustine discussed memory extensively. In his *Confessions* he seems to identify different kinds of memory, that is, memory of sense experience, of the arts, and of the affections. He also places God in the memory, but without being restricted to a locale therein, and without an image by which to represent:

> Thou has given this honour to my memory to reside in it; but in what quarter of it Thou residest, that I am considering. For in thinking on Thee, I have passed beyond such parts of it as the beasts also have, for I found Thee not there among the images of corporeal things; and I came to those parts to which I have committed the affections of my mind, nor found Thee there. And I entered the very seat of my mind . . . neither wert Thou there. . . . And why seek I now in what place thereof Thou dwellest, as if there were places therein? . . . Place there is none; we go forward and backward and there is no place.[37]

As a Christian and somewhat of a Platonist, Augustine held that our knowledge of the deity resided innately in the memory; at the same time, he held *memory, understanding,* and *will* to be the three powers of the soul, a trinity of powers mirroring the Holy Trinity.[38]

Medieval monks and scholars, drawing as they did upon Aristotle's "template" notion of memory retention, seem to have spent much time being concerned about the practical application of memory; even St. Thomas Aquinas, who was reputed to have had a prodigious memory, gave four principles for assisting memory. The last two are significant for our purposes, since they stress characteristics that are thoroughly developed in Sufi practice: "A man should dwell with solitude on and cleave with affection to, the things which he wishes to remember" and "We should meditate frequently on what we wish to remember."[39] While Aquinas was concerned primarily with means to a better memory (known today as *explicit* memory), both the flexibility of the term *memory* and the role it played in mysticism within Islam raises the question of whether Aquinas had come in contact with the Sufis, and whether he had appropriated any of their language. Beyond this, however, is the clear implication of Christian scripture that the recalling that is done in the liturgy has specific powers to transmute the bread and wine into the body and blood of Christ, a remembering that has obvious ontological repercussions.

In *Jesus, History and You,* Jack Finegan points out, "Remembrance of the past gives us a sense of stability. We are part of a continuing movement. They went into exile, but the cause did not perish. They experienced depression, but everything was not lost. The movement has continued. The past gives us a sense of direction."[40] Finegan then goes on to argue for the historicity of the death and resurrection of Christ, based upon the valid memory of the early Church. Here, a faith-constructed memory becomes the foundation upon which a history is built.[41] Subsequent historical narratives are thus dialogues between the memory-fact and the Church as it must work out the current meaning of that faith-inspired moment.

Even in its attempt to deal with mysticism, Christianity has had to rely upon memory, in some ways to see it as a constituent of the self. Consider this famous statement by the mystic Jan von Ruysbroeck: "And the bare, uplifted *memory* feels itself enwrapped and established in an abysmal Absence of Image. And thereby the created image is united above reason in a threefold way with its Eternal Image, which is the origin of its being and its life; and this origin is preserved and possessed, essential and eternally, through a simple seeing in an imageless void; and so a man is lifted up above reason in a threefold manner into the Unity, and in a onefold manner into the Trinity." (emphasis added)[42]

Here, von Ruysbroeck uses the metaphor of seeing, a notion reminiscent of Cicero's affirmation that seeing is the most powerful of the senses, transforming it into a vehicle to engage with God.[43] But even more germane, he holds memory to be the inner faculty that has the experience of the "abysmal" reality of God.[44] This motif was also evident in my Egyptian material.[45]

I turn now to enunciate a theory around which the mystical chanter tradition revolves in Islam, specifically as it applies in the Moroccan case. By doing so I will explore how one religious tradition lives and expresses itself through a sacralized memory system. The ability of music to carry religious memory into articulation and yet not to limit its meaning is the crucial foundation for the munshidūn. They see the music of the brethren as a ritual form rooted in the collective past and carried on in the dhikr and *samāʿ* (meditational song) today. So far as the individual chanter is concerned, his work can be summarized this way: The munshid operates in the milieu of a Sufi metacoding system, trying to utilize materials from the ṭarīqa's musical and textual tradition, but always retaining a memory of a previous, powerful moment when an encounter was made with "reality" and that reality became "present" or tangible. Reattaining that remembered moment is his goal. We could say that the munshid's entire career is a remembering of past-inspired occasions, reintroduced by means of his memory so that his memory of that peak moment provides a breakthrough from the past time to the present time to all who participate. In Moroccan Sufism, that auspicious moment may well be achieved through the medium of a musical meditation. Thus musical memory can play a critical role in the movement into the reality of the implicit mythic domain.

Toward a Theory of the Munshid and Mystical Experience

Two interpretive scenarios arise from this situation: the first is that the text, as a collection of pure words alone, is undergirded or connected to other systems of meaning, mythic in character and melodic in format, which together are deemed as having religious significance. Just what the signifiers are derives from distinctive elements in Moroccan religious culture, primarily recognized as maraboutic in origin but obviously rooted in an Islamic consciousness.

The second scenario is that the meaning is not in the words per se but in the interplay between the performed text and another, higher meaning level, what might be regarded as at the mythic level, based on a twofold notion: that there is, first, a transcendent domain, a spiritual reality above and beyond the articulated texts, that is held to be the locus of reference, and second, its religious purpose is to transform the regular meaning of signs and words into an occasion for entrance into a spiritual state of being. This environment operates as a metacoding system that is held to be the key to the true spiritual state. This mythic domain is foundational to Sufi understanding, for it is rooted in the Islamic worldview and Islamic consciousness. In that sense it might be designated as "nuclear," "bedrock," and "elemental." But this domain is not literal, in the sense that it can be articulated without gloss. It is mythic precisely because the only language that can truly be attached to it is myth, with its indication for a surplus of sacred meaning and authority. It is precisely because it cannot be framed in human terms that myth is necessary to explicate the realities entailed by the munshid's experience. Like Jung's recollection in *Memories, Dreams, Reflections* of his early experience, God appears to be imminent in the munshid's encounter with this domain.

Moreover, for the munshid, this domain is accessed by a ritually inspired text that is itself informed by a musical intonation and founded upon the imagery of the Islamic past. In this way the entire moment is a merging of text, music, and memory . . . an imaginative combination into a powerful tool for approaching the realities held to be constituted in this special environment. The goal of the whole exercise is to draw the listener's attention to that potentially transforming and empowering dimension.

According to my study, the munshid is the fulcrum for the process of merging the text, music, and memory; it is during his inspired interaction with the text and music that this mythic domain is accessed and brought to the foreground. The merged text-music-memory functions something like the hypertext in contemporary computer jargon,[46] that is, it operates as a metacoding system that is not regarded as random or decentered[47] by the believers but rather inspires and enlivens the memorized text and music during the rituals. The goal is to make present the realities of the mythic domain in an expressive, existential manner. Thus, the text during ritual is held to be informed by the domain and takes on inspiring hues from it.

Another distinction should be made: this metacoding system includes beliefs and conceptions of the mystical life that probably cannot be completely articulated, even by the mystical savants. At the same time, the text consciously uses conscious Sufi phraseology in verbal form. These phrasings are clearly part of the metacoding system, but their truth-value is confined by the inability of articulate speech to accurately frame their meaning. One cannot unpack the meaning just by trying to define it; one has to experience the entire process in order to grasp the significance. Thus the domain, and the access provided by the munshid's activity, is inherently not reducible to any one form of human discourse; it cannot be subject to a general kind of logic.

It follows that the mystical discourse cannot be frozen into a permanent articulation; the individual munshid remembers the words sung in the past that delivered the most powerful transformation experience, and aims to bring this kind of experience back. So the religious experience associated with a peak encounter of the past is what the munshid is trying to articulate. One could say, then, that this memory system operates with a transitory, yet foundational, experience. The memory system provides the data for the chanter's attempt to access the spiritual reality in his performance, and the chanter must learn the process of access. In order to do so, the munshid must become a master of ritual, for access to the mythic domain operates only through a specialized ritual medium. In short, Moroccan Sufi musical forms act like specialized ritual mediums through which access is gained to this expressive Islamic mythic environment.

The Cultural Distinctiveness of Memory's Implicit Mythic Domain

All Sufi groups operate with this memory structure in place, but the shape, understanding, and processes of access differ, according to each group. In general, however, the metacoding system works the same way for all Sufi groups. It follows that the exact nature of the domain itself may differ from ṭarīqa to ṭarīqa, perhaps even from one local ṭarīqa to another of the same group in another locale. Naturally, then, the precise performance of each ṭarīqa's munshid differs accordingly.

In order to understand how this system operates, we turn now to the principles that govern it. Sufism continues to have such an impact today precisely because it resides in a cohesive understanding of religious memory and what that memory can do when properly exercised. This suggests the following theoretical principles:

— Memory is a constituent ingredient in any religious expression.

— Memory deals with a basic framework both within the individual and the society.

— Authoritative models are operative within memory, and these provide guidelines for understanding, behavior, and consciousness.

— For our purposes, these authoritative models can be described as implicit mythic encounters.

— These mythic encounters are built out of and constituted by past experiences, however they are obtained.

— The Sufi chanter indicates one way that this memory-encoding system can be comprehended.

— Remembrance is the generic term that encompasses this whole phenomenon.

Let us turn then to the building blocks of this kind of Islamic remembrance.

2

THE ISLAMIC ENGAGEMENT WITH MEMORY

Remembrance as a Way of Knowing

Attempting to bring the *baraka* of the past into the present, as if it were an object, is futile and alienating. *Baraka* is attributed to manifestations of dynamic force in the world, not to nostalgic reminiscences of that force.

Paul Rabinow on Morocco's *wlad siyyed*

These are spiritual incantations, *nafathat ruḥiyya*, inspirations of the All-Glorious, conveying knowledge that is a divine gift, a secret from the Unseen World, beyond the grasp of reason and the literal meanings of texts, apart from those categories of notions that can be acquired or looked up in books.

ʿAbd al-Qādir, *Kitāb al-mawāqif*

Toutes les pratiques de la religion (dīn) sont des formes de *dikr*, de "remé-moration" du Divin.

Aḥmad Ibn ʿAgība, *Fahrasa*

Ibn Khaldūn noted something very peculiar about Moroccans: they stressed memory more than any other Muslim group.[1] Moroccan scholars had to spend some sixteen years memorizing texts before they would be accepted as authorities. This is compared to the Tunisian five. Recently Eickelman has advocated a judicious evaluation of memory as a way of knowing, and pointed out its significance for Muslim education.[2]

In fact, memory has always been of signal importance to Islam, from the Prophet's own time to today. Many of the major ideas of Muslim belief involve memory: The message of God in the Qurʾān is not new; it is, rather, a restating of a message already told by many prophets to many peoples;[3] the great ancestors of the past were prophets whose lives exemplified the way God deals with His people;[4] the Qurʾān chronicles the lives of the faithful and abjures the believers to remember God's ways of dealing with them;[5] the *sīra* (biography of the Prophet) and the Ḥadīth (traditions of the Prophet) construct a view of the Prophet that becomes normative for life and morals;[6] the Sharīʾa is constructed upon the community memory of the doings and sayings of the Prophet, so that the contemporary believer is guided by the authoritative model of the past;[7] the norms of community behavior are judged according to those arising from the exemplaries of the past; Sunnis look to the great moments of the rightly guided caliphs;[8] Shīʿīs remember the massacre of Karbala and comprehend it as universally significant;[9] and Sufis adhere to the Qurʾān's words to "remember God" and do so in rituals clothed with the Prophet's and the saints' presence.[10]

Sufism, of course, has constructed its rituals upon a deep and comprehensive notion of memory. Memory is hegemonic in Islamic mystical tradition. It drives much of Islam's experiential sensibilities, as we will see. Wherever dhikr (liturgical remembrance) has been practiced, it has generally been thought to encompass the same things and to reflect the same ritual effectiveness. While this may be true in some macro-sense, it is also the case that dhikr perceptions and dhikr use have varied considerably from locale to locale and saint to saint.[11]

Generally speaking, the group rituals of the Sufis in Morocco are known as dhikr, a word that links mystical Islam directly to a religious memory system. However, we must immediately confront the problem of translating the term into English. The dhikr tradition sees remembrance as a Qurʾānic-validated means of meditation on past verities and on the transcendent being of God, a base upon which Sufism built a structure for probing higher consciousness, engaging with spiritual forces and ultimately coming into a personal encounter with God. This is too heavy a superstructure for our word *remember*. The word dhikr, then, cannot be so translated, for it is far more organic and dynamic in meaning; it introduces the adept instantaneously to a powerful conduit that is rooted in an ontological understanding of reality, including both the cosmic and microcosmic dimensions. Hence for Sufism in general, to remember is to know and comprehend in an absolutely foundational manner. We turn now to a brief articulation of spiritual depth of dhikr in the Qurʾān and Ḥadīth.

Dhikr: Sacred and Mythological Dimensions in the Qurʾān and Ḥadīth

The Islamic configuration of memory reflects a sophisticated ontological purpose. In the *Muṣḥaf al-Madīnah al-Nabawiyyah*, the official translation of the Qurʾān by Saudi Arabian scholars, the issue of dhikr is specifically identified as a problem term with regard to its translation: "The word 'remember' is too pale a word for dhikr, which has now acquired a large number of associations in our religious literature. In its verbal signification it implies: to remember, to praise frequently by mentioning, to rehearse, to celebrate, to commemorate, to make much of, to cherish the memory of, as a precious possession."[12]

Indeed, the word dhikr and its cognates form a very complex structure in the Holy Book, far more complex than we can examine here. We shall have to content ourselves with the review of a few significant aspects.

The Qurʾān insists that the prophets were all linked together by virtue of the message they collectively brought. They were all members of one brotherhood

(23:51–52), and all brought the same *dīn* (religion). The Qurʾān identifies all of the prophets as *mudhakkirāt,* a word derived from the root "to remember or to recollect"; thus they are all rememberers. Their message is *tadhkirah,* reminder. The Qurʾān speaks of itself as *tazkirah* (*innahu tazkirah,* 80:11). Humans, however, are in a state of forgetfulness, and they need to be reminded by believers; it is the believer's chore to constantly witness (*dhākir*), both because of the human propensity to forgetfulness and because God has allowed Satan to entice humans away (17:62–64).

Like the Jewish and Christian scripture, the Qurʾān also remembers the origin of the human situation and presents two cosmic myths, both establishing important truths in the universe and in human life. In the first, critically, humans "know the names of things" and are thus superior in intelligence to the angels (2:31–33). Indeed, Adam taught the names to the angels. It is out of this superiority that Satan's downfall came, for he refused to prostrate himself before Adam as commanded by God (2:34; 20:116), with the result that he was banished to earth where he becomes a thorn in the side of all humans: "But Satan caused them both to stumble therein and thus brought about the loss of their erstwhile state. And so We said: Go down all of thee (and be henceforth) enemies unto one another; and on earth thou shalt have thy abode and thy livelihood for a while" (2:36).

The second cosmic myth shifts the focus somewhat. In it, God and Iblis hold a conversation that allows Satan to survive until the Day of Judgment:

When thy Lord said unto the angels: Lo! I am about to create a mortal out of mire.

And when I have fashioned him and breathed into him of My spirit, then fall down before him prostrate,

The angels fell down prostrate, every one.

Saving Iblis: he was scornful and became one of the disbelievers.

He said: O Iblis! What hindereth thee from falling prostrate before that which I have created with both my hands? Art thou too proud or art thou of the high (and mighty)?

He said: I am better than him. Thou createdst me of fire, whilst him Thou didst create of clay.

He said: Go forth from hence, for lo! thou art outcast,

And lo! My curse is on thee till the Day of Judgement. (38:72–79)

Thus the Qurʾān remembers the central role of God in fashioning humans . . . here God does it with His two hands, and breathes into the man His spirit (*rūḥ*), making Adam unique above all other creatures. Still greater is the ushering in of contention within the divine realm. According to this remembering, the creation of humans causes the first apparent rift within God's creation. These myths would eventually lead to much speculation on the human estate.[13]

Qurʾān 13:28 says: "Those who believe, and whose hearts find satisfaction in the remembrance of Allah; for without doubt, in the remembrance of Allah do hearts find satisfaction." The remembrance of Allah is a theme that runs throughout the Qurʾānic text. In 83:9, the remembrance of Allah is understood to embrace both acts of service and acts of kindliness, and failure to do both curbs spiritual growth. At the same time, the Qurʾān envisions dhikr as of wider significance than the formal requirement of prayer, including devotions such as silent meditation and personal contemplation (24:37). Remembrance is also linked directly to accepting Allah's guidance, a key initiative of God in human salvation, and failure to remember leads to the withdrawal of God's grace (72:17). We might summarize this theme with *āyat* 29:45: "Rememberance of Allah is the greatest thing in life, without doubt."

These notions have been enshrined in Sufism; it is in dhikr, a distinctive liturgical form within Islamic mysticism, that specific spiritual meanings and processes have been developed.

The Liturgical Practice of Dhikr in Moroccan Sufism

Dhikr is a pious ritual, designed for the brotherhood. I would not serve the tradition well if I regarded it as a public liturgy carried on in an environment open to all. Despite the popular nature of the rite and the many descriptions of its expression, and even the relative ease with which some have become members, it is a secret activity. It is open only to those "on the Way" and approved to be present by the shaikh or muqaddam.[14] During Ḥasan al-Baṣrī's time, it was a meditation on one's sinful character.[15] It evolved into a discipline established by the founder and carried on by his contemporary representative. This is signaled by the fact that dhikr is performed in the zāwiya, khāniqāh, or ribāṭ, all of which may be translated as convent, with all that means in terms of separation from society.[16] It is also characterized by its relative restriction concerning gender. It was traditionally an environment for men, even if women attended other kinds of Sufi functions. As I was told in Morocco, sometimes the shaikh arranges for a meditation dhikr for women in their own quarters. Consequently as it is practiced, it is not a popular activity even if common people join.

Clearly, there is a popular side to dhikr, since there are reports at times of orders flourishing because of their more popular nature. Shaikh Sayyid Barrāda told me that he deliberately popularized the dhikr in order to attract youth who are influenced by Western rock music and like to dance.[17] It is also manifest that many of the lyrics have been influenced by popular songs and poetry. Still it does not have the same popularity as sermons, many of which were given to the ordinary population by Sufi shaikhs and upon which some have built a considerable following.[18] Such sermonization must have attracted new numbers to the ṭarīqa, and fostered a diverse following. Furthermore, some shaikhs were gifted in special ways, and healings, granting boons, writing talismans, and foretelling events were numbered among the *karāmāt* or miracles assigned to them.[19] Such activities were regarded as part of the responsibility of the shaikh's spiritual position, and people coming with requests did not need to be known to the shaikh or his entourage. In that sense, the shaikh was like a public-spirited physician who treated all who came regardless of their status or affiliation. This more public role for the shaikh developed into what I will call a "congregational aggregate," a religious group that loosely connects itself to a dynamic and greater-than-human center, a feature that plays a distinctive role in the way in which Sufism grew in Morocco.

Marshall Hodgson argued that the role that mysticism played was not, strictly speaking, mystical; for him, the mystical aspect, or perhaps more pointedly, the ecstatic moment of the mystic, was part of a moral process of civilization. Hence he held that the mystical was but a kind of personal clarity, something like that which comes after one has had a fit of anger and then somewhat settled down . . . a clarity that allows one to see the situation from another, more convincing perspective than that during the heat of an argument.[20] That this tendency to move from the self-centeredness of one's feelings to a larger context, especially into one in which a relationship to God is the key feature, was also his perspective on recollection. For it was in this remembrance that one could be aware of one's complete humanness while being perfectly detached from one's own self-interest, in Hodgson's language, "to carry with it the moral standpoint of universality."[21] In this sense, then, mysticism's dhikr is not a closed liturgy designed for preferred adepts but a ritual with ramifications for everyone in society. It is a technique whose implication embraces the human totality; at its best, then, the concept of remembrance entails social betterment.[22]

Despite this rather formal argument for dhikr's classical meaning, dhikr as practiced was and is clearly fostered in a cloistered formation. In contrast to the *mūssem* (birth celebrations of the saint) in Morocco[23] and celebrations where a larger community of support could be found, dhikr is exclusive to the committed and functions within a secret society. One learns a shorthand code system for technical terms, one discovers the power of the local shaikh through firsthand experience, and one submits to the discipline of a guide with whom all spiritually significant secrets are shared. One does not usually communicate about the events and experiences of the zāwiyas to outsiders within Islam; nor, I must admit, does one trade secrets of the dhikr with scholars from outside Islam, regardless of how harmless they seem.

Kuper has made the telling comment that anthropologists seldom deal with the general concept of secrecy, apart from the function of so-called secret societies among Aboriginal peoples, yet she seems to think that sacred secrets become public through ritual.[24] My experience among both Sufi groups and Aboriginal peoples does not bear this out; very few initiates will immediately know the significance of everything that is said during a ritual, and others may only find out what is meant after a private counseling session, and even then only if the initiate is deemed advanced enough to appreciate the knowledge.[25]

A secret religious connection can also be empowering. For example, a distinguished Moroccan businessman conveyed to me that he owed his position in life to the baraka of a local shaikh who helped him with a business proposal early in his career, and that help was the basis of his later success.[26] While he would not indicate the nature of the assistance, it was clear that he gave immense deference to the shaikh and had reverence for the beneficent power of his benefactor, and, while secular in almost every other way, he always remembered the shaikh with gifts and accorded him undying respect. Few knew of this connection, and it is unlikely that his international business partners knew. This was a secret, though, that had a profound effect on the way he carried on his life.

Furthermore, what he implied to me was that he remained in touch with the spiritual resources of the shaikh through a personal dhikr. It was learned and practiced in the company of those who accepted certain limits on the dissemination of religious truths for everyone, in this case, in the personal presence of the shaikh when the businessman had time on occasion to visit him. In general, then, these examples demonstrate that dhikr in Islam is an expression carrying social restrictions.

All Sufi groups have dhikr, but not all have chant or singing. In some groups it is merely cadent speech. As previously noted, then, another standard applies to those who do chant: chanting is an act of spiritual expression reserved primarily for the zāwiya and zāwiya society. This is evident by the attitude toward those munshidūn who sing outside the confines of the zāwiya, as, for example, at weddings and mūlid celebrations.[27] Their confreres speak openly of the munshid having been enthralled by the prospect of a larger audience, or the money, or the popularity. Even those who do not do it regularly pay a price; some are reluctant to regard such munshidūn as having the same spiritual intensity.

One way of understanding its significance is to say that ṭarīqa life is constituted by dhikr in the same way that maintaining connection to the Catholic Church is constituted by the taking of the Eucharist. All people who are members of an order express the idea that belonging is tracked through participation in the order's practice, and they view that participation as essential for their spiritual well-being. Lack of active participation in dhikr is one of the first signs that a person has lost his spiritual perspective, at least as far as the shaikh and the members of the order are concerned. Thus participation functions as a kind of spiritual barometer, and a marker of religious intentionality and commitment.

The role of dhikr is highlighted in most writings of Sufi savants, and each has a particular way of expressing its significance. In order to give a flavor of this productivity, we will examine three masters who were influential in Morocco: ʿAbd al-Qādir al-Jīlānī (1077–1166), Ibn al-ʿArabī (1165–1240), and al-ʿArabī al-Darqāwī (1823).[28]

ʿAbd al-Qādir was the father of Sufi orders. Born in the village of Niff, in Jīlān, he emigrated to Baghdad when he was eighteen to study Islamic law at the famous

Nizāmiyya school of al-Ghazālī. Initiated into the Sufi life by ʿAbu Saʿad al-Mubārak al-Muḥārrimī, ʿAbd al-Qādir practiced his personal dhikr by reciting the names of God in his khalwa after the evening prayer. His definition of dhikr is drawn from his writings by Ainī:

> Dhikr is the impact produced when God comes fully, by eternal grace divine, into the intimacy of the initiate's heart, which is in perpetual evolution towards "God." And this dhikr illuminates and enchants the heart of the devotee. Consequently, he desires never to forget God, and wants nothing to distract him from His remembrance, he wants nothing to enfeeble, nor to trouble his well-being. In this case the initiate must repeat the Qurʾān, in the following saying: "O you who believe! recall often the name of God; recall him, and celebrate his praises morning and night" (33:41). The best dhikr is therefore that which springs up from the depths of the heart, inspired by the Glorious Lord![29]

Accordingly, ʿAbd al-Qādir developed the conception of the seven degrees within the human heart and then proposed seven different dhikrs to correspond to the needs and spiritual requirements of each level; each also entrains moral and religious values.[30]

The Qādiriyya were introduced into Morocco by the descendents of ʿAbd al-Qādir's sons, Ibrahīm (d. 1196) and ʿAbd al-Azīz (d. ?); both had settled in Spain. Their descendents were forced to flee as refugees to Morocco before the battle of Grenada (1492). The khalwa is first noted in Fez in 1692, where the order is known by the name of Jīlālā.[31]

The second master of dhikr is Ibn al-ʿArabī, who was perhaps the greatest intellectual mystic Islam ever produced:

> [Prayer] being a discourse, it is also a remembrance, since whoever remembers God sits with God and God with him, as mentioned in the tradition, "I am the companion of him who remembers Me."[32] Now whoever, being perceptive, is in the presence of the one he is remembering, he sees his companion. In such case there is contemplation and vision, otherwise he does not see Him. . . . In the prayer, the most effective element is the remembrance of God, by virtue of the words and actions it comprises. We have, however, described the state of the Perfect Man in prayer, in the *Meccan Revelations* (*al-Futūḥāt al-makkiyyah*). God has said, *Surely, the prayer prevents much evil and sin,* (29:45) seeing that the one praying is forbidden to occupy himself with anything else while he is engaged in it. *But the remembrance of God is greater,* (29:45) that is to say that, within the context of prayer, God's remembering of His servant when He responds to his request is greater. Furthermore, in the prayer, the servant's praising of God is greater than his

remembering Him, since all majesty belongs to God. Thus, He says, *And God knows what you fashion* (29:45) and, *or who listens and watches* (29:45). The listening derives from God's remembering of His servant in prayer.[33]

The third great Moroccan mystic is Mulay al-ʿArabī al-Darqāwī, whose advice on the topic of dhikr is described thus:

> Lastly, my brother, I strongly advise you—"religion is sincere counsel"—not to give up the remembrance (dhikr) of your Lord, as He himself told you to do it, "standing, sitting and reclining" (4:104) and in all conditions, for we need nothing but that, we, you and every man, whoever he may be.
>
> Listen to what I am about to say to you and do not forget it, do not take it lightly or let it go unheeded: in the course of the past fifty-five years or so, I have said to many a brother: every single man has any number of needs, but in reality all men need only one thing, which is truly to practice the remembrance of God; if they have acquired that, they will not want for anything, whether they possess it or do not possess it.[34]

The Linkages and Connections of Dhikr

As Hodgson suggests, mysticism's practice connects it with several important strands in Muslim experience. The following sections examine some of the most important ways that dhikr is linked to other aspects of religious life.

Prayer and Dhikr

Prayer is canonical. It is the authoritative action, vouchsafed by the Prophet and instituted as the required formula by which humans engage with and can be engaged by the divine. It is thus the vehicle that carries human repentance to God, while allowing God to measure to the penitent forgiveness and restoration. Each *rakʿah* (section) of the prayer is broken into eight parts, *niyyah* (intention), takbīr (saying of "God is the most great"), *qiyām* (standing), *rukūʿ* (bowings), *sujūd* (prostration), *jalsah* (sitting), second sujūd, and *taslīm* (greeting). The disengagement from the normal stance of worldly affairs is set by the niyyah; through it, the soul and mind of the believer is turned inward to his spiritual state, and he becomes aware of his position before the divine.[35] Let us refer to niyyah as "threshold disengagement," reflecting its essential function of shifting the whole reference system into another framework. The takbīr becomes then the port of entry into the prayer proper.

The threshold disengagement initiated in prayer sets the mind and body into synchronicity . . . the mind and soul establish a bilateral framework for the physical and mental self to be brought into the presence of God. On the one hand, the threshold disengagement sets the self's affections toward God, removing the believer from the profane world and placing the believer in a spiritual space. It creates, to use

Turner's language, a liminal space. At the same time, the body is engaged in orienting itself in the environment of the divine, delivering in physical movements (the rakʿah) a coded message. Whether one performs the obligatory rakʿahs (*fard*), or those extra prayers recalled and admonished in the Sunnah of the Prophet, or the *nawāfil* (those prayers regarded as superrogatory and nonobligatory but highly recommended for piety's sake), the vehicle does not change. Here is the non-oral, physical language of submission, laid down by God for engagement with Him. The Sufis have constructed on the baseline of personal piety, that is, the liminal space of prayer, a multifaceted network open to various personal, social, and religious needs. The first entry point to this network is the liturgical, that is, dhikr.

The above-noted ingredients—the threshold disengagement, the bilateral rules, and the coded messages of prayer—set the structural underpinnings of dhikr and provide the skeleton for engagement with the divine. This is important because it *grounds the ritual practices of the Sufis on the model of the canonical prayer.* This is why charges that dhikr should be interrupted when designated times of prayer intervene have usually been rejected by shaikhs.[36] This is also why the shaikh will maintain strict control over the framework of the dhikr and will "read" the progression of the dhikr in moving it from one level of rhythm and intensity to another. The framework of engagement with the denizens of the transcendent realm cannot be sustained liturgically in a limitless manner, and the speed and movement of the dhikr require careful evaluation in order to "ride the waves" of the emotional and spiritual mood to *ḥāl* (state of mystical experience). Like prayer, then, the adepts must be guided through the various religious postures at a proper spiritual pace, for the shaikh knows that the framework is more or less constructed on the basis of the spiritual progression practiced in the religious culture of his ṭarīqa.

Spoken Qurʾān and Dhikr

Spoken verses from the Qurʾān carry with them the power of the transcendent,[37] since they convey the divine intention to humans and are articulated through God's divine breath to the human plane. This spoken Word of God is the vehicle through which Muslims may know God and comprehend God's will.[38] Hence, all dhikr builds upon Qurʾānic phrase and idiom to interlock the energies deemed latent in the Divine Word into their lives and thoughts. Given that the most rudimentary of Muslim education involves the memorization of the Qurʾān, what Sufi liturgy does is to "corporealize" this memory in a liturgical form, that is, the power of the spoken Qurʾān is "physicalized" in the dhikr. Remembering the Qurʾān, then, is not a static process of memorizing verses and storing them away in the brain. One learns the verses and has them come alive within the physical movement of the ritual moment where the verses serve as conduits for spiritual energy to the devotees' inner beings.

The Body and Dhikr

Dhikr is not held to be a mental exercise only, for the assumption of Muslim liminality is that it incorporates the whole being into engagement. To use Western terminology, the body as well as the mind is enlisted in moving into this liminal space. In Judith Lynne Hanna's study on religion and dance, we are reminded that "the mediation of dance brings human and supernatural into a communication system. . . . . In the sphere of total human body in action, dance functions as a conventional sign of reverence."[39] In the same vein, in recalling the life and piety of his associate, Ibn al-ʿArabī touches on the integral relationship of the body and the Qurʾān: "When he prayed the midday prayer he would take the Qurʾān and, placing it between his knees, would follow the letters with his finger and read it to himself until the time for the late-afternoon prayer. Thus he would continue the reading of the previous night. I asked him about it and he replied that he did this so that each part of his body might acquire from his reading what was appropriate to it."[40]

A concept also related to body and the Qurʾān is breath. Haas has argued that the North African Khalwātiyya zāwiya of Raḥmānija (Raḥmāniyya) fostered a dhikr that made the ḥāl accessible to the great mass of believers. The emphasis was on rapid inhaling and exhaling, creating a hyperventilated effect. This was necessary since "the state of consciousness thus produced has nothing to do with the ḥāl obtained by years of mystic contemplation and practice." He refers to the masses' state as "pseudo-mystic" and concludes that "it is drastic and rough if compared to the methods that rule the true mystic path."[41] The ḥāl created, he suggests, is not one with divinity, but one of corporate psychological union, molded out of suggestive and hypnotic effect that overwhelms the individual's sense of separate identity.[42]

Apart from the class differential here, what Haas will have to explain is why the perfectly healthy, respectable individuals one meets throughout the Muslim world should find this state of ḥāl to be so religiously and personally enriching. Rather than declaratively insisting that these adepts were in a pseudomystic state arising from rapid breathing, it is better to hear what the experts have to say. To do otherwise is to imply, first of all, that what they said was not true, and second that they were just being led into this experience by a charlatan. A much more scientific attitude would be to ask a different question: how can we understand what the adept is experiencing? Haas's perspective belongs to the same genre of social explanations we find from Durkheim[43] to Radcliffe-Brown[44] to Evans-Pritchard[45] and Douglas.[46] They contend that they can explain to researchers what happens in rituals like dhikr without taking the local explanation into consideration. Kennedy still has the most succinct criticism of such a stance:

All sociological analyses are based upon a set of psychological assumptions—an implicit, and therefore often gross, theory of mental and emotional processes. . . . One obvious implication of such a realization is that the implicit assumptions should be made explicit, so that their validity may be judged, and their ramifications followed out. A further and perhaps more important implication is that a sophisticated psychological model be employed by the student of social behaviour. These implications are quite formidable and we cannot blame individual scholars who quail before the difficult labour entailed by the Pandora's box of psychologies which is thereby immediately opened.[47]

When I presented a sociological thesis as an explanation for the dhikr to several munshidūn, including a medical doctor among them, they replied that such explanations were prompted by atheism, not by science. A more legitimate view, they argued, was to take the view of the practitioners into account, insofar as it could account for the facts. Thus rather than ask how this can be explained using non-religious terminology, or how such a state could be promoted by disreputable people, ask rather how adepts find that one ḥal can be better than another[48] and what this tells us about religious experience in general. As was to be expected, they continued to wonder at the Western scholar's futile attempt to explain away religious experience. This point of view is also present in the more contemporary psychological research; as Hay puts it, "instead of thinking of religious experience 'as if' it were induced, we could consider it 'as if' it were something of which people become aware."[49]

The absurdity of Haas's kind of analysis is met most forcefully in the analysis of breathing techniques. He holds that breath modification is utilized during the course of the dhikr as a means to restrain the adept from a possible suspension of consciousness, since the adepts could launch very quickly into such a state if there were not two parts to the breathing cycle, presumably because they would hyper-ventilate. He does not explain why this delay should be desirable at all if the state of ḥāl , or suspension of consciousness, is the desired outcome.

The Sufi explanation is far more plausible: the adept is moving through several levels of ecstatic experience and only reaches this more peaceful level of ḥāl after great struggle, concretely denoted by the rough and difficult breathing exercises. At the more advanced level of ḥāl, having learned to discipline their disruptive minds and spirits through the dhikr, the adepts are all at peace in their relationship to the transcendent presence (whether the depicted referent is held to be God or the Prophet or the saint). They have reached a state where they experience no conflictual/separational situation between their human selves and the 'presence' they encounter. Such a notion of states of ḥāl also allows one to accommodate the obvious fact that not everyone enters into ḥāl at the same speed or intensity, and some do not enter ḥāl at all. Yet each can regard it as a "good dhikr."

Moreover, Haas believes that this use of breathing rituals is a minor survivor of yogic breathing techniques imported into the fringe area of Islam from the original founder who spent some time in India.[50] While the acquisition notion might have some validity, it is hardly true that this is a fringe element. The ascetic tradition, dating back to the time of Ḥasan al-Baṣri, has sought to reduce words to their more primal form, that is, breath, as one means of reducing the distance between the original impulse and the resulting word formation. Breathing techniques must be applied to all Sufi recitations, for the rhythm of the inhaling and exhaling plays a role in articulation and in chanting. Proper breathing is one subject that the munshidūn had to learn as they were training to be religious chanters. Thus, breathing exercises, while they are not explored to the extent one finds in Hindu yoga, nevertheless are a crucial element of the remembering structure in Sufism. This should not surprise us since it is in line with the belief that there is a reality beyond the ability of words to convey, and it is to this reality that the Sufi goal is directed. The notion is a staple in the Sufi philosophical lexicon.

Trance and Dhikr

It is important to go beyond Weber's notions of the trance or ecstasy as a singular experience. He wrote: "Ecstasy as an instrument of salvation or deification, our exclusive interest here, may have the essential character of an acute mental aberration or possession, or else the character of a chronically heightened idiosyncratic religious mood, tending either towards greater intensity of life or toward alienation from life. This escalated, intensified religious mood can be of either a more contemplative or more active type."[51]

The implication of his claim is that trance or ecstasy is a stand-alone experience identifiable by the distinctive "possession" or "idiosyncratic religious mood." In fact what occurs is neither of these descriptors, but a morphological modification of the person through remembering past spiritual models. The articulation of these pasts, however, ultimately falls back on group-approved descriptors. Yet it should be noted that ecstasy always takes place through a communication medium, of dance, music, language, visions, stylized motions, stances, and so on, and the mode of expression arises out of the cultural milieu in which the trance takes place. It is important to note that the trance never takes place as an unconnected experience. While it appears *just as if* it were a unique experience, it finds validation in the signification of the group's remembrance. The trance is *expressive of* a religious system, then, and not a type of religious mood or a self-deification arising out of some kind of suppression.[52]

Indication of these perceptions arises from my fieldwork. The following are my notes from a visit to the zāwiya of the Darqāwiyya al-Shādhiliyya in Tetouan for the mūssem of Sīdī al-ʿArabī al-Darqāwī; I reproduce them here in their entirety because they deal directly with this topic:

After maghrib prayers, we proceeded to the main zāwiya on the second floor of the newly painted white complex, built into the hillside. Already adepts were milling around the door, removing shoes and placing them against the wall along the south side of the room. The room itself was large, approximately 15 meters by 30 meters, with a raised dais along the east wall enclosed by a guardrail. The shaikh, an entourage of officials, munshidūn, and musicians entered and moved to the northern end of the hall, where they sat against the wall or, in the case of musicians and munshidūn, cross-legged on the floor. The chanting began with the *Bourda,* and the slow recitation of *wird.* Then began the chanting of the dhikr, with the younger and training singers going first and contributing one song. A drummer wandered among the adepts who were now stretched out in a rough circle around the room, with arms linked. They began a slow rocking back and forth, but moved to a little jump when the rhythm increased and the cycle changed speed. All the while the *naqīb* of the dance, a man of over sixty years, kept time by clapping his hands and directing the musicians. Throughout the evening, a cycle of dhikr would be followed by a cycle of rest and drinking of special nectar and tea. During the jumping dhikr, young men, dressed in very fine robes, moved into the centre of the circling adepts, and suddenly were seized by great excitement. They began moving rapidly back and forth within the circle, now jumping straight up in the air and waving their feet back and forth like wings before descending again to the floor. All this they accomplished with eyes tightly closed. They appeared to be in trance. Some broke off and began racing with great abandon around the inside of the ring. With several running with their eyes closed, it seemed only likely that they would collide; that they did not was a further sign, I was told, of the baraka of the saint. The dhikr lasted until about midnight, and all kept up the running or jumping for considerable lengths of time. Finally, at the climax of the evening, the whole group performed a small jumping pattern. The youths gradually ceased to run, the music ended, and the adepts slowly moved from the hall. The next evening, I had an opportunity to talk to the young men. They were euphoric, and reported tremendous joy and lightness from the trance state. Three of them indicated they were training to be munshidūn.

Religious trance is distinguished in the literature from a wide range of changed perceptual states, such as hypnosis, lucid dreaming, daydreaming, and REM (rapid eye movement) sleep; in the West, the religious trance has received very bad press because it was the focus of the Freudian analysis of neuroses.[53] Perceptions have changed somewhat since Bourguignon's study in the 1960s found that 92 percent of 488 small societies around the world demonstrated what could be called trance behavior.[54] Indeed, ritualized trance, that is, trance operating within the bounds of religious ritual and responding to signals from a ritual custodian, may well be universal. Eliade rooted the experience in the archaic shaman, seeing this as the genesis of a fundamental religious form.[55]

Even the most cursory familiarity with altered states of consciousness indicates that there are different kinds of experience, of different duration and goals. Goodman addressed this variety by breaking the experiences down into episodes with a port of entry or *start* (usually with the impression of a boundary that must be crossed); a *sojourn* (with various kinds of physiological effects such as swooning, trembling, or twitching that may involve a peak experience, such as ḥāl); followed by *dissolution* (return to normal consciousness) and *aftereffects* (joy, euphoria, heat).[56] What she has forgotten is the interpretative structure that frames these elements. Two areas that apply to the sojourn phase are critical. First, the shape of the experience is often driven by a set of needs or is directed toward the benefit of the "self-in-a-better-state." And, second, memory is the necessary ground for the structure to function. It is remembrance, then, that provides a way both of knowing the primary intent of the sojourn and judging the effectiveness of the experience. Memory is the fuel cell that runs the ecstatic experience, because one remembers the way of ḥāl and proceeds along it. With this in mind, Kotre's tripartite requirements (see chapter 1) might well find a place in this analysis.

Wajd, the Arabic word for trance, is the term used most often in Western materials for what occurs. This category of experience would, however, be better translated as "altered state of consciousness," since, on the basis of the Moroccan material alone, there are great differences in the experience. Some of them vary widely from the category descriptions outlined by Goodman.[57] What seems clear is that the sojourn phase can be given multiple tasks according to the spiritual requirements of the individual, all because some basic spiritual needs are being addressed in the ritual. For example, ʿAbd al-Qādir identified trance as follows: "It is the abundant felicity of spirit, provoked by the exercise of dhikr and the graceful plentitude of the soul, in communion with the spirit. The overpowered consciousness becomes free, with a liberty such that one is no longer enslaved to any object estranged from God, with a freedom which one bequeaths solely to one's Beloved Lord."[58] ʿAbd al-Qādir's description is a fine example of the three elements in Kotre: the trance, the interpretation of the trance, and the blending of the fact and interpretation in a summary statement depicting the meaning of the whole phenomenon.

Given its place in the establishment of Sufism in Morocco, we should then expect that the trance is a commonplace among Sufi groups;[59] it is, but interestingly, it is not universal in Morocco. Those groups influenced by reformist tendencies, such as the Tijāniyya, are one exception.[60] What seems evident is that, once past the threshold of disengagement, there are several ports of entry for the Sufi, each with different goal-oriented trajectories: The most important seem to be telic, mergent, and assertive.[61] Telic, from the Greek word *telos* (goal), affirms that the prime intentionality of the religious behavior will have a shaping impact throughout the activity. Thus, for example, if trance is the vehicle for healing, the telic quality of addressing the health issue will remain uppermost throughout the ceremony. This latter characteristic is evident in the dhikr of the Ginawa, as several studies have indicated.[62]

In al-Darqāwī's *Letters of a Sufi Master* we read: "I was in a state which was a very intense combination of spiritual intoxification and sobriety as, one evening, I entered the mosque which contains the tomb of the Husaynī Sharīf, Aḥmad as-Siqāllī in Fez."[63] This is quite an extraordinary statement, because intoxification is generally a word for advanced ḥāl, a totally altered state of consciousness in Sufi parlance. The sobriety indicates that he nevertheless was not exuberant to the point of losing his mind but had passed beyond that experience to quiet mergence with the divine presence.[64] Mergence thus indicates a neutral position beyond the separation of self from the other, however that other may be conceived. Sufis have traditionally called this *fanāʿ*, usually translated in English as "extinction," a word with little plasticity in its meaning. *Mergence* has the advantage of implying movement and dynamism within the relationship, a characteristic that is lost in the concept of union; even *wuṣūl,* usually translated as union with God, is more elastic than the English word, for it implies being involved in movement toward and arrival at an end point in one's relationship with God.

Mergence also identifies the ground of the experience . . . a mutual redefinition of specificity arising out of the encounter itself, a point that lies at the heart of Ibn al-ʿArabī's mystical philosophy. According to Austin, Ibn al-ʿArabī contends that "there is rather a relationship of mutual conditioning going on by which each, at once, experiences and determines the other."[65] The great Andalusian mystic sees a dynamic relationship as essential because love, the framework of his interpretation of the divine-human relationship, requires differentiation in order for love to be possible. At the same time, love is a kind of infidelity, because it requires a movement away from absolute cohesion of the pair. Thus what the Sufi is constantly engaged in, from a theoretical point of view, is the paradoxical movement toward merging with the divine presence, at the same time that love pulls toward individualization. No wonder, then, that when Haas analyzed the dhikr of the Raḥmāniyya, it appeared to be constructed of two contrasting and differentiating sections.[66] It was because of the dynamic at the heart of the adept's reality; understanding the process requires a ritual formula reflecting the paradox of the mystical experience. While this paradox may pose problems for exclusionary logic, it is intellectually quite conceivable and understandable. We might say that, for Ibn al-ʿArabī, as for many practitioners in Morocco, love has its own logic of separation.

Finally, there is the assertive trajectory. Sufis speak of freedom from a range of inhibitors, beginning with their households and including rules laid down by society and religion. Shaikh al-Darqāwī stressed how dhikr delivers freedom from the drives and needs of the self: "Every single person has many needs but in reality all people need is only one thing, which is truly to remember God; if they have acquired that, they will not want for anything, nor whether they possess something or do not."[67] One group of Sufis, the *Malāmatiyya*, deliberately sought out situations in which the more orthodox would react with criticism or blame, as a means to set themselves apart for spiritual disciplines.[68] Such assertiveness directs the self to take stands on issues that are not popular. The intention is to be only what God wishes regardless of the norms of society or even of one's own achievements. Within the spiritual state, self-abnegation becomes a program of rejection of one's heart's desire, all for the greater good of Sufism or Islam. In such a case, the self denies the self for the pursuit of a greater spiritual good. The metaphor of blame also plays an important role in the chanter's lyrics, as we will see in chapter 4. Assertiveness also requires the Sufi to actively forget his personal self, making forgetfulness into a positive religious expression. But it further highlights the paradoxes inherent in the Sufi way, paradoxes that require the Sufi to step aside from the ordinary affairs of life and trust in God, while at the same time trying to be true to the Sufi's personal identity as a mystic. That paradox requires the sensitivity of effective evaluation and decision making, for which direction one chooses has implications for the religious outcomes. There is a logic to this that arises out of the framework one is maintaining. It does not surprise us to learn that the saint spent much of his time in counseling his adepts on weighing and balancing. Teachings of balance, of course, derive from the balance deemed constituent of religious life in the Qurʾān and Islamic religious life.

At the same time, Sufism teaches that ordinary life is awash in forgetfulness; forgetfulness functions in the Sufi realm as *māya* does in Hinduism, or as sinfulness does in Christianity. It is the natural state of nonawareness that has dire consequences in terms of religious perception.[69] One of the screening devices that comes into play as one moves through a *wajh* or altered state of consciousness is the change of perspective. This mental movement allows one to remember the proper motivations for life and to adjust one's priorities, as in the story I encountered in Morocco of the Sufi who required a businessman who was a suitor of his daughter to spend some time in the zāwiya in order to prove his determination to marry her. He became so enthralled with the spiritual life that he gave up his business and became a Sufi.

Movement and Dhikr

We have touched on physicality through a discussion of breath; evidently this is a problematic relationship. The Moroccan munshid Ashḥab indicated that it was impossible to be in the presence of God and the Prophet and not physically *move*, citing as proof that human response patterns to God have been codified in the movements of prayer. For him, this meant that God expected the human, *as body,* to respond when He was present; Ashḥab noted that before prayer, the body was the first to express a prayerful pose, as was evident in the Abraham story in the Hebrew Bible.[70] The primacy of movement and gestures as a necessary language before God, even before the articulation of any phrase, is likewise affirmed by the fact that only one canonical prayer of the day is audible. This requirement is not offset even though recitation of the prayer formula requires an inner rehearsing of words. Audible articulation is clearly subservient to the outer movement of body and the inner vocalization of sacred text.

Without doubt, then, Sufism has enshrined gesture communication as fundamental to its ritual expression; all dhikr sessions, even of the most judicious and restricted kind, are accompanied by head or body movement. In religious ritual generally, the gesture carries considerable weight, as I discovered in my research into the Oblate missionary Roger Vandersteene among the Cree.[71] In fact, research now makes it evident that gesture communication either precedes or subsists with the verbal.[72] What seemed evident to me is that in Sufi movement we encounter a structure of movement that unites body, mind, and self in a more fundamental manner than Western scholarly analyses of Sufism to date have grasped. It embraces not only the movement within the rituals themselves, but configures attitudes of mind and displacement along with journeys of discovery. Some of these are addressed in the next chapter, but here we will sketch the ritual aspect associated with dhikr.

In dhikr, the physical motions and gestures carry with them several formative influences. The first is the way in which the culture of the group has learned and carries out the whole program of gesture, a remembering that links the practitioner to the original formula established by the saint. This remembered formula can only be broken if granted by the contextual approval of the muqaddam or shaikh in charge of the dhikr. One can hear complaints that the participants are raw or young, meaning that they cannot move in a sophisticated manner and thus do not move appropriately. On one occasion I saw the director of the dhikr pull someone out of the line and put him down with the young initiates; he explained to me that this was a way of disciplining him for not attending regularly and for thus being raw in his dhikr. In the past, he obviously had moved appropriately and was therefore placed within the line of seasoned and trusted adepts. This is a principle, it was explained, that applies to both sport and spiritual fitness: If he forgets who he really is, through his involvement in the forgetfulness of the world, then he needs to be, so to speak, retooled or retrained. It is the responsibility of the shaikh to gauge the depth to which forgetfulness has overtaken the adept and deal with it within the ritual.

Connerton addresses this important issue in a general manner, building on Merleau-Ponty's remark that the phenomenon of habit requires a restating of the notions of "understanding" and "body"; he insists that "habit is a knowledge and a remembering in the hands and in the body. In the cultivation of habit it is our body which 'understands.'"[73] Using habit instead of disposition because it focuses on "the sense of operativeness, of a continuously practised activity," such that "the body comes to co-ordinate an increasing range of muscular activities in an automatic way, until awareness retreats, the movement flows 'involuntarily,' and there occurs a firm and practised sequence of acts which take their fluent course."[74] In the case above, the irregular dhikr of the lapsing member is evidence already that he has entered into the territory of forgetfulness, his spiritual muscles are untoned, his habit decaying. Dhikr is a bodily understanding that must be kept in training, and like the hockey player whose movements from forward to backward skating should be without flaw and whose handling of the puck on his stick should be so automatic that he knows what the puck is doing on his stick every moment even if he is not consciously looking at it, the committed dhikr participant "knows" the movement up the spiritual ladder *with his body* in such a way as to circumvent self-conscious awareness. Thus in the Sufi case, Connerton's definition should be modified to include the notion that, when the bodily movement of dhikr begins, the *self*-awareness of the adept retreats. At the summit of the dhikr, self-awareness is abandoned for the bodily merging into a higher process of engagement than what the conscious self can arrange for it.

There is also sensed evaluation of the dhikr: one often hears from the participants about the effectiveness of a dhikr, indicating that there is an evaluative ingredient attending every performance that involves a wide range of factors. Among the factors are the spiritual tone of the chanter, the energy infused into the dhikr, the presence of God, the Prophet, or the saint, the spiritual presence of experienced adepts, the inspired insight of the naqīb, and whether the day itself was auspicious or not. There can be widespread agreement on this evaluation, so it is not just a personal judgment.

Performance and Dhikr

In contrast to personal meditation, and even to canonical prayer (save, perhaps, the Friday noon prayer), both of which may well be solitary activities, dhikr is necessarily a group activity; the blessings attendant only come when the members perform it together. Moreover, as it is constituted in Morocco, it is composed of the blending of oral/sung narration and body movement, both components of which involve the group *performing together*. Thus both the form of liturgical expression and the performance are social events that are integrated through the ritual. As such it constitutes a system of language and movement codes. The performance of the munshid is only one element in a coded system that has as its goal the transcending of the corporate into a telic experience of significance.

When asked whether he chants anything new, Nabīl replied with an indulgent smile and a shaking head: "No! Definitely not! What I sing are the words and lyrics of the past. It is through them that God's blessings come to the adepts—they are related to God—I can't change them." The point is not that dhikr as a movement, in and of itself, is deemed to be beneficial, heedless of the initial spiritual outcomes. Rather, there are codes of performance that come into play both from the perspective of the munshid and the participants in dhikr. The basic stance is found in Ibn al-ʿArabī's affirmation: "Do not abandon dhikr because you do not feel the Presence of God therein. For your forgetfulness of Him is worse than your forgetfulness *in* the dhikr of Him. Perhaps He will take you from a dhikr of forgetfulness to one with vigilance, and from one with vigilance to one with the Presence of God, and one with the Presence of God to one wherein everything but the Invoked is absent. *And that is not difficult for God.* "(Qurʾān 14:20)

Ibn al-ʿArabī was insisting on something very important about dhikr as religious activity: The very performance of it has beneficial effects, *even when the effects are not articulated or consciously encountered.* Carrying out the performance has its own intrinsic graces . . . participation with the brethren, obedience to the liturgical cadences, adjusting one's demeanor, subjecting oneself to a ritual act, etc. These effects are positive, even if, as Ibn al-ʿArabī says, the presence is not felt.

But his critical point is forgetfulness. For him, there is the *religious* problem of forgetfulness. Forgetfulness is part of the normal awareness of life, a kind of attendance to a packaged meaning that is most deadly because one is not aware. Better to be engaged in dhikr, even if inner engagement is not there, than not. For in the participation, one is, to change the metaphor, at least speaking the language of remembrance. Performance makes engagement possible. This notion is also expressed in the fact that dhikr does not have an audience: those who are not in the dhikr will eventually be considered as outsiders, for dhikr is a validated religious and emotional field of its own. This was brought home by the statement of the shaikh who insisted that an adept who had not participated in the dhikr for several rounds "get in line" (that is, into the dhikr position), "lest you become cold." In this regard, Rappoport has indicated a critical element in performance:

> To say that performers participate in or become parts of the orders they are realizing is to say that transmitter-receivers become fused with the messages they are transmitting and receiving. In conforming to the orders that their performances bring into being, and that come alive in their performance, performers become indistinguishable from those orders, parts of them, for the time being. Since this is the case, for performers to reject liturgical orders being realized by their own participation in them as they are participating in them is self-contradictory, and thus impossible. Therefore, by performing a liturgical order the participants accept, and indicate to themselves and to others that they accept whatever is encoded in the canon of that order.[75]

Being an observer does not deliver the same cohesion, even, I think, as an audience.[76] We might say, then, that as the adepts become fused with the dhikr of the order, they *become* the exemplification of the order. They *are,* so to speak, the order for that time and place. Thus Nabīl *cannot* chant anything but the words of the order from the past, because those words are the means to the fusion. At the same time, he chants these words anew because what we have is really *memory made present* in a way that removes its past history. We might call this the archetypal content of dhikr's ritual performance.

At the same time, this content cannot be understood as a relic, as Rabinow's comment above indicates; it is enlivened and embodied in the present moment. Participation is participation *with*—, not with the brethren, but with an interactive Presence. It is because the dhikr engages God in the same kind of dialogue as that constructed by prayer that dhikr takes on a current life: fresh spiritual outcomes occur. Hence from the standpoint of the Sufi adept, the most important thing about performance is not that he carries out the liturgical requirements perfectly (as Rappoport seems to imply)—there is room for the nonmandatory here—but that it promises a fusion with Presence.

Sufis make a distinction within the experience of fusion, basing it upon grades of awareness built into the dhikr. Thus, for example, Nabīl's chants, as words, do not deliver Presence in and of themselves. Rather, as he understands the teachings of the ʿAissawiyya, he is only providing an aural platform through which the deeper adept can hear the true message. Hence it is not the case that he can deliver a "flawed" text, for even if he makes a mistake, it may be understood by someone as providing a way into tawḥīd (lit. oneness) *for that person.* Thus it is not the text itself, in terms of pure diction, that carries the power, but the intentionality of his heart in delivering the message that then conveys the platform for spiritual insight. It is his inspired heart, so to speak, transcending the limitations of the words and mediating the spiritual power to the listener through his own spiritual state. This notion is close to that expressed by Ibn ʿAṭa'illāh; he insisted that the whole point of dhikr was to lead to God's *tawḥīd,* a notion that arises out of the *Shahāda (lā ilāha-illā-Llāh).* Tawḥīd was juxtaposed to everything that stood "alongside" God, meaning that everything that claims existence apart from God is, in actual fact, only illusion. The real problem in dhikr is not keeping to the formal order, as Rappoport insists, but realizing that those who participate in dhikr do so starting at quite different levels of spiritual sophistication. Thus Shaikh Ibn ʿAṭa'illāh says: "Dhikr has three stations: the dhikr of the tongue, which is the dhikr of the generality; the dhikr with the heart, which is the dhikr of the elect amongst those having faith; and the dhikr with the Spirit, which is for the elect of the elect, and is the dhikr of those of maʿrifa (gnosis: spiritual insight, awareness or knowledge), who are extinguished from their own dhikr by the contemplation of the Tawḥīd who is their Rememberer (i.e. one of the names of God)."[77]

The same conception was spelled out by munshid Ashḥab Ibrahim:

"What we see in dhikr is not one kind of trance. There are really three kinds of fanāʿ . . . fanāʿ fi'l-shaikh [extinction in the shaikh], fanāʿ fi'l-nabī [extinction in the Prophet], and fanāʿ fi'llāh [extinction in Allah]. The first level is reserved for all believers; the second is for the muqaddam and ṭarīqa specialists. The third is for all those deep in the way, the full initiates. We chant knowing the limitations of those to whom we chant."

For the munshid's performance, then, the text as text is only a proclamative device for those of "the generality"; those who have "gone inside" already understand the referential importance of text, that is, the text refers to or points to the inspiration of the heart, thus bypassing the hegemony of the text itself. Those at the highest level do not pronounce dhikr themselves but already are aware of how God's Name of Dhikr remembers them in the very pronouncement of the Name, for all expressions of dhikr are conceived of as but a recollection of the Divine Remembering. Only when the munshid is aware of the three levels of meaning in the words of his message can he adequately be said to have chanted in dhikr. Thus the munshid already knows whether he is chanting effectively if all three levels of adepts can be said to be merging toward the experience of tawḥīd. This is his measure of the success of his performance.

Performance also provides something else: a situation in which the very mood associated with the sainted memory of the founder is initialized into the action. Hence, whether it is one of contemplation, expectation, reflection, or submission, a religious mood is rescripted as the medium of remembrance. This is why the meeting at which dhikr is carried out is called *ḥaḍra* (presence), for it is conceived not as a group meeting, nor as an organization of adepts, but as a collective occasion for the feeling of presence. This is an encounter with a level of reality along the path toward mergence; as one adept put it, "The air is electric from God taking over the whole atmosphere."[78]

Thus transcendent presence is both new each time and a replication; it is new to the extent that both sound and motion triggers will be unique to every occasion, but it will be replicated by the scripting that takes place. Of the several issues in these statements, we can note these: what presence *is,* that is, how it is known to be the proper emotional presence (and not, for example, a figment of emotionalism, or the *ifrīt*); and how conviction comes that it is available and present (that is, how the group will agree that it *is* present). All these reflect a type of scriptedness. It is familiar yet new. The adepts and their leaders recognize and go with the flow of this genuine emotional encounter. This means that the presence will have a character exemplifying the "objective subjectivity" known to each group—in Western social science parlance, the cultural experience of each group has its own texture and identity deemed to transcend the group. Once this is present, it is the responsibility of the muqaddam or shaikh to make sure that the reaction to presence is properly carried out.

Once the presence is acknowledged, some dimension of the properness is measured by the reactions, one of which is by trance. The munshid chants for this reaction and reads the emotional power of the moment in order to continue the theme, or reaffirm the phrase that was part of the moment he had chanted just prior to the one that precipitated the current rise in anticipation and the sense of the objective subjectivity's evidence being increased. He remembers the kind of mood that contributes to his group and tries to move the emotional structure of the dhikr in that direction. By recalling a previous electric moment, he appropriates its power to this moment, and his remembering contributes to the emotional impact. Recently, research has been carried out in the area of mood-congruent memory, by which the content of memory is aided and makes tangible a moment of the past. Thus, for example, Riskind argues for mechanisms that bridge mood and memory and prime the recall, resurrecting powerful emotions and reintroducing them into experience.[79] This suggests a religiously driven template, very like what dhikr provides in this research.

One could even go so far as to say that there is a scripted reaction to the presence, because those who have experienced the trance recognize its legitimacy and move to encourage it. Yet it is surely true that trance recognition, while not exclusive to the group, has a certain group feature that makes it familiar and recognizable to them. It has an element of group scripting to it because the trance has to fit the parameters accepted by the group. [80]

Performance also has a "place" character. As one munshid commented after the Ḥarrāqiyya dhikr, "I love this place. So many great followers of the shaikh have been present here, so many great ḥaḍras have taken place, so many have been blessed. I feel it in the very air. It's like being at a (spiritual) home." Hence it should not be lost on us that the performance is taking place within a certain environment imbued with a history. This is true even when the Ginawa perform outside someone's home rather than in a sacred precinct of a zāwiya. Genuine dhikr comes already staged, in the sense that it occurs in a predetermined space, a space formed by the participants. Dhikr space is always organized properly, and the director of the dhikr, regardless of the group, will establish the boundaries and the space first. This terrain is controlled by the dhikr. Expectations of the space's contribution are built in, even if that means that the general locale may have to be discounted, as in the Ginawa performance. Still, even in this case, a space is ritualized, as can be seen in the description of the seating arrangements in the dhikr. Moreover, the meaning of space may be positive as, for example, in dhikrs performed in an environment made sacred by the saint's tomb or by the space of the zāwiya constructed for the dhikr. For most ṭarīqas, however, the space contributes to the memory, either as a place where the adept first engaged in this bodily dialogue with God, or as a remembered ingredient in the saint's baraka. So the space of the zāwiya may play a role in the imaginative environment created for the dhikr, and, like staging *Hamlet* in the Globe Theatre, it contributes an air of authenticity to the proceedings. The point is that the spatial framework of memory provides certain guidelines for the meanings expected in the proceedings.

Presence and Memory

It is clear that the adept is not a passive receptor of a presented emotional experience but in some ways both contributes to and helps shape what is encountered. This is an activist kind of remembering. It is important to note that the presence within dhikr is not some imprint upon the soft wax of the adept's soul; rather, it is in some measure tailored for the experience level of the participant. There is, in short, a projective ingredient in Moroccan Sufism: "We will have a good dhikr if the brethren come wanting it to be so" was Ashḥab's way of stating it.

How is this to be perceived? While we have already insisted that Sufism goes well beyond a mentalist position on human experience of the divine, it is worth indicating that the mental projectivist account really derives from very ancient sources, Plotinus to be exact. Deliberately rejecting the concept of sensations as imprints or "seal-impressions" on a passive mind, Plotinus opted for a more dynamic view of human interaction with the divine overflow. He saw the mind as an act, a power that "gives a radiance out of its own store" to sense data.[81] The influence of Neoplatonism lives on in the shaikh of Andalusia, Ibn al-ʿArabī:

> The world above gives movement to the world of sensation, such that the witnessed is under its subjugating force, as a wisdom from God, not that this belongs to it by right. There never becomes manifest in the world of the witnessed the property of movement or stillness, eating or drinking, speaking or silence, except from the world of the absent. This is because the living thing moves only as the result of an intention and a desire, and these two are deeds of the heart. Desire is from the world of the absent, while motion and such things are from the world of the witnessed.
>
> The world of the witnessed is everything we habitually perceive through sensation, while the world of the absent is that which does not habitually become manifest in sensation and which we perceive through the Shariʿite report or reflective consideration.
>
> Then we say: The world of the absent is perceived through the eye of insight, just as the world of the witnessed is perceived through the eye of eyesight.[82]

Ibn al-ʿArabī, then, wants "the absent" to be integral to and perhaps responsible for this activism. While this might be true of some aspects of the mystical experience, it cannot be for the normal trances we see in Morocco. They are much too scripted, much too recognized for their group character. Crapanzano identifies one such,[83] but, generally speaking trances do not depend on "the absent," and this likely holds throughout most of Morocco.

In fact, Ibn al-ʿArabī may be speaking of the highest level of interaction with deity. At the lower levels, where trance is also present, performance involves memory . . . memory of past dhikrs of outstanding presence, of evident, powerful trances, and the group recollection of a proper trance as authorized by the shaikh and the ṭarīqa. All these interplay with an awareness of the presence validating the experience. These surely cannot be reduced to a sole cognitive awareness, since the body responds with an articulation that moves in consort with its training. There is a merging of external referent and inner production. With remarkable similarity did Wordsworth express this perception of a law of intermingling in poetic form:

> Which do both give it being and maintain
> A balance, an ennobling interchange
> Of action from without and from within;
> The excellence, pure function, and best power
> Both of the object seen, and eye that sees.[84]

There are, then, many aspects of the human expressive system involved in dhikr; emotions are surely an important aspect. But what analysts seem to have missed is the constructive setting of ritual. It is the dhikr formula itself that provides both the potential and the constraint necessary for encountering deity. A good dhikr will provide a normative framework through which the religious presence is encountered, experienced, imagined, and submitted to, yet dhikr is not a system with predestined emotional patterns. Those participating must clothe the dhikr—dhikrs fail, adepts "can't make it work," maqaddams "don't feel it," munshidūn "just can't get into the right place." No one writes a successful performance for dhikr unless both the external presence and the inner group dynamics gel into "an ennobling interchange."

But when the ingredients do gel and the adepts break through to a distinguishable sense of presence, a spiritual aesthetic swings into play. "A good dhikr tonight," one often hears. Shaikh Idrisū Maḥjūb notes: "When we have a good dhikr, people learn things about themselves, about their brethren, about the spiritual life, about the saint, about God."[85] There is an educative, revelatory dimension to the performance of dhikr, a factor found in the Egyptian study.[86] This function is particularly to be associated with the munshid, who sees it as part of his contribution to "bringing a message."

Finally, performance and memory are essential in another way: dhikr moves through cycles to completion. It has expectational guidelines built in for emotional release. During dhikr, the munshid mimics the structure of a spiritual short story. There is an introduction, in which the main themes are propounded and laid out and the rhythm is established. Then there is intervention of conflict, of the world of forgetfulness and self slowly in retreat before a new life experience. Following is the intensification that comes with remembering, or the intrigue of the situation, by which phrases that have been powerful in the past are invoked and added to the impact. There are the shifts in speed that move the adept from an exterior mode to an interior. There are the moments of blending, in which layer after layer of images are cadenzically arranged. This is deliberate, for snatches of phrases can have built-in energies that, taken together, can deliver a shock. The munshid weaves replication and new articulation together to contribute to the rising emotional sophistication of the dhikr. There is, at the last, the climax, the deliberate mantric-like repetition, the merging of tune, image, and motion in intensity until the whole transcends the part and a new experience of Presence is born. The birth of this moment signals the spiritual end of the dhikr process.

What my research indicates is that this birth is scripted by memory, to stand as a possible normative model for the next encounter in the next dhikr. Otherwise, it can quickly retreat into a blur with other dhikrs, to be activated as a standard collectivity for memory to resurrect as part of the code of the order's dhikr. Performance, as a structure, is always waiting in the wings for the next event. For the munshid, memory transports the whole script of that good dhikr forward from this moment to the future.

Islamic Memory: Remembrance as a Way of Knowledge

These many patterns constitute a complicated and sophisticated ecology of knowing; together they sketch an epistemology of religious remembering of quite some consequence. The remainder of the discussion here will focus on the munshid and his role in utilizing this knowledge in his performance.

The munshid is a Sufi master . . . a master of "power" music. He does not understand his words as *just his words*. They come from a transcendent dimension, he believes, in that their origin is not in him, and the power to sing them is not from him. His goal is to be part of a process of transformation. The words he chants are something more than mere words. The notion here is very much akin to the Hindu concept that the priests chant the words because the words have the power.[87] Only through this power dimension can the munshid have proper access to the imaginal dimension of the performance.[88] The text is regarded as a composite of energies, with each text having its own power and potential. He reads the emotional direction of the dhikr, senses a spiritual direction associated in his memory with a particular verse, and fits it to the current situation. His role is thus to engage the spiritual resources of the texts in his imagination and to plumb them for the one that will best respond to the opening he sees in the dhikr.

This is not just a remembering of the text. It is a remembering of the power, or even of the potential for the power. Hence his performance, like that of any theatrical performer, is not just remembering words in a literal fashion and singing them; rather he should perform with the emotional authority embodied in the words, because it arises out of his conviction that this phrase has the appropriate power to move the dhikr beyond where it is now. Such a process is a complex task involving his own spiritual memory, the power of the words, and his ability to engage creatively with his imagination. Successful preparation for his chanting is both learning the process sketched here and preparing his own spiritual state so that he can read the dhikr appropriately. In fact, he regards this as an attesting function: he is trying to get the dhikr participants to see what he has seen, to know what he has known, to share what he feels.

Several related themes arise from this attesting function. First is that he chants in a creative environment: both his imagination and that of his brethren anticipate the Presence, configured at the level that each is able to relate to. The process is described by al-Darqāwī in some depth:

> It consists of visualizing the five letters of the Name while saying Allah, Allah, Allah. Each time the letters dissolved in imagination, I re-visualized them and if they dissolved a thousand times during the day and a thousand times during the night, I continued a thousand times a day and a thousand times a night to visualize them. This method gave me moments of intense insight when I practiced it for a little more than a month at the beginning of my spiritual path. It brought me great knowledge as well as intense awe (*haybah*) but I paid no heed to it, occupied as I was in calling the Name and visualizing the letters until the month ended. Then a thought forced itself on my attention: God (be He exalted) says that "*He is the first and the last, the outer and the inner.*" (57:2)[89]

Here is the method distilled from one of the great Moroccan masters. After initiation into the order, the adept is trained to disengage from forgetfulness and to actively engage his imaginative powers, harnessing them for spiritual dhikr. In this activity, he is taught to bring the sense of Presence into relatable form through visualizing. Al-Darqāwī began with the ninety-nine names of God, focusing upon them and holding them in his inner being. The imagination is an unruly mental tool; if it can help with the visualizing process, it also is unstable. What he found was that no sooner had the process begun than his imagination would be off on some other direction. Once he learned to control its wildness, however, he found that the names themselves were not empty of content. Rather, he realized that behind the names that he was holding so close was the presence to which the names gave access. There was, so to speak, a genealogy of the names, and that process introduced him to the spiritual force. Hence dhikr is an active creative process that calls upon the visualizing powers of the chastened imaginations of munshid and the other adepts.

Ibn al-ʿArabī regarded the knowledge gained from this kind of active imagination to be the third spiritual route sanctioned by God. Indeed, the Great Shaikh (the nickname of Ibn al-ʿArabī) called it *kashf* (unveiling), a type of knowledge that can take four different forms: tasting, witnessing, opening, and insight. Chittick summarizes the relationship between imagination and unveiling this way: "Generally speaking, unveiling is associated with imagination, because it typically occurs through the imaging of various invisible entities or realities. In other words, things that are normally inaccessible to sense perception or to reason are given form by God and then perceived within imagination by those to whom the door to unseen things has been opened. Unveiling is an everyday occurrence for prophets. For the friends of God, it is an inheritance from the prophets. The folk of unveiling are the highest ranking friends of God."[90]

For the Moroccan munshid, heir to the theosophy of Ibn al-ʿArabī, he has a noble calling that issues in the potential unveiling for the brethren. This imaginal force links him to absolute Islamic value . . . to embody in lyrics and vision a message that will have salvic benefit.

All this is very difficult to translate into Western religious theory. How are we to address what is happening in this phenomenon? Sīdī al-ʿArabī al-Darqāwi cautions us that one possible alternative—conceptualization by standard rationality—is suspect:

> Men with knowledge do not run away from things as others do, for they contemplate their Lord in everything. . . . And know that nothing prevents us from contemplating our Lord but the fact of being preoccupied with the desires of our souls. Do not say that it is existence which veils the maker of existence, for by God, it is imagination/illusion (*wahm*) alone that hides Him from us, the wahm which gives rise to ignorance. If we only knew, it would lead us to the knowledge of certainty and certainty would distract our heart and inmost consciousness from the sight of ephemeral things.[91]

In this reading, that is, that of classical mysticism, the Sufi does not see rationality functioning in the same way. Rather he sees it as a logic of enactment; it has a logic to it, but it is not the logic of the Greek philosopher or the Western rationalist. Rather, the munshid is the master of the beneficent enactment,[92] and his maneuvering through music, drumming, hand-clapping, lyrics, and gesture appears to be a following of an emotional cognitive map.[93] This is the logic of the spiritual savant. It provides adepts the potential to find their own level of spiritual insight in the dhikr.

Let us turn now to examine a crucial dimension of the map: the mythic domain that the chanter is attempting to access in his performance. As we begin our analysis of the textual forms of memory, we note again that they should be conceived as specialized ritual scripts through which access is gained to a spiritual environment. They are the tools that lead to the sense of power and authority attached to the munshidūn's place in Moroccan Sufism.

3

THE CHANTER'S RELIGIOUS SCRIPTS
The Transformation of Memory's Heritage

I want to tell you how I feel in the ḥaḍra. I live in several worlds—I have many friends, I have my work, I have my social connections, I have my family. But the true meaning of what I am is not expressed in any of these environments. Where I am truly myself and am truly real is when I am in the ḥaḍra. There, all the things that I am are truly united. There all these other parts fit together. That is the true world.

> Nabīl, ʿAissawiyya munshid

Archaic and neoclassical poetry remains always their model. Memory exercises on them a tyrannical power; imitation becomes second nature.

> Aḥmad Salmī

Ritualization becomes the means of memorization.

> Eric A. Havelock, *The Muse Learns to Write*

Religious Scripts and Textual Memory: Integration in the Munshidūn Tradition

The Qurʾān's language and verbal quality shapes the way remembrance was conceived for the contemplative life; it also helped generate a philosophy of dhikr or remembrance that undergirded an entire way of seeing the religious life. It furthermore bequeathed a compendium of terms that have been formative for understanding the Sufi life: terms with special significance for Sufism, such as *ghaība, ṣife, bard, hor khain, ṣafāʿ*, and so on. These terms articulated a reality validated by the Qurʾān that, in turn, supported the world of the Sufi. These terms were also essential for providing a unifying ideology for the diversity of religious experience. When incorporated into a systematic perception of religion, they provided a key dimension of Sufi consciousness and shaped a metaphoric inner script.

In this chapter the focus shifts from the strength of remembrance in the dhikr to the content, themes, and motifs of Morocco's rich munshidūn tradition. In keeping with the analytic framework in chapter 2 above, these literary scripts appear to be the tools through which the encoded system is encountered, activated, and expressed. In terms of the ordinary munshid, these scripts are the storehouse by which realities beyond are engaged. From the perspective of the munshid, then, the reality of the spiritual world is expressed within these texts, and he sees no difference between what is performed and recited and the powerful experience that comes with the litany's expression. Remembrance always carries both the expressed text and the mythic domain together in performance.

My treatment of the lyric scripts is influenced by Susan Stetkevych's work on pre-Islamic panegyric and draws upon Havelock's notions, which were foundational for her study. Havelock insisted that "ritualization becomes the means of memorization." As such, ritualization provides the platform for the role of the munshidūn: rituals transform Sufi memories into living texts. Having been immersed in dhikr from youth, the chanter articulates a tradition seen to reside in the very shadow of the Most High, registering and reregistering it for the believers in a manner that brings the past to life and makes it powerful in the experience of each adept. The object of chanting is a ritual reactualization of a remembered normative experience at the heart of the Sufi tradition; hence, chanting is a transformative, integrative act. The chanter is the master of this ritual process.

Analyzing this process is not without its problems. When does a secular poem become sacred? What changes a secular text into a sacred one? At what point does a text derived from a different, even contradictory source become accepted? How does this discourse achieve its standing, and how does its meaning change in time? These and scores of other questions come to mind. In effect, then, we are not just examining a literary form that has some antiquity, as, for example, an epic that occupies some hoary position in high culture, retaining both an aura and a power. Rather, we are examining the network of ideas and beliefs whose content is somehow rooted in a religious consciousness, yet is clothed with the rich inheritance drawn from many aspects of Muslim art and culture. What seems to be happening is a process of continually renewing the experiential life of a community through the ritual handling of the literary culture of the past.

It is also important to see that connecting with this textual tradition integrates Morocco's Muslims in ways that lie outside the formal structure of the Sufi orders. Even if people believe in the saints and seek their assistance at crisis points, they may not be members of an order per se. Rather they may articulate a linkage through the signage of a textual history seen to unite them with Islam but nebulous enough not to demand total allegiance. For example, Geertz noted that in 1939, one-fifth of the males in Morocco considered themselves formal members of one of twenty-three Sufi groups,[1] and certainly that is a significant number. But that still means that 61 percent of the men and an undetermined number of females were not formal members of any order. It is far more significant that Dwyer found in her sample areas in southern Morocco that 92 percent of both genders "had been linked to Sufi orders and/or to the cults of individual saints at some time in their lives and continued to cite these loyalties as meaningful to them."[2] According to my own unofficial probing on these matters, Dwyer's figures are likely more reflective of actual religious affairs. Thus, one of the ways in which a Moroccan is integrated into this system is through the vehicle of literary culture. I need hardly add that this culture is not necessarily "literate," in our sense of reading and writing.

Moreover, we are not looking for one source of text for this process. It is, for example, enshrined in musical and poetic traditions that reach back to the earliest days of Islam in the region, to the first immigrants from Arabia. Indeed, for some, the munshid's roots reach well beyond the Arabic confines to the outposts of pre-Islamic Berber and African cultures . . . outposts, because my research leads me to believe that important roles and patterns seem not to derive solely from Islamic sources but also come from indigenous and southern cultures that are poorly known.

There are five principal foci for our examination of oral and textual materials: the "Oriental" Arab, the Moroccan Arab/Andalusian, the Berber, the Ginawa, and the Visionary. Each of these is related to the others in a complex interwoven way, with each maintaining a kind of core tradition while interacting or reacting to the others. Overall, the result is a diverse tradition that belies any simple configuration. The current chapter spells out the broad outlines of the first focus; chapter 4 examines the Moroccan Arab/Andalusian; and chapter 5 discusses the Berber, Ginawa, and Visionary materials.

Given the superior position accorded the Arabic language of the Qur'ān by all Muslims, we might pause to sketch where the Arabic background fits in studies of the Moroccan data, for clearly Arabic is only one influence that dramatically shapes the munshid's expressive system. Also to be considered is the local dialect of the people, which includes a massive Berber influence.

The Arabic tradition that came to Morocco was not unified, either in language or in codification, and the Arabic utilized in oral discourse is colloquial, having been amalgamated out of various influences. We may safely conclude that the Arabic of the Qur'ān and the Ḥadīth remains as a standard reference for all "high" or classical occasions and that Sufis adhere to that language when intending to draw on the basic texts of Islam. Beyond that, however, there is Moroccan Arabic, which arose out of diverse influences: the dialects spoken by the early Muslim conquerors; the diplomatic Arabic as represented in the language of the courts of Andalus and Qayrawān; the dialect associated with the Banī Hilāl and the Banī Salīm—the early immigrants to Morocco; the crossover Arabic of Berber-speaking people who learned Arabic imperfectly from some source; the imported Arabic of Moroccan travelers, businessmen, and other sojourners who had spent time in the Arabic centers of the East and then returned home with their learning; and, finally, the Arabic of visiting officials, scholars, and poets who brought their own distinctive accent with them and imparted it to the native Moroccans. Such diversity could only logically lead to a distinctive tongue.

It is important to note that this is an oral tradition that grows within the ongoing concerns of everyday discourse and only obliquely accepts the rules of classical Arabic. Indeed, there is an attitude toward Arabic that is distinctly Moroccan, and it has considerable history, judging by this statement from the great North African historiographer Ibn Khaldūn:

> Knowledge of grammatical rules is merely knowledge of how to do the work (of communicating), and not the work itself. That is why we see that many illustrious grammarians who are skilled in Arabic sciences and well versed in its grammatical rules, make mistakes and commit *lahn* (grammatical errors, break the rules) when they are asked to write even two lines on any given topic. Conversely, there are those who write excellent prose and poetry, even when they do not know the grammatical rules well, such as the subject, the direct object, the nominative or the genitive, nor any of the canons that underlie the Arabic sciences. Talent, thus, is something beyond this (knowledge). What's more, true talent can dispense with it.[3]

The poetry Ibn Khaldūn uses as examples of this excellence are drawn from the Sīra Banī Hilāl, collected by him from the Bedouin peoples, samples of which are still to be found in North Africa today.

Thus, what the student has to deal with is a very distinctive kind of Arabic that is rooted in the formative dialects of tribal Arabia, with its own rich and colorful past, a past that plays a direct role in shaping the materials utilized by the Sufi chanters. This is a topic too vast to study here in depth. However, three important Arabic influences on Sufi oral cum textual development must be discussed: the Banī Hilāl tradition, the poetry legacy of al-Andalus, and the corpus of the local *malḥūn* writers.

The Remembrance of the Banī Hilāl

The tribes associated with the Banī Hilāl and Banī Salīm were originally from Najd in Central Arabia and existed there before the coming of Islam. They continued to live there largely unaffected by the events of Muḥammad's life. Some time around the end of the ninth century and the beginning of the tenth, the tribes began to leave their ancestral homes for reasons that are not clear. Some of them had been involved in the Qarmatian revolts, and the Fāṭimid caliph of Cairo, ʿAzīz ibn al-Muʿizz, disciplined them by moving them to Upper Egypt. Some of the best studies on the Sīra Banī Hilāl genre today are associated with Egypt,[4] but M. Ben Rahhal wrote about them in Morocco in the 1880s,[5] and Loubignac studied the language associated with a Moroccan group claiming Hilalian inheritance.[6] Several conferences over the past twenty years have examined the Banī Hilāl phenomenon in North Africa.[7]

What influences might best be focused on in the cycles of Banī Hilāl for our purposes? Certainly one is the quality of the remembered past. Connelly depicts some important aspects succinctly: "The word dhikr, used so prominently by both oral poets and the redactors of folk editions of the *Hilāliyya,* sums it up: The mention contains the recollection and the memory that give knowledge and renown. That mentioned recollection transmitted and spread in shared oral discourse can become a written record of the oral transaction, just as the speech of God dictated to the Prophet became inscribed in The Book. Classical Arabic written discourse retains in its vivid narrative style the aura of oral speech on the model of the speaking voice contained in the Koran and in the early oral poetry."[8]

From Connelly's perspective, the Arab poet deals with a past that is powerful precisely because it is somehow present and current in the meaning of the recited version. This remembrance has an existential element in it. It also has vestiges of the sacred attached to it, by virtue of the association with the language of the Holy Book. Moreover, performed, affirmative spoken word is viewed as carrying a kind of inspiration within it that is not present in the written literal text. These issues are wedded to what might be called the phenomenology of memory to deliver a specific kind of power to those who listen. Beyond this, is the power of the qaṣīda form itself that could be utilized to map out and affirm positions of power, as Bürgel has indicated.[9] So the Banī Hilāl do have a significance, but the extent becomes the central issue of academic analysis.

From the beginning, it is important to indicate that the extent of the Banī Hilāl contribution continues to generate debate in Morocco, so the issue has resonance within the Muslim community. For example, Muḥammad Ben Cherīfa of Muḥammad V University held that there was little direct influence of the Banī Hilāl on the development of Moroccan Sufism:

A central feature of the munshid's repertoire is the *madīḥ* (praise or eulogy). But the madīḥ al-nabi (eulogy of the Prophet) is a phenomenon of the city. The Sufism we are discussing is an urban matter, dependent upon the masses to follow it. Look at the Shādhiliyya, they are maghribian in form, but they now thrive in Egypt. The same applies to Shaikh al-Badāwī in Tanta, Egypt. He was born in Fez and then left on the hajj, and stayed there because he had a following. This is because in Morocco the *inshād* (song, chanted text) is a phenomenon of the city, while in Egypt it is a phenomenon of the countryside. There is no influence [contra Jirārī] of the Banī Hilāl on inshād. This is because the Banī Hilāl are a country phenomenon.

There may be, of course, some regional modifications to this. In Chaoui, there were families from the country who were descendents of the Banī Hilāl. They had and have "popular" inshād so there may be some influence. Certainly there are some affiliations and parallel patterns. For example, there is the notion of an ideal text—the qaṣīda based on the Arabic language . . . so there is something like the "spirit" of the Arab text operating in the repertoire. It has a pre-Islamic form, but is an ʾamāna. . . . It continues the same form as from the time of Ḥassan ibn Thābit. The Banī Hilāl also used this form. I also think the madīḥ and inshād reflect some of the same themes, with some of the same concerns, as those in the early writers. People live in the same vein, and this is part of the patrimony of Morocco, and so it is to be found in the inshād.[10]

While Ben Cherīfa may be technically correct in terms of direct familial and social expression, it is doubtful that the urban/rural distinction is very effective as a means of evaluating the development of Sufism—as has been seen, Sufism took different shapes in different areas of the country.[11] Nevertheless, his point about forms and parallels certainly is crucial, and hence the discussion here examines three: the *rāwī* tradition, the structure of madīḥ, and the bourda element of the Banī Hilāl cycle, since these relate directly to the munshid's repertoire.

Both the rāwī and the munshid "recite," so there are interesting parallels in the roles they play and the material they recite. Both deliver a text, both perform, and both bring the words of others. Rāwī also has strong connections to poetic expression, since both the rāwī and the *shāʿir* (poet) are directly related to the creative involvement with literary expression: the rāwī in the memorization and reciting, the shāʿir in the composition. The structural difference of activity in this whole process has generated a long and vigorous debate in Arabic literary tradition, since it seems evident that pre-Islamic poets composed and recited their own materials. Nevertheless, once the poem was recited, it was picked up and repeated by the rāwī, who then could deliver an evening's entertainment with collected oral poems. Connelly reminds us of the processes involved: "He wants the reader to *hear* and to *remember* in his mind's ear the ceremonial performance of the *Hilāliyya* by a rabab poet. The muʿallif's rendition of the *Hilāliyya* is but a recollection of a true performance; or, to use the scribe's own words, a dhikr—a mention and a retelling of the sīra which commemorates the ceremonial, ritual telling before the assembled community."[12]

Reciting itself must have gained immensely from the role of reciting the Qurʾān after the death of the Prophet, and the traditional story is that it was the death of so many reciters that spurred the written collection of the Qurʾān.[13] Whatever the original situation, the distinction between the two social and cultural roles is well established in modern Arabic studies.[14]

The use of the word munshid may be fairly late, in terms of use in Morocco, but there is no doubt that the rāwī is more related to a fixed spoken text, while the munshid is understood to chant or sing from an accepted repertoire. On this issue, Zākī ʿAlī, munshid from Zerktouni, notes that "one is either a poet or a munshid," and that it is too much to expect both in one person.[15] Despite that, both rāwī and munshid are intensely loyal to the authenticity of the original text, and there is a sense of the preciousness of the words. Thus among the Ḥārrāqiyya, the tradition rests close to an aesthetic of the fixed word. Its antiquity, its phrasing, its rich cadence of memory, its history of restating the great themes of the heart before God, all combine to energize the recitation. There is an attitude of nobility to the text whose meaning, by its very chanting, lifts the soul. This does not mean that the text as written or as published is regarded as the "true" text. The true text is the inspired literary script within the dhikr of the group. It is not the text as one finds it published in various chapbooks. But it is the word as inspired script that is illuminated during the presentation.

In this context, even the trance seems to have a muted place. The trance, when it comes, comes to the few, and comes in the midst of the munshid's meditation as if, in the wave after wave of enlightening phrase, the solitary adept is swamped by the words themselves. That this can occur, I take to be a reflection of the honor accorded to Arabic poetry at the dawn of the Islamic era.[16]

In the Banī Hilāl material of the Najd, collected by Alison Lennick in the early 1980s, we find that the rāwiya remained quite true to a version even if it was orally performed without a written text, and even after a year's interlude in the performing. This implies that the oral tradition remains quite firm despite the variations in performance: "The kinds of variations occurring between such subsequent renditions were solely the omission of a line, which was frequently added at the end of the poem with the comment that the rāwiya (reciter) had forgotten it or the transposition in order between a line or two. It should be noted that these kinds of variations can only be attributed to a brief lapse of memory. Most significantly, the actual wording of lines *in no case* varied, even after a lapse of more than one year between performances."[17]

Similarly, the munshidūn constantly told me that the text was always a text of the past and that therefore memory was the key to performance. Commenting on the issue of the adepts being faced with modern problems, unheard of in the days the texts were composed, Ashhab put it this way: "We are really governed by ʿamana (bond of allegiance)—this prevents any change in the text on the part of the munshid. Moreover, the music of the zāwiya and the madīḥ texts stays traditional because this is the foundation of life. People in the zāwiya can explore these (modern) issues in their lives outside, but in the zāwiya, it's like classical arabesque, with fixed connections and fixed borders."[18]

The text is from the past, but the quality and style of presentation are contingent on the training of the munshid. Memory is not just a rigorous rendering of an original text. The English word "recite" suggests a mechanical repetition of the text. But Nabīl indicated that this is not the case for the true munshid:

I have great reservations about the young munshidūn that are coming up. When I was growing up in the *taifa* (order), I learned the songs by listening to the great munshidūn, writing down their songs and going over them with them and the muqaddam. Now the young munshidūn listen to tapes and copy the singer. But this is not enough. There are many qasidas that are hard to understand, and their meaning is not clear during the ḥadra. So just listening and repeating the words is not enough. One has to be taught the depth of meaning in the words to convey them properly. I spent hours with my muqaddam. A wonderful old man who was over forty years in the ṭarīqa. He had so much depth. When I listened to him sing, he would explain the words to me, thus when I sing the songs, I don't just mimic him, I have a feeling for the depth of the words, and the things I learned while he taught me the song, and his spirit that was conveyed to me. That's the way a song becomes a living thing. Tapes can't do that for you.[19]

Moreover, the munshid is called upon to remember in another way—to honor the living memory of the dead. This role is an outgrowth of the fact that he is associated with the great people of the past and also that he is in contact with the unseen world. He links the hearers with that domain: "The munshid does not just sing in the dhikr. He plays a role in the life of the zāwiya and the community that is larger than that. He will, for example, sing at memorial services. Three days after the death of a loved one, the family of the deceased holds a remembrance service. During that service, a munshid will recite Qurʾān and will sing the praises to Muḥammad. He will also sing inshād. His repertoire will depend upon the relationship of the deceased to the ṭarīqa and upon the family requests. The same remembrance takes place forty days after the deceased's death."[20]

These factors indicate that the munshidūn do not just sing the same words, without modification. They change their repertoire depending upon the occasion and their audience. They can, by dint of utilizing materials from different poets and shaikhs, convey a contemporary message. But what they do not do is use their own material, the way a poet might. What they use is always drawn from memory, from the great Islamic past. Remembering the deceased is not a personal recall but rather a fitting of the person's memory, resident in the memory banks of the audience, into a familiar pattern indicative of a common meaningful life. This is a process of allusion rather than direct association. It is closer to a ritual calling to mind that collectively represents the spiritual potency surrounding both the individual and the community. There is, then, a kind of ritual pre-text underlying the text. This is the imaginative text, a type of lyric script, to which the munshid is committed.

From the standpoint of lettered tradition, the munshidūn carry on a role that itself is not only associated with regional memory but is laced through and through with linkages to the great moments of Arabic and Islamic religious experience. The munshidūn see themselves as part of a tradition that reaches into pre-Islamic Arabian culture, and they affirm a role that encompasses handling the great literary expressions of the past that deal with the age-old matters of the spirit. They conceive themselves as functionally parallel to the poets and professionally akin to the rāwī. At the same time, their cultural role is really subservient to the religious purpose, that is, conveying the spiritual truths that are timeless and inspirational today. Moreover, their role today helps define relationships with those who have recently died and are still fresh in memory. From that perspective, the munshidūn are constantly involved in a transforming process, transforming both the word and the memory of the past into the inspiration of the present.

The Paradigmatic Madīḥ

If there is a genre deriving from the time of the Banī Hilāl that still has influence in today's Morocco, it is the madīḥ. The munshid, as part of the tradition, has taken that form and transformed it. The madīḥ al-nabī is a central feature of the munshid's repertoire. These eulogies are performed by a distinctive group of chanters called *musmiʿīn,* who may or may not be considered munshidūn. Ben Cherīfa says *madīḥūn* as a recognizable group dedicated to *madīḥ,* or eulogy, emerged during the Merinid period and then gradually became known as munshidūn, that is, those who chant songs, inshād.[21] Morocco's munshidūn, however, claim that they are also musmiʿin, that is, those who sing the samāʿ. Munshid Nabīl says: "The munshid can do both madīḥ and *musamaʿ* (meditational chant), but not all can do *mawwāl* (improvisational song). Only those who are really good can do mawwāl. On the other hand, the samāʿ is something that must be learned from the Sufi teacher, and is specific to the ṭarīqa. As to the form, the *baḥr ṭawīl* is basic. One must stay in that form. The experts combine it with ʿala and other forms of music."

Of all the eulogistic types, that directed to the Prophet is the most powerful and compelling in Morocco. As Ḥajj Ḥusain Toulālī, perhaps one of the best singers of malḥūn in all of Morocco, stated: "Of all the many themes of malḥūn available to me, the theme that is closest to my heart is the madīḥ of the Prophet."[22]

The madīḥ of the Prophet have many forms that are similar to the earlier model of panegyrics and eulogies that reach also into pre-Islamic times. Madīḥ is dressed in the qaṣīda form, that Arabic poetic form rooted in the jāhiliyya period of Arabian history that has dominated high literary poetry right down to our day. That dominance has not been without its critics, both within and without the Islamic fold. The madīḥa (or madḥ) (panegyric form) mode of expression is, after all, directly related to tribal achievement, and, crucial from the standpoint of its religious critics, it is deliberately focused on braggadocio, a praising of humans untoward in proper religious circles. Writers like Ibn Qutaybah (d. 889 c.e.) castigated the qaṣīda as lacking in cohesion and high-minded purpose.[23] The result was that the qaṣīda itself came under fire as existing solely for the panegyric component of the poem. Typically, the qaṣīda opens with a prose *akbār* that ostensibly gives the story's setting; this is followed by an amorous reflection, a *nasīb.* The journey through the desert toward the vanished love follows (called the *raḥīl*), and the entire poem ends with the panegyric segment, known as madḥ. Madḥ, then, is not a neutral form, without political and religious consequences. It has often been regarded as the real purpose of the whole production. Yet it can be argued that this form is chosen precisely because of its absolutizing of relationships. The form utilizes its particular beat-like resonance pattern to portray powerful relationships and to anchor social positions in a concrete, historical continuum. There is reason to believe that it is not, however, the symbolism of the Ancient Near East's dying and rising gods that is its basis, as Susan Stetkevych has argued,[24] but perhaps another powerful, more enduring one: the Female as the mystery of life.[25] The meditation, inspired by a remembered place, focuses on a female figure and portends a quality of elation, of transcending issue. Indeed, these odes are more apt to be derived from honoring Mother Goddess than from any other religious mythology complex. Love of these godlike creatures has a kind of oracular bliss attached to them. [26] The divinities incite his muse. The resulting emotional intensity leads to longing, quests, agony, slander, social ordering, and death.

A few important aspects of this tradition will entertain our discussion here. Panegyric is a necessary ingredient of the Banī Hilāl. The wars, skirmishes, treks, intrigues, victories, and deaths all rest within an idealized frame of reference, a frame that reflects a heroic intentionality. The eulogies presuppose an audience, one that anticipates being affected by the praise and, at the same time, one that will prove beneficial to the eulogizer. It is important to see, then, that madīḥ is embedded in a particular remembering situation, for that situation contributes to the tension of the poem and sets up the logistics of praise. It also highlights the social meaning of this special poetic *ritual remembering*.

The Bourda Story: A Legacy from the Banī Hilāl

Of all the legacies of the Banī Hilāl crucial to Moroccan Sufism, no other comes close to the *Burda* (generally written as *Bourda* in Moroccan and French sources). The story of the cloak of the Prophet is what might be called a metasymbol; it informs and energizes all activity of the munshid. The authoritative version, penned by Busayrī, is a fundamental icon of Moroccan spiritual discourse, playing a role as essential in that tradition as the icon does in Orthodox Christianity, or the sense of balance in Chinese religions. In effect, ṭarīqa life is unthinkable without it. All the munshidūn interviewed pointed to it as the fundamental structure of the inshād; they insist that the qaṣāʿid of the *Bourda* and the *Ḥamzīyya* are the foundation of the inshād in all the zāwiyas of Morocco. They do this because the qaṣāʿid encompass the principal themes of the qaṣīda ideal in praise of the Prophet, and because all the melodies of the inshād are dependent upon the qaṣīda forms in their melodic expression.

An ʿAissawiyya chanter stated:

We commence with a poem of the shaikh and then finish with a poem of the shaikh. The *Bourda* is next, followed by poems that develop parts of the *Bourda*'s themes, that is, we take the same theme as in the *Bourda,* and the same rhythm. If we change the *baitiyya,* then we change both the rhythm and the theme. The *Bourda* is the foundation of all ḥaḍra singing, so we weave in and out of its themes, depending upon the *hefqa* or the leader of the group. However, as a rule of thumb, we change after *Bourda* and one poem. We always end finally with a poem of the shaikh. In Berber territory, we usually sing the *Bourda* and poems of Ibn al-ʿArabī or any other Sufi poet either in Arabic or Berber. Most of them have been translated into Berber.[27]

Moroccan historian Muḥammad al-Nouhī affirms that the *Bourda* is a trans-Morocco phenomenon, existing in the South, where no musical instruments are to be found, and in the North, where diverse musical forms are used.[28] It harks back to Kaʿb ibn Zuhayr's *Banāt Suʿād,* or, more commonly *Qaṣīda al-Bourda* (the Mantle Ode). Kaʿb ibn Zuhayr was a poet of the pre-Islamic era whose satirical poetry attacked the Prophet, and that put a price on his head when the Prophet triumphed. The poet, condemned to death by the Prophet for his satirical lampooning of his message, appears in Medina, approaches the Prophet, who did not know him, and asks whether, if Kaʿb were to appear and repent, his life would be spared. "Yes," says the Prophet. When the Prophet's supporter hears that this is Kaʿb and threatens to kill him, the Prophet prevents him, indicating he wishes to hear what Kaʿb has to say. Following the recitation of the panegyric qaṣīda, the Prophet was so moved he threw his mantle about Kaʿb.[29] Kaʿb became one of the few poets tolerated in the new Islamic order and the robe, bequeathed to Kaʿb's heirs, was eventually purchased by Muʿāwiyah for twenty thousand dirhams and was worn on feast days.[30] It therefore appears as a symbol of prophetic authority and spiritual power.

What is it that was conveyed, and how have the Sufis conceived of this gift? Brockelman notes the ancient trophe of the robe of honor (*ḥullah*) given as a reward by kings as a reward for the poet's verse, and Stetkevych then argues that the robe takes on religious and political meanings of legitimacy, deriving from Mauss's idea of the object being imbued with the spirit of the giver, in effect, the gift of immortality.[31] As attractive as this interpretation is, it misses the direct individual situation of the gift. Muḥammad gives Kaʿb acceptance, first as one who has submitted to Islam, then as one who has the Prophet's protection (line 40). The Prophet stands between Kaʿb and any who would deprive him of his existence. It is the personal forgiveness of the Prophet that is key, and the force of the *Bourda* for the Sufi is that it is the Prophet who has wiped out the condemnation and provided Kaʿb with a new life in Islam. It is not the qaṣīda form itself, then, that is the basis for Sufi rootedness, but the antiquity of the form. It returns the reciter to the beneficent interactional moment of Kaʿb and the Prophet. Chanting the *Bourda* is a resituating of the hearers to the foundational time when the Prophet welcomed the condemned into Islam. The mantle is both a symbol of the individual's submission to Islam and of the Prophet's ability to confer an Islamic beneficence upon the seeker.

Stetkevych convincingly argues that, rather than the qaṣīda being a form restricted to self-aggrandizement, it can reflect far more seminal purposes. The *Banāt Suʿād,* for example, is a poem of ritual exchange, a poem for a life. She sees in the story a ritual form with sacrificial intent by which an exchange of a poem is made in lieu of one's death sentence.[32] This raises the meaning of the qaṣīda above the mundane, self-congratulatory purpose of the initial form, giving it a superhistorical significance. Thus the qaṣīda is grounded in an ancient system of ritual exchange, whose language is mythological. Hence the potential for the qaṣīda form to reflect a deeper religious meaning. These characteristics make it available for a deeper ritual purpose.

Where Stetkevych sees the purpose as the social function of ritual exchange and roots its meaning in a sacrificial death-for-life principle, our analysis holds that, if exchange is involved, it cannot be a reflection of a ritual exchange of the sacrificial sort. The reason is simple. Under the sacrificial regime, a price must be paid for the sacrifice to be acceptable; Abraham must sacrifice Isaac. But there is none here. No persona (or animal) dies that Kaʿb may live. Nor is poetry perceived to carry the equivalent of the individual's worth in it—there is not a great tradition of poets buying their life through the quickness of their tongue among the pre-Islamic Arabs.

Moreover, there is no shedding of blood as redemption, the sine qua non of ancient Hebrew sacrificial notions, and predominant in Semitic religious tradition. Nor, unfortunately, does Kaʿb "possess" poetry in a manner that would make his poetic talents so worthwhile as to stand for a valued and tribally honored treasure that could vicariously cover all the jāhiliyya poets in the land. Kaʿb is saved for himself, alone.

Finally, the *Bourda* could not have found a place in the piety of Morocco as a qaṣīda honoring the Prophet as a spiritual mentor, had the thrust been on sacrifice. While the Prophet can be a measure of one who forsakes the benefits of the world in order to seek a more spiritual way, he is never perceived as one who fulfils the role of a sacrificial person. While blood sacrifices are still carried out in Morocco, especially those associated with the king and the court,[33] the thrust of the qaṣīda seems to be much more on the poem as an inspired gift exchange than as a sacrificial exchange. Hence, at least among Sufis, when one chants the *Bourda,* one is tapping into a form associated with this past inspiration and spiritual power.

The central focus of the *Bourda* is iconic patterns affirmed in the Prophet. The qaṣīda harks back to or creates a past in which the poet is on a quest to regain his beloved, Suʿād. In that quest he will need a great Arabian steed whose beauty and fortitude alone can take him there. (The literary trope of the hero and his dependable horse has significant elaborations in ancient Arabic poetry.) Rather than focusing his mind on his love, however, the steed's rhythmic movement recalls the lamentation of a middle-aged and childless woman. Suʿād, his beloved, is unreachable. His memory does not, cannot, complete the trek to Suʿād. The reality of the situation presses upon him. The present interrupts and he must face his death sentence. That is the fact that leads to the famous verses in which the poet addresses the Prophet:

My slanderers on both sides
denounced me saying,
"You, O Son of Abū Sulma, are
as good as dead."
And every trusted friend in whom
I put my hopes
Said, "I cannot help you, I am occupied
with other things."
So I replied, "Out of my way,
you bastards!"
For all that the All-Merciful decrees
will come to pass!
For every man of woman born,
though he be long secure,
Will one day be borne
on humpbacked bier.
I was told God's Messenger
had threatened me,
But from God's Messenger
pardon is hoped.
Go easy, and let Him be your guide
who gave to you
The gift of the Qur'ān in which
are warnings and discernment!
Don't hold me to account for what
my slanderers have said,
For, however great the lies against me,
I have not sinned!
I stood where I saw and heard
What would have made
The mighty pachyderm,
had it stood in my stead,
Quake with fear unless
The Messenger of God,
By God's leave,
granted it protection.[34]

The *Bourda* plays such a role in Moroccan life because it enunciates many of the crossover themes within Sufi and general piety. It also encompasses ideas relative to the role of the Prophet in Moroccan popular culture. The *Bourda* reflects these features of Moroccan tradition: first, the conviction of the ritual effectiveness of spiritual exercises, of which dhikr is the bedrock. Remembrance takes one back to authentic beginnings, to the "first love," to Suʿād or, as the name means, good fortune and happiness; this nostalgia for an old love, a woman known and lost, is a common theme in the oldest Arabic poems, the *Mufaḍḍaliyāt*.[35] One returns to an idealized love. Second, this return in memory sets the stage for a process of empowerment. That process involves contention, thus discourses on the dangers of the trek, the reliance on the camel, and the treachery of friends and associates, the struggles encountered in the journey, and confrontations. These contentions raise the bar, test the poet's mettle, and weigh his dedication. Third, the process ushers in the praise section, by which the social efficacy of the praised one is highlighted, stressing the notion of collective elevation and accomplishment. The panegyric is a stylized remembering of where the poet has been and why he now enjoys a new status.

There are further ramifications: the hero is dependent upon his social connections. Despite all the skills and luck accorded the lover, he needs the assistance of someone beyond himself in order to succeed. The goal of the qaṣīda is to revisit and re-cite the social dependencies and statuses that are essential to religious understanding; it is to affirm that even the most accomplished warrior is beholden to the fortuitous and ennobling assistance of others. The *Bourda* spells that out with regard to the Prophet.

In addition, the process of empowerment has been assimilated into Moroccan public consciousness in many different ways: through notions of touching the garment of some holy figure, to kissing the hands of the powerful, to visits to the shrine of the saint, to the recitation of sacred verses. For example, the people of Salé utilized the melody of Buṣyrī's famous *Bourda* in order to pray for rain. Brown indicates that the prayer for rain, ṣalāt al-istisqaʾ (known as *al-Laṭīf*), or Praise to God), had often been used by the government of the day in the face of crises, to forestall some pending evil, such as the French invasion of 1911 or to expel invaders from Morocco. Thus, when urgently needing rain the townspeople sang one hundred times:[36]

> *Yā'l-laṭīf fī-l-azal, antāʿ l-laṭīf wa-lam tazal; alṭaf binā fī mā nazal, bi-ḥurmati'l-Qurʾān wa-'alā man nazal.*
>
> *Oh God, the Gentle One of all times. You are Benevolent and have not ceased to be; be gracious to us in what is to come, out of respect for the Qurʾān and Him to whom it was revealed.*

When the city revolted against the French attempt to split Berber and Muslim law by approving the institution of local Berber legal codes, called the Berber Dihar, it was the *al-Laṭīf*, sung to the tune of the *Bourda*, that galvanized the city.[37] During the times of my research in Morocco, similar prayers were being carried out because of a long-standing drought.

While we will examine the malḥūn tradition in the next chapter, it is important here to identify that the panegyric motif is also expressed in Moroccan Arabic, that is, it is not just expressed in classical Arabic writings. Thus the history of the malḥūn also represents the history of certain poets, their battles, and their relationship to the state and society. The malḥūn reciters used poetry as a weapon against their enemies, and they used references in poetry to illuminate many of the social issues that agitated them; that is, poetry had a current impact. For this reason it is not an artistic form just prized by a few.[38]

The role of the poet in general is not elitist. Indeed, the poet in Islamic society would laud the recent North American phenomenon of placing poetry on subways and buses. The poet is understood in Islamic society to be speaking to the people, and hence modifies themes and expressions even as they do. Moreover, the Moroccan poet understands his or her field to be socially reformative, in the sense that poetry can effect moral change. Much that the poet does is concerned with embodying eternal things in poetic form so people can grasp them. Poetry has an educative function. So, for example, in madīḥ, the popular poet does not create many texts because he does not think his problems and themes are important judged against the crises at the time of the Prophet. The honorific position of the Prophet in society means that one can praise him without fear, and only good taste and general religious approval act as guidelines. Consequently madīḥ for the Prophet is really a social expression, not one of personal piety per se.

Thus, in Jirārī's analysis, he commits almost fifty pages of his text to various aspects, themes, and conversations enshrined in popular Arabic poetry in Morocco to the Prophet (pp. 457–500). Led by long devotional sections of love for the Prophet, one can find more than ten pages of discussion of the personal characteristics associated with the Prophet, stories of his birth, details of his early life, and details mostly derived from the classical biography.

Parallel madīḥ developed from the Prophet's family connections, including his grandfather, his father, and other relatives, add to these details. This is followed by meditations on the Prophet's home life, Mecca, Medina, his contemporaries, and his trials, all reflecting the traditional picture of the Prophet. These themes are widely known and lauded among the population.[39]

Where it becomes personal is when the madīḥ of the Prophet is seen to have some impact on one's own spiritual life. And it is in that arena of meaning that the Moroccan Sufi has developed a wide range of texts and understandings. In addition to the role of the Prophet as a statesman and lawgiver, the spiritual role of the Prophet in leading Muslims into the mystical life is stressed. This is accomplished in many ways, but one of the most crucial is that of the creation of fictive conversations. These imaginary conversations between people, the *nās ʿarabiyya,* constitute an important element in Sufi development,[40] for they incorporate classical Arabic words and phrases into popular lore and thus give shape and form to local piety. The life of the Prophet becomes instructive on how to handle personal problems and issues. One "reads" the Prophet's life and actions in terms of one's own spiritual needs. Included in that, of course, is the problem of personal circumstance (Can one be powerful and rich and still be a Sufi? Can one be a sinner and still be a Sufi?). The conversations between the Prophet and his contemporaries illuminate how the spiritual life of the past uses remembrance as denoting present standards.

A significant portion of madīh texts deal with the *miʿraj,* the Prophet's ascension to the Throne of God. Some of these texts reflect the belief that the *akhlāq* (spiritual characteristics) of the Prophet are crucial to his journey. This theme has much occupied the Sufi poet, since the ascent is crucial to the mystical life.[41] Through the ascent, the poet moves into themes associated with the spiritual context: the mores of the Prophet, the heavenly world, the pardoning of the Prophet, the pilgrimage as a heavenly motif.

Other madīh stress the grandsons of the Prophet, Hassan and Husain, and other saintly individuals, from Fāṭima, the daughter of the Prophet, to ʿAlī, as well as the sharifian ("sacred" relations of the Prophet and their genealogical line) conception of great value to Moroccan society. Constructed on the same model are madīh to the *awliyāʿ* or saints, there are also praises about the zāwiya as an environment of blessing.

For Sufis, there is specifically the madīh of Mūlay Idrīs, and the whole Sharifi tradition associated with the saints. Jirārī mentions that the malhūn sing in Fez during the mūlid of the Prophet but the madīh was directed originally not at the Prophet but at Sīdī Farag: "This madīh to Sīdī Farag has been going on since the twelfth century," a view that contradicts the idea that madīh of the Prophet predetermined all elements of the saint's praise.[42]

All of these themes indicate the spiritual world of the Prophet, in which the Prophet is the center of a universe of love. This love is expressed in one ideal form toward women, but the Prophet also constitutes another mode of this universe of love. Its meaning is expressed in meditations on tears, wailing, and the way of rūhānī.[43]

The Paradigmatic Memory: *The Bourda* as Spiritual Inspiration

Let us first examine the *Bourda* in the light of Sufi texts, specifically that associated with the Great Shaikh of Morocco and Andalus, Ibn al-ʿArabī, especially as expressed in the work of ʿAbdallāh Badr ibn al-Ḥabashī, his confidant and close disciple. He first appears at Ibn al-ʿArabī's side in Fez in 1198 C.E. and accompanied him thereafter for twenty-five years. ʿAbdallāh may thus be a Moroccan by affiliation, although Ibn al-ʿArabī describes him as Abyssinian,[44] and we know he was originally a slave from Ethiopia.[45] Whatever his place of residence, he expresses a viewpoint that is enlightening without much of the highly esoteric language associated with his master. By explaining his work and comparing it with Sufi texts we can demonstrate the deeper purposes of Moroccan mysticism. Such an analysis should reveal the "subtext" of both the *Bourda* and Sufi writing.

It is immediately evident that the piety of the *Kitāb* is not one of excessive spiritualization; it does stress that the end of the Way of his master (Ibn al-ʿArabī) is wisdom (sections 69–73), but this is a wisdom that embraces pragmatic understanding (52). Throughout, the text is a step-by-step guide for the murīd (devotee) on the true path as perceived by Ibn al-ʿArabī (Introduction). Like Kaʿb, the murīd is an itinerant (*sālik;* 57, 66) on a quest. The goal, according to this tract, is to travel back to the origin, to God, and then to return to this life to complete a cycle (65–66). This is a spiritual process, based on a special kind of exercise: "The spiritual exercise (*riyāḍa*) consists of improving one's character and of carrying on a spiritual struggle/battle (*mujāhada*), to force the soul to endure hunger, thirst, sleeplessness, being without clothes, and seclusion. Without riyāḍa, one cannot have struggle/battle (*jihād*); without jihād, one cannot have contemplation/spiritual insight (*maʿrifa*)."[46]

Here, we can detect the structure of the Path reflecting the same mental framework as the *Bourda* poem above: In the poem, it is to return to the beloved, to happiness (*Bourda,* 1–13). Through memory, the return to the most meaningful, to the most exemplary, is facilitated. On the other hand, in Ibn al-Ḥabashī's tract, the focus is a different beloved, a beloved encountered through the inner processes of the true self (*Kitāb,* 79). The essential fulcrum for these processes is the mind (55–56). What drives the mind, urging it on, is a veiled sense of personal well-being, of completeness (cf. sections 69 and 79). The seeker in Ibn Ḥabashī must determine which reality is the true reality, which data are the primary data. In Muslim terms, the question is which is the correct perspective: the contingent law (*sharīʿah*) or the cosmic law (the transcendent law of love) (64)—in philosophical terms, which is contingent experience and which is undifferentiated truth (72–73). The pattern dominates the *Bourda* as well, for Kaʿb is pulled in two directions, remaining true to his forebears and their loyalties (and thus reaping his own death) or embracing the new religion of the Prophet (and hoping for release from the death threat).

Like the camel in the *Bourda* (14–27), the seeker must rely upon inherent strength. The soul in Ibn Ḥabashī is the beast of burden, the carrier of the mind's search (*Kitāb,* 2). In the *Bourda,* the mighty camel is filled with strength, determination, and fortitude (20, 24, 27). Yet in each, the vehicle has the potential to fail; in the *Bourda,* despite the camel's greatness, its imagery recalls the lamentations of the woman, past her prime, whose firstborn perishes (29–31); in the *Kitāb,* the soul must contend with its own tendency to deception . . . all the veils of the soul have the potential to detain and defeat the destiny of the seeker (68).

Both pieces require confrontation with serious personal problems. To return to Suʿād, the calumny of the slanderers and false friends must be weathered (*Bourda,* 32). Kaʿb must deal with friends who promise and never deliver (33). He must deal with people who gladly would see him dead (34–35, 47), and with his own frailty that would say "why bother" and then die. He must decide to seize the day, to choose the way of life over the path of death, even if it means going into the very lair of trouble

(40–43). No one would condemn him if he died in the process, for if he died, he would be a hero to his family and tribal traditions. If he lived, he would live in a new community, with new goals (49). In the *Kitāb*, the murīd must deal with the perfidies of the mind and the contentions of a dubious heart (56). The search for true being must deal not only with the problem of determining which path to take, but also with the very deception of the path, once one is upon it (57). Ibn Ḥabashī sees the one pathway as defined by servitude and poverty (*Kitāb*, 32), the other by terms of normative empowerment (33). Each path implies its own set of struggles and activities, and each is a possible and acceptable way. But one is clearly superior: the way of empowerment (35). This way, however, can only be achieved by the person who throws worldly discourse to the wind and pursues the goal with abandon (61).

In both, the key to survival is spiritual personality. The *Bourda*'s hero is the Prophet, who throws his robe in protection over the bereft poet. In the *Kitāb*, it is the shaikh, the spiritual guide, who saves initiates by providing them with the protection of spiritual intuition and leads them into full awareness (29). Symbolically expressed in the patched frock, the Sufi adept regards the *Bourda* as a conferring medium, reflecting symbolically the hierarchy of baraka reaching from God, through the Prophet to the saints, and culminating in the local shaikh.

Only the intentionality of the panegyric is different. In the *Bourda*, the Prophet is recognized as the sword of God (48), whose prowess has ushered in victory over his enemies. The *Bourda* is an exploration of the power resident in the Prophet and his message. It is he who provides purpose; it is he who defines the destiny of the new community (49–50). In the tract, the knower (*ʿarīf*) comes to know the wisdom hidden in God, a wisdom that is nondifferentiated (33–35). It is a wisdom that exists only in a contemplation that removes the difference between the contemplator and the contemplated. It is the successful knower who is lauded. The knower is empowered (36). For, once the knower truly *knows*, then contingent law finds its proper place, and the social fabric of life is reknit in its true order (16–17). Any attempt to depict this state of knowledge requires a return to the world of language, and thus a loss of *ḥaqq*, or truth (77). The knower understands the failure of ordinary discourse and comprehends reality from the perspective of one who has transcended it (79).

Note specifically the similarity in the release that comes with the "deliverer." In Kaʿb's case, he is delivered from death to new life in Islam (*Bourda*, 34). From the *Kitāb*'s point of view, the knower is delivered by the shaikh from the shallowness of life to intuitions about cosmic reality (58). Here is where Moroccan Sufism abandons Ibn Ḥabashī's (or Ibn ʿArabi's!) blueprint of the spiritual life: The *Bourda* is chanted because of the role the Prophet is deemed to play in the murīd's life, becoming a metaphor of spiritual protection and religious achievement in Islam.

Within this framework, the role of the Prophet is sketched in several ways, but from Ibn Ḥabashī's perspective, the murīd is the inheritor (*wārith*) of the Prophet:

"If the path that leads to union is followed by a *wārith,* he will return with the attributes of lordship, such as those of commanding and forbidding, the power, the grandeur, the guidance, the teaching, the tenderness and compassion, the endurance and the rigor, and the domination. (Even) if he is not a wārith, he will follow that (experience) by acceptance, renunciation, negation of ordinary attributes, the permanence in the company of God on the carpet of contemplation and serenity in the face of destiny's fluctuation, without saying a word."[47]

Such a person does not vacillate between the ḥaqq and *ḥaqīqā,* between the Law and cosmic reality, for there can only be a synthesis of the two in the oneness of God. In effect, the Prophet is a pattern for the murīd in choosing the route to empowerment, and by reciting the *Bourda,* the murīd is rearticulating the ideals of the spiritual life he has chosen. Following the Prophet is therefore a liberating, transcending scenario that puts both contingent and cosmic law into practice in the life of the seeker. This is the Suʿād of goodness and happiness that the Sufi is seeking.

The *Bourda* of Busayrī is a paeon of integration—a critical one at that—of Berber and Arabic (a topic examined further in chapter 6). Busayrī, a Berber, composed the *Bourda* in Egypt, where he was residing. Berbers claim him as their own, indicating that he is an extraordinary example of the way their people have responded to the claims of Islam. Moreover, they see Busayrī as one who made Islam great in North Africa. Whether or not he was Berber probably cannot be determined now, but for our purposes, Busayrī represents a prime example of the integrating power of the Prophet within a divided Muslim community.

From another perspective, the *Bourda* is the way in which the Arabic language has been utilized as a cohesive element in Eastern Muslim civilization. Here is evidence that Arabic was perceived as a liturgical and scholarly language, espoused by Berbers for its spiritual potency. The Berbers' willingness to embrace Arabic in this way signals a stance toward bilingualism that has been essential for Islamic triumph . . . learning Arabic was not held to be a loss of one's identity as a Berber. But above all, it is the way in which the eulogistic form in Arabic has been wedded in the creative response to the figure of the Prophet; in Sufi piety, it is of the highest significance. The Arab munshid sees Busayrī's lauding of the Prophet to be a model of the way in which the Prophet continues to relate to his people. So the *Bourda* is a quasi-sacred medium of an ancient praise form, united with conceptions of the salvic propensity of the Prophet in the Sufi cult. Busayrī's work provides an integrating vehicle at several levels of spiritual and cultural expression. The result is a culture of prophetic madīh of importance both in Sufi and larger Moroccan contexts.

Changing Remembrance and the Arabic Munshid

Despite the predominance of the past as a theme in the munshid's repertoire, Morocco's chanters have not focused solely on the aged texts without regard to the general Moroccan context. There are several ways in which the context affects the message. One certainly is the emotional tone and religious fervor of the munshid. Thus at the munshidūn gathering held in Salé in 1995, I repeatedly heard that the energizing effect of the singing really depends upon the munshid and his special training. For example, he develops technical listening skills to detect changes in the emotional atmosphere, and then can make a movement within texts. The good munshid knows the du'a Nasiri, the *Bourda,* the *Hamzīyya,* Ibn al-ʿArabī, Ibn al-Fāriḍ, and the leading saints of the past and knows from the signals by the ʿamdah when to shift from one to the other.

But the munshidūn are also aware that the spiritual world in which they operate has changed. Some of them are responding to these changes in creative ways. For some, the inshād is in danger of being modified or forgotten, so steps must be taken to preserve it in its original form. In Fez, in June 1995, I met with Ḥajj Muḥammad Bennīs. Now forty, Bennīs was raised at the knee of his grandfather, who was a muqaddam of the Tijāniyya ṭarīqa. He is now regarded as perhaps the most outstanding munshid in Fez and, for many, in the whole of Morocco, with invitations from far and wide to chant in a wide variety of venues: "I am not connected with a specific ṭarīqa now. I'm with the ṭarīqa of God. I am with all the ṭuruq . . . because all the ṭuruq take the same way . . . the way of the Prophet. This is the right route because all have a central difference of mind in them, and I've decided to take a proper direction. . . . That is why I now assist with all ṭuruq."[48]

From age eight, Bennīs has been chanting the *Bourda* and the *Hamzīyya* in the zāwiya. He regards these texts not just as poetic expressions but as inspired embodiments of a way of life: "The inshād is something confided to us by our ancestors, and consequently, nothing should be changed, since what is important about this legacy is the message inscribed in it. The object of the munshid is to convey that message. It follows that this message must be safeguarded from distortion, and specially to be defended from being modified by contemporary interests."[49]

The urge to preserve this charged memory is so important that Shaikh Bennīs has organized the *Association of the Imam al-Būṣayrī,* dedicated to preserving madīḥ and to documenting both the textual and rhythmic legacies associated with it. Several important points lie behind this collective effort: "It is typical of the Moroccan material that local artisans and performers learn the texts of madīḥ and malḥūn, since they chant these every Thursday at the shrine of Mūlay Idrīs in Fez during the ʿamdahs. They chant texts in classical Arabic as well as in regional dialects, using poetry in the form of malḥūn, *barāwil,* or *zajal.* There is a controversial move on now to change this tradition, to modernize it, introducing new texts and new rhythms. I am opposed to that. We must maintain the literary tradition bequeathed to us by our ancestors."[50]

Asked whether he will preserve all texts, Bennīs admitted that he was principally concerned with the madīḥ in general, and he pointed to the ṭarīqa Tijāniyya, his own ṭarīqa, "because it once had the ʿamdah and the ḥaḍra, but now neither occur there." So he will concentrate on teaching the texts of the Ḥarrāqiyya, the Dar-qāwiyya, the Bu Dshishiyya, and others.

But it is not just the text that he regards as imperiled. He holds that the very rhythm of inshād is beginning to disappear:

> This is why some of us want to preserve the inshād and its basis in the material derived from Imām Būṣayrī. The Moroccans, of all Muslims, are known to understand and use the texts of Imām Būṣayrī. The other countries do not learn the entire texts of Imām Būṣayrī. In addition, we want to preserve the actions [style]. When Moroccans work they sing, and they sing either malḥūn or inshād. That is why they know many texts. So with my classes, among the activities each Friday morning they chant the *Bourda* at Fez, and in the afternoon they chant with the malḥūn. Each Friday they go to the mosque of Mūlay Idrīs to chant the *Hamzīyya* and the *Bourda*.

Shaikh Bennīs has formed an association in the mosque of Tajmuti because he thinks he can teach the *Bourda* more effectively in a group than by just having the group attend the ʿamdah at the Sīdī Mūlay Idrīs shrine as individuals. Despite this, he acknowledges that, from a historical perspective, Mūlay Idrīs is the best school of inshād in Fez:

> All munshidūn must climb the steps of Mūlay Idrīs in Fez. Each day I assist at the ʿamdah and inshād and recite *Hamzīyya* and *Bourda*. I have been teaching this for eight years. I have been singing in the ribāṭ for thirty-two years because I learned from my father and my grandfather. My grandfather was the muqaddam in the ṭarīqa Tijāniyya; my grandfather was also in the ṭarīqa, the Kittāniyya, when I began my career in Sufism. My grandfather was the leading munshid of Fez; therefore, I am at home in the tradition of the munshidūn. My father was a true craftsman, and he worked all the time in the dhikr. Now, in my family, everyone knows dhikr.

The shaikh agrees with the modernizers that new songs and new rhythms are attractive to the younger generation, but he argues against moving in this direction, since it will cut Morocco's ties with its past. He wants instead to renew the madīḥ by building on a solid foundation of the madīḥ of the past, and integrating it into a comprehensive art form. To that end he has broadened his perspective from that associated only with the Tijāniyya; he now wants to incorporate the best madīḥ from all the ṭuruq. Acknowledging that it has been a struggle, since he has been roundly criticized by his fellow Tijāniyya murīdīn, he nevertheless believes that systematically organizing this material will lead to its regeneration. Hence two of the key elements in Moroccan spiritual conceptions as represented in this Sufi writing, *remembrance* and *struggle*, are reflected in the life of a leading munshid in Morocco, a kind of metaphor for his colleagues all across the land.

Spiritual Remembrance: The Classical Sufi Tradition in
Ibn al-ʿArabī and Ibn al-Fāriḍ

If the two themes of remembrance and struggle predominate, they are, however, filtered in their understanding by what might be called the classical Arabic Sufi tradition. Contemporary Sufis in Morocco look to the writers of the thirteenth century as the culminating point of a long and rich poetic tradition . . . a tradition that set the norms used by the poetic shaikhs and Sufi writers to this day. This tradition draws on great poets and savants of the Sufi past, reaching back to Rābiʿa al-ʿAdawiyya (d. 801) and Ibn al-Fāriḍ (d. 1235) and Ibn al-ʿArabi (d. 1240)[51] to incorporate them into the oral world of the ordinary murīd. Sufis see individual differences in these poets' styles, but regard them as inspired in the same way, by the same mystical life in God.

Even when the words and phrases are not understood, the classical tradition links the ordinary person with the richness of the great Islamic past, especially the artistic and poetic past. This connection roots the religious experience of the present with a "high" literary and cultural tradition, one in which Sufism embraced most of the official Islamic world. Grasping this history channels it into the "now" of the seeker.

The classical Sufi Arabic tradition in Morocco functions in a number of ways that set it apart from other forms of munshidūn activity. Immediately recognizable by its formal language, it is associated with permanence, stability, and continuity. It is viewed as a prime signifier of the illustrious past, both of Islam's intellectual mysticism and its literary quality. The point is that even people who know little or nothing about the classical language regard it as an indicator of the matrix out of which the Qurʾān, Ḥadīth, and early Islamic religious language were developed. Classical Arabic language is thus a "memory" language, called upon to shift the sentiment to the truths of Islam and its great intellectual past. Citing it is a way of moving out of the compromises and fuzziness of the morals, slippery ideals, and shallow pieties of the modern world that plague the community today. It is "safe" in that no one but recognized scholars can deal with it, and few of them are expert in its meaning and structure. In a way, the munshidūn who chant it are removing themselves from the present time frame and introducing the time frame associated with the past, while at the same time affirming that those past truths apply at this moment.

A number of shaikhs indicated that they use the classical language with the savants of the order, but that everyone uses dialect for ordinary people. It is purely a strategy of communication. Thus, while the precision and sophistication of the ṭarīqa's beliefs might better be expressed in classical Arabic formation, the fact is that only the most educated understand it, and this limits its availability as a teaching medium. Only if one is called upon to theologize about an issue would the classical language be used to sct the discussion.

The Art of Remembrance in Ibn al-ʿArabī

Ibn al-ʿArabī's legacy continues to have an impact in three ways: first, in the role played by his presence in North Africa and Morocco; second, in the ideas and mystical concepts that were enshrined in the institutional structures of Abū al-Ḥasan al-Shādhilī (1196–1258), whose initiative in establishing disciplined organizations for meditation and prayer gave rise to the ṭuruq; and third, in the written texts, commentaries, and poems that he left for the brethren.

Ibn al-ʿArabī left a lasting legacy in Morocco through his visits there early in his career. His first trip to North Africa must have been in 1190 when he journeyed to Tunis to work on a commentary on *The Doffing of the Sandals* by Ibn Qisya.[52] A short time later he returned home to Andalus and then moved to Fez, where he spent less than a year. He was back in Fez for a more extended period the following year, where he had several crucial mystical experiences that forever after made this part of North Africa a special place for him. It was here (1197 c.e.) that he learned of the state of being entitled Seal of the Muḥammadan Sainthood, and received a vision to the effect that he was that seal. Nevertheless, he was to learn also how quixotic rulers could be, for the Almohads were very suspicious of Sufism. On one occasion he was nearly arrested.[53] Despite this, he seems to have gathered quite a number of disciples in the region, and it was in Morocco that he received a personal directive from God to carry his Sufi message to the eastern territories of Islam. This period of his life was most rewarding and brought about the writing of works such as *al-Futūḥāt al-Makkiyyah* (The Meccan revelations), *Fuṣūṣ al-ḥikam* (The bezels of wisdom), *Rasāʾil Ibn al-ʿArabī* (The commentary of Ibn al-ʿArabī), *Tarjumān al-Ashwāq* (The interpreter of desires), and *Diwān* (a collection of his poetry).

Yet it is clear that Ibn al-ʿArabī's importance in Morocco is based more on his spiritual impact than on his published materials. What his trips to North Africa established was the validity of his messages beyond the scope of al-Andalus. They served to universalize his activity in Islamic culture. In this sense, his successes in Morocco were foundational for his more aggressive trips to the East. First, of course, is the relationship of his writing to his spiritual life. He notes, in fact, that he has written not just to record or to publish, but rather to unburden his heart from the energy unleashed through his mystical experiences; that is, his writing was spiritually therapeutic: "In what I have written, I have never had a set purpose, as other writers. Flashes of divine inspiration used to come upon me and almost overwhelm me, so that I could only put them from my mind by committing to paper what they revealed to me. If my works evince any form of composition, it was unintentional. Some works I wrote at the command of God, sent to me in sleep or through mystical revelation."[54]

In effect he is reflecting a principle still dominant today in Morocco: written text is important, but only an indicator; it is not *the* text. That text is a matter for the devoted heart to comprehend. Thus, for example, Ibn al-ʿArabī interprets the Noah verses in the Qurʾān (71:21–28), and particularly the verse "grant Thou no increase to the oppressors but confusion" (71:24), as "It only increases those who oppress their own souls by self-denial in spiritual perplexity," a meaning that bears no relation either to the written context of the Qurʾān or its general usage of key words.[55] Such interpretations, of course, rain literalist condemnations down upon the heads of Sufi followers, but they are regarded as an expression of esoteric verities venerated by the initiated. They are only expressive of the fact that true life is not lived in normal discourse of existence.

Beyond this, however, is the impact of this experiential Islam on the notion of an independent religious system. Ibn al-ʿArabī attended Averroes's funeral, and clearly was skeptical about arriving at truth through philosophical disquisition;[56] he lauded shaikhs who took a stance different from the political leader.[57] This notion of a self-subsisting system apart from the normal appearance of things is still quoted by Moroccan Sufis, where it justifies a pathway different from the culture around them:

> He praises me and I praise Him,
> He worships me and I worship Him.
> In my state of existence I confirm Him,
> As unmanifest I deny Him.
> He knows me, while I know naught of Him,
> I also know Him and perceive Him.
> Where then is His Self-sufficiency,
> Since I help Him and grant Him Bliss?
> It is for this that the Reality created me,
> For I give content to His knowledge and manifest Him.
> Thus did the message come,
> Its meaning fulfilled in me.[58]

What is crucial here is the notion of self-sufficiency. Ibn al-ʿArabī had a protracted debate with an Andalusian shaikh who did not teach the possibility of assuming the attribute of self-sufficiency. He records that he argued effectively against the view so that the shaikh capitulated.[59] The problem surrounded whether or not the true seeker can be said to gain the attribute of self-sufficiency through the mystical encounter. The attribute of self-sufficiency, of course, derives from the belief that God exists completely separate from His creation and does not need that creation to exist. At the same time, the cosmos itself is dependent upon God. Again, God does not have any need to create, so that what He does is totally a free act of will, and noncontingent.

The question is whether, when the adept experiences the oneness of His being, the adept also reflects the attribute of self-sufficiency. Clearly if one has encountered God in this way, the implication for one's own life in the here and now will be affected. It will, at one level, promote a sense of superiority and identity that is not mediated by the normal Muslim community. But this identity, according to Ibn al-ʿArabī, has no permanence. It is merely the summation of what is known at the moment. As Sells puts it: "In apophatic mystical texts, there is indeed a sense of the extraordinary, but the extraordinary, the transcendent, the unimaginable, reveals itself as the common. . . . In Ibn al-ʿArabī, the relinquishment of the reified 'God' of one's belief to accept the perpetually changing image of reality is nothing other than the eternal self-manifestation of the transcendent in each new moment."[60]

At one and the same moment, then, the individual is important because the experience of the divine is being known through his or her experience, while all other moments are rendered insignificant (because God's form could not appear that way without the existence of the individual).[61] Such notions make the uniqueness of the person of transcendent significance. Thus is the sense of self-sufficiency of the person sustained and supported by mystical doctrine in Morocco.

Ibn al-ʿArabī also affirms a special sense of remembrance. As Roger Boase points out, he drew inspiration from the brilliant Andalusian poetry of Ibn Zaydūn, especially his *Nūniyyah*. Thus, "I weep out of loyalty even if you do not generously accord me love's union; yet a dream image will suffice us—a remembrance will suffice us" became transformed into Ibn al-ʿArabī's concept of remembrance as an encountered reality: "If union with the beloved is not personal union, and the beloved is a superior being who imposes obligations on the lover, then the fulfilment of these obligations sometimes takes the place of personal union, producing in him a joy which obliterates the awareness of sorrow from his soul."[62]

Clearly Ibn al-ʿArabī's "memory" sustains these experiences in such a way that he can argue for some sort of permanence within them. That is, what is known in each mystical experience is not absolute reality, but a kind of dialogue of the sacred in and through these experiences. No mystic of the true way, then, can claim that any one experience of God is definitive. Rather, each constitutes a ground for learning of the infinite possibilities in God. It is not that humans cannot "know" God; they can and do. But they cannot root that knowing in the structures of the mind and certainly not in the structures of language. The best that can be done is to hold the experiences in memory and to dialogue with their collective power as to what they say about reality, for it is in this image or form that God has deigned to express Himself: "When I (God) love my servant (ʿabd) . . . I become the hearing with which he hears, the seeing with which he sees, the hand with which he grasps, the feet with which he walks, the tongue with which he speaks."[63]

Poetically, Ibn al-ʿArabī states:

> If you affirm transcendence you bind
> If you affirm immanence you define
> If you affirm both you hit the mark
> You are an imam in knowledge and a master.[64]

The thrust of this poem is much more to the point than the oft-quoted poem "My creed is love / wherever its caravan turns along the way, / that is my belief / my faith." What is permanent is the nexus point of divine and human that takes place in the mystical moment. It is the remembrance of the beloved as encountered in the previous moment that is at this instant both transcendent (and therefore God), and immanent (and therefore self), held not as polarities but as interfused reminders of the task ahead, that is, to move beyond where one is:

> Whoever binds him (in a belief) denies him in any belief
> other than that in which he has bound him
> And affirms him in the belief
> in which he bound him in his manifestation
> But affirms him in every image into which he transforms
> himself
> He gives him(self) of him(self)
> in accordance with the image in which he appears to him(self)
> Infinitely, since the forms of manifestation
> have no end at which to stop
> And, likewise, knowledge of Allah has no limit for the knower
> at which he might stop
> Rather, the knower asks in every moment for an increase in his knowledge of
> him
> "My lord, increase me in knowledge" (Qurʾān 20:16)
> "My lord, increase me in knowledge"
> "My lord, increase me in knowledge"

So it continues, perpetually, from both sides.[65]

As Sells points out, the repetition of the Qurʾānic verse is an indication of dhikr, a repetitive engagement with the words of God designed to bring the speaker closer to God.[66] Hence, Ibn al-ʿArabī's remembrance utilizes the words of God as a vehicle to continually alter the adept's vision of God. The result is a notion of constant transformation of the remembered experience that then leads to new knowledge of God's meaning. Here, then, is Ibn al-ʿArabī's modus operandi for the munshid: rehearse the powerful words that will lead to a transformed perception of God in the life of the adepts, providing the language of new awareness for them. What, then, of the text?

In Ibn al-ʿArabī's view, the grounding of the "word" in language is part of the human requirement for God's disclosure. This means that the images that the individual relies upon to formulate the spiritual encounter have a grounding in human culture. Language is therefore essential as a building tool, but it cannot become the ultimate in the experiential world of relating to God. Ibn al-ʿArabī's use of classical Arabic rests upon the conviction that that language is refined and sophisticated and carries with it the wealth of imagery that is just as necessary as the stages and stations of the mystical life.

Within the context of a powerful and mythical memory is that of the Primordial Covenant, based on God's question in the Qur'ān, *"Alastū bi rabbikum?"* (Am I not your Lord?), and the reply of the spirits, *"Balā"* (Indeed!). The theory that all humans stand before God pledging their allegiance to Him derives from the early Sufi Sahl ibn ʿAbdullāh al-Tustārī. In his commentary, al-Tustārī sees this paradigmatic event out of time as the basis of human meaning; Moroccan Sufis, like Sufis everywhere, view this moment as the first dhikr and the remembered moment of unity to which all humans desire to return.[67] Ibn al-ʿArabī builds on this mythical moment by viewing Adam as the exemplar and ultimately the ideal human being, completely unified in both the physical and spiritual senses. It is in Adam that God's mystery became known, specifically through the metaphor of the mirror (i.e., God provides the means for Adam to know himself). Thus memory rehearses for all humans the basis for overcoming the sense of separateness inherent in the human condition, and the return to God is the ultimate purpose of life.[68] For contemporary Sufis in Morocco, this original dhikr is fundamental to all remembering.

We can now see how Ibn al-ʿArabī's insistence on the imagery of God in the mystical moment is a critical one for the munshid. Under the jurisdiction of language, the munshidūn have a transformative role to play that reaches to the very knowledge that the adepts grasp. This indicates that they are more than speakers of dhikr; they are handmaidens for the deepening spiritual processes of the brethren. They do not just sing; they articulate phrases that remind the participants of true origins. They chant the liturgies of the inner heart in a language that will remind the listeners of their Primordial Covenant. Their ability to use the text is a key part of Sufi creative engagement with the divine.

Memory's Engagement in Ibn al-Fāriḍ

Ibn al-ʿArabī once asked Ibn al-Fāriḍ if he could write a commentary on Ibn al-Fāriḍ's poem *al-Tāʾiyyah*, to which the latter demurred, saying that Ibn al-ʿArabī's book *The Meccan Revelations* was sufficient.[69] Ibn al-Fāriḍ (d. 1235) was thus Ibn al-ʿArabī's contemporary, and Ibn al-Fāriḍ's emphasis on love certainly must have had an impact on the Great Shaikh's writing of *Tarjumān al-ashwāq* (The interpreter of desires).[70] They had met briefly while Ibn al-ʿArabī was in Cairo in 1201 and 1202, during which the above exchange took place. *Al-Tāʾiyyah* illustrates another feature of Moroccan Sufi character, for in it another motivation, at once more common and yet more articulated, is declared. It is a meditation on an ancient love, an honoring of the beauty, sagacity, and agonies of a monumental relationship with the beloved. It taps into the perceived eternal mysterious attraction inherent in love as a force in the universe. *Al-Tāʾiyyah* drew upon the skills of the greatest qaṣīda writers and combined with it the fundamental Sufi conviction that what attracts the individual to the Sufi way also empowers life itself. For love allows the Sufi to speak of an experience beyond the specificity of Islamic belief to those of other religious beliefs, as was documented in my Egypt study.[71] Where Ibn al-ʿArabī elucidates the connectedness of the person to God and the universe, Ibn al-Fāriḍ points to the glue that holds that unity together.

The inspiration, if not the source, for the textual tradition of love is Andalusia. There Ibn Zaydūn (d. 1071) and a number of other love-inspired poets developed a whole genre of love odes, the theme of which was taken up in the next century by Abū Madyan "al-Ghawth" (1126–1198). Abū Madyan was an Andalusian mystic who was the spiritual progenitor of Abū al-Ḥasan al-Shādhilī, the founder of the ṭarīqa institution in Morocco. Here is a segment from his qaṣīda recorded in Meknes in 1995:

> We live in your memory (remembrance)
> for love of the lovers revives and moves us.
> Without your love inside us, we could not live
> the spirits dance, longing for a rendezvous.

Here several of the themes that would bear fruit later are found: memory is the vehicle that brings back the revivifying love; love is empowering because through love humans are truly motivated; "your" love refers either to God, to the *ahl al-baīt*, that is, the family of the Prophet, or to the love of the shaikhs or that of the brethren (hence the multiplicity of referents quite usual in Sufi writing); and engagement with love in Arab Sufi chanting tradition.

Memory and the Revivifying Power of Love.   The revivifying character of love is part of the ʿUdhrī poets' basic theme.[72] Ibn al-Fāriḍ is yearning to return to the beloved, and as a means to do so, he revisits in his memory the events of the encampment. The well-known pattern, as summarized by Ibn Qutayba (d. circa 888), is as follows:

> I have heard a certain man of letters remark that the author of a *qaṣīda* began always by mentioning the encampment, the dung-heaps and other relics. He then wept complainingly, addressed the deserted site and begged his companion to halt, in order that he might furnish an occasion for mentioning the folk who once dwelt there but were now departed. . . . To this he joined the amatory prelude: he complained of the violence of his sentiments and the pain of separation, as well as the extremity of his passion and yearning, so as to incline men's hearts towards him and win the attention of their eyes and ears; for love-poetry is very near to the soul and readily cleaves to the heart.[73]

Memory becomes the vehicle to transform his anguish into joy. Ibn al-Fāriḍ writes:

> And when I remember you, I sway with emotion as though I have been given
> to drink of wine, because of the fragrance of your memory.

> And when I am urged to feign forgetfulness of my bond with you, I find my
> bowels are very jealous of that bond.
> Fresh forever be the recollection of those days passed by, with neighbours in
> whose company our nights were festivals indeed.
> Never did the breeze wafting from the East sway the sweet-scented worm-
> wood of the sandhills, but that it brought new life from you to the lovers
> slain by passion.[74]

It is the significance of this recollection that is paramount; it articulates Ibn al-Fāriḍ's most meaningful relationship. The notion that memory carries the meaning of his deepest passions is depicted in several explicit ways throughout the poems, but these relationships reflect more than just amatory extravagance. In effect, the specific references to memory and remembrance constitute a catalogue of psychological movements in his mind, each of them encompassing a different way in which memory has affected him. Thus, in the first poem, he begs God to preserve his memory of the times spent together with the beloved, in the second, his memory reconstitutes his beloved, so that he is "at his side." In the fourth poem, the entire festive moment returns with remembrance. In the fifth, he begs the reproacher to destroy everything of his past save he "who mastered and possesses the whole of human beauty" (that is, the Prophet). In the seventh poem, he begs for a return to the intensity that the relationships of the past had; in number eight, his memory of the beloved is activated by a fragrance that brings again the beauty of the beloved. In the ninth poem, though near death, the beloved flows "like blood in me," and the very remembrance revivifies him so that he "mounts on high." In number ten, remembering the beloved turned into a wine preexisting even the creation of the vine, and number eleven, memory is like wine, aiding in the articulation of tales about the beloved. In the twelfth poem, the past may appear as relics, but though they be destroyed, he will remain true to their existence. In number thirteen, remembrance provides his soul's food, and in number fourteen, the remembrance of his passion for the beloved has killed the tragic memory of his friend's destruction.[75] These explicit references to memory and its functions indicate a sophisticated comprehension of the role of the mind in constructing one's self, for obviously the writer sees this functioning as far more than a simple artistic trophe. Rather it is a means of articulating his conviction about the role of memory in defining the most meaningful parts of his existence: memory is the critical means by which one constitutes reality.

The Motivational Power of Love.   Ibn al-Fāriḍ's poetry also deals with the motivational powers of love. These ideas of the empowerment deriving from a source beyond the self are expressed in a number of situations, but we will focus only on one poem, the second in the collection. In the first line, the writer shifts the scene from the ancient meeting place of the qaṣīda form, the encampment, to the trysting site of the soul. This place is well known because it is the location where lover and beloved meet constantly: "In the midst of the battlefield of enchanting glances and amorous hearts hold me, slain, and that without sin or guilt." This setting is not an ancient battleground, however, but an existential one, since it is the situation of the Muslim believer: constantly in jihād with the inner nature. It is familiar, then, because every day the sparring takes place, with glances and longings the weapons. He is slain, not in a historical war but by his own perception . . . the beloved is so beautiful that he dies of ardor (line 14), and like a gazelle (line 13), God's beauty is ever evasive and thus ever beyond, creating the motivation to continue doggedly to pursue Him on the way (line 16), now understood to be metaphorical for the Sufi path. All his senses are refined into remembering the beloved, who is then revealed to be none other than the Prophet: "For that home is my home, when my beloved is at my side; and be he but manifest to me, the ascent of the rugged ridge is likewise my ascent" (line 36). Here the poet uses code words for the Perfect Man and the Mirror of God; both Sufi concepts[76] stress the nonspecificity of space related to God, and the results of the adept's existence in fanāʿ, that is, in the state of passing away into ecstasy (line 6, "invisible to myself"). This ushers in a new awareness that the poet is alive to God, despite his waywardness, and regardless of all his perceived faults, "thou has been remembered yonder" (line 44). Remembrance maintains his existence in God, even as al-Suhrawardī and the other Sufi shaikhs remember His being present to them in Mecca. He is assured, then, that his love has secured him a permanent place in God's firmament, even when there is nothing left of him. With this type of love language, Ibn al-Fāriḍ has rooted his true being beyond the fray of the physical world in that realm of the Prophet and of God. In a wonderful denouement to being slain on the battlefield, he is slain in God and exists evermore in the memory of God.

Love Related to Sacred Islamic Figures.   Relating to the object of the deepest religious emotions is a constant concern for Sufis. Giving these sacred denizens their proper respect and affection is a theme found in many poems. Whether these sacred figures ore held to be God, or the family of the Prophet or the Saint, one's comportment to word is always evaluated and measured. The focus of the discussion here will be the Spirit of Muḥammad, but similar analyses could have been made of any of these figures. In poem number eight, described by Arberry as a hymn to that spiritual notion foundational for Sufism of the time, and often heard in present-day Moroccan samāʿ:

Indwelling in thee is a truth that hath adorned thee to my reason's eye; wherefore my sight is busied with thy adornments.

Thou hast excelled in beauty and goodness all the people of loveliness; and they have dire need of thy inner truth.

All lovers at the Last Day shall be raised under your banner, and all the lovely ones shall be raised under thine indwelling love. (lines 37–39)[77]

Here Ibn al-Fāriḍ is exploring the problematic of the mystical life; specifically, how can the mystic speak of the dichotomy of the lover-beloved when one embraces the Spirit of Muḥammad? In that sacred state, there can be no longer any "thing" so that his inner eye sees only the essence (*maʿnān*), even as his tongue has to speak of the attributes (*ḥila*). This distinction between essence and attribute is the stock in trade of the theologians, who argue that humans can only know the attributes of God; the essence lies beyond human experience. Sufis of this time saw the Spirit of Muḥammad as a means of bypassing the problem. For the attributes of God are known only as a series of adornments, that is, as descriptors of qualities like mercy (*al-raḥmān,* the Merciful), whereas in the mystical embrace, the physical seeker vanishes away, leaving nothing of the human frailty available by which one can know. It is then that the Spirit of Muḥammad becomes available as a divine attribute, pointing the mystic to the essence beyond the attribute. It is at this point that all language fails, and the Beauty of the Beloved can only be depicted in the most elevated of human symbols, the full moon:

> The moon at its full might have deputy been to the phantom of thy bright countenance, shining upon my wakeful eye, so close it resembled thee:
> And so thou showest thyself in a form not thine, to an eye that rejoiced in thee: and naught else but thee I beheld. (44–45)[78]

Among the members of the ṭuruq in Morocco, Ibn al-Fāriḍ is a classical Sufi poet whose words carry extraordinary authority. The formulas he uses, and the imagery he explores, are regarded as a clean depiction of the spiritual life. He is therefore a safe and legitimate author. His writing, though acknowledged to be elliptical, is generally simple and straightforward. This makes his lyrics widely appreciated by the shaikhs in maintaining a high standard of language while providing a special discourse that is beyond most people and therefore not subject to the ordinary limitations imposed by the Sharīʿa. It also links them with a writer of the past whose work demonstrates how refined the mystical life can be.

These two classical writers, Ibn al-ʿArabī and Ibn al-Fāriḍ, enunciated a system of understanding that harnessed the most basic of human needs and wed it with the most abstract of mystical thought. Despite the internal conflicts between the two systems that they represent, they are compatible enough that they have been able to carry the meditation tradition from their day to our own. In retrospect this is quite an amazing feat.

Engagement with Love in Sufi Chanting Tradition

Love is a code word found throughout Ibn al-ʿArabī and Ibn al-Fāriḍ. Yet it is also central to the notion of Sufi performance. The material examined in this chapter demonstrates that the Arabic-speaking munshid is immersed in articulating a spiritual world comprised of several dimensions, a key one of which is love. Love involves an engagement with a world quite beyond his personal domain, an encoded domain belonging to a prized and powerful memory system. That world is directly related to and rooted in the literature of classical or, as it is known in Morocco, oriental Islam. It is defined by tradition (*ṭurāth*), by the past, by the rituals he is involved within, and by the character of the group within which he performs. Clearly the text of his performance is a singular element in his purpose, but he does not regard that text as just a set of words. Rather the text is a vehicle to transform lives around him, for love is held to have transforming power. Thus the "oriental" text is interpreted as a feature of a religious culture, rather than as a literary expression. This makes the meaning of a text, even one that is "oriental," subject to subtle change and reinterpretation. It can be a vehicle for education, for development. For the Sufi chanter, a traditional Arabic text is never just a text. It is enshrined in the elemental structure from which he draws his spiritual sustenance. That is why the engagement is described in terms of love. In his performance, this conception of love acts like a lyric script or metaphorical model providing the bedrock for his inspiration and content.

In the next chapter, we turn to another part of the tradition, this deriving from the great days of Moroccan and Andalusian achievement. To the oriental Arabic related to the Qurʾān and the Ḥadīth, to the Banī Hilāl and classical poetry, came another, in some ways more powerful, force: Moroccan Arabic. This language allowed for a distinctive Moroccan identity to be forged, an identity with its own sense of place and execution. Under its genial guidance the repertoire was broadened and deepened.

4

THE CHANTER'S CLASSICAL TEXT
Tools for the Master of Memory

We are bound by ʾamāna. ʾAmāna prevents any change in the text, like a dam holding back the flood.

Muḥammad, Ḥarrāqiyya munshid

The majority of civilized mankind do not possess the organ by which poetry is perceived. Can you hear the shriek of a bat? Probably not; but do you think less of yourself on that account? Do you pretend to others, or even try to persuade yourself that you can? Why be unwilling to admit that perhaps you cannot perceive poetry? Is it an unbearable thing, crushing to self-conceit, to be in the majority?

A. E. Housman, *The Name and Nature of Poetry*

Memory of a Grand Past: The Moroccan Arab/Andalusian Tradition

The Moroccan memory-encoding system also involves literary and artistic influences from Andalusia, and after an evening of Andalusian poetry and song, there are few who would not grant its grandeur and vigor. Hearing children mimicking its cadence, memorizing short phrases, and using images in conversation is convincing proof that remembrance encompasses a wide swath of Moroccan cultural life. Those who know poetry are convinced that snippets, phrases, and iconic statements become templates in the mind. These templates do not so much direct Moroccans' lives as provide them with images with which to play, and in the playing we come to know something about what is real. Of such stuff is the Andalusian tradition in Morocco. One cannot deal with the munshid tradition in Morocco without reference to this prized heritage.

According to Professor Muḥammad Ben Cherīfa, with the fall of Andalusia, Morocco became the inheritor of Spain's great literary tradition. Henceforth, maintaining the tradition became Morocco's great destiny. After Andalus was lost, Morocco sent its poets and scholars to study in Damascus and Cairo. The families of Morocco also sent their sons to engage with Muslim culture in the East, and in this way the families became vehicles for cultural advance. Where Andalusia had previously attracted many students and scholars and had been the catalyst, now few came from the East in search of knowledge. Morocco had to develop its own resources.

According to Professor Ben Cherīfa, "Maybe the zāwiyas have maintained the Andalusian poetry as the 'pure' form of Arabness because they saw it as their responsibility to maintain this in the face of the great crisis in the eastern world with the invasion of the Turks, etc. Besides, Arabic was the sacred language of the Qur'an and even the most dedicated Berber honored the language of the Qur'an and the Prophet."[1]

Still, as Zwartjes argues, it was the superior poetry of Andalusia that continued to influence the Berber-Arab communities of the Maghrib, for they adopted the popular forms and embraced it so fully that it became *the* classical tradition for their literary culture.[2] This is very much different than the Eastern Muslim countries, where the sophisticated classical Arabic of the court won the day.[3] Zwartjes's point highlights one of the enduring differences between Morocco and Egypt and its import for religious texts. In Morocco, local saints, venerated by radiating circles of believers, are the center of Sufi identity. Some of these collectivities developed into what has been called by French scholars "maraboutic states," especially in the South,[4] but even in non-Berber areas, sainthood takes on a hereditary cachet, with agnatic affiliation a mark of distinctive status. These saints, known as "tenth-century saints" (*aṣ-ṣaliḥīn al-qarn al-ᶜāshir*) because, like Sīdī Muḥammad al-Jazūlī, they were able to provide an integrated religious community that survived their deaths and became solidified into religious institutions that maintained their presence through to our day. Even when the "maraboutic corporations," to use Hatt's apt phrase,[5] underwent significant change, the sense of family connection, whether real or imagined, had deep and lasting resonance. Perhaps this was another legacy of the social impact of Arab tribal groups such as the Banī Hilāl on northern Moroccan culture. The transformation that occurred was that belonging was mediated by the religious qualities associated with the saints, and a measure of the saint's charisma was routinized into a patrilineage sacrality that still operates in Morocco in the loyalty of Sufi murīdīn to their ṭarīqa.

Still, Sufism did not just follow the southern model of the maraboutic states or the individual family model of the main cities. The Kaybele, as Montagne indicates, are a northern tribal affiliation that are constituted as a family of varied social classes. They did not institutionalize themselves as ṭuruq because of a basic conflict between themselves and the sultan. In this case, the Idrīsiyya represented the centralizing tendencies of the government by the consolidation of political and religious power. Rather, the ṭuruq that were organized in that region promoted a common cultural world because the orders had individual family rapport with the sultan. They were not, however, attached to the sultan by means of their membership in a ṭarīqa. Nevertheless, some zāwiyas were also attached more or less directly to Ibn Idrīs, as for example, the Sharqāwiyya.[6]

In short, it was not just one kind of Sufi political culture that promoted Andalusian connections in ṭarīqa/zāwiya rituals. The malḥūn tradition, rooted in an Arabic more or less regarded as classical because it was associated with the immigrant Arab tribes from the Ḥijāz, drew its inspiration from the earlier zajal and *muwashshahāt* forms.[7] The "mission" Sufism promoted by Abū'-Ḥasan al-Shādhilī fashioned out of it a new aesthetic, redirecting its language into a vehicle for deep piety among its devotees.

The Distinctively Moroccan Malḥūn Tradition

The word malḥūn derives from *laḥana*, which has two distinctive meanings: singing and musical chanting; and making errors in grammatical form. While the connection may be difficult to see at first blush, the fundamental notion is that of verbal communication; thus both are specialized, perhaps even slightly deviant forms of Arabic cultural expression. In Morocco, both senses of communication have had an impact. The question is whether the malḥūn tradition constitutes a distinctive Moroccan Arabic genre.

Abbās al-Jirārī insists there are three areas that convince him of the uniqueness of the Moroccan malḥūn genre.[8] The first is his belief that each nation has a national patrimony, that is, a cultural, social, and political character or soul. He believes that one can untangle the threads that make up this national character by analyzing the various folk elements that constitute its basis. One can, then, examine how it is constructed. Jirārī thinks this analysis is of the utmost importance: "It gives a clear vision and a profound insight into the soul of a nation. The role of the popular culture of the malḥūn is critical to this partrimony; in popular culture one finds the picture of the national soul. Classical Arab culture in Morocco, on the other hand, is less clear. What is evident is that local Arabic expressions are the locus of such studies, not the texts of the larger Arabic world. Local literature is quite different than classical literature, and one must make a study of each."[9]

Secondly, Jirārī bases his views on the distinctiveness of Moroccan Arabic. It is quite unlike classical Arabic; Jirārī sees it as an Arabic foundation with an admixture of Berber and the Kaybele dialect, as well as residual classical forms. Thirdly, he sees the Sufi malḥūn formulation as reflecting a fundamental difference in its musical derivation. He holds that several aspects of Moroccan culture have had a bearing in this area: language, rhythm, personnel, attachment to religion, and types of singers.

Moreover, when this Arabic tradition began to gain speed, it was not based upon classical forms of Arabic but upon popular and local Arabic . . . on "court" Arabic. Furthermore, it is likely that not all the early poets were Andalusian, and, despite the fact that scholarship seems to ignore their contribution, some were Moroccan. Nevertheless, the Andalusian tradition did have a preponderant influence on the Arab culture that developed.[10]

Al-Jirārī, whose work on the zajal is formative for all further studies on the content of the munshidūn's repertoire, holds that the malḥūn tradition dominates all Moroccan ṭarīqa expression; his model insists on an integrative distinctiveness constructed upon the Moroccan conviction that Moroccans are custodians of a distinctive Arabic culture. Ashḥab, munshid from Rabat and a Ḥarrāqiyya devotee, regards this as an oversimplification of the munshidūn's tradition, and he insists that the repertoire is far more sophisticated than this.[11]

Jirārī's central thesis is that Moroccan poetic and musical tradition is a unique creation, not deriving from either classical Arabic or from a regional folk literature. Rather, he sees Moroccan creativity at work in the way in which the various elements contribute to an organic cultural expression. He remarks that, to some extent, Arabic and Islam were seen as contrary to the culture of Morocco, and the lower classes did not accept all that the Arabo-Islamic culture brought. The consequence has been that Islam and Arabic have adapted to the will of Moroccan culture.

This has meant that the Arabic language and Islam have been adapted in ways quite different from other Islamic cultures, while retaining the essential unifying strain in Islamic doctrine and cultural style.[12] It also means that there is a crucial oral dimension to its development.[13] Jirārī notes that much of what the munshid chants is called brūla. This means that it is really a distinctive combination: brūla in inshād is near to the qaṣīda, but it is also near to the zajal of Andalusian music. One finds in the rhythm a *quddām* or *draj* distinctly Moroccan.[14] Yet today, no one knows who these brūla poets were, or how their texts were passed on. Nevertheless, their creations have become a basic part of the munshid's repertoire.

Al-Jirārī tends to see the malḥūn tradition as *the* tradition, reducing all other forms to this one. He contends that Muslims like zajal because they can understand the texts, in contradistinction to the classical texts. There is another perception: The zajal is used because it has sufficient depth in social consciousness to be educative; the people comprehend its message and relate to its popular form. As a consequence, a writer can get a hearing on an issue when popular phrasings are used. Relying on malḥūn becomes a way of making a statement.

Unfortunately, Moroccan Sufism is probably too diverse to be reduced to this particular form. While al-Jirārī's notion of integrativeness is attractive, and there is no doubt of the originality of Moroccan artistic culture, it is unlikely that Arabic and folk cultures can remain so clearly defined (and separated). In my fieldwork, I found that texts could vary widely. For example, in Meknes, at the zāwiya of Shaikh Maḥjūb, an old munshid began by chanting ḥizb ʿamdiyya.[15] Then began the ḥaḍra. Said Shaikh Maḥjub: "We really don't have a text, per se. The munshidūn take a little something from malḥūn, something from our shaikh, something from poetry . . . most of it is malḥūn on the Prophet [that is, madīḥ]. The ʿAissawiyya are a very popular group, and we use malḥūn material quite a bit. We use the dialect of the populace. We also have ecstatic words and sayings that fit in the context of our dhikr."[16]

Thus one should not become too enamored with the notion of a "pure" text as the basis of all meaning. While there clearly are commitments to the texts of the past, including the classical Arabic of the qaṣīda in some groups, there is also the constant blending and metamorphosing that takes place in the use of texts under the impact of Sufi ritual and cult practice. What seems to obtain among Moroccan Sufis is a sacred language that has evolved through amalgamation and modification of earlier forms.

Nevertheless, al-Jirārī's work remains fundamental to an understanding of the genre. He presents zajal as an important artistic tradition; as such it has several identifiable elements: the zajal poem, the *mawwāl* and other related forms, Andalusian music, modern Eastern Arabic singing, labor songs and children's dancing tunes, and the religious songs and anāshīd being studied here.[17] As important as he holds it to be, it is not clear that zajal is the key to understanding the development of the Sufi textual form, which seems too shifting and fluid to be limited to the zajal.

Indeed the religious songs and anāshīd continue to be separate, in some sense, from the other elements, and, one should note, from each other even until today. For example, the madīḥ or eulogies of the Prophet are performed by the munshidūn or, more technically, the musmiʿīn, that is, those who help others hear the eulogies. These eulogies are set to distinctive patterns and musical meters, all derived from Andalusian sources, and largely performed without musical instruments. The songs chanted by the various orders are called a nāshīd or spiritual songs.[18] These occur primarily in ritual dhikr or related spiritual occasions. Most of these songs had their origins in one of the great Sufi writers, such as Ibn al-Fāriḍ or al-Shustarī, or the Moroccan al-Ḥarrāq. Anāshīd also encompasses another kind of devotional material, *wird*, along with the recited formulae and sung sayings of the shaikhs of the orders.

Moroccans take great pride in the fact that Arab North Africa has been party to the growth and flowering of two distinctive (and original) poetry genres in the Arab world: zajal and muwashshaḥāt. Moreover, they are usually at pains to point out that the influence of these two genres went far beyond the Arab world and has left an important legacy in European literature of the Middle Ages.

Muwashshaḥāt and Zajal: Backbone of the Munshidūn's Text
The Muwashshaḥāt in Sufi Performance

Arabic is a flexible language, and its use in Moroccan Sufism is a good example of how fluid it can be. While it is held to be rooted in the Qurʾān and Ḥadīth and exemplified in law in Morocco, the Sufi tradition has adapted it to a wide variety of ritual situations. It is the Moroccan poets and their singers and chanters, including the munshidūn, who have been instrumental in that formation.

The masters among the munshidūn, such as the chanters of the Ḥarrāqiyya, sing classical qasāʾid and maintain strong connections with so-called classical pronunciation. They see themselves adhering to a high tradition reaching back to the foundations of Andalusia. The language they espouse is not, of course, the classical language of the Qurʾān, but the "classical" language of Andalusia, however that be defined.

On the other hand, in some ṭarīqas, like those in Meknes, munshidūn sing in local dialects, using local images and phrases and even local "songs." Such is the range of tradition. It would seem, then, that traditional inshād is very much defined by the *ijmā* (common understanding) of the ṭarīqa. This allows for modifications of tradition with the munshidūn tradition and proposes a possibility for adjustment in the tradition subject to the changes perceived as acceptable with the ṭarīqa. Clearly the shaikh or the muqaddam will have an important say in this process of modifying the tradition. For the most part, though, ʾamāna prevents the modification of that long-standing Arabic commitment to the received text, in effect, demarking an "Arab" textual memory.

One way of defining this ʾamāna is to consider it as an intellectual, conventionalized form. In many studies, the predominance of metric patterns exemplified in the language of poetry is regarded as artistic convention alone. Drawing on Gill's work, what is espoused here is that the commitment to a certain text is not just an artistic choice, responding to artistic sensitivities, but is more deeply embedded in the Moroccan consciousness through patterned modes of thinking: "Familiarity with metrical patterns is taken to represent, in most part, the *tacit*—rather than conscious—*knowledge* possessed by poets and their hearers and readers. Moreover, since each and every person is endowed with the same prosodic competence, similar metrical patterns typically occur in a variety of geographically and temporally distinct speech communities. In such cases, metrical patterns are not culture-specific properties spreading from one community to another by diffusion. Instead, metrical patterns in poetry may be viewed as representing *cognitive universals*."[19]

Unfortunately, Gil's cognitive universals are difficult to establish, since by definition one would have to find the same kind of metrical patterning among the literature of all peoples. That is likely to be impossible to establish. Rather than viewing these metrical patterns as cognitive universals rooted in the mental construct of the human mind, I maintain that certain intellectual patterns are generated in culturally or linguistically specific shared environments, which, in turn, take on an embedded character in shared assumptions about what should be known. This directly links us to the factor of memory, for it is in the repeated patterns, remembered from past performances, that the possibility of a shared discourse is formulated. Memory is enshrined as the vehicle of reality.[20]

In keeping with this view, I suggest that we have here patterns related to Arabo-Iberian cultural expression, growing out of the bilingual and bicultural environment of Muslim Spain, with Jewish, Berber Mozarab, and Arab participating in a cultural and linguistic commonwealth. Such a perspective allows for some aspect of the cognitive to be retained, but in relationship to a shared language and artistic culture, with a common sense of the role and function of memory as the essential ingredient of any embraced convention.

In that way, the metrical patterns identified by Gil demonstrate a way of understanding that is implicitly connected to Western Islamic civilization through the poetic forms of the troubadors. They are, however, limited in their application, owing to their marginal role in Western culture as a whole. Such a cultural-generator view of the patterns can take into account the fact that the muwashshaḥāt developed at a particular moment in Andalusian history, arising out of patterns of understanding deriving from the confluence of several strands of cultural input. Thus muwash-shaḥāt were "probably introduced as both a literary and musical genre by a poet and singer who lived about 900 and was born in Cabra near Cordoba."[21] That singer is usually identified as Ziryāb, who had escaped to Andalus from Baghdad where he was persona non grata to the caliph:

> Educated in Baghdad, and trained in Persian and Arab traditions, Ziryāb brought to Andalus not only expertise in performing and teaching, but also a musicotherapeutic system, known as the "tree of modes," or the "tree of temperaments." The system was based on concepts then prevalent in Arab medicine: relationships between parts of the body and elements of earth and Heaven believed to underlie human physical and psychological states and behaviors. Ziryāb's system, which he presented as revelation rather than theory, associated specific modes with body organs (heart, liver, brain, spleen) and human temperaments (anger, calm, joy, sadness.) The musical modes were further linked with natural elements (air, fire, water, earth), colors (red, yellow, white, black), and conditions (heat, cold, humidity, dryness).[22]

In time this system became widely embraced so that writers of muwashshaḥāt and zajal were Arab, Berber, Jewish, as well as mixed.[23]

His emphasis on the therapeutic role of music relates quite nicely to the contention made in this book, that is, that dhikr is a way of understanding, or a particular pattern of the mental frame of Muslim culture arising out of the deep religious roots. In common with dhikr, recurring metrical patterns may well have taken on a quasi-sacred character, intimately related to a specially validated way of perceiving, in effect, a religiously endowed memory system. Such a view is congruent with that of Kugel in *Poetry and Prophecy* for the early period of Near Eastern culture: "I suggest that among the predominantly monotheistic milieux . . . there had evolved a reasonably conventionalized, perhaps even sacralized, mode or genre of discourse for representing instances of divine intervention and communication. . . . Since the second century (maybe even earlier), typological interpretations, speculations, and representations had been essential ingredients of that discourse and the standard stuff of its language and imagery."[24]

Extending this argument, the repetitive patterns espoused in the muwashshaḥāt form were seen to be encoded in the discourse of basic human responses to life, thus making the language acceptable and recognizable by a broad range of ethnographically diverse peoples in Andalusia and North Africa. This accounts for the fact that Jewish interaction with Andalusian culture allowed the Hebrew *šīr ezor* (Jewish form equivalent to zajal) to develop, since common cultural patterns were embraced by the Jewish residents of Andalus when they became bicultural if not bilingual.[25] When the form matured enough to move beyond the singer's performance, the muwashshaḥāt became a distinctive contribution to the arts. Thus the Andalusian pattern of poetic expressive language probably arose out of oral performance and then took on its most literary form in the materials that have come down to us as the muwashshaḥāt.

Beyond methodological issues, we also see the interweaving of religious orientations and literary form in these materials. Sufi material capitalized on this interweaving, and both religious and secular writers drew from a fund of prominent metaphors and allusions in writing their poetry. This trend continues to today.

Furthermore, some overarching connections obviously bridged the divide between the Sufi and the literary poet—both were performed in a formal structured space, for example. So the performance of the poems was dependent on proper locale, that is, Sufi poetry would be utilized in Sufi ritual situations, while literary material would be quoted in entertainment and public events.

The first connection is the dominance of a discourse of antisociety criticism. Whether on the topic of Moroccan lack of hospitality or on the theme of the uncouth Berber, the muwashshaḥāt is a fitting venue to indicate some social malaprop or lack. But more, it is a way of regarding the meaning of life in a given society. Thus, according to Abu Nāsr al-Fath, Abū Bakr Ibn Bākī (d. 1134?) wrote scathingly about his reception when he went looking for a more congenial environment than Andalus across the straits in Morocco, and received nothing to sustain his art:[26]

> I am among you despite my misery and situation; If I had been free, with a proud soul, I would not have stayed. . . .
>
> There is no means of subsistence among you; I would therefore search for it around the world if good people were sent away in equitable fashion. . . .
>
> If, an Andalusian, after I have crossed the straits, rejects me, I will go to Iraq and there everyone will rise to receive me.
>
> What hope, what nobility can be found in a determined and vigorous prince who makes expeditions against enemies during sacred truce months! . . .
>
> Living for his concern is an expedient that has lost all force and is now a profession which embarrasses even men of base extraction and of vile manners! . . .
>
> I have thrust myself too long into Morocco without any success in obtaining significant gifts, so much so that I will return with regret (at having undertaken this trip).[27]

Second, as Pérès notes, the criticism of "men of base extraction and of vile manners" was directed against the learned classes of traditional religious scholars, the legists, the theologians, the religious authorities, whose toadying to the Almoravids so incensed Abū Bakr Ibn Bākī. This was castigation of a very powerful group, reflecting an almost prophetic denunciation.

Such criticism indicates a measure of indifference and disconnectedness that implies an independent literary establishment. It is satire with a radical critique of the religious establishment. The ability to criticize this establishment was a delicate and important trait that allowed for the development of alternative ways of perceiving truth, society, and the divine. Without that trait, the growth of a ṭarīqa culture would have been difficult; with it, the infrastructure of centers of the sacred could thrive.

A third dimension relates to the conceptual: here was formation of another universe, accessed by literature, quite separate from the standard world of the government and the religious scholars. Abū Bakr Ibn Bākī's entire poem expresses a strong rejection of the world, but this critique of the learned members of Muslim officialdom was turned in the first instance to an antidiscourse against Andalus and its people ("This one [that is, a disgraced Almohad vizier] is an Andalusian / he doesn't number among the Berbers / he sought to lay his hands furtively / On the realm to the detriment of the Berbers")[28] and then upon Sunni doctrine, as when Ibn Habus (d. 1202) recited the following poem before ʿAbd al-Mūʾmin, the first Almohad caliph:

> Lady Fortune has arrived, thanks to your assistance, as she had hoped and her days learned to (treat us) fairly.
>
> It suffices him, by the fact that she has arrived at a favourable moment, to have found the image (of a government impregnated with principles) and of good guidance and to be fashioned after her. . . .
>
> You are The Truth [al-Ḥaqq], which no one would doubt, and which none is permitted to ignore.
>
> You are the secret of God and your commandment, exemplified in the tiniest as well as the grandest manifestation, fills the earth.
>
> Those who wish to understand beauty have been beset by the impossibility of perceiving Him. He is the Pure; it suffices that he is known by intelligence.[29]

This is panegyric with a real difference; this directly challenges Sunni doctrine. For example, the use of al-Ḥaqq, one of the names of God (see Qurʾān 2:142, 3:53, 4:114, 10:94, 15:63–64, 19:35) to describe the caliph is a flagrant violation of social probity and standard interpretation of the words of the Qurʾān. Yet it is congruent with the growing Almohad notion that they (the Almohads) are the embodiment of the Mahdī. Still al-Ḥallāj's use of this descriptor while in mystical union led to his execution.[30] Despite that, the idea continued in an analogical form in Sufi doctrine.[31] Under normal circumstances, such a claim would put the spokesperson outside Islam, making him *kafir* (an unbeliever). The fact that Ibn Habus apparently got away with this demonstrates the independence of the poet from the judiciary and the theologians while in the employ of the caliph, even as it illustrates the power accorded to the caliph in the Western reaches of Islam, that is, to allow expressions of poetic license that breach the codified law. The acceptance of another realm of discourse not driven either by government or by Muslim authorities lays the foundation for Ibn al-ʿArabī and the institutionalization of the saints.

Perhaps this rendering of scriptural formations was regarded as acceptable under *ṭawīl*, a special anthropomorphic interpretation espoused by the Almohads.[32] At any rate it demonstrates the way in which the Qurʾān's words were subjected to the over-riding ideology of local leadership. Ṭawīl opened the possibility of other systematic visions of the Islamic experience that could be just as sophisticated as that established by Mālikī law.

In addition, it affirms the service function of the Arabic language. This means that language must be put to the service of spiritual versions of truth, not that spiritual versions are derived from language. Doctrine has to be contextualized; it does not ride above the currents of Muslim life. It is not enough to believe certain dogmas as if they were not grounded in the time and place of their expression. Doctrines are to be suborned to the systematic structure, rather than taken as given from the language passed down from on high.

In actuality, only those words that fit the needs of their ideological believers can truly become dogma—consider Ibn al-ʿArabī's dhikr, bequeathed to him in a special vision: "I saw while I was sleeping as though God was calling out to me, saying to me: 'O My servant, if you want to be close to Me, honoured and enjoying delight with Me, then constantly say "My Lord, cause me to see, that I might look upon You!" Repeat that for Me many times.'"[33]

Such a dhikr clearly violates Sunni doctrine about the ability of humans to see God, if the literal meaning of the words are taken as normative. In effect Ibn al-ʿArabī utilized a different interpretative system, closer to that of the Almohads.

Interweaving also links remembrance and identity; as we have seen, Abū Madyan demonstrates a deepening of the connection to the saint complex. With Abū al-Ḥasan al-Shādhilī his spiritual grandchild, and then, the mystical order, the Jazūliyya, the notion that "we live in your remembrance / Without your love inside us we would not live" becomes a direct reference to the conception of spiritual progeny.[34]

Such a notion of embodying the spiritual heroes of the past was broadened to encompass the spirit that they encapsulated. It was extended to poetry, which, in its ideal form, was like the purity of a virgin, in the full flower of her beauty, brimming with pride and presence:

Receive my poetry, said Ibn Ruḥaim to one of his friends, just as if I guided your fiancée toward you, giddy (from her beauty) and trailing the flap of her nuptial cloak with a regal grandeur.[35]

What a beauty! said Abū Muḥammad Ibn as-Sid al-Baṭalyawsī in response, this virgin that you have bestowed upon me, like a bride enwrapped in the evening.

For dowry, I offer you my sincere affection and for domicile, the most secret corner of my heart.[36]

Note too that the Almohad panegyric above utilizes language found in Sufi circles, that is, "the secret of God." This phrase was generated by Sufis to conceptualize the mystical moment of union.[37] This demonstrates how poetry was the vehicle for new and potentially radical ideas with a measure of freedom from censorship; through this medium, writers could open up metaphoric uses of Qurʾānic language in ways that in some contexts would not be acceptable to the ʿulamāʾ.

What emerges is a network of ideas and notions, perhaps more thematic than systematic, that links the conscious world of Andalusia and Morocco. Some sense of how this material formed critical religio-poetic linkages is evident in the chanted qaṣīda recorded in Tetouan at the ḥaḍra of the Ḥarrāqiyya.

If we examine the material sung during the Ḥarrāqiyya ḥaḍra, what appears evident is that the muwashshaḥāt function as a textual platform upon which the performance is constructed. In its language, the classical Andalusian material is spiced with Moroccan popular Arabic. Themes are stated and inferred through the choice of phases or snatches of texts, but there is no slavish adherence to the muwashshaḥāt text per se: it operates only as the channel within which the Sufi inspiration can flow.

Zajal in Sufi Performance

We know that muwashshaḥāt were never considered a bona fide Arabic form of poetry, since the first "oriental" scholar to consider them as legitimate, the Egyptian Ibn Sanāʾ al-Mulk (1155–1211), was the only one of his contemporaries to include them in anthologies of Arabic poetry.[38] This may be because the presence of colloquial or "Spanish" Arabic was present in some of the poems, or because of other technical details. Compton lists three identifying elements in the differences between zajal and muwashshaḥāh:

> The primary differences between the *zajal* and the *muwashshaḥāh* are in the former's use of colloquial rather than classical Arabic and in the repeating pattern which is woven into each stanza throughout the poem. The second element of every strophe in a *muwashshaḥāh* is an exact metrical duplicate of the entire opening *matlāʿ*, when there is one, or of the entire closing *kharja*, whereas in the zajal the end of every strophe matches only one line of the opening *matlāʿ*. Moreover, a *zajal* does not have a *kharja* at the end, although there are exceptions to this rule: Ibn Quzman did compose some *zajals* that look like *muwashshaḥāhs* in the vernacular.[39]

When and where muwashshaḥāt and zajal developed independent existences (if they did) has been the subject of much debate. Nykl mentions that the form was said to have existed in Ibn ʿAbd Rabbīhī's time (860–940) but that none of his muwash-shaḥāt are extant; zajal is known to have existed in Andalusia before the time of the Almohads (1129–1275), but whether Moroccans themselves composed it before this time is not clear. Al-Jirārī believes they composed zajal in Morocco during the time of the Almoravids (1038–1129), for two reasons: Moroccans closely imitated Andalusian culture; and even during the Almohad reign, which was officially hostile to this kind of composition, an unofficial underground culture flourished. Drawing on ancient sources, he contends three Moroccans were instrumental: "They were divided on who invented the art of zajal. Some said Ibn Ghurla, others contended it was Yakhlūf b. Rashīd and others still that it was Ibn Quzman (the poet), or Magha-lis, or ʿAbd al-Muʾmin (the caliph), or Rumayla (his sister). The consensus of opin-ion is that the first poet to recite zajal was Ibn Quzman, followed by al-Qayyim Maghalis, then Ibn Ghurla, then Yakhlūf b. Rashīd, then Sabuʿ al-Andalus, that is, ʿAbdul-Muʾmin, and then Rumayla."[40]

Al-Jirārī argues that the Moroccan composition of zajal was in competition with and not an imitation of Andalusian styles, and that examination of Ibn Ghurla's texts with his Andalusian counterparts indicates no appreciable differences. Hence he holds that this is evidence that the style already existed during the Almohad period.[41] In another book, al-Jirārī dates the origin of the muwashshaḥāt to the third century A.H. (ninth C.E.),[42] while Alan Jones, in listing the most important writers of muwashshaḥāt, also indicates that the earliest dated person is Ibn ʿAbdi Rabbīhī (d. 939 C.E.).[43] The earliest poem to have survived is that of ʿUbada b. Maʾ al-Samāʿ (d. 1027 C.E.). Ibn Ḥayyān confirms the Moroccan/Berber connection of zajal by refer-ring to a man of prodigious memory and intelligence, Muḥammad ibn Saʿīd ibn Abī Sulayman, as al-Zajjālī (that is, the writer of zajal) (d. 843 or 846 C.E.).[44] Thus, even if Andalusian masters developed the genre at a more prolific rate than Moroccans, there is ample reason to accept that zajal had impetus from Moroccan poets.

Wulstan has argued for the precedence of zajal to muwashshaḥāt, largely based on a structural analysis of musical samples, and holding for its genesis in oral perfor-mance,[45] seeing these two forms as more or less growing in tandem with Romance refrain songs. Schuyler has perhaps summed up the most plausible explanation for their growth:

It seems more appropriate to point to the aspects of *zajal* that departed from Classical Arabic models: vocabulary, syntax, and prosody, as well as form. The blending of poetic styles, like the fusion of languages themselves in a mixed tongue, could take place more freely on a vernacular level. The flexi-bility of the dialect would have made it easy to fit Arabic into Iberian mod-els. As the form gained attention in literary circles, the *zajal* must have been purged of its colloquialisms in order to gain respectability. Vocabulary and syntax were Arabized, and line form was recast in "bogus" prosody. But the strophic design of *zajal* posed little threat to the sanctity of the classical language. Indeed, the *zajal* could not be "classicized" without losing its essential appeal; rather, the form was elaborated in the *muwashshahāt*.[46]

This view coheres with the slow Arabization of Morocco. It also is congruent with the interest of the missionary saints who wished to utilize vernacular modes of communication in order to establish their ṭuruq. Utilizing a mixed form of poetry like zajal and then muwashshahāt would allow the local people to relate better to the content, thus justifying the use of poetry and idiom sometimes quite foreign to the religious environment. Jones lists three religious poets who composed muwashshahāt, all in the same time period: Ibn al-ʿArabī, (d. 1240), Ibn al-Sabbagh (whose poems were collected during the reign of al-Murtada, 1248–1266), and al-Shustarī (d. 1269).[47]

Moreover, al-malhūn, as it is designated in Morocco, is a form related to the Moroccan *nūbat*, and it reflects some of the formalization that Schuyler mentions (that is, vocabulary, syntax, prosody). It is also strophic in form, while the nūbat is not. What is significant is that malhūn is given a special place in the firmament of Moroccan musical text because it is known as the "Moroccan zajal" and hence it represents a later evolution of the literary/musical tradition from the muwashshahāt / zajal complex.

With regard to Sufi malhūn, it may be possible to argue that it is related to the flowering associated with the rise of modern ṭarīqa development, that is, those translocal organizations associated with the nineteenth and twentieth centuries, when the appeal was to a clientele affirming Islamic hegemony over against Western (French) influence. In that case, malhūn could be seen to be sufficiently allied with the past to represent tradition, while adapting creatively enough to the current moment to accommodate the universalizing interests of the shaikhs.

It is rare that a writer of zajal also performs; while it is not impossible, within the Moroccan context, it is the munshid who performs and not the poet. Thus the munshid is commonly called the *shaikh al-nushshād* or the *shaikh al-ḥuffāẓ*, by which is meant that the munshid is the chief singer of *anāshīd* or the head or leader of those who know the anāshīd by heart. Al-Jirārī quotes a common saying, "Al-zajjal (the writer of the zajal) creates the poem but cannot sing it, and needs, accordingly, al-rāwī [the reciter or, more commonly, the munshid] to popularize the poetry."[48]

What might constitute the malhūn genre? During a performance, it is often easy to tell this because of the Moroccan Arabic context, but al-Jirārī has a technical definition: "The *qaṣāʾid* of the malhūn genre are poems composed in an Arabic dialect mingled with both literary and archaic words, according to rules much different from classical poetry. Instead of being constructed on one of the sixteen meters of regular prosody and terminated completely in the same rhyme, the verses of *qaṣāʾid* are generally longer and carry up to six hemistiches; they are arranged in strophes like those of Andalusian *zajal.* The whole is divided into several divisions or *qsam,* comprised of the *qsam* proper and a refrain (*al-ḥarba*), sometimes along with one or other little strophes in short verse called *naʿara* [from the verb for *"to gush"* or *"to cry"*], which can in turn have a separate refrain, *ḥariba* or little *ḥarba.*"[49]

He also notes the strong connection between Arabic poetry, the court, and the development of malḥūn: "The first known authors of malḥūn are from the sixteenth century. The period when the genre flourished the most was during the reign of Sultan Sīdī Moḥammed (1859–1873), a poet himself and Mecene. Many continue the tradition right to our day. Unquestionably, and not less inspired, are the simple artisans. All have an elevated notion of poetry, which they call *al-ʿilm al-mawhūb,* the science or law of love."[50]

If one were to accept the malḥūn as the basis of the munshidūn traditions, this would place their development fairly late. In fact, the *maddāḥūn* or reciters of praise emerged under the Merinid period and then gradually became known as munshidūn. They are rooted in the relationship between the composer and the reciter: "The authors of *qaṣāʾid* compose poems in their heads that they then confide to the memory of a *haffaḍ* [ḥāfiẓ] or *rāwī* who then teaches them to the *siah* musicians. These [ḥāfiẓ] also chant accompanied by a violin and the *taʿrija,* then with the *aliyīn,* who sing classical Andalusian music, having an orchestra formed of lute, two-stringed *rbab* (rebec), the long-bodied drum, the *ṭarr,* and violin."[51]

Yet when one speaks to the ordinary Moroccan, munshid, rāwī, and ḥāfiẓ are often used interchangeably. So obviously the popular perception of the relationship is not sufficiently articulated to form the basis of an analysis. It is only when one discusses these matters with professionals or with the Sufis that the differences become clear. Then it is evident that there are important differences between the performing public malḥūn, and the traditions and ideas associated with Sufi malḥūn. And the Sufi malḥūn are not always accepted as the determinative ingredient by the munshidūn. For example, Ashhab insists there are at least five differences between a public malḥūn singer and a munshid:

1. The use and styling of the voice is distinctive in inshād.
2. The text and performance of the munshid is geared to the dhikr.
3. The metric cycle in inshād conforms more or less to the time measured by the drumbeat in the dhikr.
4. When the munshid sings, the quality of his earnestness is critical.
5. Munshidūn utilize distinctive performance codes. These include special entrances during the performance, stylized phrasings deriving from Sufi tradition while chanting, contextual responses from listeners to phrasings requiring adjustments to texts, and, finally, important closure signals geared to the completion of the cycle of dhikr that are accommodated textually.[52]

To this must be added the fact that some munshidūn will not sing malhūn apart from what they chant in the zāwiya. That is, they will not sing for a wedding or in a public place. These munshidūn regard such activity as degrading to their spiritual ministry, and likely to impact on their relationship with their brethren in the tarīqa, as well as their relationship with God. Some told me if they did such things, they would expect it to impact negatively on their inspiration during the dhikr.

It is also the case that each tarīqa develops its own textual stock of phrases and stylings. Even if they sing malhūn-like material, as, for example, among the ʿAissawiyya, and these munshidūn also perform much the same material at weddings, this cannot be equivalent to the kind of material one finds at the Ḥarrāqiya or with the Ginawa. Hence the emphasis on the malhūn style is more noticeable among the Darqāwiyya and ʿAissawiyya ṭuruq than it is among the Ḥarrāqiyya, who sing the more traditional Andalusian texts that have a stronger classical Arabic emphasis. One result is the further blurring of the line between the zajal and muwashshaḥāt.

We can conclude, then, that, while the Sufi malhūn and the munshidūn traditions have intermingled and reacted against each other, they nevertheless evolved as separate traditions because they arose out of different contexts, and they have played different roles in the growth of the repertoire. Certainly they have mutually interacted as part of Morocco's literary development. However, they are not integrated, and it would be incorrect to hold that the Sufi malhūn tradition, important as it may be, defines the repertoire of all the munshidūn. These caveats must be kept in mind as we examine the malhūn/Sufi interplay in Morocco.

Memory's Outline: Moroccan Sufi Malhūn Material

There is no doubt that the use of poetry and chant among the orders originated with the coming of the first of the missionary shaikhs, Abū'l-Ḥasan al-Shādhilī. He himself traveled widely in the region and established orders, utilizing popular song and easily understood phrasings as the basis for discipline. Since his time, spiritual achievement and popular artistic expression have been integral to the tarīqa in Morocco. What is evident is that Sufi memory has created a distinctive compendium of malhūn material.

The close connection between the malhūn tradition in general and Sufism in particular can be easily seen in the poetry of Abū al-Ḥassan al-Shastarī, who traveled extensively in Morocco and whose zajal poems are still recited by the Darqāwiyya. Much of his material expressed notions of what we would call social analysis or even social criticism. For his perspective, the original malhūn tradition contained an element of political and social concern within it. This could take many forms, but one of the most common was to write poetry that was intimately linked to the experience of the commoner, including the geographical and political landscape. For example, the popular settings of al-Shastarī's poetry reflect a Moroccan environment:

> The old man from Meknes
> Sings in the suq,
> "I worry little about others,
> Nor do they care much about me."

This secular, devil-may-care attitude toward the establishment of Moroccan society was picked up by the Sufis and transformed into a trophe on the life dedicated to social ostracism and the mystical experience. One can see this often reflected in Sufi poets; for example, Muḥammad Sharqī carries on this theme of seeming lack of concern for personal affairs:

> Nothing is wrong with me . . .
> Nor do I care about my "self's" opinion
> Why despair in the earning of a living
> Since God sustains me.

As Jirāri notes, Sufis like Shaikh Aḥmad Zarrūq and Ibn ʿAjība both glossed Shastarī's works, using bits and pieces from them in their own poetry, while Ibn ʿAbbad al-Randī says directly: "As for Shastarī's pieces and zajal poems, I am strongly attracted to them. Do not hesitate to embellish them with good voice and tunes, and be sure to write them down, whatever you can find of them."[53]

The role of poets in Morocco has shaped the usage of malḥūn material. For example, in the history of poets and malḥūn writers, local turbulence and political battles have colored the text. As a result, various wars and jockeying for protection have dictated that the malḥūn use poetry as an arm against their enemies. Consequently, one sees in ṭarīqa poetry a reflection of this trend that might be called "current" relevance.[54] These poetic usages mean that there is an intimate relationship between the political context, the religious environment, and the people the poet is addressing. The Sufi poets always have this special relationship to their people and continually adjust what they write in order to address the world the Sufi inhabits. This means that, if the text cannot be changed, the way the texts are woven together and the emphasis they are given play a key role in the presentation. From the standpoint of the Sufi poet, there is no poetry that is not popular.

This places some immediate restrictions on the poet. Language must be clear and direct, and despite the Islamist or fundamentalist criticism that Sufis are obscurantists, the Sufi poet uses only a language that is well recognized by the murīds. The writer operates quite strictly within the parameters of this special language.

Two types of specialists can be noted in the malḥūn tradition, those whose focus is performance, that is, singers, and those who write, that is, poets.[55] Only rarely do contemporary singers or chanters write qaṣāʾid. The chief concern of the performers is to relate the material they sing to the context, to integrate it into the performance situation, and to test material for public response. Most good munshidūn will say, however, that if the text is not solid, that is, arising out of an inspired soul, it will not be effective regardless of what they do. At the same time, writers will acknowledge that they cannot tell how a poem will play in the ṭarīqa, in effect recognizing the distinctive role of the munshid.

On the other hand, the poetic shaikhs are very important because they draw upon and affirm the poetic tradition. They view their work as fundamental for the brethren, weaving it into a rich and diverse cultural tradition. Despite the inspired environment from which it comes, there is an underlying practical political message: Sufism is the way to the satisfied life. A quick analysis of the themes within a malḥūn poem from the Nāṣiriyya ṭarīqa demonstrates this:

> The ṭarīqa is the way to arrive at truth
> Dhikr gives clarity to the way
> The poem is like the Prophet—through it I begin to see
> During dhikr I understand love and verity
> Wird and dhikr, I am saved by them
> Whoever hears the poem is aided
> Through it I know love in my heart
> It expresses love of the sharīʿa
> It speaks to me in my language
> Through it I am content
> A visit brings peace, problems disappear
> Love satisfies me.[56]

Al-Jirārī also notes that the diversification of ṭuruq cult has modified the text of the munshid. For example, some ṭurūq do not incorporate samāʿ into their rites; others do not technically have ḥaḍras. Each of these tendencies has had an impact on the textual development in Morocco: "When, during the eighteenth and nineteenth centuries, the Nāṣiriyya dominated Moroccan Sufism, they did not use samāʿ. The Tijāniyya were not yet in place. The Nāṣiriyya did not condemn the ḥaḍra explicitly but tried to make it sunna (that is, without mixing men and women during their rites and without musical percussion, like the ṭabla). In fact, ḥaḍra was connected to the lower classes, and it was used as a kind of social therapy, to help them escape some of their crushing problems."[57]

This means that there is no uniform development of a textual tradition among Morocco's Sufis, and it is impossible to sketch it as one tradition reaching back to one root. The best that can be done is to reconstruct the various streams that make up the current reality. One of the most crucial is that fundamental element in the malḥūn's repertoire, the zajal text.

The Structure of the Zajal Poem and Classical "Remembrance"

Generally speaking, the zajal poet (*al-zajjāl*) does not use the classical word qaṣīda for his or her creation; it may be called a *liqṣīda* or *liqṣīd* or even *qiṭʿa,* piece (pl.

qiṭāʿ). This serves to indicate that, while the zajal creation is regarded as related to the metrical poem in the classical tradition, it has its own character and interest. It also has its own history, since clearly the internal construction of the zajal poem has been modified over time, probably as a result of performance. Thus, in the original poems of Ibn Quzman, the structure of the poem was fairly clearly set out, that is, the poem had an opening section called *al-saraba* (pl. *sararīb*), entrance; the middle segment that bore the name of the poem itself, that is, al-liqṣīda; and an ending hemistich called *al-radma* (from root meaning to fill with earth). The saraba set the metrical pattern (*mīzān*) of the poem and hence was regarded as the controlling element for the rhythm of the poem.

Today, one scarcely ever hears the munshid chanting the saraba in its entirety, because the intention is not to preserve the integrity of the poem per se but to inspire the hearers. Instead, the introduction to the poem may include several phrases from a variety of sararīb, even if sometimes the fit leaves something to be desired. As often as not, there is no saraba at all. Zajal purists regard this casual attitude to the saraba with disdain and consider the metric structure flawed when it is not present. It is a major criticism of contemporary munshidūn that they ignore this important part of the poem's character.

Eventually, of course, the pressures of performance and the disruption of the flow from the opening into the main body of the poem led to sararīb taking on a life of their own. Famous opening lines were combined with others and the whole attributed to well-known poets even if they never wrote any part of these cohesive sararīb. One can hear these combination sararīb utilized as interjections or transitions in a performance. In popular parlance, these collective lines can sometimes be referred to as a separate species of zajal.

Technically the saraba is made up of two distinctive sections, *al-dukhūl* (entry) and *al-nāʿūra* (pl. *nawāʿīr*, from root meaning to gush, bellow, cry). The dukhūl is easily recognized because it is the traditional opening of any formal speech segment among Muslims: the bismillah. Although the dukhūl can vary, it situates the speaker or chanter within the framework of the Prophet and his spiritual accomplishments, a pattern that frames the whole poem, since the ending will also usually involve some reference to the Prophet. The naʿūra sets the tone for the poem by determining the rhythm and the rhyme scheme; within two or three lines, the structure is set by this important aspect of saraba. The munshidūn today do not think this section is necessary, since the whole poem may be known to the hearer, and the naʿūra may only serve to introduce the structure of the poem. Consequently the munshid moves directly into the body of the poem as a means to deliver the power of the poem immediately, to "test the emotional waters," as one munshid put it, with the phrases that will remind the hearer of the theme of the whole poem. Thus performance in dhikr or samāʿ determines the commitment to the poem; it is not the integrity of the poem as a whole that is required.

Traditionally, zajal poems were constructed in sections or chapters (*lifṣāla*), broken by an *al-ḥarba* (refrain). In original zajal, the ḥarba could be heard immediately after the dukhūl, and thereafter at the end of each section of the poem. It is usually composed in the same meter as the poem. In fact, the ḥarba is the "identity" feature of the poem, since hearers will associate the entire poem with the ḥarba, and they will often join in and sing the ḥarba with the munshid during a performance. In some orders, there will be a choir or chorus who will perform this function. The lifṣāla are usually regarded as made up of individual *aqsām* (sections), and poets distinguish themselves by the number of sections they have in their poetry. The intentions and abilities of the writers show up here, for the poet may wish to deliver a short, powerful piece by keeping the number of sections to a minimum, or contrariwise, to tell a long story through the use of many sections. Obviously the number of lines in each section, too, may play a role in the delivering of a message.

One of the techniques that great zajjāl used was to introduce each qsām of the poem with distinctive openings (*muqaddimāt*). These muqaddimāt may be called *ʿarūbiyya* (lit., women), which are comprised of a few lines that then end with a hemistich called al-radma. The second part of the aqsām is the nawaʿīr, which is usually from two to four hemistiches long.

As indicated above, the ending of the poem is called al-radma. Traditionally the radma was an occasion for the poet to include his or her name and to acknowledge the blessings of the Prophet or the shaikh. It could also be utilized to lampoon one's enemies or to laud the rāwī or munshid. Additionally, it was supposed to summarize the theme of the last aqsām; today, the ending may be called a *dūraydika* (deriving from *dardaka*, meaning to pound rapidly on the ground with one's feet or to rapidly recite something), which is really a sign of closure, and may have any length that the munshid might wish, ranging from blessings on the Prophet to a pious phrase from the Qurʾān. Since the munshid performs these zajal in the rites of the orders, the shaikh may decide to cut the song off quickly, in which case no formal ending can occur. If this happens, the munshid's dūraydika may be nothing more than a short "amīn."

Memory's Message in the Sufi Mawwāl

In general there are two underlying modi operandi in the poetry of the Sufi in Morocco.[58] At one level it is concerned with the whole world of Sufi learning and experience, seeking to inspire devotion and awareness of the Sufi way. At another level it is directly political, since it regards its task as educative in the broad sense. One could argue that the Sufi poetic text, in general, is shaped to educate in that it uses a special language to formulate certain ends. In that sense all malḥūn material could be considered political.[59]

Malḥūn utilized in Sufi orders are constructed upon themes arising out of the Andalusian zajal, with the incorporation of what is crucial for both the head of the order and the murid; this is what is known as *maqāmāt mawwāl.* These maqāmāt mawwāl are inspired phrasings drawn from the Qurʾān, the Ḥadīth, and special sayings of the saints. A whole range of terms finds its way into Sufi malḥūn, terms such as ghaība, ṣife, bard, *ṣaff al-Qurʾān,* and so on.[60] The goal is to construct a distinctive landscape of the world for the Sufi.

The mawwāl form is drawn from classical Arabic and is recognizable in the munshid's performance. In Morocco, however, the munshid extrapolates from this form to construct the form called *timwila,* which is like mawwāl in that it respects form and language of the text in its rhythm, even while adapting its usage to the needs of the dhikr and samāʿ, but it is smaller and shorter. Still, one recognizes the qaṣīda structure[61] as well as the themes that are associated with the Andalusian poetry in that form. As we have indicated earlier, it also can mix classical and Moroccan Arabic in performance.

Munshidūn also chant much longer poems, called *simāwī.* Like mawwāl, these can be long and involved chants. Most mawwāl utilize classical Arabic, but under the pressure of performing in dhikr or samāʿ, the loyalty to the form and shape of classical poetry is subjected to the rhythm of the music.

In general the themes pursued by the Sufi poets include the following:

Women, love, and the poet and lover
Wine, vineyards, and wine cultivation
Sufi drinking, the cup, the server, and the occasions
Teachers of abstinence, *zuhd,* discipline of the soul
Madīḥ of the Prophet
Madīḥ of the ahl al-bait and the saints
Special prayers and praise for God

Each of these categories—not an exhaustive list—takes a certain shape for the Sufi, and the poet keeps within fairly clear (and traditional) parameters sanctioned by the shaikh and the order's mores.

When the poet explores the theme of women, they are not particular women, or even national representations of culturally defined women. Rather, women become the metaphor on which a wide range of beauty, characteristics of the "good" woman, and pleasure are explored. In general, the majority of poets speak of several women, not of one woman, so that the poet is really addressing a symbolized reality rather than any particular person. Second, love is understood to be very diversified, ranging from a vague form of compatibility, to love as adoration, to what might be called a "proper, acceptable" love relationship. Third, sometimes poetic language speaks directly of a male lover, not necessarily using this as an intimation of homosexuality, but rather as an indication that intimacy of a spiritual kind can and does exist between men. Moreover, as it was explained, there is a love that transcends the sexual among humans. Fourth, the poet speaks of what he believes about love, not what he holds is, in fact, the case. The problematic the poet is encountering is trying to represent the intensity of emotion in a language that will be comprehended by his hearers.

Moroccan Sufis are very sensitive to criticism concerning the use of love imagery. They are aware that the roles and positions of women in Muslim society have been strongly attacked in the West, and they view the emphasis on love to be an important rejoinder to the impression the West has of male dominance. They take some pride in the language of love that is their heritage, especially since it addresses the "ideal" relationship between God and humans.

The centrality of love and women's imagery bears further elaboration. When raising the issue of the role of women in the orders, responses varied. I noted that there are very few female public munshidūn in Morocco, and, in any case, I was never able to interview one. I was told that there always have been female chanters in Morocco, and this was confirmed by Benchekroun's study.[62] There were female chanters among the Ḥarrāqiyya. The shaikh has a special dhikr for them in his quarters, and at least one woman performed at the great festival of ʿamdah at Fez in 2000.[63] Ḥajj Barrāda of the ʿAissawiyya in Fez was blunt: "There are no female chanters in the ʿAissawiyya." However, his confrere, Shaikh Mahjūb al-ʿAissawi in Meknes said equally categorically: "There are dhʾkara (female chanters) in the ʿAissawiyya ṭarīqa, and they chant in the same fashion as men." I took this to indicate that traditions varied depending upon the shaikh and his social views.

Generally speaking Morocco seems to be more conservative about the place of females and their participation in rites than was evident in Egypt. Yet I could see no lessening of female attendance at the ṭarīqa celebrations, nor, for that matter, their ardor.

Those women with whom I was able to discuss the issue (friends of my hosts in Fez and Tetouan, wives and daughters) were fairly straightforward: Women see themselves as a complementary force to men within Sufism, and see the use of love imagery as an expression of the true role they play in all spiritual life. In effect, the argument is that the most powerful and most advanced spiritual states are depicted with the language of love, a domain with which women are intimately connected. This factor alone is indicative of God's view of the lack of differences between maleness and femaleness. When encouraged to speak of role models for women, they will refer to the well-known story of Lalla Zaynab, the shaikha who handled the French with great skill.[64] In this way, they believe women's role in Sufism undercuts what they contend are improper understandings of the role of women in Islam. As one exasperated murīd commented when asked if this was all tradition without reference to the present: "Why would we [Sufis] spend so much time talking about love if it had no grounding in our lives? Of course it relates to our understanding of what relationships should be in this world!"

It is also worthwhile indicating that love language becomes interlaced with many other symbol systems. Note the ways love is integrated with other trophes in the following:

The *Ṭarṣūn*, of Ben ʿAlī Cherīf, is one of the *qasaʾīd* still well known in Morocco. The musicians sing it frequently in festivals, reunions, marriages, and dinner parties. *Ṭarṣūn*, which is close to the Spanish *torzuelo*, is a poetic name for a little falcon, and the poem continually unites alternatively the ideas of the bird as hunter and as the object of love. As has been remarked by Henri Pérès, it is convenient to note at this juncture that, in the Arab tradition, which is to a large measure the source of the "courtly" tradition, the poet of love, enslaved to his beloved, extended the image of his vassalism to the point of calling the one he loved by *Sayyidī*, Lord (Sir), or *Mawlānā*, my master, in the masculine form: but it is well known that the poets employed every bit as much the masculine as the feminine to speak of their beloved, so as not to make a distinction in the verses between those which addressed children and those whose object was a woman.[65]

This characteristic has allowed the malḥūn singer to incorporate lines from secular poetry and use it in the service of the mystical experience, creating a very dense, ambiguously referenced literature.

Moroccan Sufism has a creative relationship with wine. Not only does wine provide the conceptual background for the mystical experience, but it is also the imaginative link to several related notions. Wine is an icon of the Moroccan Sufis' spiritual endeavor, rich in poetic reference, polyvalent, and sustaining throughout the many linkages. The diversity of views about it allows for an exploration of tasting the mystical life. This is accomplished through ranking different kinds of wine according to the stages of the mystical experience. At the first level are meditations on *dalīʿla*, that is, the general principles of adding fruits from the tree of wine (the grapevine) to the cup of one's inner life; to this is added, in increasingly powerful images, the increasingly heady wine of the spirit (*ilḥām*, or inspiration): *sākī*, *ṣāhī*, *kumāra*.

Wine references can be used in a number of ways. There are long discussions about the different kinds of Sufi wine tastes, such as *kūmriya hilāya*, *rūmwiya*, *ḥarrāq*, and *shuqor*, but one of the most popular is to relate the mystical life or a great saint to wine. Thus one can hear phrases such as "This is the wine that Ḥallāj and Rifāʿī drank before us." It is possible to see how this imagery can be extended into many permutations. The munshid Ashḥab is somewhat skeptical about the predominance of such wine imagery. Where at one time it was widely understood for the positive role it played in the concept of the mystical life, he regards modern society as too fragmented to understand the allusions properly. In his view, the contexts in which wine imagery is found now vitiate its proper understanding: "In our society today, we have people who are munshidūn, but they no longer have the religious experience to make it living or to comprehend the real mystical life behind the references. For example, ʿAhl al-Jamāʿah was written by the Darqāwiyya in the nineteenth century, and it is full of wine imagery. Yet this is now translated and published in London by a Sufi convert. How can these Western people understand the original meanings of wine?"

The themes of cultivation, of the time of harvest, climate, drinkers' tastes, and so on draw upon social awareness of farming and its pursuit. The labor involved in wine making is incorporated into the vision of working to rid oneself of nonessential interests so that God may be pursued. These are connected to natural elements contributing to wine's character, the sun's setting, the night, the trees, air, flowers, birds, and the moon. These ingredients are related to the pleasures of drinking, the joy of shared moments of delight, and the exquisite palate of vintage wine.

Themes of discipline, zuhd, and learning are also well developed. Thus, the pain of separation from the beloved is transmuted into the language of sin and the need to seek forgiveness. These states promote rites of zuhd, by which one's ardor in weeping over one's distance from God is assuaged by the loving kindness of a God who forgives. The mourning soul is placed within the framework of the other world, the transient nature of life, and the passage to the realm beyond. Much is made of the inferior state of this life compared to the life beyond, and comparisons give rise to a whole range of details that enlighten the seeker. Still, such penitents do not arrive at the level of the Sufi, who wants not just to deal with sin but wants to move beyond the awareness of sin to the ground of knowing all things. From the standpoint of zuhd, love is expressed in terms of the loving Prophet for the great example he provides. The collective purpose of these texts is to stir the heart to remembrance of those who saw a deeper purpose in life than the normal standards of society. Discipline and learning form a trajectory of meaning that trains the soul for the more difficult route to the presence of God.

In today's world, emphasizing zuhd can be a covert way of depreciating the more ecstatic and inspirational forms of Sufism. Zuhd can be a code word for reformist Sufism such as that espoused by the Tijāniyya. The dedication to rational definitions of the Sufi life, a closer honoring of the Prophet as a lawgiver and less as a spiritual guide, and less credence given to the miraculous all can be implied by an allegiance to zuhd. Even among some independent-minded Berbers, whose historical orientation to talismanic Sufism puts them at odds with Tijāniyya asceticism, could fully and vigorously support the Tijānī saint Sīdī Lḥajj Lehsen u Muḥammad.[66] It can also be a way to justify curbing the popularity of impressively talented munshidūn. Overall then, the glorifying of the zuhd trend can be a modernist tendency in the face of a sacred that cannot be controlled by either government or the zāwiya.

In light of these factors, al-Jirārī's interpretation of Sufism is quite conservative. In the section of zuhd, he indicates that the goal of the exercises is to ready one for the other world and that humanity's purpose in pursuing the good is directed primarily to that end. If, as he contends, zuhd does not lead to the level of the Sufi, the spiritual import of zāwiya rites is restricted to a few insiders. In fact, the most that one can do is to compare this world with the world to come. Moreover, zuhd texts limit notions of the love of God strictly to that enjoyed by the Prophet—he is the exemplar in love.[67] Such a depiction of ascetic practice narrows the mystical life in ways quite out of keeping with popular perceptions of the Sufi way in Morocco. The necessity of the female aspect of love cannot then be overemphasized.

The Prophet as a theme of spiritual exploration is second to none. Malhūn constructed on a madīh superstructure related to the Prophet and the norms he established for the spiritual life constitute an absolutely premier area of development. Special place is given to his birth, and the signs attending it. Following this there are themes on the Prophet as a person, his qualities, habits, and attitudes. Meditations on his qualities, his khalūq or manners, and the moral excellence of the Prophet are a predominant fixture. In the world inhabited by the Prophet, love predominates. This principle of love is found throughout the universe and is, in its essence, the same as that encountered in women. Out of the tears of joy comes the way of rūhānī, or the spiritual life. The Prophet's ability to deal with his loneliness is an important theme, and the issue of his mirʿāj as a reward for being faithful is often heard. There, too, one can hear, in the malhūn sung by the Harrāqiyya, about the other world and Muhammad's role in it.

As noted above, the cloak of the Prophet has become a predominant theme within Moroccan Sufism, leading to meditations on many aspects of the religious power of the Prophet. In that connection, no summary would be complete without some exploration of *tawassul,* or supplication. Many zajal deal with the Prophet's intercession for all believers before God on the *Hawl al-Qiyamah,* or Day of Reckoning. So significant has supplication become that it has generated its own set of themes, some of which raise interesting theological issues. One of these, the theme of the Prophet's pardon for wrongdoings, is interwoven in many qasāʾid and has caused some concern by one munshid I interviewed. Nabīl tells the story:

At the founding of the ʿAissawa, there was a poet who would write songs for his tarīqa. He would take the qasīda to the fuqahāʾ and ʿulamāʾ at Qayrawān. Someone would check the words for their validity according to fiqh, and someone would check the Arabic. One of these songs came into my hands to sing. I could not understand how I could sing it because it asked the Prophet to forgive his sins. Muhammad, after all, was only a man. So I asked the muqaddam. He said to ask a man who was at the university, and he agreed the words were acceptable. I asked him why. He said that, had the words been said early in the Islamic period, they would certainly have been bidʿa. But as Islam developed and the hadra came into existence, words take on different meanings. "Besides," he said, "words sometimes cannot speak the whole truth about a religion. With regard to this statement, in the context of the hadra, people know the phrase is a short form for asking forgiveness from God, but He does it through meditation on the Prophet."[68]

Another interesting area is the exploration of texts about the Prophet's family, his grandfather, father, and near relatives and, finally, the mourning that take place at his death and the response of those near to him to his demise.

The popular poet does not make many texts focusing upon contemporary issues because he does not think his problems and themes are as important as a Sufi text. Madīḥ of the Prophet is a "safe" text, since no one will be critical of favorable things said of the Prophet. That's why one finds maddāḥin, the madīḥ of the Prophet, on all official occasions, even in those dominated by prestigious people like the king. While the modern poet can make up stories in his imagination that reflect modern problems, these issues are never stated directly. Rather they are hinted at by changing the emphasis in traditional wording or juxtaposing a variety of themes. The same effect can be achieved by means of different methods of presentation.

A special genre of madīḥ is reserved for the saints and the *ahl al-bait* (lit., people of the house, that is, Muḥammad's lineage). Panegyric for the Prophet is supplemented with praise for ʿĀʾisha, for Ḥassan and Ḥusain, for Mūlay Idrīs, the entire range of awliyāʾ, and other statesmen of piety throughout Islamic history. For example, Sīdī Faraj is celebrated at Fez, and has been continuously since the twelfth century. This kind of madīḥ is prized because it has been a continuous source of blessing. The malḥūn to Sīdī Faraj is modeled after the Prophet's, in that that moment is regarded as having had great poets. Each saint may have special praise bestowed upon them, depending upon the group. Not all groups stress this kind of madīḥ, especially not among the reformist ṭarīqas. One can also hear malḥūn texts dedicated to those who journey into the inner space of the tombs, where conversations and blessing are imposed by the marabout.

The *Hubb Allāh* genre is based on the view that there is a significant difference in treatment of the love of God and the love of the Prophet. Some malḥūn cultivate the notion that love for God is for Sufis, or even for the saints, while the love for the Prophet is for everyone. Some writers, however, focus specifically upon love poetry to God, the joy of the pilgrimage to Him, and the exultation that the karāmāt provides to the believer, coming, as it does, directly from God. Even in malḥūn not specifically written with the love of God in mind, one comes upon terms like *hubb illāhī* (i.e., love to my God).

Where direct reference to God may not be acceptable, the zajal poet resorts to *jalāla*; this means being related to God because it is an attribute of God. Comments and meditations upon these features of God's relationship to humans are sometimes explored. Oftentimes you will hear both jalālī and samāʿ-based material in a funeral, in which case, the goal of the reference is to alert the hearer to such concepts as destiny, death, and the afterlife. The love for God is regularly associated with the saints and exceptionally spiritual people. Chanting zajal that deal with this usually signals that the focus is on what might be called absolute situations.

Memory and the Arab Andalusian Heritage

If the Arabic of the Qur'ān and the Ḥadīth provides the basic mythological structure, with their foundational language and conceptual framework, it is the Andalusian inheritance that imparts a literary and cultural patina to the repertoire of the munshid. With its richness of imagery and its vivid memory of the greatness of Andalus and Islamic character, these materials give considerable cultural sophistication to Sufi remembering. With its brilliant expressions, exotic allusions, and high-cultured and powerful language, the Andalusian legacy has directly impacted on the Moroccan, providing metaphors and models for the spiritual life. The Arab-speaking munshid draws deeply on this heritage in constructing the discourse of the spiritual life of the orders and for his means of relating to the denizens of the other world.

In the next chapter, we turn to the munshidūn who do not belong to the Arabic-speaking segment of Morocco's population, and examine the nature of religious memory in their perception of reality.

5

ALTERNATIVE AND VISIONARY PASTS
The Impact of Other Memories

I leave my world, I pilgrimage into my Life,
He guides me, mediates for me, loves me,
His heart is a world for me.

Munshid's Song, from Shustarī

I came to be what I am first through my experience, and then by studying
under the great connoisseurs of madīḥ in Fez.

Muḥammad Bennīs, 1995

I served him [the Prophet] with my eulogy to be redeemed thereby,
From the sins of a life of poetry and servitude.

al-Būṣayrī, *Bourda*

Memorable Pasts in the Present: Divergence in Morocco's Legacies

The notion that a mythic moment of the past is important in the present and shapes
it without reliance on any other moment is as basic to religion as the existence of the
subatomic particle is to physics. It signals the dramatic movement away from the
ordinariness of the current act and directs it to a normative occurrence in the past.
That past is sacred, inasmuch as its meaning remains normative and definitive. The
result is that the text itself is neither set in the time in which it is recited, nor is its
moment confined to the past; rather, it enshrines a kind of dimorphic time outside
of normal time. As such it is adulated because it represents a powerful religious
occurrence of the past, yet is present at the immediate moment of rehearsal.

In Islam, the most obvious expression of this quality is found in the Qurʾān. Yet
there are other forms of this type of text whose referent is less specific in its
moment in the past when it occurred, and just how it is to be conceived. In effect,
the "sacred" represented in these examples of the past is not necessarily a historical
event but a normative event that *may* have taken place throughout an unspecified
time period of a sacred past. The materials examined here have the same dimorphic quality, but the past is much more vague and the referent more ambiguous.
Moreover, the language of the text itself is less a vehicle of the normativeness than
is the meaning enshrined in or attributed to the text. It is such diversity of approach

that provides insight into the way memory functions in Morocco and specifically within the role of the munshid.

This chapter explores just such areas of religious sensitivity. First, we will examine the Berber and Ginawa traditions, as they indicate pasts of quite a different order. Then we will move to the varied spiritual settings in which the munshid is operative, outlining how the past is modeled differently according to various layers of meaning, all of them laminated into a finely textured experience.

Shifted History: The Charged Berber Memory

How are we to understand a people who do not read Islamic history the way the textbooks describe it? Or to put it more potently, who experience their Islam through their identity as Berbers, before they experience their Islam through the medium of language? Indeed, the Berbers have been noted for their independence from any particular designation or authority for so long that their territory is often referred to as *bilād al-sibāb* (land of vituperation).[1]

These distinctions are clear to me since I have similar experience in Canada. In my country, speaking French may well be a measure of one's independence from a monocultural English, and the entry into a distinctive experience of self and person. In Morocco, in many Sufi groups, Berber language is used for all but the most official of religious duties. Thus a text is recited in Arabic if the point of the exercise is to link the believer to a social and spiritual order of the larger Islamic world. It is apparent that Berbers move back and forth between these worlds without difficulty. Language is not rendered as otherness, nor has it been a deliberate vehicle of marginalization.

> It is important to remember that most of the big Sufis did not speak Arabic at all. For example, we have a book dating from the thirteenth century that includes a selection of biographies of the great Sufi shaikh Abū Muḥammad Salé, and up to that time it is obvious that they were all Berber speaking, that is, before immigration of the coming of the Andalusians. Nor was this culture just assigned to the countryside. Even to today there is some indigenous poetry now among the Berbers, and they have translations in Sous in southern Morocco, of Arabic works like the *Bourda*. There are also a few important poets who write in Berber.[2]

Still, there are a few poets who stress their Berber background. Yusuf bin Yahyia al-Taḍilī (known as Ibn al-Zayyat, d. 1220) had his book, *Tashawwuf ilā rijāl al-taṣawwuf*, edited and published in Morocco by Aḥmed Toufīq in 1984. His book indicates that, in the past, most Berber did embrace samāᶜ, but they also participated in dhikr without music.[3] The most characteristic experience is in the ḥaḍra, with the repetitive ṭabla to help in the trance.[4]

Muḥammad Darīf has argued that the Berbers formulated different kinds of social organizations because of their propensity to independence and resistance. Since zāwiyas are associated primarily with Berber locales, he holds that the zāwiya rested upon a political base, arising out of the tribal nature of Berber identity. At the same time, these zāwiyas never achieved religious power. Thus there is a difference between the zāwiya and the orders in this regard because the orders did achieve religious power.[5]

There are limits to this interpretation. Can it be strictly a Berber-Arab structural variation? The Kaybele, for example, are found in the north and constitute a family of social classes, yet the Kaybele (an Arabic word meaning clan) dialect is composed of Berber and classical Arabic intermixed. The Kaybele did not openly espouse the orders because of a basic conflict between them and Sultan Idrīs. The Idrīsiyya provided an opening to both political and religious power, because everyone attached to an important family participated in a common Islamic cultural world. If they did belong to the orders it was because the orders had family rapport with the sultan. Thus, while some zāwiyas were also attached to Idrīs, for example, the Sharqāwiyya, in the main the zāwiyas remained closely tied to local saints and local power structures.[6]

Moreover, as Hatt suggests, there are really three intermingled institutional forms among Berber-speaking populations: *madrasa* systems, systems of tribal affiliation, and maraboutic zāwiyas. These can be distinguished from each other if they are considered as reflecting a continuum, with madrasa-type forms at one end, and small saint-focused cult groups at the other, and the tribal confraternal groups operating between them. Thus between the poles, one finds an intermix of all forms.

Būsayrī's *Bourda:* A Berber "Memory" of Paradigmatic History

Berbers have produced important key cultural and religious elements that are crucial for understanding Morocco. The most outstanding of these, from the perspective of this study, is the *Bourda* of Būsayrī. Every ṭarīqa in Morocco bases its liturgies upon the *Bourda,* and every mūssem (birthday celebration) features its recital. Very little Sufi life would exist in its current form in Morocco without the *Bourda*. Quite simply, the *Bourda* (and al-Būsayrī's other qaṣīda, the *Hamzīyya*) is to Moroccan Sufism what the Qurʾān is to Islam.

The *Bourda* has long been hailed by Berbers as a distinctive Berber contribution because Būsayrī is claimed to be of Berber parentage (the *nisba*, al-Sanhaji, of his father is indicative of Berber origins, but al-Būsayrī himself was born in Dilas or Abu Sīr in Banī Sueif province of Upper Egypt). Because the *Bourda* has recently been translated into English[8] (that translation has served as the basis for the evaluation here), we will only analyze the distinctive "remembrance" elements, and try to relate the whole work to the Berber/Arabic integration mentioned earlier. In this way the paradigms that undergird Berber participation in Islam will become clearer, and consequently the role of the munshid's chanting of the *Bourda* more transparent.

It is a vibrant and recurring motif among Berbers that they provided the hospitable basis for Islam . . . that it was because Berbers carried out the ancient codes of hospitality that Islam has been able to take root and thrive in Morocco. This motif they see exemplified in the text of the *Bourda*. As Sperl points out, the thematic center of the *Bourda* revolves around two concepts: hospitality (*dhiyāfa*) and protection (*jiwār*), the former allied with the ancient codes of Arabian hospitality and the latter an ancient equivalent to the modern word asylum.[9] Berbers believe that both of these concepts were operating when Islam originally was brought to the Maghrib, since the Berbers embraced Islam and became its champion before the Arabs were able to muster the strength to capture the land through military campaign. In effect they provided protection for the fledgling religion long before it took shape politically in the land. Moreover, it was they who spearheaded Islam's expansion in the region. Thus we read:

> Religion alighted upon their courtyard like a guest
> Bringing chiefs hungry for their enemies' flesh,
> Leading armies vast as the sea, mounted on swift steeds.
> Foaming with surging waves of heroes.
> Each answerable to god and trusting in His reward,
> And wielding swords that uproot and shatter unbelief.
> Until the faith of Islam, exiled from them at first,
> Became part of their lineage and kin,
> And was provided through them with the best father and husband,
> And would never be orphaned or widowed.

These lines are a trope for Berber convictions. Today's Berbers perceive these verses as directly related to the Berber role in Islam—of their late coming to Islam because of their distance, and their initial response to a religion that came as a stranger to them in the form of powerful armies poised to wipe them out. But they sidestepped this outcome by converting immediately to Muḥammad's message. When they accepted Islam, it became as much part of their lives as it had among the Arabs. Indeed, it was they who pushed Islam into the nether reaches of North Africa and across the straits to Spain.

This theme is picked up in the central eulogy of the Prophet, where, after addressing the Prophet's character and known qualities (29–33), the object of deserved love and adoration (36–58), the poem shifts to the power of Muḥammad to cure and produce miracles (73–104). It culminates with a ringing endorsement of the Prophet's military accomplishments: the victories of Ḥunain, Uḥud, and Badr are "Seasons of death more calamitous than the plague" (128), and even "lions of the thicket are stunned" (135). His protection of them was the model for their protection of his faith, for "Never will you see an ally of his not aided / By him, nor an enemy of his not crushed" (136). His lifework founded their nation:

> Good tidings for us people of Islam, for in him we have
> A pillar of kind care which none can overthrow.
> When God called him—who calls us to obedience of Him—
> His noblest messenger, we became the noblest of nations. (116–17)

The theme is underlined by the return to the concept of neighborliness in line 148: "Far be it from him that a supplicant should be deprived of his gifts / Or that a neighbour seeking his help should remain unprotected." Such conviction is based upon the knowledge that Muḥammad is the origination of "this world and its counterpart (154)," an affirmation that roots their faith in the transcendent realm. By their commitment to Islam, they, too, became children of Muḥammad.

This notion is essential to comprehend the growth of Sayyidī consciousness in the Maghrib and especially among the Berbers. While even a cursory examination of this issue is beyond the parameters of this study, it is nevertheless important to note that Berbers do not draw a hard and fast line between themselves and Arabs. They regard themselves as having absorbed and transformed the Arab presence. Jacque Berque was quite right to affirm: "The analysis of Maghrib societies requires, not a distinction between what may be 'Berber,' 'Arab,' or 'French,' but criteria that would trace, with respect to the Maghrib personality, the greater or lesser coherence or dynamism achieved in the integration of heterogeneous characteristics and in the responses of a group to its milieu."[10] Indeed, it is possible to hear Berbers argue that they became a kind of tribe like that of the Arabs in the early Muslim period, that is, a tribe that belonged to a larger collectivity called Islam. Thus the sayyid concept, linking the Berbers to that pre-Islamic figure of authority in Arab culture, is key to this understanding. Watt indicates that the sayyid notion did not involve absolute authority, a requisite that Berbers could rarely tolerate. Watt points out these limitations in the pre-Islamic concept:

> The power of the *sayyid* (in pre-Islamic Arabia) was also limited by powers and functions given to other persons. Leadership in war was usually given by special decisions, and might be for a fixed period only. Mostly, it would seem, it was not the *sayyid* who was appointed as war leader. In some tribes, again, before adopting some new plan the soothsayer (*kāhin*) would be consulted, and this would give some power to the soothsayer at the expense of the *sayyid*. Finally, there were disputes to be settled involving traditional law or custom. If the *sayyid*'s wisdom was respected, disputes between parties within his tribe would be brought to him. In other cases, however, and where he was not sufficiently respected, recourse could be had to those men of wisdom and integrity who were widely accepted as arbiters (sing. *ḥakam*).[11]

Berbers had no difficulty recognizing the local leadership of someone who represented the respected values of the group. They also were willing to accept those who could show some ostensible connection to the lineage of the Prophet. Regardless of their early history, then, they ultimately disagreed with the Khārijīs, who wanted to separate completely political leadership from the religious.[12] The Sayyidī tradition has bequeathed certain valuable themes to the munshid. This legacy includes a sensitivity to obedience to the Divine, whether that Divine is experienced in personal life and faith or through the law imposed by the Qurʾān.

Furthermore, texts that stress closeness to the Prophet, particularly as a militant response to detrimental attacks on the ummah (Islamic community) or God's word are highly valued. Some would argue that a special depth of spiritual perception is open to those who fall under the influence of the Eastern sayyidī tradition. Finally, Berbers are particularly sensitive to the power of the Prophet's family, where they are regarded as directly connected to God.

Here, too, al-Būṣayrī expresses notions close to those of his brethren in the Maghrib. Muḥammad is not just a respected individual who provides the neighborly hospitality of the tribal mores; he also brings transcendent reality, for, by appropriation of his protection—"And he is mankind's most faithful protector" (146)—al-Būṣayrī himself will be saved: "Since I have devoted my thoughts to his praise / I have found him the best guarantor of salvation." (149)

Thus, the Berber notions are grafted onto an ancient interpretation of Arabic history, and cultural redefinition is established. It is through this reinterpretation of religious lore that the role of Moroccan identity becomes integrated into Berber/Maghribian consciousness.

In this way, when the munshid is reciting the *Bourda,* he is also affirming his sense of identity within the Muslim community. No wonder, then, that as an expression of this culturally defined role, one can hear special programs every Friday on radio and television stations in Morocco dedicated to these themes in Berber language. This particularly applies to programs destined for the Middle Atlas region. Since the themes noted above recur frequently, the munshid will rehearse these poems later to be heard in the mūssem. In this way the tradition continues to rephrase itself in the modern world. And Berbers see themselves with a divine destiny: The protection and good-neighborliness of the Prophet is their birthright.

The Spiritual Alternatives of Africa: The Ginawa's Memories

The African connection arises out of quite different social realities. The "black" person clearly comes from some other place even if he or she has roots in Morocco, but that is not necessarily evaluated in terms of racial difference.[13] There are perceptible differences in the way Arabs, Berbers, and Africans see skin color, for example.[14] Yet many ancestors were slaves, and the implication that many blacks came from such circumstances has skewed perceptions, at least for that population segment. The issue of color puts an entirely different structure into place than the minority situation of the Berbers. Some sense of this difference is reflected in Pâques's descriptive comment on the central rite of the Ginawa:

> The Ginawa carry out their ceremonies at night because it is during the night that the tree penetrates the heavens [the tree associated with the seventh heaven at the Qurʾānic "limits," with additional mythological meanings]. It is also during the night that marriages are celebrated. The celebration of the cult,

the *derdeba,* brought about by sacrifices and dances, actualizes cosmic events that we can only summarize. All rituals are constantly undergirded by reference to marriage. The derdeba has as its goal to divide up the sacrificial animal as was the world first divided, and divided in the same manner as adepts are, then all the elements are reassembled, incarnating the seven categories of possessedness, to rise toward heaven in a vast whirlwind. [The entire dividing and reassembling process] accomplishes also the unification of the universe. During the course of this regrouping, the souls of the dead come to possess the living, and they even will return to reunite with a spouse in the same manner as her husband had penetrated her during their (first) night. Also, in assuring through the consummation of marriage the cycle of reincarnations, the woman becomes a girl, wife, and mother of the dead. In the *derdeba,* all the souls gathered together by the muqaddam are revived by him during the night and like a great psychopomp blacksmith, he unleashes a double whirlwind, ascending and descending, and thereby, the reincarnation of souls [takes place] in the corporate body of the adepts, all reunited under the seven colors of the universe.[15]

With such cosmic, mythological, and physical meanings intermingling, it is evident that we are dealing with an entirely different religious system than we have so far encountered. Similarly, there are different perspectives on the way memory functions. We turn to the information provided by Bilāl, the Ginawa adept, provided during an interview in Rabat in August 1995.

Bilāl, the Ginawa, and the Memory of Islam's Beginnings

I think the history of the Ginawa is tied up with the development of the Arabic dimension of Islam. How is it that Bilāl, a black African, became for a time Muḥammad's son, yet there are few ḥadīth traced to him. Why? It is almost as if the black dimension of Islam was systematically erased. Bilāl seemed to have had a special relationship with Fāṭima, for when he was with her, Bilāl seemed able to overcome her moments of dismay by means of his speaking. What kind of speaking, of language, was this? Hidden in this history is a special language, a hidden language of refreshment and invigorization. But it was not a dimension that the Arabs wished to acknowledge. Consequently, they have erased the stories that Bilāl told the Prophet, considering them to be different from their idea of Islam. But the Prophet knew the truth, and he recognized Bilāl. There is therefore something quite tragic and hidden in the Ginawa and Bilāl. This is the key to understanding the munshid in the Ginawa.[16]

As Bilāl's statement implies, Africans in Morocco are intimately connected to the issue of color in Islam.[17] The role and significance of the Ginawa cannot be divorced from the way Africans perceive their history to have developed in Islam, since it is that history that is the operative ingredient in the Sufism that we are examining. Bilāl was the name of the African who was one of the first converts to Islam, served as the first muezzin of the fledgling ummah, and for a time was adopted by the Prophet as a son.[18] All of this predisposed Bilāl to be a kind of patron saint of the black in Morocco: "He was a slave manumitted in the first hours of Islam, and he was one of its first converts. The pain of being in bondage, the obsession with an original blemish that legend had attributed to them (they were the descendants of Ham, son of Noah, who was white at birth but became black as a result of being cursed by his father), the confidence in a divine clemency are the essential themes of their [that is, black Moroccans'] refrain."[19]

It is also worth pointing out that Bilāl has a further religious domain connected to his name. Bilāl is especially associated with shoes. The Ginawa make their musical instrument par excellence (*karkorru*) from the sole of the shoe. It is because Bilāl was held to lead the Ginawa procession to paradise, and because of his importance to Islam, he alone wore his shoes into paradise. The sound of his shoes on the floors of paradise was indicative of the charged spiritual atmosphere. In this way, the Ginawa recognize the special function of the karkorru sound to lead one into a mystical samāʿ.

The role Bilāl played in early Islam is taken as indication of God's attitude toward all dark-skinned people, that is, they are necessary for the development of true Islamic piety. Yet that elevated place of prestige in Islam has not been maintained. The history of the African in North Africa has been complicated by forced labor, various types of capture, and social displacement. Indeed, blacks were slaves in Morocco from Roman times, and the practice was carried on with the victory of Islam because of the commercial value of slave trading.[20] Moreover, black slaves from *bilād al-sūdān* (the land of the Sudan) people the popular stories of Morocco, and are likewise regularly part of the malḥūn tradition.[21]

Morocco's political stance within Islam has also played a role in the position of Africans. Generally resistant to centralizing tendencies in Islam, right from the beginning of Islamic dominance in the region, Moroccans have looked to their geographical and economic position at the top and west of Africa to keep them at a distance from the Eastern hegemonic proclivities of the caliphs, and they relied on African soldiers to help them maintain the distance. In addition, the Almoravids tapped south into Senegal for the soldiers that helped conquer Spain.[22] Black militias also were used to control the local population, a factor that distanced them from the Berbers; under Mūlay Ismāʿīl (1672–1727) more than one hundred fifty thousand soldiers of Sudanese origin were recruited to control the Berbers.[23]

According to a letter written by Sultan Ismāʿīl in 1706, all marabouts were descendants of the great saint Sayyidī Abū ʿAzza; furthermore, he regarded himself as directly involved in the existence of the zāwiya, designating it as "our zāwiya" in an official letter, even though there is no evidence that he was ever a member.[24] In the same letter, he castigates the ruler he had placed over a nearby garrison, who was apparently mistreating some of the local zāwiya members, who he identified as the servants of "our cousin" Mūlay Muḥʾammad, son of the late Mūlay Muḥʾammad Aḥʾmad al-Gnawī, and founder of the Ginawa zāwiya.[25]

At any rate, this connection to the symbols of power catalyzed lesser peoples with the result that important families paid handsome sums to have a collective of black slaves in their households as indicators of wealth. Moroccan blacks believe that, in many ways, the "curse" of Ham still is operative, despite the beneficence of Islam and the decisive acknowledgement by the Prophet.

In addition, Bilāl, my informant in Morocco, noted that there is a relationship between the Banī Hilāl and the text. My own hunch is that their poetry speaks of the Arabs in terms of slavery and servitude, so that the Banī Hilāl, as representatives of ancient Islam, are regarded as more Arab than Muslim. As a poet himself, Bilal reinforced the idea that there is an ancient connection between the Banī Hilāl and the poetics of the Ginawa, but he did not know what it was. Perhaps it has something to do with capture. Here is an ancient text chanted today by the munshid:

> Peace to our Prophet, our Lord Muḥammad
> Come to Allāh (*repeated four times*)
> O ʿĀʾisha, O ʿĀʾisha of Bornu
> O ʿĀʾisha, slave of the Turk, O ʿĀʾisha
> O ʿĀʾisha, the Sudanese, O ʿĀʾisha
> O ʿĀʾisha, slave of the pasha, O ʿĀʾisha
> O ʿĀʾisha, O Allāh, O ʿĀʾisha
> O fire, O fire, O fire that consumes me, decree from Allāh
> They have carried me off from my country, the Sudan
> The infidel Touaregs have captured me
> Dragged off to Shʿamba by a surprise attack
> Delivered over to the sand carriers of Suafa
> Sold off to the wine-drinking people of Jerid.
> And as for me, I search for mabrūka [grace, beneficence]
> My shoes are grass, my staff tamarind
> With overburdened back, dagger in my sash
> I seek mabrūka and I never find it.
> O misfortune! Guide me, wherever I may go
> I've not found it [mabrūka]!

Here the munshid rehearses the bleak history of many an African in Morocco, whose ancestors were enslaved and sold to the "Turk" (Ottoman Muslims) or to the rich landowners. He remembers this indiscriminate past. The memory is not one specific event, but a paradigmatic event that encompasses the story that Africans in North Africa hold as oral truth. The "history" becomes a mythic story deemed as replicated in their ancestors' lives. In this way, the myth explains the abject position many find themselves in, and gives credence to the belief that blacks, as a group, have been systematically discriminated against. At the same time, the story explicates their peripatetic lifestyle, and provides a rationale for the many travels and instabilities among their people. Here is a burden they must recall, for they acknowledge that the story is not of their own doing—it is God's decree. The retelling is a revisiting, then, of a primary religious issue with God: why has the African suffered such degradation? The problematic of their lives in the economy of God's plan creates spiritual tension and a personal quest. Bilāl then connects the story to the ritual of the Ginawa: "When one enters the mūssem [here, Ginawa ritual dhikr], one must recite one's family tree. This traces one's ancestry back through a spiritual tribe to Bilāl, the black man who was the first to call the Muslims to prayer. This may well be a fabricated history, but it has mythical significance precisely because one's lineage is the key to one's spiritual level."[26]

One's spiritual level is not just expressed in terms of political power within the group; it is also replicated in one's public behavior. The most obvious example of this is clothes. The kind and color of clothes one wears are a barometer of spiritual status both within one's heart and within the community at large. Thus Bilāl says:

> The clothes of the Ginawa are very important, for they demonstrate his sense of identity. The white jalibiyya is from the Arab, representing our distinguished origin. The red sash is indicative of one's personal status among the Ginawa. The hat is particularly indicative also, of one's moral and spiritual behavior. One can wear a black hat or a green hat. I asked one man why he no longer wore his green hat.

> "Because," he said, "when one wears one's hat one signals that he not only understands one's moral responsibilities but is willing to shoulder them. Wearing a black hat is easy, because it means just being part of the group. But by wearing the green hat, one signals that one is, like the Prophet, energized to bring about God's world. It is a tremendous responsibility. I cannot do it with my life as it is right now. I cannot be like the Prophet in my community. If I wear the hat, I must live the law exactly."[27]

In fact, the color of the clothes reflects a philosophy of the spiritual world to which the murid belongs, as noted above in Pâques's description. In effect, the Ginawa believe that the murīd may live in any one of three ṭbīqa (levels or degrees) of existence.[28] The first degree is that of the jinn. Activity in this world is influenced not just by the character of individual people, such as those who live and act aggressively, or timidly. The Ginawa believe that each person is engaged with a counterpart spiritual domain, a domain of the jinn. Here there are both good and evil jinn. Some people choose to engage with the evil jinn. One chooses the evil jinn if one wishes to progress in the spiritual life, or one wishes to have one's inner life challenged beyond that of the ordinary believer. By winning out over evil jinn, one allows oneself to gain insight into spiritual matters, and the triumph over the evil jinn is a signal to the spirit world that you are a serious contender for deeper spiritual insights. Like the Zoroastrian belief, human life is an engagement with the forces of evil and how one comes out of this encounter has important ramifications for one's future. Struggle, or jihād, is an essential part of this motif. The Qurʾānic injunction to jihād is believed to have been downplayed in early Islam, to have been turned over to the state. This move, according to the Ginawa, was illegitimate. It represents a distortion of the true message of God, which sees struggle as endemic to the spiritual environment. It also signals that the Qurʾānic material on the jinn has not been accorded its proper place in the Islamic theological system.

Accordingly, if one chooses the evil spirits, it is to get to the stage beyond the preliminary stage. Once beyond it, one finds the second degree of spiritual attainment. This is known as the realm of the shaikh. It is a degree of spiritual power of a genuine mystique. This is the realm to which all the great shaikhs of the past belong, and it is a mysterious realm because it is really the realm that maintains the physical world in which we live. In effect, the saints actively support the earth, the sky, and the cosmic realities that we experience. At this level, one encounters the systems that run all things.

Bilāl notes: "There is another level, a very difficult degree or level to define, because it is that of the sultan. This is the third level . . . the level of the orange color." This is a realm of deep religious experience, and generally beyond the ken of ordinary believers.

The Ginawa Munshid and Ritual Experience

Crapanzano indicates that parts of the ḥaḍra among the Hamadsha come from the Ginawa. There are, he reports, three parts to their ḥaḍra: the hot part, the cold part, and the *ḥaḍra gnawiyya* that draws its central ritual section from the Ginawa. In it, some respond to certain tunes while others do not, and it is the responsibility of the munshid to change the *rīḥ*, or musical phrasing, in order to maintain a sense of the presence through trance dancing.[29]

There are actually two kinds of Ginawa.[30] The traditional Ginawa of Marrakech practice an enthusiastic, trance-type tradition with dramatic dhikr. But there are also the Ginawa of the leading families of Boufkraine, situated near Meknes. Members of this ṭarīqa practice an ancient kind of Ginawa in which the songs and music play a spiritual role. They are not dramatic but very low key, one could almost say gentle. These Ginawa have a long genealogy of singing about religion. The text noted above belongs to this group of Ginawa. We turn now to the trance-type tradition. Bilāl states:

> I recall returning to my people one time. I was very tired and fatigued. The Ginawa were beginning a séance. I sat back to relax. Arrangements continued

around me. Then began the song. As soon as the drummer hit the drum, I was startled. I knew of the drum. Something shook me to my roots. An energizing force overtook me, of which I was quite ignorant. I was no longer tired. Later I asked my father what it was. My father, a leader in the Ginawa, smiled and said . . . Good, I know you are truly a Ginawa now. Those who are not, do not respond to this sound and this rhythm.

The Ginawa will tell you that when the munshid sings the text, the text is not the most important element. The texts are very simple, with few words, endlessly repeated, it seems. Yet at some sign, the munshid interjects another word into the text, and another meaning is produced. Yet it is not possible to say what that meaning is, for the Ginawa say that that meaning is not resident in the text but in the context of the word and the occasion. There appear to be trigger words that simply announce another stage of spiritual intent. The result, however, is evident: people go into trance even if none of the "classical" context of mysticism is present. Perhaps this indicates different kinds of Sufism.[31] Clearly there is a relationship between the words interjected and the spiritual development of the meditation, but there is no evidently defined meaning of it. All one is able to say is that these terms function as a kind of portal through which one is propelled by the trigger words or sounds, and on the other side, we do not know what happens. Yet there are no doubts among the Ginawa of these mystical portals.

Bilāl continues:

I was at a marriage. The chief commenced to sing and almost immediately the groom fell down. His new wife was startled, crying and beating him in desperation. When his trance was over, I asked him if he had lost consciousness, and he replied, "No, I was aware of everything going on around me . . . the people, my wife, and the brethren." So you see there is a rhythm of another world, unknown, that is spoken through the rhythm of the Ginawa, and when one hears this sound, one must follow it. Yet it is impossible to say anything about that world because I have no idea what it is. I do know that when one sings that text, the spirit enters into the munshid and influences both the singer and the text. The text is empowered by the spirit that spins toward the singer and suddenly enters him.[32]

Like the ʿAissawiyya, the electricity of the experience predominates. The Ginawa affirm that the text and the music are placed at the service of ecstasy. Even when the fire only lights on one or two, the appearance of power in their midst in the form of trance is the cherished factor, and everything bends in the direction of that flame. What one might say is that the trance experience becomes a normative means by which the transcendent realm is visited and appropriated. That appropriation potential is the common ingredient of the Ginawa with other munshidūn, for they all use that past extraordinary experience as a guide for their contributions to corporate good. It is what might be termed an existential moment that is continually affirmed as the norm for collective experience.

In addition, the ideology of the female plays a much more central role in the ideology of the trance, for possession is conceived as replicating the intimacy of marriage, and the birthing of a personage from within oneself. Blin also indicates the importance of blood and alcohol among some Ginawa, as a way of integrating the physical and spiritual during the rites.[33]

An Alternative Field of Memory: The Paradigmatic Moment of Visionary Experience

If ethnic and national memory provide the vehicle for connecting to certain kinds of realities, these are not the only imaginative materials available to the Moroccan munshid. Indeed, one could argue that it is the personal dimension of these memory banks that is the most telling, for the munshid thinks its content is crucial. Instead of religion defining one kind of past, however, it provides several. Yet they are all integrated in the performance of the munshid.

Such a strategy allows many different kinds of paradigms to blend and intermix, and collectively to provide a living environment from which to draw inspiration. In this section I illustrate a very complex part of this intermixing by pointing out the visionary or spiritual perspectives that are operative in the munshid's life. Touched on only briefly here, this critical aspect of the munshidūn's life should receive further study.[34]

While on the surface the immediacy of the experience would seem to militate against memory being involved, on closer look, the munshid operates with past visitations and visions in mind, and he tries to bring these past moments to life in the present context. This is a recovering notion that does not intend to reconstitute the same moment but rather to recreate the same potential in ritual so that the same kind of power can be felt and experienced. These encoded moments of power express highly personal images of past spiritual highs that become paradigmatic for the munshid's current performance.

These encoded moments introduce us forcefully to the mythic dimension of Moroccan religious life, because the selection and expression of these pasts constitute a religious re-creation and affirmation. In them we can see the shift from a shared history to a transformative life force, stated simplistically here as heritage within and beyond the individual performer. Consider these statements:

The munshidūn receive ilhām like lumʿa, or the twinkling or flashing of stars in the night sky. This is a sacred presence delegated as *Tawhīd*. . . . We don't see the Prophet as God but feel the presence of the world beyond, and when I have ilhām, it carries my soul out of my body and I can sing as if it were not me singing. . . . The ʿumda begins at 8 P.M. and sometimes continues to 2:30 A.M. . . . We use many different kinds of texts, and each poet has nafas-like style, but each zāwiya has a few words and a kind of universe of performance that is distinctive to it. But a good munshid is also rūḥ . . . and if he feels a powerful text outside, he has to change it to make it conform to the ṭurāth of the order.

According to my sources, the munshid operates in an intermediary realm between this world and the spiritual one inhabited by God and the angels. One sees in those worlds something like paradise, only it is not the paradise at the end of life. It is a state into which the munshid arrives when he sings well. It is defined both as ilhām and as a gift from the heart of the shaikh. Clearly, then, if we are to understand the munshid's tradition, we have to confront his visionary memories, for these also constitute part of the elemental-mythic script upon which he draws. The munshid's art and performance incorporate a significant dimension of remembrance of past exemplary moments of performance where the spiritual verities dominated.

Twenty-seven-year-old Nabīl al-Jaiy, munshid of the ʿAissawiyya, sketched the modus operandi of the munshid this way:

The structure of my chanting is fixed: I begin with a chant of praise to the Prophet, continue with a selection of praise to the awliyāʾ (sing. wālī), move to praise of Idrīs I, then to praise for Idrīs II. When these elements are complete, I may then turn in love to my shaikh and chant lyrics to him and his great baraka. This structure is firm, because it leads the listener from the foundation of our religion, Muḥammad, praise be to him, deeper into the personal authority of the path we follow. We come to know the great blessings of God through the persons of this history, all of whom are known to us and the brethren, and who present for us the personality and character of true spiritual inspiration. We need this power of personal authority, not just because the experiences of the ṭarīqa are oral, but also because only an experienced person can teach you the meaning of the words. This means that I cannot chant just any words. I must chant the words that have been created through the power of the shaikh and the ṭarīqa. The saint's words have power, not only because they come out of his inspiration, but because I love the saint. So my love empowers the already powerful words. The ʿAissawiyya use the texts from all the saints, because some great saints die and leave no ṭarīqa. We take their songs and chant them. Our sources are very diversified in comparison to some other groups who only chant their own shaikh's songs.

I learn the songs in the samāʿ, usually from a shaikh or nuqabāʾ or muqaddam. These are songs from the malḥūn of the ṭarīqa. They have a great sense of what belongs to the tradition, so when they write a song for the ṭarīqa, it is prized. We can write these words down, but mostly we rely on memory. I heard a song in the samāʿ one time, and it did not seem right to me. I told my muqaddam I thought it was a mistake. A phrase was different from what I remembered as a boy. I went to the shaikh, and we checked it in a book, and the mistake was there, too. We studied it for a long time, and then we agreed that the book was wrong and my memory correct. I sang it the way I remembered it after that.[35]

So chanted texts are twice-embodied powers; they are first the articulation of love expressed in the saint's baraka[36] through the form of words and his spiritual genius preserved as memorabilia within the group. Then they are the inspirational love that the munshidūn brings to the performance through their own personal devotion to the saint. They therefore see themselves as involved in a revelatory process, for it is through them that the relatedness to the presence can be expressed and engaged by the adepts. In a very real sense, they are not just chanting words; they are attesting to a reality that lies behind the words. The adepts accept the munshid as a guide if they *hear* the power of his words and recognize it.

As Ashḥab says, "The munshid can only sing to the level of his spiritual understanding, he cannot go beyond his own spiritual growth. It is like you can only describe what you have seen." Hence the munshidūn's words will carry the adepts along if they are sufficiently elevated in their own spiritual life. Thus, attestation is one fundamental requirement of their calling.

The second point to be made is the mundshidūn's reading of the mood of the dhikr. Their role is not mechanical; they do not sit down and choose a repertoire for the evening, as, for example, a choirmaster might choose songs with a particular theme for a church service. Ashḥab again:

The munshid starts his chanting under the guidance of the shaikh and the anāshīd of the dhikr. Then he will move into a call-response relationship with the brethren, by which is created a kind of umbrella of sound for the group. Once the sound is strong and envelops everyone, he can move in and out of the sound with his text, and the sound moves everything along. Then he reads the dhikr to move the dhikr beyond where it is by introducing a new theme and moving in a new direction. He just feels an opening in the dhikr and moves that way.

Here is testimony to a spiritual directive that is central to the performance. Only through it can the chanters have proper access to the imaginal dimension of the performance. The text is regarded as a composite of energies, with each text having its own power and potential. They "read" the emotional direction of the dhikr, sense a spiritual direction associated in their personal memory with a particular verse, and fit it to the current situation. Their role is thus to engage the spiritual resources of the texts in their imaginations and to plumb them for the one that will best respond to the opening they sense in the dhikr. This is not just a remembering of the text. It is a remembering of the power, or even of the potential for power. An example of how this power is conceived is related by this munshid from Meknes: "There was a man who had not been here for six years, but the muqaddam knew what his spiritual state was. During the laila, the shaikh began to sing, and the man immediately went into a trance. The spiritual power is there, and the muqaddam knows just what he needs."

Such validations lend authenticity to the munshidūn's contributions. Hence their performance, like that of any theatrical performer, is not just a remembering of words in a literal fashion and singing them; rather, they should perform with the emotional authority embodied in the words, because it arises out of their conviction that this phrase has the appropriate power to move the dhikr beyond where it is now. Such a process is a complex task involving their own spiritual memory, the power of the words, and their ability to engage creatively with their imagination. Successful preparation for chanting involves both learning the process sketched here, and preparing one's own spiritual state so as to read the dhikr appropriately. In fact, the munshidūn generally regard this as an attesting function; they are trying to get the dhikr participants to "see" what they have seen, to know what they have known, to share what they feel. Ashhab notes:

> When the munshid sings he is in the *ʿālam al-mithāl* or *ʿālam al-rūḥ*. One sees in those worlds something like paradise, only it is not paradise. It is an extraordinary environment, an environment of emotion and personal meaning . . . an environment of one's soul. It is a state into which the munshid arrives when he sings well. It is both ilhām and a gift from the heart of one's shaikh. A ḥadīth concerning dhikr says, "When one hears dhikr, all the angels gather around and enter into the place and transmit praises to God."

We can summarize how the model arises from this attesting function in the following fashion:

First, the munshid places his performance within another realm of consciousness—*like paradise, only it is not paradise*—whose language and sound patterns are not dominated by spoken or written expression. It is not a language of the tongue but of the heart. The performance is based upon a lyric script that is part mythic, part memory and part transcendent/paradisal.

Second, the munshid believes his/her performance has an emotional level to it that is both personal, yet is recognizably religious. The responsibility for the emotional power residing in the performance is seen by the munshid to come from a transcendent source (the founding shaikh, the Prophet, God), while the members of the order feel the munshid's emotion to be central to the good dhikr. His/her performance "attests" to the reality beyond.

Third, the visualizing capability of the munshid's imagination plays a key role in lifting the words that he sings from the level of ordinary discourse to the level of inspirational insight. For example, visualizing the names of God brings religious reality associated with those Names into the realm of discourse, providing a focus for enshrining that sacred existence in the performance. This is what Ibn al-ʿArabi regarded as (unveiling).

Fourth, the munshid strives to reach a certain kind of religious and emotional state that is fixed in his/her memory as a normative spiritual state. Under the influence of this enlightening experience from the past, the munshid moves the level of discourse into the realm of "Presence," that is, language is used that "strikes fire." Striking fire depends upon the spiritual tenor of the dhikr and the participants, that is, the munshid searches for the right words and lyrics in his repertoire so that the words can provide the excitement and insights for this particular emotional situation.

Fifth, every performance is new, because different lyrics are required to promote the sense of "Presence." The munshid cannot plan on what combination of texts will inspire the dhikr, so he/she must rely upon the munshid's processes outlined to explore the spiritual lyrics for that performance.

Sixth, the munshid must keep his/her spiritual perceptions in line with the leader of the dhikr or samaʿ . . . for it is above all the priorities sensed by the head that dictate what the spiritual agenda is during each session.

Seventh, the entire performance: sound, music, text, emotional states, visualizing abilities, choice of texts, selection of spiritual emphases, interaction with the members, relatedness to the shaikh of the order is an elaborate attestation. It is an imaginative attestion to a deep lyric scripting that encompasses all those present.

Al-ʿArabi held that from this comes a singular kind of knowledge.[37]

For the Moroccan munshidūn, heirs to the theosophy of Ibn al-ʿArabī, they have a noble calling that issues in the potential unveiling for the brethren. This imaginal force links them to absolute Islamic value to embody in lyrics and vision a message that will have salvic benefit. Said Ashḥab:

> There is a belief in the *rū'yā* [a vision of the shaikh], but that is not all. There is also belief in a hierarchy of appearances—sometimes a munshid can be meditating in the zāwiya, and the deceased shaikh will appear to him and give him songs. Some may also see the Prophet, who gives satisfaction to all people. It also has something to do with one's state: if someone is upset, he sees [a vision of] the shaikh.

Thus the munshidūn are more than just regular participants. Clearly the quality of the dhikr is dependent, in some sense, on how successful they are in "reading" the dhikr and moving it in the proper direction.[38] So presence is not just a mood or atmosphere that happens because the rituals are carried out in a regular manner. It is also The Reality, insofar as each is able to envision it through the method taught. Moreover, this presence is not experienced as divisible, one kind for the advanced adept, one kind for the beginner (that is, one kind for the tasting level, one kind for the insight). Rather, there is a collective sense of presence that is engaged, even if the theoretical understanding of it may vary.

There is another dimension to this visionary power: healing. Many of the rituals are designed to bring about a transformed person, either in terms of the inner human or of the physical or social world in which the petitioner lives. Consider the munshidūn of the Jahjouka, as reported by Schuyler, who are technicians of healing as well as musicians:

> If someone is sick or crazy, we bring him and we step on him. Or if a woman comes to us and asks for male children, we do the same. We say "In the name of God, O Messenger of God, O Prophet Moḥammed, O Sīdī Ḥmed Shikh, may your hand become our hand." Then we tread on her and we touch her with the drum and the ghaita. When we have finished the treading, we say another prayer. . . . Well, the Lord finishes the job, and the woman gives birth. Whether it's a boy or a girl, that's in the hands of God. And that's the baraka that has come to us with the authority of God and the Saint.[39]

We could, perhaps, analyze it this way. There are, in every religious group, icons of power. Not raw political power, but individuals who, at some charged moment, transcend their ordinariness and touch the depths that lie beyond human understanding. But what if it was not a person who had this power but it was really an iconic quality that shifted from person to person, according to a spiritual script? Then we comprehend the unity and validity of the system behind the dhikr. During the dhikr, the collectivity of brethren encounter religious *tawḥīd*, which is held to be the fundamental spiritual value of the great master Shādhilī and the basis of Muslim belief in God. This is the foundation of the ḥaḍra, and the munshid has the responsibility of leading the group in its encounter.

The munshidūn regard this as being in a state of affliction. While the dhikr is technically being directed by the muqaddam of the dhikr, within the bounds of the ritual itself, it is the munshid that carries the emotional texture. He or she delivers the mood, clothes the feeling. The real authority is in having an emotional sensitivity to spiritual movements. Most performers acknowledge the crucial notion of experience in allowing them to deliver a powerful performance. The munshid must learn to winnow the joys and sorrows of his or her life and universalize those into the heartaches and triumphs of a spiritual quest.

Nabīl added:

> There is no doubt that this is an environment of great spiritual power, because I am aware that Satan is behind me. He is just waiting for some opportunity to destroy. But I go into a munshid's trance at a certain point with which I am familiar, and then I need not be concerned about Satan, for I am protected by the spiritual circumstances. You must also be aware that in being a munshid, I am also part of a great family . . . A ṭāʾifa is a great family, with many powerful people. We all belong to a strong group, from the faqīr,

to the munshid, dhakrān, muqaddam, and shaikh. [We] will all help and protect each other.

Alternative Memories and the Munshid's Legacy

We have now surveyed the principal alternative "pasts" that influence the way in which the munshid works out his chanting; while there is no doubt that textual aspects predominate, it would be false to say that texts constitute the only memory that incites remembrance. Indeed, with the introduction to a visionary component in the performance, it is evident that any simple description of the mythic domain to which the munshid directs a yearning soul cannot be distilled to one descriptive metaphor. Despite the fact that the spiritual environment appears to be encountered as a stable template resident in the munshid's memory, we can see that across the spectrum of performers that template takes many forms and is described in different ways. Such a result contradicts our Western notion of abstraction, even within religious studies, where we find succor in descriptors like "the sacred." Still, regardless of our ability to comprehend a reality that seems to take so many rich forms, the munshid knows of this reality and embraces it in chanting. What we have to acknowledge is that, however it is conceived from the discourses we have here, it is powerful and real.

Interaction with this reality provides the basis for the munshid's religious experience in the zāwiya, but we must now add another dimension to his remembering—the music. No matter how well the munshid knows the texts, and no matter how powerful his experience of visionary elements, he will be unsuccessful if he cannot chant in a pleasing and knowledgeable manner. We turn now to this aspect of his remembering.

6

REMEMBERED SACRED SOUNDS

The Music of the Munshidūn

Music is regarded as a form of ritual procedure that must be performed correctly.

Herndon and McLeod[1]

Poetry . . . is the felt consubstantiality between language, music and myth.

Paul Friedrich[2]

The Memory of Religious Music in Morocco

When thinking about the issue of music in Islam, one is chastened by McAllester's comment after working among the Navaho:

> Perhaps the most basic question, and one of the hardest to approach, is *what music is conceived to be*. A striking example of my own cultural bias in this respect became apparent when I had the first section of my questionnaire translated into Navaho: There was no general word for "musical instrument" or even for "music." A "fact" in the Navaho universe is that music is not a general category of activity but has to be divided into specific aspects or kinds of music. I learned, moreover, that beating a drum to accompany oneself in song was not a matter of esthetic choice but a rigid requirement for a particular ceremony, and a discussion of musical instruments was not an esthetic discussion for the Navahos but was, by definition, a discussion of ceremonial esoterica.[3]

It is quite possible, then, that music in Islam, and in Sufism in particular, operates according to quite different rules than in the West. Or it may be that music is to be conceived as a coding system only within Sufism, not as a widely understood and acceptable framework of expression within Islam in general. This means, among other things, that we cannot comprehend Sufi music as we would comprehend other kinds of music, precisely because it *is* liturgical music. Undoubtedly the debate about its legitimacy is one that occupies Muslim sensitivities, but from our perspective, understanding it *as liturgical* fits fully with the notion of being part of a religiously encoded system. Nevertheless, we must examine the issue of music and Islam in order to put our comprehension of music in its proper perspective.

Ostensibly, the role that the munshid plays as a chanter immediately brings us into a conflict within Islam itself—the role of music in religious life. Despite the current negativity about music, the fact is that it was so popular during the Merinid period (1269–1465) that it was taught even in mosque schools; it reached the highest echelons when Muḥammad al-Ayrārī taught music at the university attached to the Qayrawān mosque toward the end of the thirteenth century.[4] Music and religion are really closer in Moroccan Islamic consciousness, then, than is generally acknowledged by ideologists. Despite the fact that Muslims are moved by music, a characteristic noted by both Islamic and Western writers,[5] still the image persists that music is frowned upon in Islam and that Muslims are generally opposed to any form of it. The fact is that religious music, that is, music that officially serves a distinctly religious purpose, assumes a complicated position in Moroccan culture. As we shall see, its origin is rooted in times and places no longer ascertainable. This gives it a hidden quality that does not necessarily justify the "mystical" label, but the fact that religious music has survived in a tradition that was careful to reject non-Islamic forms as jāhiliyya certainly means it has more than a little staying power. Then again, despite its current religious character, religious music has been and continues to be impacted upon by cultural forces not always sacred in intent: everything from political Islamism to marketplace pressures is evident in the religious music of Morocco today.[6] Nor is it possible to distinguish the purely religious piece from its close secular associate: they sit together in collective awareness, and only the occasion or setting may indicate the directed intent. Indeed, the same words may occur in two different settings, inspiring secular responses in one and leading others into ecstasy. This is one reason why some Sufi music can apparently make the transition to everyday listening pleasure without being out of place.

Were one to listen to the advocates of Islamist doctrine, one would think all forms of traditional Islamic music were slowly dying, gradually being eradicated as "true" Islam expels it. Either that, or Moroccan ears are giving way to the onslaught of Western music. Before I went to Morocco, I was half convinced that I would find traditional religious music on the wane; although totally unscientific as it was, my early experience there seemed to confirm this, as I rode in taxis whose radios were set to some kind of Western music. But I thought differently after several train rides. Thus when I visited the Rabat train station, the familiar and obvious strains of Andalusian song wafted over the public address system, followed by the *Bourda* chanted by a popular group. Or, when riding in a local bus bound for another part of the country, munshidūn could be heard for hours over the bus system. I suppose I should have realized earlier the truth of the matter: Taxis deliberately play Western music for Westerners in order to attract their business, while services to the Moroccan public are more likely to reflect the common taste.

Hence Islamic tradition in Morocco is very much steeped in musical memory, and that memory carries its own significant freight. No account of the Sufism in Morocco is complete without an attempt to delineate a theoretical basis for these facts, and no account of the quality of Islamic life in Morocco is understandable without it.

Music as a Liturgical Event
Music and the Sufi Spiritual State

It would seem that the role of music in shaping any understanding of the spiritual realm would differ from that of text. In some groups, the absence of certain kinds of music or the absence of musical instruments requires the spiritual to be triggered through a sung or recited text alone. Different ṭarīqas constitute access to this reality differently, some using musical phraseology as an integral unit in the spiritual state, others imbuing certain words themselves with spiritually powerful meaning. Some groups, such as the Tijāniyya, have largely abandoned music as a means to engage the divine, but they retain melodic oral recitation in dhikr. Limiting music so would not be possible for many other Sufi groups, such as the Ginawa, where the entire healing dimension functions in and through a musical idiom.

We have to conclude then, that the spiritual domain must include the assumptions about negative or positive attitudes toward music within each group. For some, there is integration between musical structure and text, so that the relative importance of one or the other is part of the metacoding system. One finds this when a visiting member from the same ṭarīqa may find it difficult to openly participate because "the rhythm is somewhat different."

Even in cases where there are restraining views toward music, but not disapproval, attitudes to music are a key ingredient in the access to spiritual realities. Sufis generally distinguish their music from the ālah by insisting that the proper word to define their musical form is *samāʿ*, not just "music," not "singing," not "folk" music, and not "entertainment" music. Moreover the kind of listening involved is the same as that in hearing God's word, as opposed to music with a secular focus. Thus samāʿ is not really music in the conventional use of the term, according to Sufis, even if it is music in the generic sense. As Aydoun notes, drawing on the Sufi exponent al-Qushayrī, there are really three types of listeners to samāʿ: those who only pretend to "hear" during the moment of samāʿ, those who truly hear in a mystical state (*bi-ḥāl*), and those who wait upon God (*bi-Allāh*) by means of the samāʿ.[7] The Morocco material, then, would seem to indicate that the negative attitudes toward music in Islam apparently cannot undercut its power within the Sufi situation; this is because samāʿ is a critical element in Moroccan spiritual life.

Moreover, to claim that it is all music, even if spiritual in intention, guarantees controversy. It follows that the precise nature of sacred music is difficult to portray. It is not just the long-standing antipathy to music of all kinds within Islamic cultural tradition. As a result of Islamism and conservative religious policies, one would think that music would be retreating. It is not. So the real quandary is this: What is it that makes religious music thrive when the dominant religious ideology of Islam tends to condemn all its forms?

This is not a new problem, of course, since the early ḥadīth graphically betray more than a gentle antagonism: "Music is fornication's magic," Muḥammad is reported to have said.[8] Islamism adopts similar points of view. If some form of Islamism is increasingly representing Muslim views, it follows that Sufi musical forms should be retreating. Yet, by most measurements, religious music, including Sufi music, is expanding its circle. Apart from the public places mentioned above, it is now heard on the radio and television and through cassettes around the world. You might even say that adopting Sufi music is a deliberate attempt to rebuff the conservative ideology. Moreover, the Internet has brought the sacred concert into the hearts and lives of far more Muslims than ever attended a Sufi samāʿ. Sufi music is not drying up. How can these contradictions be measured?

Scholars have developed various strategies or explanations. Some look to the supposed origins of music in order to explain the problematic. Orientalists sometimes lay the contempt for music at the feet of the Prophet and his propensity for writing, that is, to the Prophet's favoring of literary institutions over oral. With the dominance of the Qurʾān in the aural life of Muslims, and the emphasis on the human voice in the daily devotions, this is hard to accept. Moreover, this is regarded as a ridiculous claim by most Muslims.

One might root the musical resistance in the ethnicity of Islam's founding peoples, the Arabs, as Farmer seems to claim.[9] This allows one to hold that the ethnic character of the people, their "folk nature," so to speak, carries the musical imprimatur, and those who do not share that heritage may resist what appears to be non-Islamic elements from being reified into Islam. If Islam came to purify Arabs, it did so at the expense of the jāhiliyya, with its free-wheeling embrace of folk expression, including music and poetry, but the continuous use of musical phrasings within Islam indicates that what was embraced and modified for Islamic rituals was the result of some negotiation within various groups and tendencies in developing Islam.

For many, music is a product of the interaction between sonal qualities implicit in Arabic cultural preferences, particularly the Arabic language.[10] Music is but one expression of this implicit musicality. Thus scholars from Marcais to Pellat to Guettat affirm that music itself arose out of the pre-Islamic Arabic rhyming system, itself derived from the interaction of the duality of consonants and vowels. As Guettat points out:

> A better proof for us [of the origin of music] is given by the Arabs of the jāhiliyya, who invented the rhyme founded on a profound sense of rhythm, which, in turn, ruled the whole metrical system of poetry, seen as "the Arab prosody." As Massignon said, "Music preceded language and language succeeded it, emerging from silence."

Similarly, Guettat quotes with approval Pellat's declaration:

> An Arab (word's) root, according to W. Marcais, is therefore a lyre to which one does not touch a cord without making vibrate all the others, and each word, in addition to its own resonance, awakens secret harmonies of related words. Beyond the limits of (the Arab's) direct sense, there arises in the profundities of the soul a whole procession of sentiments and images.[11]

The assumption behind this view is, then, that the oral structure of the Arabic language was informed by a musical sense, and that that musical sense was passed on to all peoples who spoke Arabic, including those who revered the Holy Writ itself.

Yet, holding that the Arabic tonal system has a transcendent meaning has important ramifications for Islam: It undercuts the specifically Islamic quality that Muslims affirm to be at the heart of their musical repertoire, replacing it with an ethnic one. Theologically Muslims have difficulty accepting such a notion, since Islam's claims are deemed far more fundamental than the sense of tribal or ethnic identity, and are held to be more basic than the truths expressed in even the language of the Qur'ān. In addition, music as found in Morocco today only indifferently relates to text, a fact that would seem to indicate the separateness of language and music. For example, everyone agrees that Arabic as expressed in the Qur'ān and presumably spoken by the first Arab immigrants to the Maghrib was not sung to tunes that fit with the tonal pattern, a factor that would seem to militate against the notion that language arose out of musical forms, and certainly would vitiate the idea that current music is but a development of Arabic rhyming systems. It could be argued that music is rather a result of Islam, that is, that it is expressive of basic Islamic values. A species of this argument is that of al-Faruqi, who holds that music is a branch of the artistic expression of Islam, that is, that it developed out of rhymed prose forms of expression (*sajʿ*), which themselves were informed by the Islamic doctrine of *tawḥīd*.[12] Thus music is a derivative, yet vigorous form of the Islamic arabesque aesthetic.

This is an attractive idea that maintains the Islamic-ness of music in any spiritual evaluation. It acknowledges the transforming power of Islam, and particularly its ability to provide a larger cultural and aesthetic framework within which local and even folk elements can find a place. Monts has pointed out how Islam has had a similar impact on another musical tradition in Africa, that of Sierra Leone. There the music of the secret societies has slowly been transformed by the introduction of Islam.[13] While it cannot be true to say that Islam changes everything, the presence of Islam does provide a transcultural reference point that gives the local music a more universal panache. So obviously Islam does have an impact within the musical environment.

Still, while no one who has listened to the cantillations of the Qur'ān in the hushed environments of a crowded mosque will ever doubt the powerful emotions the vocalized performance conveys, it does seem quite a stretch to hold that all music in Muslim countries derives from this source. In the Sufi case alone, we know this does not fit, since there has been cross-pollenization from popular music, that is, from sources hardly religious, let alone Islamic. This fact alone would render Monts's idea limited to Qurʾānic-type music. Moreover, given the negative impressions of music that one encounters within Islam, it is difficult to see how tawḥīd can be said to be expressed in it, since tawḥīd is often held to be a fundamental religious value in Islamic culture, leaving one to explain how Muslims could express antipathy to something so essential to Islamic awareness. Finally, the Sufi groups that utilize music do not regard it as a utilitarian matter. They believe music provides a special kind of communication medium. They hold it is just as much subject to sacred inspiration as are words. They reject any assertion that makes music derivative in communicating God's praises.[14]

Consequently, those who seek to define the musical dimensions of Sufi realities with reference to music's origins, whether religious or not, cannot base their understanding solely on origins ideology. To be sure, the primacy of music in conveying religious value is evident, but the roots of that primacy does not seem to be either Arabic itself or official Islam. Something broader in the religious repertoire is operative.

The Issue of Influences on Sufi Music

Al-Jirārī, in an interview in 1993, identified several influences on Sufi music. First, he insisted that inshād holds a special place within the Moroccan musical corpus, arguing that it functions as an equivalent in Moroccan culture to other people's popular music and song. Since such music and song are a living tradition within a realm of popular music, many of the usual influences applying to popular songs also apply to inshād. He identified the following influences as crucial in understanding the development of inshād: the qaṣīda of al-Jazūlī; the classical qaṣīda-influenced music, such as mawwāl; the Andalusian heritage, including āla; modern songs from the "orient," that is, music deriving from popular modern singers like Umm Kulthūm of Egypt; and popular and contemporary tunes or themes deriving from children's dance or work songs. It should be noted that each rests upon a remembered past. Let us consider each of these.

Qaṣīda al-Jazūlī.   Current Moroccan Sufi music constitutes a different rhythm than that supported by the classical qaṣīda; nevertheless, the classical qaṣīda still provides the bedrock out of which the musical tradition comes. The foundation for this music is the songs developed by Shaikh al-Jazūlī (d. 1465?), whose early mission utilized the qaṣīda form and modified it to the language of Morocco. At the same time he wed it to popular songs to ease the learning. He had been a follower of al-Shādhilī (d. 1258), who himself had left no writings but was a well-recognized teacher. That teaching was embodied in zāwiyas by al-Jazūlī, particularly in the Sous in southern Morocco, and when he died, he was buried there, only to be disinterred by the

Saadian sultan fighting a war against Portugal and transported to Marrakech as a way of uniting Moroccans against the foreigners.[15] Al-Jazūlī's odes were composed to encourage the participation of the common folk in his orders, and they constitute one of the principal sources for the ʿAissawiyya. His book *Dalāʾil al-khayrāt wa-shawāriq al-anwār fī dhikr al-ṣalāt ʿala al-nabī al-mukhtār* is full of material used by the Sufis: prayers and litanies for the Prophet, a description of his tomb, the ninety-nine names of Allah, qaṣāʾid to the Prophet and Fāṭima, and so on,[16] who, he insists, are his ancestors through Shaikh al-Kamal, Moḥamed bin ʿIsa al-Mukhtārī (d. 1525 or 1526). Hence the musical tradition of Moroccan Sufism returns to the founder of the mystical way for its validity, and connects itself with the Prophet and his family.

Classical Qaṣīda-Influenced Music

We have considered the qaṣīda as text at some length in chapter 4. With regard to the musical aspect of qaṣīda, Jirārī held that since the mawwāl are mostly in classical Arabic, and the music fits improperly with the text, what really happens in performance is that the text is subservient to the rhythm conveying the textual message. This should be treated with some reservation, though, because, as Bürgel has argued, the repetitive element in Arabic literature signals a structure of abiding importance for understanding:

> Repetitive structures in Arabic literature are more than mere display of formal devices. They reflect what we might call ontological structures, structures perceived in the universe, in human society, in the sequence of generations and in one's own individual fate.[17]

Thus the *rubāʿiyyah* (s. *rubāʿi*) or quatrains may be lengthened or shortened musically, depending upon the desire for an enhanced emphasis on the deeper message the munshid is trying to connect to, in this case to repetition of some fundamental image. The munshid also respects what we might call musical flow, and a good munshid will try to develop a *sinād*, a profound type of chant with elaborate vocal stylings and emphasizing graceful and highly nuanced singing. The focus then will be to utilize the music to add to the profundity of the text, through the expert use of vocal stylings. In addition, a wide variety of tonal changes can be introduced by a good chanter who elucidates the textual material. The chief alternative to this conception is the *ṭawīl*, which respects the form and language of the text in its rhythm. In short, there are several elements involved in expression of classical texts, not just the accurate repetition of the words.

The Memory of Andalusia

Arab Popular and Secular Music.   There was apparently little known of Arabic music in Morocco before the development of the so-called Andalusian tradition.[18] As indicated above, with the modernizing tendencies during Ziryāb's time, a new form was constructed that came to be known as *al-āla*, a form that has defined Andalusian music ever since. In addition, two other quasi-classical forms of music are known in Morocco, the *malḥūn* and the *gharnaṭī*. As we have seen, the ālah tradition is made up of *nūbat*. These nūbat were at one time connected to the time of day, with a different kind of nūba for each hour. Now, however, there are only four full nūbat; together with seven partial nūbat, these make up the current repertoire. Each nūba involves a long, complicated performance; a full nūba may last as long as seven hours and thus must be performed over a period of several days. Indeed, most scholars argue that the genre's internal construction of five distinctive *mīzān* or parts of various lengths means that different sections of the nūbat should be performed at different times during the day. Each section has its own *īqāʿāt*, which requires that the sections be performed in sequence so there is a progression from *basīṭ* (6/4), *qāʾim wa nisf* (8/4), *draj* (4/4), to *bṭāyḥi* (4/8) and *quddām* (6/8).

Each mīzān has introductory instrumental preludes followed by a collection of songs (*ṣināʿa*); usually there are three or four ṣināʿa to a mīzān, but some munshidūn said they have heard upward of twenty during festivals, and it usually has something to do with the time of day and the expectations of the listeners.

The musical genre in these performances is the *muwashshaḥ*. The muwashshaḥāt are characterized by vocal music involving either a single voice and a chorus or, more rarely, just a single voice. A small group of instruments also accompanies the vocal form. The rhythmic pattern is repeated throughout the song, vocalized by the soloist or the chorus, and the whole is broken by a recurring refrain. The musical form of the muwashshaḥāt has three basic sections, here described by al-Faruqi:

> The first of these is the *dawr* or *badaniyyah* (from "body"). This is a setting to music of the opening *juzʾ* or strophe. Most often this initial dawr is accompaniment for only one stand-alone segment, or bayt, of poetry. Or perhaps it carries only the first hemistich of that line. This dawr is repeated to accompany the second poetic bayt or the second hemistich. The second section of the muwashshaḥ is called the *khānah* (inn, or square of a chessboard) or *silsilah* (chain, or series). This is either a completely new musical presentation or has new elements at its outset and then a return near the end of the dawr to a musical refrain previously presented. There is new poetry for the khānah, but this section may contain poetic as well as musical repetitions. The third section is called *qaflah* (key, or closing), *rujʿā* (return), or *ghiṭoʾ* (cover). It presents new poetic material set to a repeat of the musical elements of the dawr. Occasionally a literal poetic, as well as musical, repetition of the dawr replaces the qaflah. This succession of three sections can begin again with a new juzʾ of poetry, the end of the performance determined more by the inspiration and inclination of the performers than by the actual number of strophes or lines in the poem.[19]

Muwashshaḥ is a distinctive invention of Spanish Islam, even though there were earlier writers of the stanza poem, such as Bashshar (d. 783) in the East.[20] Scholars say that the muwashshaḥ tradition dates from the time of the great musician Ziryāb, even though the earliest mention of the term muwashshaḥ was by al-Kindī (796–874).[21] One such scholar is Ben Cherīfa of Muḥammad V University. Here is his statement during an interview:

> There is also some Arabic influence in the patrimony of the early musical form. There was an Arab form that was found in Andalusia, which had its origin in the East in the singer Ziryāb. The caliph invited him to Andalusia, and he constructed a new school of music in Córdoba. He incorporated both Andalusian and Arab music into another form. The classical Arabic text could not be sung to this music, so another textual form had to be developed. This is called muwashshaḥāt. This form became a fully developed musical and literary form. When Andalus was lost, then the leading poets, savants, and Sufis came here. This meant that Andalusian tradition was transferred to Morocco. At the same time, it met the cultural forms of African and Berber, and out of this interaction came another mélange of musical traditions.

Muddyman also held that the form derived from Ziryāb at the court in Córdoba, where he originally developed it.[22] But this view is not universally accepted. For example, others say it was a local poet and singer born at Cabra, near Córdoba, who invented the form.[23] Moreover, we have to deal with the fact that North Africans also had an impact at the court in Córdoba, so it is conceivable that the impetus for change derived not only from Ziryāb's dream (see below p. 133) but also from the fact that Andalusian Arabic already did not fit the patterns of the East, especially those whose first language was Berber. In effect, the sharp distinction between Morocco and Andalus culture may exist more in theory than in fact.

Regardless of the circumstances of invention, the form became so popular and spread so widely that the form of music became known as the Andalusian muwashshaḥāt. The zenith of its perfection is usually dated to ʿUbāda ibn Māʾ al-Samāʾ (d. 1028 or 1030), who was the first to have his poetic work saved in written form and thus to have it survive to today. From Córdoba it was exported back to the East, where it became increasingly popular when linked to classical Arabic verse.

D'Erlanger identified seven types of muwashshaḥāt; but the most predominant is that which he names *tawshīḥ simple* or *tawshīḥ muʿlūf*.[24] Yet it is clear that the relationship between the text and the music is not a simple one. Haxen argues for a close interrelationship between the text and music, quoting Reese's statement: "In penetrating to the essence of the troubadour and trouvere songs, it is necessary, as Gennrich has shown, for musicology and philology to make a joint approach. Music and text are here one entity, and a full understanding of either form is impossible without a comprehension of the others."[25]

That is, the text may encompass several different themes, but the music will not alter accordingly. One can hear poetry sung in muwashshaḥāt that is related to any of these great themes: *madīḥ* (panegyric), *ḥubb* (love), *waṣf* (description of nature), *fakhr* (boasting/pride), *hijāᶜ* (satire), *ḥamās* (inspiring to courage), and *rithāʾ* (lamentation for the dead). Clearly some of these hark back to the earliest form of qaṣīda in pre-Islamic Arabia. Yet, there will be no change in the way the muwashshaḥāt are performed for these different themes, and it is quite possible that the same form may be used for two different themes. Hence it is not apparent that the music drives the text, or supports it with a particular mood.

Another form of musically adapted poetry, called *barwal* by the munshidūn;[26] it is near to the qaṣīda form, in zajal language, but its rhythms are near to the draj of the Moroccan music. Apparently no one now knows who the brāwīl writers were or what their goals were, but one can still hear their music today. The music appears to be a further extension of the Andalusian form, taking on a Moroccan hue.

In performance, the muwashshaḥāt contain words and phrases that are not central to the theme of the poem and, indeed, may have no meaning whatsoever. Terms such as *yā Ghānim* or *lalalalli* have no meaning, yet they may be repeated often throughout a performance and may be used to introduce the song. Phrases like *yā hilālan* (Oh new moon) can recur throughout the performance and can be used to establish a consolidating theme of love, even if the major theme is something else, such as rithāᶜ. Within one performance, then, the singer of muwashshaḥāt may be making allusions to another level of meaning even while voicing ideas related to a different abstract concept. Such layering gives an oceanic or boundless quality to the performance. The presence of such words has led Schneider to argue that these phrases function as magical intrusions, designed to charge the atmosphere, and the listener, with their power. The munshidūn encountered in Morocco during this research, however, indicated that these were often stock phases generated within Sufi circles that triggered other levels of awareness and that, even if used in secular circumstances by professional, non-Sufi singers, they still pointed to another level of meaning in the performance. The result is that regardless of the principal theme of the words, the song was to open the listener to this other dimension. They were indicators or triggers alerting the listener to listen for other meanings and hidden connections, not to take the words and phrases themselves as literally significant. In fact, we know this kind of disjunction between words and meaning was well recognized in Arabic literary studies. Ibn Khaldūn notes, "Poetry and prose work with words, and not with ideas. Ideas are secondary to the [words]. The [words] are basic."[27]

Musically, then, the tune is there to present the text within a pleasing, formal structure, not so the listener will be enamored with the music as such, nor even of the text per se, but will become attuned to the text that gives meaning to the text itself, that is, the religious scripting that gives meaning to the whole piece. Thus the music is but an outward frame for the text, which is then to be understood to point to deeper structures of more powerful and relevant meaning. This is the coding system that exists in Sufi music, which justifies the munshidūn's activities.

This does pose a problem for the analysis of the relationship between the text and the music, for this means that neither can be taken as the ultimate indicator of meaning in and of itself. This is of great significance to the munshid, for this fact alone suggests meaning only can be determined in performance; just reading a text does not deliver its true message. Performance is necessary for the unleashing of the potential in the words to convey the level of meaning the munshid wants to articulate.

When Islam was expelled from Andalusia by the Christian conquerors, the strongest schools of music were reestablished in North Africa, with the school of Valencia moving to Fez and that of Granada to Tetouan and Chaouen.[28] The school at Fez has continued the Andalusian tradition to this day. Its Andalusian orchestra is still the pride of Fezzians. But local orchestras in Tangier and Meknes are just as popular to their supporters. Generally the orchestras are comprised of rabāb (fiddle), oud (lute), kamenjah (larger violin played vertically on the knee), qānūn (zither), darabouka (goblet drum), and tarʿīja (tambourine). Flutes may be used on occasion, but the nāi is not as important for Andalusian music as it is for Turkish or Persian music. Wind instruments like the ghiṭāʾ (oboe) can be found in some Sufi circles in Morocco, such as among the Ḥamadsha.[29]

Malḥūn and Gharnāṭī Music of Morocco.   Ben Cherīfa mentioned the mélange of music that came with the blending of cultures in Morocco, and certainly one of the results of the interaction in Morocco has been the growth of malḥūn music. This music is really sung poetry, but it is not as "classical" as Andalusian music, and as is noted in chapter 5 with regard to the poetry, the music, though directly related to Andalusian forms, is much more exuberant and diverse. The music is shaped by the predominance of a string and percussion mix: kamenjah, swisen, hadhouj, and oud all carry a heavy load of musical nuance, while the tarʿīja, darabouka, and handqa (small brass cymbals) maintain the beat structure. The dynamic interaction of these two kinds of sounds provides a musical framework for the text.

Malḥūn musical performance has two distinctive styles or sections; each piece follows the same pattern. The first is a *taqsīm* (overture), which sets the mode for the coming piece. It is usually a violin or oud that plays the taqsīm. Following this introductory styling, the qaṣīda (poetic rendition) is sung by a soloist and a choral group. The qaṣīda segment is not sung as a literal poem from start to finish, but rather is divided into three sections: *al-aqsām* (solo verses), *al-ḥarba* (refrain by chorus), and finally *al-dridka* (an increasingly fast choral segment announcing the end of the entire suite).

Malḥūn performance allows far greater flexibility in text than Andalusian music. Indeed, texts can be folk stories set in poetic form, or they can be phrases that no one understands. In some Sufi settings a large admixture of mystical and unknown language can find its way into the performance, as was obvious in the ʿAissawiyya case in Meknes. The important element is the rhythm, which must deliver a certain kind of enthusiasm and joie de vivre, and provide for the possibility of raising the adept's spirits toward a trance experience. This means, then, that text is not as authoritative as it is in Andalusian cases, and the music is partially responsible for raising the participant's expectations to exhilaration. Moreover, the devotees appear to feed off the ecstasy voiced by the munshid, and believe themselves to be touched by the spiritual enthusiasm they hear coming through his experience.

Hence the munshidūn are not just delivering a solid performance, they are also a cipher for the amount of religious enthusiasm felt by the group, a measure, if you will, of the potential for entering the other dimension through this expressive means. This understanding is predominant among Sufi groups because the quality of the spiritual experience cannot depend upon the words. The words as text may not make sense, so they do not necessarily deliver any particular message in and of themselves. It is the relationship to religious scripting, the higher meaning of the total performance, that delivers the spiritual insight.

Gharnāṭī is not a word used everywhere in Morocco. It can be heard in Rabat, the capital, and in Oudja, near the Algerian border. The word gharnāṭī derives from the area around Granada, where the term nūba was designated as gharnāṭī, indicating the same suite of music others call āla.[30] According to Muddyman, there are two differences. The first is in the instruments used, for gharnāṭī usually includes plucked instuments, along with bowed and percussion. Hence one can hear banjos, mandolins, even kwitras (a type of lute) in gharnāṭī performance. The second is in the order in which one hears the various rhythms. For example, a typical suite begins with *msaddar* (4/4), followed by *draj* and *btāyḥi* in reverse to what is normal (that is, btāyḥi, 4/8 before draj 6/8), then a totally different rhythm, *inṣirāf* (5/8), then *makhlaṣ* (6/8).[31] Not only is there a different ordering of rhythms, but fewer rhythms are found in gharnāṭī. Thus, while one might attribute these differences to local flavor, they do constitute distinctive musical stylings.

All these facts indicate that Sufi music has a very dense root. Guettat contends that the Andalusian school was built upon three essential "facts": first, the importance of mystical conceptions in Andalusian music; second, the chant called *nūba;* and third, the predominance of musical rhythm over the poetic rhythm.

As to Guettat's first contention, his thesis can be summarized in this way: The key concept among Western Arabs was the *ṭabʾ*, in contrast to the notion of *maqām* in the East. *Ṭabʾ* (pl. *ṭubūʾ*) is far broader in scope than the Eastern word, for it encompasses in its meaning not only modal levels but also a coherent system underlying Andalusian music in all its various forms. Ṭabʾ encompasses certain characteristics that can be co-related to psychophysical realities in that they trigger awarenesses about both beings and things in general, held together in a pattern like a symbolic tree called *shajarāt al-ṭubūʾ*. In short, Guettat holds that ṭabʾ brings to consciousness a cohesive cognitive system of abstract realities, much like our notion of religious scripting.

The system described by Guettat was founded upon the work of the *Ikhwān al-Ṣafāʾ*, the thinkers at the end of the tenth century who wrote about music based upon a school he identifies as the ʿUdists, whose sonal patterns have certain affinities to the Berber language. The system is also based upon the same harmonic principles as the Pythagorean system.

The system differs fundamentally from that espoused in Eastern Arab territories.[32] While Guettat admits that much of his theory is based on imperfect sources and therefore must remain hypothetical, he nevertheless holds that it explains the facts the best.

Guettat's second basic contention progresses from these ideas. The *nūba* was integrated into this system. As a name given originally to the scenarios at court for competitions between poets, singers, and so on, the nūba came to define a psychological reality:

> Like ṭabʾ, the nūba of the poetic texts evoked a sentiment, a particular state of the soul; and according to a formal rule, it should be executed at a particular moment determined during the day. Each ṭabʾ with its nūba possesses a particular effect and also an atmosphere and a determining moment during the day. Then, in a twenty-four-hour cycle, each nūba possesses a [specific], propitious moment. . . . If this "specific" interest began to change beginning in the eleventh century, according to the writings of Ibn Ḥazm (994–1064), it continues no less vibrant today, especially in the music or nūba of the religious orders, for which musical art constitutes a way of leaving the automatic mental world, liberating [one from] anguished emotions and obsessing preoccupations.[33]

The consequences of Guettat's ideas are of the first order for our thesis. For, if he is correct, his ideas will go a long way toward explaining how Sufi music is able to survive and grow despite the interdiction of Islamic conservativism and Islamism. Indeed, like the importance of dhikr rituals, this form of music is integral to the cognitive understanding of reality among the people within Western areas of Islam. It has been traditionally *the* way that Islam was construed. Moreover, it fortifies the significance of the mystical point of view, for it says that the grounding of all knowledge is in these unseen but felt patterns in human consciousness. Accordingly, it is because this mythic domain is held to be eminently knowable to human awareness that Sufis are convinced of the veracity of their system.

The final category supporting Guettat's ideas of the distinctiveness of Andalusian artistry relates to a story about Ziryāb. According to this story, as related by Ibn Khaldūn, Ziryāb awoke from a dream, got out of bed, and asked both his favorite disciples to bring their lutes. He asked them to repeat the tune with which he had been inspired during his dream, playing it until they knew it. Then he returned to bed, where he composed the words that went with the music. Thus was melody, formulated on the basis of ṭabʾ, held to be independent of text, allowing the musical imagination to shape tunes to which poetic verse had to conform. This later fact allowed for the growth of muwashshaḥāt and zajal.[34]

Al-Jirārī adds another dimension to the issue. People appreciate zajal, he maintains, because they understand the texts, in contradiction to the classical texts. At the same time there is another conceptual feature: the zajal is educative because the people comprehend its message and relate directly to its popular form.

It can be seen, therefore, that the relationship between musical form and mystical expression is essential. In 1995 I recorded the entire performance of Andalusian Sufi meditations performed during Ramadan. The munshidūn sang the entire corpus of poems by Ibn al-Fāriḍ entitled *Diwān Ibn al-Fāriḍ*.[35] Thus the great poet forms a living link with the literary traditions of the past through contemporary performance.

If we then turn to the individual performances by the munshid that one can hear within the dhikr and samāʿ, a different pattern emerges. Rather than chanting all of Ibn al-Fāriḍ, we find one line serves as the basis for the whole performance and the meditations branching out from there, all still utilizing the same *baḥr* and *wazn*. A published expression of this integrating of disparate sources is found in Abū al-Laṭīf Muḥammad bin Manṣoura's *al-Kuwakba al-Yusefiyya*[36] (lit., "the Stars of Yusef," a reference to Surah al-Yusef, Qurʾān 27). This text is a compendium of meditations often utilized by the Andalusian-based munshidūn in performance, and it demonstrates the fundamental role that the Andalusian musical form plays in the whole expression. As we can see from the following, meditations from Ibn al-Fāriḍ provide the basis for a process of weaving a musical tapestry. The process begins by citing a single theme, followed by Sufi meditations, which shape the background for Ibn al-Fāriḍ.

It is also important to note that the performance incorporates the meditation (in classical Arabic) followed by meditations in draj form (in Moroccan Arabic), then selections from several Moroccan shaikhs' writings, and, finally, popular Sufi phrases. To take one segment (that is, one "star") of Abū al-Laṭīf's work, his second, we find multiple structures informing the performance. Note that there are eight segments to the following textual representation of the second star, heard in concert during the Ḥarrāqiyya dhikr; and in the printed text it reads:

I. Meditation in Nūba Gharība al-Ḥusain (based on words from Ibn al-Fāriḍ)

If I plead to perceive you as Truth [reality]
Permit me, and do not give "no" in answer.[37]

II. Inshād describing the sand by Shaikh ʿAbd al-Ghany al-Nābulsy

Yā, signified of all signifiers, By everyone he was "the entertainer"
In every scenario, by You, my eyes were entertained.

III. A small "veiling" by ʿUmar Ibn al-Fāriḍ

Whenever you are far away from me
Every pleasant urge is activated
Like the melody of the guitar and the plodding flute
Blend together in harmony.

IV. Description of sand by Muḥammad al-Ḥarrāq

My eyes were not without sight,
My love rose up endlessly
It would all be over, If someone else took my place.
I returned home happy, My heart received his desires.
Perceiving, after a long search, the hungry love.

Barwal by the same author:

Fortunate are those who / Could see the mystery revealed.
Happy are those who / Could find all justifications
in [nearby] dwellings
To chant a song for the lover, / And intoxicate people
with love.
He whoever won his lover, / Would dwell
in the Present radiance, [so that for]
All the tenderness in the world, / Scarcely a glimpse would be its
    equivalent.
Whoever won his lover, (would be) / Healed instantly
from every illness.
His heart would shine like the sun and the moon,
And good news would fill his time
Whoever gained thoughts of love and honesty,
Light would encompass his life.

V. A reflection by *Shaikh Sīdī Ḥajj Aḥmad ibn ʿAshīr al-Ḥaddād*

Rain fell, watering my garden
with blossoms and leaves, Yā Baba
Yā, Everything around about me, filled me with self-assurance and
    elevated me in dignity, Yā Baba
Time moved me and my tongue praised Allāh, Yā Baba.

VI. Short rendition by Ibn al-Fāriḍ

Musing about my youth, flattering me with your beauty,
Your land, even though your neighbour, yet barren and dry.
My eyes saw no sleep, staring at you in my daydreams.

But in a night filled with the Truth, in a place wherein dwells blasphemy
Surrounded by those who loved you,
Who could ever think of sleep?

"A Veiling"

I roamed about, and nobody was there save you
And even my heart's love was shining in the galaxy above.
Searching for your purity deep within my heart
My mountains rose higher up, fearing the Highest.
My secret was no more a secret to all those like me
And I became "Moses" of my era
For death lived in my life, and my life lived in death.

VII. A meditation by Shaikh al-Ḥarrāq

The light of my lover, I would never doubt . . .
I watched it close to me.
Nothing would keep my heart away from the light
It was not there but it was everything to me
If ever you saw the light of my love,
You would never want to wake from your dream.

VIII. Short selection by Ibn al-Fāriḍ

To rule over the people, lest the cloistered be enslaved
From loneliness; only blasphemy could I see.
Ah Brother!! You who condemned me because of my kindness,
I was lost on my path and my senses and thoughts were torn asunder
I would not covet your brotherhood;
All the beauty that prevailed, you would not be able to comprehend.
"An eye for an eye"; but, then, thought I—I should forgive myself!

We are now in a position to note some crucial features of this material. We will look
closely at four: the writers, the integration of Andalusian forms, an analysis of the last-
letter rhyming system, and the integration structure of the lines from each writer.

We begin with the various writers as they are presented during the "star"; note
the dominance of Ibn al-Fāriḍ.[38]

Ibn al-Fāriḍ (modified poem) in Nūba Gharība al-Ḥusain, Moroccan musical styling associated with Sufis

Shaikh ʿAbd al-Ghany al-Nābulsy, famous Eastern mystic and writer
Ibn al-Fāriḍ, Egyptian poet and mystic
Shaikh Muḥammad al-Ḥarrāq, Moroccan saint, of the Darqāwiyya al-
  Ḥarrāqiyya

Shaikh Aḥmad ibn ʿAshīr al-Ḥaddād, Moroccan saint
Ibn al-Fāriḍ
Shaikh al-Ḥarrāq
Ibn al-Fāriḍ

The second structural element is the integration of Andalusian musical forms; there are two principal nubāt:

Gharība-Ḥusaīn(ḥsīn), principal mode in Morocco
Ramal, an integrative mode in Morocco

The third structural element is prosodic meter. Here one hears *basīṭ* for the first phase of the Moroccan nūba, then brāwīl, that is, verses of unequal length, chanted to Andalusian tunes. Then follows *khafīf,* which is a rhythmic mode, then muwashshaḥ, expressed as a fairly significant rhymed chant, then khafīf again, this time as the key rhythmic mode. Then comes *taghtiya,* literally a "covering" (translated above as veiling), a kind of postlude after a significant mawwāl, and before the final phase.

We then move to *mutadarīk,* which is a poem continuing in the same meter, followed by khafīf again, that is, the final rhythmic mode.

Then there is the structure of text by last letter or phrase endings: *rā, zā, jīm, a(h), rā, ney, kā, ly, a(h), kā.*

Finally, the structure of the text occurs by integration of selections into a whole performance. Here we find the following, each identified by a distinct number:

1. Single-line verse from Ibn al-Fāriḍ (rhyming verse ending in *rā*)
2. Partial inshād in ramal form, a two-line meditation from Shaihk ʿAbd al-Ghany al-Nābulsy
3. Basīṭ form by the chanter from Ibn al-Fāriḍ (two lines ending in *jīm*)
4. Ramal fragment by Shaikh Sīdī Muḥammad al-Ḥarrāq (five lines ending in *ah*)
5. Brāwīl fragment (seven lines ending in *ra*)
6. Muwashshaḥ from the "knower" Shaikh Sīdī Aḥmad Ibn ʿAshīr al-Ḥaddād (three lines ending in *ney,* then Yā Baba)
7. Segment in form khafīf from Ibn al-Fāriḍ (five lines ending in *kā*)
8. Summation based on previous lines (four lines ending in *kā*)
9. Segment from Ibn al-Fāriḍ (four lines ending in *ly*)
10. Segment from Shaikh al-Ḥarrāq (three lines ending in aspirate *h,* followed by two lines ending in *ra*)
11. Fragment from Ibn al-Fāriḍ (six lines ending in *ka*)

What is impressive about this structure is the way that the music integrates the words into a more comprehensive whole. Where a strictly literal reading of the text would leave one grasping for meanings in several instances, with the music, the concepts break down and meld into one another. Far from being a group of inchoate words and phrases, the entire performance is integrated through the music. The textual nuances listed above are not text per se, but rather textual effects that respond to a musical sensitivity. Put another way, this is a musical text, utilizing the oral text of Arabic as a prime element in an opening to the mystical. By integrating spoken text into the musical framework, Sufi music establishes a new kind of significance, a vehicle for the spiritual environment to be expressed in and through the rituals being performed. The form of the two kinds of texts is modified by joining them this way, and the result is a new, enhanced form, symbolic of the religious possibility of transformation within the meditator. Thus, the munshid is master of this musical/spoken form, and his goal is the articulation of a transformation within the listeners.

Modern Songs from the "Orient."   Another category is that of music deriving from popular modern singers like Umm Kulthūm of Egypt. A supreme songstress known all over the Arabic-speaking world, Umm Kulthūm had almost a cult following. In Morocco, the public was equally impressed. The king invited her to perform at the palace in 1968–69 to great fanfare. For her part, Umm Kulthūm went on record as indicating that her calling was to bring the Arab poets out of the libraries and put their words in human souls. She particularly was enthralled with Aḥmad al-Shawqī's material, often regarded as confrontational and passionate: "Before I sang his poems, Shawqī was unknown among the people. He was considered difficult. But when the people heard me singing his poems, when the words sank into their consciousness, then they began to love him as I love him."[39]

Apart from the awareness of the riches of Arabic poets, what left its impression on the religious music was the popular praise of the Prophet, especially a song about the Prophet sung by Umm Kulthūm during the mawlid al-nabī. This was well received in Morocco, according to my informants, and traces of the song can be found in phrasings and even in some snippets of styles. A much greater impact is felt in individual ṭarīqas. For example, the Casablanca ṭarīqa is noted for its adaptation of "oriental" music to its ʿamdah. In an interview, munshid Ḥajj Muḥammad Turābī of the ʿAlawiyya ṭarīqa in Casablanca noted that, in their ʿamdah, they began with the wird of the Ḥamziyya, then, in the malḥūn section of their repertoire: "We sing in Eastern musical style, a style reminiscent of Egypt or Syria. . . . For some reason, the oriental style has had a great influence here. While we sing the texts sung by other groups and we use the same texts as others, we switch the style to the Eastern style musically." Neither he nor his fellow munshid, ʿOmar ʿAbdūl Ḥaqq, could explain why they like the Eastern style over the Moroccan style of music.

The fact is that they begin with Moroccan rhythm but then move to the Eastern style almost immediately. During the duʿa they then return back to a Moroccan style. It was suggested that this was a phenomenon of the eighties and nineties, perhaps even of the cassette trade, since it has no foothold among any of the other groups. This gives an appearance of being new and recent. Since this is the first evident group to take this direction, I attempted, unsuccessfully, to learn who had begun the tradition of utilizing Eastern styles; both munshidūn, however, thought it earlier than this century.

Nevertheless, Ḥajj Turābī did mention that while there were around five hundred munshidūn in all of Morocco, "only perhaps fifty to one hundred are really good." This means that the pressure to be innovative is perhaps not that significant in Morocco, while the ʿAlawiyya chanters try to belong to a more international fraternity of munshidūn as their commitment to uniqueness. This could help explain their use of these rhythms.

Popular and Contemporary Tunes or Themes Deriving from Children's Dance or Work Songs.   Shaʿab songs, or *"chaabi"* as they are known in Morocco, are so diverse and inchoate that they defy description. This kind of music probably started first in the streets and lanes of Morocco, and gradually built a following in local festivals. Popular songs have diverse ways of impacting on Sufi repertoire. First of all, they are usually mixed with malḥūn and other forms of popular or classical songs as part of an evening's entertainment. In Morocco today, the *Jīl Jilāla,* a theater group based loosely on Sufi loyalty to Mūlay ʿAbd al-Qādir al-Jilānī, has incorporated Ginawa rhythms into its "traditional" entertainment package. When the group became popular, chanters in Sufi ʿamdah imitated some of their stylings. Popular at weddings and fairs, they draw on a wide variety of material, including some traditional Sufi songs.

These popular settings can also bring out social or political statements, some of which can land the singer in jail.[40] But it is also interesting that the leadership of the Sufi order can fall victim to lampooning and criticism:

> The poet, the qādī and the shaikh are all the same;
> They want money from everyone they encounter.[41]

The fascinating aspect of this is that the Sufi chanter may sing in a public setting and sing songs that express popular perceptions even while still a member of the ṭarīqa.

Sufi-Enriched or Sufi-Originated Tunes and Songs.   A good example of this category is the *bouji* text. In the version I recorded, the sorrowful tone arises from an internal debate between the poet and his own muse—the bouji. The bouji comes upon the poet, forlorn and defeated.

> "Why are you crying?" the bouji asks.
> "Ah, I have many problems . . . You wouldn't know of these human problems, every person knows these troubles."
> "Then tell me," coaxes the bouji.

What follows then is a recital of his heart's torment:

"I have this story to tell you . . . the problems of my heart, the love of my heart, a heart that can never seem to be satisfied. My beloved is gone and I am lonely, without direction, lost."

After speaking at length of his soul's forlorn state, he articulates his sense of alienation. In stating the theme this way, we lose much. Actually, in the dialogue between the poet and the bouji, a sense of the poet's inner life comes alive. This is a wonderful genre of music exploring the inner life, but it is based on Sufi premises. Still it is entirely psychological, even nonreligious, in intent. In effect, the inner state and stations have been transformed into the normal problems that weigh on people's imagination, and their inner dialogue is replicated in the bouji text. The music reflects the spokesperson's sad state of affairs and reflects the inner and outer dialogue taking place, with changes in tone and articulation to indicate shifts of inner and outer voice.

Spiritual Realities and Vocal Music Memory.   The movement from Andalusian music to a Sufi ritual medium is not well documented. After all, Andalusian music may have been a male domain, following Ziryāb, but it was the women singers who made it popular, as Ibn Bassam commented about the training of a female chanteusse:

> No one in this epoque had seen a woman with a voice so soft enshrined in a better singer, excellent also in the art of writing, in calligraphy, with a more refined culture, a diction more pure. She was a fount of all minor dialects in which she could write or sing, [and in the dialects] she knew the morphology, the lexicography, and the metric system; she [also] understood (even) medicine, natural history, and anatomy besides other sciences the knowledge of which she could render the savants of the period inferior.[42]

Here women's vocal music is linked to a cultural effulgence that raised Andalusian society to its zenith and charted a distinctive Spanish Muslim type of singer, one that was a cultural repository of depth and sophistication. Music, performed by women highly trained and refined, became the symbol of this rich civilization.

What, then, of the movement from Andalusian female singer to Sufi mystical chanter? As a result of our investigations, the predominance of the male chanter derives not from any favoritism in the gender issue, nor even from the social position of women in Islamic society, but from the role accorded to the male human voice by the Prophet. By selecting his slave Bilāl as the means to call the believers to prayer, the Prophet was indicating two things: the superiority of the human voice in communicating spiritual truths to the believers, and the predominance of the public position of the male voice in delivering God's messages.

As for the first point, the Qur'ān itself is authoritatively delivered only in speech, where it has a direct impact on the listener. The ability of the human voice to affect emotions, to reach to the soul, was thus confirmed in the early days of Islam by the way that the Qurʾān was recited. This underscores, at least for the munshidūn of Morocco, the hegemony of the voice over instrumental music in carrying the message of God to the human spirit.

As for the second point, the problematic of women munshidūn relates to the public role of women in society, not to the preference of the male voice over the female.[43] We cannot debate here whether the female is subjected to social status loss in Muslim culture, the issue being an ongoing debate within Islam itself. But we can say something about the human voice and female chanters. There are good female munshidūn, but their role in public expression is closely regulated and constrained in Morocco, far more, in fact than would seem to be the case in Egypt.[44] For most Moroccans, there are no female chanters in the dhikr or samāʿ although there may be occasions when female chanters make public appearances, as, for example, on television; many people I talked to insisted that there are no female chanters, that is, *faqirāt,* who sing in front of men, but certainly there are female chanters. I was told that there are faqirāt who chant in the Ḥarrāqiyya, before the prayer ashūra in the shaikh's house, to which only women and the shaikh himself are admitted. The munshid Ashḥab was very definite: "Even the women prefer to stay in the corner and hear male singers. There are just very few female chanters in the zāwiya in Morocco. There are, for example, none in Rabat."[45]

The tenor of what Ashḥab said was validated by others: there is a clear preference for the male voice as the vehicle of spiritual messages, even among women. The central role of the male voice seems to be in keeping with the practices of the Prophet, and since this is religious music, men should follow that model. Here the memory of the Prophet's society still determines singing policy.

But even the issue of females chanting does not vitiate the fundamental point: the human voice is superior and must retain the dominant position in music over instruments. Sufi music in Morocco is overwhelmingly vocal, even where instrumental music is part of the performance. The longevity of Sufi music, then, has to be partly explained by the position of the human voice in ṭarīqa life, and its importance as a carrier of inspiration. It is not just in the fact of it being a musical form in itself.

Spiritual Realities and Mystical/Philosophical Provenance.   There are those who see a mystical mental pattern as the basis of Sufi spiritual realities. Jean During holds in *Musique et extase* that Sufi music is linked to the mythic Covenant (*mīthāq*). In his view an absolutely hard-wired mental awareness is established when the child is first born and has whispered in his ear "*Alastu bi rabbikum,*" that is, Am I not your Lord? From that moment on, the remembrance of the true origin of one's life plays a role in human consciousness, connecting the person to that ecstatic moment at the founding of all individuals when one realizes one's true ancestry.[46] What obtains, then, is a mythizing experience linking the person forever to a God-consciousness. While somewhat related to al-Faruqi's tawḥīd thesis above, it places greater emphasis on the experience of God as the base upon which to build the musical awareness, holding that this visionary moment at birth sets the thought pattern for life. This is a view not likely to appeal to many Western scholars, including some who are Muslims, who might view the notion of a templatic experience of God during one's first few moments of birth just too radical to accept. Moreover, those who convert would appear to be left out of this scenario. Nor does it explain how nonbelievers can be inspired by Sufi music.

Of greater promise is the view that song produces a kind of awareness, perhaps some would call it mystical, but not of the otherworldly kind. In this, song creates a special state. One might argue, as does Rouget, that music and trance demonstrate sophisticated relationships in behavior, much more complicated than appear on the surface,[47] and Monts writes about the Vai women singers this way: "For the dancers, songs are used to promote or create a state of "other-awareness," or "other-self"; they evoke change in the dancer's state of being, not inducing trance, but in some way altering the state of consciousness or personality from human to spiritual."[48]

Such a conception would hold that the Sufi's mythic domain is a psycho-mental process, involving an internal shift of perspective toward a kind of spiritual consciousness. This pattern fits with the obvious religious emphasis that Sufis give, and tallies well with the fact that the munshidūn must articulate the emotional power of the encoding system but do not themselves go into trance the way other participants do. This conception is also easily adapted to the ritual perspective suggested below.

The late Fazlur Rahman favored the view that Sufism retained a genuine place for human cognition by developing and sustaining what might be called metaphilosophical views. Sufi wisdom, therefore, was attempting to grapple with realities that the more institutional Sunnī and Shīʿī theologians had eschewed.[49] In the light of the import of memory in this study, his view has much to recommend it.

Spiritual Realities and Ritual Memories

Another explanation can be suggested: this is a ritual formulation born in Islamic cultural situations. Rituals embody remembered codes. The individual who hears these codes recognizes their ritual potential and responds to them as ritual markers. I suggest that musical forms, and especially the vocal musical forms of Sufism, arise naturally out of a coding system that is ritualistic and therapeutic; Sufi music is indeed linked to Islamic awareness through dhikr, but also through the very practical knowledge of handling the problematic issues of life. Islamic cultural forms bear the potential for transformation of the person, both spiritually and otherwise. It is precisely because the mythic domain of the Sufi includes a wide range of memory triggers for inspiration that it is able to appeal so widely to so many kinds of people. Some attempt to identify these, and to describe how they appear to operate, will be suggested below, but before doing so, it might be helpful to sketch the complex field within which Sufi music operates.

Berber and Arab: Melodies of Musical Morocco.   Religious music begins, as it does in all Muslim environments, with the Qurʾān and the attending rituals of the Islamic prayer. From the moment the sun elevates her head above a Moroccan community, the muezzin lifts his in calling the faithful to prayer. Muḥammad may have believed that the sound of the human voice was more natural than bells, but the aural landscape of the contemporary Muslim's life is so intertwined with the sounds from amplified speakers that life is woven around this repetitive framework. One cannot escape the sonic structure. Once joined together in reverence around the recitation of the Qurʾān, the community can never revert to a careless attitude toward communication theory: God speaks in words too powerful to ignore or forget. This sacred communication provides benediction at weddings, funerals, and celebrations of saints, during Ramadan, and even at the opening of new restaurants. It bathes believers with soothing tradition. The line between musical aesthetic and oral speech is eroded in these moments, and linguistic and ethnic distinctions are dispelled. This is as much a national music as it is international, and everyone participates in its presence.

The most ancient forms of music in Morocco are not Arab but Berber. Salvador-Daniel notes:

> It appears certain today that the Kabyles are the descendants of the people that the Carthiginians and then the Romans had found on the coasts of northern Africa and [consequently is the origin of] the generic name of the Berbers; this name became the Roman epithet *Barbare*, which was applied much later to all conquered races. The Berber people had not become subjects of the Roman Empire, but were for the most part Christian. Saint Augustine was originally a Berber. He spoke the language utilized in North Africa, and according to him, the Berbers were descendents from Ham through Ham's son Shanaan.[50]

Salvador-Daniel goes on to argue that the music that arose out of these peoples was lumped together with sacred musical languages of the Greeks by the Roman writer Plutarch so that their musical forms were identified as sacred because of the cultic use of music of a certain type. There is, then, according to him, a very ancient tradition of distinctive Berber religious music.

Traditional Muslim Berber religious music, in addition to the normal muezzin and Qurʾān reciting, uses the same instruments that are found in marriages, agricultural celebrations, and circumcision parties, that is, hand drums called *bendirs* and flutes called ghaita*s* or *rhaïtas*. These community gatherings are shaped into large circles of participants in the local square, where both men and women engage in a call-response chanted prayer called *ahouach* before beginning the dances in the western Atlas mountains. Among the Berbers, music clearly has a therapeutic ingredient; when I was there in 1995, prayers were given for rain during some séances. Much is made of controlling the jinn in these ceremonies, especially if the jinn are held to be the cause of some local misery or personal malaise.

Celebrations normally bring out the professional musicians, who form a group to entertain and assist in creative community expressions. They may also appear at the local market, where their leader is known as an *amydaz* (poet), and they perform his improvised lines accompanied by the drums and *rabāb*. The text of these performances sometimes includes social commentary of a contemporary sort. Some groups, like the *Jajouka* in the Rif mountains, have a long history of excellence in the genre and have gained both national and international acclaim. The ṣūq at Marrakech is a favorite locale for fledgling groups to perform, and after the ṣūq closes in the evening, such groups take over the square. Other professional Berber musicians are from Chleuh in the Sous Valley. These groups, called *rwaīs*, are also headed by a poetically endowed leader, but they are generally known to have a well-polished repertoire, and their performances are highly structured, even if the parts of the performance can be moved about in any given order so long as the cohesion of the whole is retained.[51]

As noted earlier, almost none of the founding Sufis spoke Arabic but were instead Berber-speaking; Berber dominated the religious landscape before immigration of the Andalusians.[52] Indeed, even today, as Crapanzano points out, Meknes is a kind of borderland between Arab and Berber.[53] There is some indigenous poetry now among the Berbers, and of course they enjoy good translations of pious Arabic works like the *Bourda* in the Sous in southern Morocco. In addition there are also a few nationally recognized poets in Berber.

Professional Berber musicians may participate in Sufi celebrations if they are members of an order, and the best musicians of the zāwiyas may also be co-opted by the rāwīs. Generally, though, the musicians have to be professional to perform up to the standard required, and even in some Sufi ḥaḍras, professional musicians are hired.

Such a state of affairs does not usually apply to the munshid. There is an inherent critique of someone who sings both as a Sufi chanter and as a public performer, as has already been noted. Professionals also perform with Sufi groups during processions and mawlids. So far as I was able to determine, no Sufi songs would ever be performed by a rāwīs group during a celebration. Berber-speaking Sufis in the singing orders may utilize Berber poems during their ʿamdahs, but they are translated into Arabic. The relationship to classical Arabic music is more complicated than this simple sketch would indicate, however. Al-Farābī identified seven well-known īqāʿāt or rhythmic modes in Arabian music, but over the centuries twenty-three others have been developed, as well as combinations among them, providing a rich rhythmic texture for the Arab musician. Today, there are īqāʿāt that reflect origins quite apart from the Arab. For example the *hindi* represents a rhythm done in the Indian style, while an *ifranji* is in the Western or French style. Among these there is also one called *maṣmūdī*, named after a Berber tribe, but which may represent a more general Berber rhythm.[54] In addition, Berber music also plays a role in the structure of

Ginawa music. All this indicates that rhythm is far more complex in Moroccan music than it is in the West. Normally we can figure out the time in a Western piece sufficiently to tap out the beat. In Sufi music, the interweaving and layering is too complicated for most of us to identify. So music of the samāʿ, that is, meditations primarily for listening, may have very complicated rhythms. On the other hand, music used in the dhikr has to have a relatively dominant beat, since it relates to the dance (requiring a simple beat) and is much easier to follow. The issue of a dominant beat, however, brings us to the African content of Moroccan music.

The African Contribution to Maghribian Sufi Music.   Of great significance to any study of Sufi music is movement, and Sufi movement highlights the interaction of music and movement or dance. In this regard, the most telling point is made by Lester Monts concerning music and dance among the Vai people. Elaborating on Herndon and McLeod's statement that "music is regarded as a form of ritual procedure which must be performed correctly,"[55] he notes, "As a mode of communication, music is often directed to the ancestral spirits impersonated by *zoo-ba,* a plea on the parts of the sande membership for the spirits to cast their benevolence upon the *sande* society."[56]

The close relationship of musical dance and religious states in African music raises key questions for this study. There is an expectation built into the Moroccan material that ritual dance brings about a change in emotion—in Sufi terminology, that a change of state will take place. Sufi music "religions" the atmosphere, sending out signals that attest that something of a personal, altered state may take place, constructing an anticipation of interaction with the spiritual world. It may well be that this close relationship with music/dance and ecstatic expectation is not African in origin, but certainly the expectation, found in earlier religions of Africa, that music will make present the spiritually powerful ancestors is. It is an open question as to how much the munshid is integrated into this construction. Certainly the well-being involved in contacting the divine in the Sufi worldview, and the therapy of engagement with higher powers, underlines one possible way in which the African context has influenced the material.[57]

Furthermore, from my work in Egypt, it is evident that percussion, long a dominant medium in Africa, plays an important role in the musical framework of zāwiya culture. It is similarly critical in Morocco. As was noted in my previous study, both the speed and the tone of drumming are important indicators of the expectations of religious outcomes.[58] Slawson's contention, then, that there are features in drumming that are similar to those we find in phonetics is an interesting proposal. Drawing on Locke and Agbeli, he suggests that the primary features of a drumming communication may be *place, manner,* and *source.*[59] Whether this analysis can help in comprehending individual dhikr performances is a fertile field for exploration, one that will have to await future examination. What we can say is that if it is possible to establish such features, it may well be possible to, at least, identify the distinctive beats related to the collected material of some Sufi groups in Morocco. If it proves of significance, we may be able to show how the drumming language is peculiar to the dhikr of certain groups, a feature with solid African connections. Of course this aspect is most evident in the healing rites of the Ginawa, whose ritual performances are directly connected to therapy, and spiritual as well as physical well-being is crucial. Their history connects them directly to Africa. It is interesting speculation to consider drumming communication as the inspiration for the Moroccan Sufi's ecstatic dance. The relationship of beat to trance could then be part of a long-forgotten memory of an African religious origin.

The Parameters of Religious Music in Moroccan Sufism

The Musical Dimension of "Remembered" Codings

The mystical dimension in Moroccan Sufi music begs definition, and despite attempts, eludes. There are a number of reasons for this, but, in this study, the shear size of the subject matter is a decisive factor. Primarily, the recorded music encountered in this research dealt with Arab-based musical systems. Discussions with distinctive Berber musicians were limited, and, judging from Schuyler's study, the musical tradition is complex in other ways, such as the predominant use of professional musicians.[60] Nevertheless it is a factor that cannot be reduced to something else. It is very reminiscent of Jonathan Hill's description of the sacred chanters of the Amazon:

> Musicalization, or transforming the taxonomies of mythic speech into the dynamic language of music, is a turning inside-out and upside-down of mythification. Musicalization is a process of expanding, opening, and augmenting the miniaturized vertical creation into a horizontal dimension of exchange relations among a plurality of peoples from different places. [Through] musicalization the ceremonial bringing and mixing together of foods and peoples [helps to] create a cultural landscape of rivers, peoples, and places, including the clthonian underworld of spirits of the dead.[61]

Change some of the descriptors here and you begin to see what the munshid sees, and understand how she or he performs. The music of the munshidūn is polyphonic, constructed upon a music language that informs the intentionality, presenting a unifying codex by which the listeners are assured of familiar patterns, and solutions to the chaos of their life's clamor. Each performance is marked by shifts from one time frame to another, from one speed of meditation or articulation to a more advanced, a mirror of the replicative pattern of stations and states in Sufi ideological belief. We can recognize the various planes that the munshidūn operate within; these we can designate as lamentation, tranquillity, affirmation, exhilaration, and transformation. Each of these has a musical tone and expectation. Thus the encoding brings with it comprehension of several moods of spiritual attainment. I have made selections from a vast repertoire here.

In the lamentation mode, the munshid's meditations are structured by a slow movement of inward meditation, a deliberate slowing down of the hectic pace of life toward an open embrace of the stance of prayer . . . like shoes . . . the removal of the mind from the regular and public to the inner and secret. This is the domain of personal emotion and meaning, and the munshid's recitation of the *Bourda* begins on a slow and deliberate note, in rap-like speech to focus attention, reduce disarray, and introduce mystical order to thought. This is the zuḥd (ascetic) strain of Sufi music, with its deliberate weeping and open personal condemnation . . . a remembering of the soul, concerned with the precarious situation of the personal being in view of the condemnation of the law and an acute awareness of the distance from God.

What is fascinating about this mode is the connection to the earliest strains of Sufi remembrance, a returning to the ascetic strain of Sufis rooted in the wailing of the devotees of Ḥassan al-Basrī, who urged his followers to consider how little they had to offer to God and how corrupt they were in contrast to the purity of God's requirements. Remembering through lamentation is not just a recalling of one's own sins but a return to the founding of the Sufi tradition itself, through meditational procedures.

Here is a selection from the "crying" dhikr of Ḥajj Ḥusaīn of the ʿAissawiyya of Meknes. In this fragment, the munshid uses a very simple movement, filled with half tones, repeated over and over as a mantra of lamentation. The atonality of the crying sound shifts the thought patterns from the poses of adult living, with their supposed toughness and resilience in the face of life's crises, toward that of a child contrite and pleading for some amelioration and acceptance. The shift is toward interiority, a retreat to the inner person, where the outward façade of self-assured human falls away and we discover the brokenness and fragility of the inner self. Note the narrow range of the tonal base, and the predominant shadings implied in the rapid move from flats to natural notes:

Musical notation from dhikr of the ʿAissawiyya of Meknes, May, 1995, by Ḥajj Ḥusaīn

Like Mozart, the munshid begins with an adagio that redirects the human to the inner side of meaning, toward the calm of another clime, toward an origin firmly

Musical notation from dhikr Sīdī al-Saʿ of Salé demonstrating hand-clapping rhythm change beat when ritual moves from one level to another

established in the presence of God *in illo tempore.* Here is the Prophet's domain, for in his presence one is made aware that one is forgivable and transformable. Once the munshid moves upward from this tonal base, he does so in a faster tempo (see rhythm changes above), indicating that a different level of consciousness is being opened, one that is beyond the normal. This higher register signals the domain of the spiritual world and invites listeners to examine their inner realities. When the exploration comes to a climax, the munshid then returns to this tonal base, and life returns to normal.

From the litanies of the devotees of Sīdī al-ʿArabī b. al-Saʿ of Rabat comes a meditation that renders *tranquillity* into tonal encounter; rather than demonstrating a taqsīm here, which would set the musical idea firmly within the Western expectation, I have replicated that of hand clapping and hand drumming. In the regularity of this beat, a certain structuring of the world takes place. This structuring is reassuring and convincing and comes across as inspired, just because maintaining the constancy of the beat reflects an environment quite different from that in which we normally live; here the beat not only replicates the conception that there is a certain nuclear beat in the cosmic plane, but also holds that the heart itself must move in tandem with this beat to bring it into cadence with the universe. In our selection above we demonstrate two aspects of this drumming structure; the first indicates how the drumming changes in response to the switch from one cosmic level to another, implied by the different rhythm change and speed. The whole performance suggests an ordered movement from one level of consciousness to another.

The second structure demonstrates the way drumming integrates the two musical groups (along with the guitar as background) in the same ṭarīqa. The intent is to provide an aural experience of integration and order within the same beat pattern:

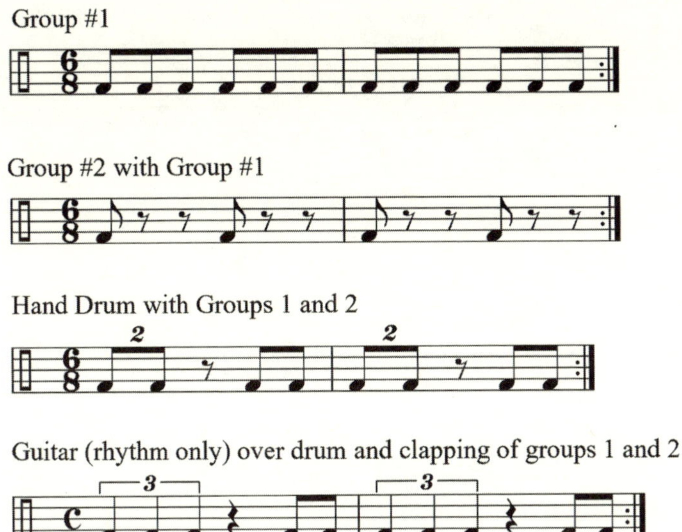

Musical notation from dhikr Sīdī al-Saʿof Salé demonstrating use of drumming and guitar as integration features

But human existence, even of the most dedicated spiritual visionary, is not permanently invested with such calmness. The lover has departed, the ashes of love appear to be cold, and immediately the memory delivers a discordant note: life is filled with tension and conflict far from the gentle breast of the beloved. Beyond this, one is not free just to engage the lover without social cost. So reality is constituted by social metaphors: they are necessary to sustain as a conduit for the spiritual residue of memory and, it is hoped, to enliven it. The shaikh as father, the ṭarīqa as family, the religious life as community, all provide the framework for eliciting the vividness of memory. Yet none of these exist without the clash of opinions and the turmoil of difference. The ṭarīqa handles these issues by resting in the permanence of *affirmation,* as in the *Bourda;* in Morocco, and among the devotees of Sīdī ʿAbdallāh b. Ḥassun (d. 1604), patron saint of Salé, there can be no other intoned text as crucial. Affirmation in this case is dependent on stress, extension of the word, and loudness. On page 150 is a brief selection with stress pattern signified by circumflex over letter; extension by long parallel line, and loudness by wavy line above text.

So far, then, moments of lamentation have given way to the tranquil awareness that the cost is too great, there are not sufficient tears to provide enough wailing. Somewhere the soul must find rest. Thus does affirmation from the Holy Word or the Prophet bring a sense of release. The soul moves on to a new resting place. Still, this has really only removed the great weight of despair, it has not lifted the soul to its natural source; this pattern of music provides a pathway to a transformed inner person.

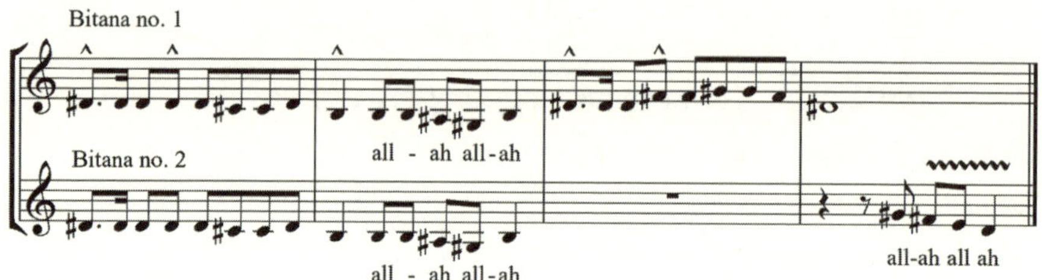

Musical notation from dhikr al-Ḥarrāqiyya demonstrating stress patterns

Once again the munshid leads the devotee through affirmation toward *exhilaration*. It is this pious joy that connects with tender moments in the past and, together with the jubilance of the present, creates a moment of effervescence; this selection, from the Tetouan Ḥarrāqiyya, features a movement from affirmation to exhilaration, signaled by a modification of rhythm (see below).

In short, this is a kind of memorable mapping, the encoded system that fosters and undergirds the munshid's performance. Thus is the munshid's musical journey; an unfolding of these relationships and the text and style of music reflect the whole

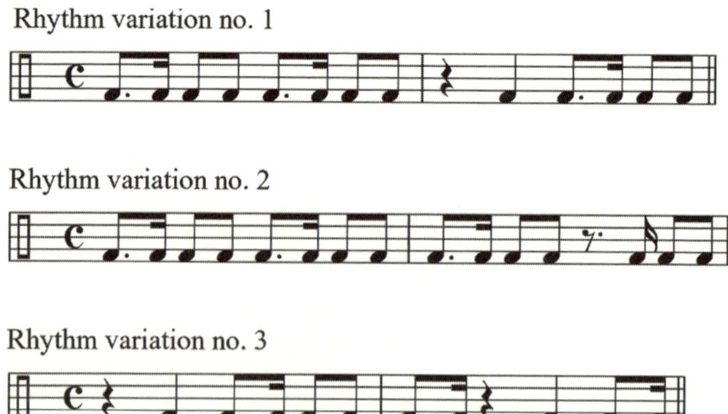

Musical notation from dhikr of Ṭarīqa al-Ḥarrāqiyya demonstrating rhythm variation

Two musical segments from dhikr al-Ḥarrāqiyya demonstrating pattern of notes

complexity inherent in the religious life: the ludic joy of love, the freeing exultation of wine, the pristineness of nature, the universality of the Prophet, and the mystery of God, all these are musically expressed in the styles of time and tempo (see violin and oud above). This is the Sufi's Mozartian andante. At some point, unknown to outsiders, transformation takes place, and the spiritual environment of the soul becomes a reality indicator.

Note the variegated role of religious memory here; the very polyvalent nature of this music intimates problems, for memory reminds that the last dhikr perhaps was not successful, that the family is not without its claims and demands, that the shaikh may be above the fray but his followers strangely are not. So the music must move beyond this concatenation of metaphors to an ecstasy of union . . . to some sort of transcending of the metaphors to a unity grounded beyond the metaphors themselves. This is the experience of discovery, a recasting of remembered exaltation into new forms of awareness . . . new but obviously founded upon the mind's visitation of the old. In this terrain, the munshid comes to know of his or her own dichotomy, an irrelevance to the true state of being, but yet a necessary accomplice for this overthrowing of the metaphors. Here is the zenith of musical exhilaration in the Ḥarrāqiyya dhikr, stressing a quick, almost staccato sound shaped by a limited range of notes, as if the energy of the blessing must be kept within a very narrow range (note line 2 above).

The code of the human encounter with spiritual presence is delivered in autobiographical terms, and each finds the level of God-consciousness attendant to each person's capability. In effect we have journeyed from the slow movement to the fastest, along a musical path whose goal is suggestive rather than literal. Here is the move from verbal score to percussion, and through percussion to transformation of sound into emotion. This moment leads beyond the amalgam of sound and word, into an experience that is connected through memory to past moments "out of oneself." Yet this is not some kind of wizardry. It is a kind of enhanced consciousness that is translated through integration of music and text as a hastened and enthusiastic *transformation*. Using the language of this study, the transformation moves the listeners through a collective participation in sound into the extraordinary tones of an encoded experience of what is understood to be truth and reality.

The Musicality of the Munshidūn

Ashḥab, Ḥarrāqiyya munshid, indicated:

> We do not sing the *Bourda* in ṭab but in nagham, which means it has a different time structure, and nagham means the same things as maqam in classical or Eastern music. In my view, nagham comes out of classical music, but it is not directly present in our Sufi music. Nagham is found here in modern Moroccan music, but it is not in Andalusian music. The reason the malḥūn can use nagham is because his music is interwoven. . . . It's an interweaving of malḥūn traditions and Andalusian traditions. . . . It's the musical variations that allow this. The malḥūn sings the ṭabʾ of Andalusia, but he introduces sometimes an oriental naghma. In the ṭabʾ of Andalusia one finds a distinctive form; nevertheless, the munshid may introduce some features from the oriental naghma, like "ah-ah" into his singing. This is popular with the people. Badjdūb [the well-known singer] does this to great effect, but it is not regarded as proper by the munshidūn and is not done in Andalusian music. We have to learn these distinctions when we chant in the zāwiya.[62]

Nagham is the plural form of *naghma*, a word that has various meanings. It can refer to a musical note, or to a mode or modal characteristic.[63] Clearly Ashḥab is not referring to the first. Nor can he be arguing that there are no modal characteristics; rather, he is contending that there is no overriding mode assigned to Sufi music. Diversity allows for a richer expression of the divine-human relationship and the munshid's capabilities to express it. But not all zāwiyas have the same freedom of expression. Some, like the zāwiya ʿAissawiyya, use the same chant all over Morocco, while others, like the Ḥarrāqiyya, may technically use material for any ṭarīqa. On the other hand, the Naṣīriyya zāwiyas all have their own poetry, and Saif al-Naṣīr poetry is even published in manuscript form in Rabat.

There are also distinctive techniques that the munshidūn use. In fact, my informants stress that four genres of musical expression dominate their chanting, along with four other distinctive musical terms of significance to Sufi chanting:

Mazluk.   Sufi chanters claim they can tell by the mazluk if a voice belongs to a genuine munshid. It is a special quality of the voice that allows for a broad range of meaning. One sings in a tone ranging from fine and elegant to strong and aggressive. In effect, this is a quality that speaks of values beyond the words that carry power regardless of the tone. There is a sense of authority and confidence in this type of singer.

Gubāhī.   This is a very assertive, authoritative tonal quality. It is usually accompanied by strong claps. Most zāwiyas use this form during the introduction to their wird. It is the quality reflecting attestation, as identified and discussed below.

Hudhārī.   Under the influence of the spiritual state, a munshid will move quickly through a text as if, by singing fast, he is collapsing the spiritual energies of each individual word into a kind of pressurized form. When the whole is compressed, a potent form of spiritual power is available. There is a kind of rapid chanting that leads to an increased tension between this world and the spiritual world, and pushes the participants to another level of spiritual awareness. Here the munshid is operating under the influence of previously remembered energy releases, anticipating transformation within his listeners. This form is often encountered at the zenith of the dhikr, when excitement runs high.

Tayyʿ.   This is a quality of voice that reflects a humble attitude, a heart that is broken because it cannot reach its goal. Generally designated as weak or small, it can also mean pliable or flexible, indicating that the intent is to be broken before God, but willing to do what is bidden by the spiritual powers. A broken munshid is a powerful munshid.

Haniyya.   When someone sings with haniyya, their voice reflects a spiritual softness and gentleness. Being able to chant this way reflects the spiritual state that the chanter is in, that is, it reflects that he is in harmony both with himself and the spiritual forces surrounding him.

ʿAsāla.   This is a chant that is, as its name implies, thick, sweet as honey, and as refined as a beehive. It is usually laden with love imagery, perhaps even layers of such imagery. By connecting various unrelated statements about love, the munshid "glazes" the meanings, giving them depth and sweetness.

Simāwī.   This is not a vocal tone per se, but a musical text that is like the mawwāl but much longer and more involved. It purports to slowly draw the listener in, all the while emphasizing the difficulty of encountering the spiritual world and reflecting the long Sufi path to enlightenment and transcendence.

Dandanah.   Dandanah is a malḥūn form of chanting that was introduced by Abū al-Azīz al-Maghrāwī. It is described as soft humming, but it can mean that the munshid hums as a way of releasing the mind from the text and as such utilizes the tune as the means to convey the words that are no longer discreet, but implied. It is a technique of distilling and enhancing the meaning of the words into a form beyond words. The implication is that the basic sound is closer to nonarticulate humming than to spoken words, because it is closer to the inner person.

Taqmas.   The munshid, if he is to perform properly, will not appear to be singing, that is, the words and the music will appear to come effortlessly, as if from the realm of a mythic script, that other dimension. He will bear a relationship to the *taqlīd* or imitator, in that he is trying to personify exactly the inspiration embodied in the text. The goal is not to add something of his own to the recital but to be "enrobed in the presence" that is quite beyond him to manufacture. This embodied music presupposes the body as a kind of instrument, a conception that rests upon the assumption that the body can be enveloped by a force quite outside its normal reality.

My sources suggest this is an African notion, deriving from a belief in possession. Possession is the highlight of both the Ginawa and Ḥamadsha ṭarīqas, and suggests that the person can be taken over by another spirit. But it is difficult to make a distinctive case for the origin of this as African, since we know that Dionysian dancers did the same thing. Moreover, Morocco has a long and very complex musical history, since Berber, Islamic, sub-Saharan, Christian, and various African indigenous traditions have left their imprint there. The munshid does seem to respond to an emotional trigger and moves into another state of consciousness, quite short of the trance state that some experience, but nevertheless regarded as beyond the normal. It is my perception that this state is highly controlled and disciplined, in order that he can provide the means to assist the brethren into trance. This notion of a refined trance condition may derive from the patterned behavior of African trance itself. Nevertheless it was evident to me that the place of possession through the medium of music is quite different than in Western music, where listening has become mainly a passive activity, so trance through music is a forgotten pattern.[64] In that sense, this part of the munshid performance is closer to the African model.

Music serves more than one master in Morocco's inshād conglomerate. In dhikr it bears a language of relatedness to a sophisticated and rich spiritual life. In samāᶜ it celebrates a many-sided artistic tradition. Among the Ginawa it is the vehicle that transports the individual into an inner world of power and connectedness with wholeness. With the Ḥarrāqiyya it is the music of the spheres, a glimpse of the Andalusian musical medium that is linked to both greatness and Arab brilliance. The fact is that performing outside the confines of the order is a very recent trend; the context has traditionally been an essential element in performance. Those who are masters within their own context perform where they carry out a familiar and well-patterned function. Music of that function cannot be transported to another environment; the memory of its past greatness dictates that because one needs the memory to activate the spiritual realities. Memory is thus the basis of this religious encounter.

Musicality and Regional Ṭarīqa Differences

Given the great variety of peoples and cultures present in Morocco, much diversity is to be expected. There is no doubt that this diversity impacts on Sufi music. The masters among the munshidūn, such as the singers of the Ḥarrāqiyya, sing classical qaṣāʾid, and maintain strong connections with the so-called classical pronunciation, and apparently they adhere to a high tradition reaching back to Andalusia. On the other hand, in some ṭarīqas, like those I found in Meknes, chanters sing in local dialects, using local images and phrases, and even local songs. So the range of meaning of ṭurāth, or tradition, is sizeable. Indeed, it would seem that traditional inshad is very much defined by the consensus of the ṭarīqa. This allows for modifications of tradition within the munshidūn framework, which poses the possibility for adjustment in the tradition subject to the changes perceived as acceptable with the ṭarīqa. Clearly the shaikh or the muqaddam will have an important say in this process of modifying the tradition.

But there are other specific differences encountered in the Moroccan material. For example, while some groups make no real distinction between the songs of the ḥaḍra and the songs of the samāʿ, Bin Mansour says there is a vital difference in the fete of Salé between ʿamdah and samāʿ:

> Madīḥ in the Salé ʿamdah is directly related to the ʿamdah one finds in the *Hamziyya* and the *Bourda,* while in the samāʿ, one hears the rhythm of the Andalusian tradition. In general, in public festivals, only texts from ʿamdah are used. Also, in general, one changes the text and one changes the *hūdūd.* On the other hand, one can have different subjects but use the same *baḥr.* In samāʿ, no time belongs to it alone.[65]

There are also differences in style. For example southern chanters go up and down the scale very quickly, from low to high. Some call this *naghamāt muttaʿid,* which is a melody that has an ascending character to it. Northern chanters tend to follow the rules laid down by Andalusian music.

There are other specific differences, summarized from a conversation with key munshid Muḥammad al-Turābī of Casablanca:

1. There is now a considerable distinction between popular "traditional" music, even the music that is based on the Sufi ṭarīqas, and ṭarīqa music. There is great resistance to modifying the ṭarīqa music. Thus there is not much new because the munshid sings the ancient texts and keeps to the old patterns, since that is where the inspiration is held to lie.

2. The munshid can play different roles: one can sing in a group or as a soloist, and the potential to have an impact on the samāʿ will differ depending on the role.

3. There is a difference between īqāʿ (rhythm) of the secular song and īqāʿ of the dhikr, and the crucial difference is the rūḥānī, that is, the basis for a shift during the dhikr is "the rhythm of the heart." The munshid senses when to change. Beyond that the munshid also varies the rhythm because different texts require different rhythms. Where the music carries on during the dhikr, the principal intermediary is the inshād solo, tahlīl, or mawwāl. This phase is called baitīn. So the munshid must carry that transition and the message over the music being chanted by the group.

4. There are major differences in accompaniment. There are, for example, no instruments in the ʿAlawiyya, while there are several different kinds in the Ḥarrāqiyya.

5. There are some differences generated by age differences. Most of the good munshidūn are old, and they were trained for a long time under the shaikh or his muqaddam. Now a munshid learns how to sing in the ʿamdah, or even from popular singers via tape cassettes, and then he comes to the zāwiya influenced by outside sources. He won't quite get it right until he has learned to do away with his secular stylings.

6. Learning the rhythm is different from learning the text. In order to learn the text, the munshid can just recite it over and over . . . memorize it. But he has to learn the differences in rhythm of the different songs by beginning to practice in the zāwiya. He has to listen to how it is sung to gain the experience. Then he can see the differences between the way a Sufi sings and an outside singer.

7. There are differences in pronunciation between Berber and Arab, even when they all sing the same language. In the southern inshād, one finds most texts are closer to classical Arabic, whereas, in Berber areas, even texts translated from Berber into Arabic will be Berberized. Despite that, though, one finds the rhythm similar, that is, one does not change the rhythm from Arab to Berber-Arabic.[66]

Finally, in an interview, al-Jirārī indicated that there are considerable differences in religious expectations. The orders make a clear distinction between those who are deeply into the mystical tradition and those who are just listeners, or even transients who come for something to do. Thus, he pointed out that songs that stress loving God, that is, the "Ḥubb Allāh" chants, are for exclusive use during séances of intimates of the shaikh and the mystical brethren. Structurally, then, there is a difference between the love for God and love of Prophet. Love for God is for advanced Sufis, implying long mystical encounters, while love of Prophet is something that all Muslims have. It is for everyone. This means that there is little criticism of the munshid if he chants of Muḥammad or his achievements and spiritual gifts, since the Prophet is beyond the stigma of criticism. On the other hand, to talk of experiencing God raises the whole issue of theological language and the threat of anthropomorphism.[67] By framing the terms musically, one envelopes them in another system of meaning that renders them indeterminant. The munshid "remembers" the goal beyond both word and music.

The Modifications and Innovations in Sufi Music

While the Sufi chanters claim that their music is strictly guided by tradition, in fact there are some modifications that can be indicated. For example, the draj is apparently a recent development in Moroccan music. My sources say it was begun in the Moroccan zāwiya but then spread to other areas of music. The draj is translated as "a rhyme or chant, a series of vocal or rhythmic cycles, the fourth of the nūba in Morocco" by Guettat,[68] and he notes that it is one of five rhythmic phases of vocal music in Morocco. He notes that al-Ḥāyik, the writer of the manuscript he draws from (writing circa 1730–1800) did not record it in his general detailing of the various Moroccan forms.[69] Al-Jirārī regarded it as distinctly Sufi in origin. Draj is played, however, only in one tempo, 4/4; all the other forms are regarded as of Andalusian or mixed Arab/Andalusian origin, and, of course have a variety of tempos assigned to them. Since draj is a major ingredient in the Sufi repertoire, however, it suggests that the music is not as static as one is led to believe.

In addition, ʿAbd al-Ṣadīq Shaqāra, the now deceased master of the Ḥarrāqiyya Darqāwiyya ṭarīqa, introduced a new form of inshād, called the Tetuoan inshād. In it he used Andalusian music drawn from the malamut tradition (that is, the "extremist" or radical Sufi tradition) and combined it with other texts to make a new form of inshād.

Another evident innovation is the development of the tape cassette market. There are several ways that the tape has altered the world of the munshid. First, the munshid can now record the master's chanting during an ʿamdah or samāʿ and learn from his stylings. Second, tape cassettes of famous chanters are now available commercially, and this allows the student not only to hear the current popular chanters but also to learn new lyrics. Third, tapes can be used in the teaching process by a munshid who is trying to improve the chanting of a student. Fourth, the better the munshid is, the more apt he is to have cassettes demanded of him, so that there is a tendency to encourage the best to record for the commercial market. Fifth, the munshid who is in demand may leave the ṭarīqa simply because he feels he can reach a far wider audience with his voice than just the local brethren. The new world-music market is attractive to some Sufis who are weary from lack of challenge in the local zāwiyas, or because of a falling-out with the leadership. Finally, the local samāʿ used to be the only place where this kind of music could be heard. Now that it is available on tape, it can be brought into the home, business, or train station. This completely changes the role that Sufi music has had in local culture. As Muḥammed al-Nouhī observed: "Before, Morocco used to be samāʿ from shore to shore. . . . It was 'secret of the brotherhoods.' Now the cassette has changed all that."[70] Sufi chanting has now become part of world-music entertainment.[71]

As noted, contemporary topics cannot be incorporated into a munshid's singing. But, as Ashḥab says, there are ways of bringing recent issues into the ṭarīqa: one can chant a traditional song in a way that implies a new meaning. The munshid can, in his imagination, make up stories that reflect modern problems and then hint at them through emphasis within a song. Thus he can comment upon Islamic attitudes toward fighting with Israel by singing chants that stress the jihād, or the struggle against an intractable problem at home.

The fact is that malḥūn performers throughout history have used poetry to influence wars; poets were also operating during the French Protectorate, and the malḥūn have used poetry as an arm against Morocco's enemies. Thus if a munshid wants to refer to some current clash, he can use these references already existing in poetry to illustrate the same themes. In effect, he is not addressing the precise moment at the poem's creation, or the situation when the poem originated; his brethren catch his allusion.

In addition, different methods of presentation can also indicate modern problems, so that by using a phrase from a popular song during his samāʿ, a munshid recontextualizes the chant in the minds of the listeners. In sum, these referrals cannot be direct, but they can and are hinted at during performances, providing fresh perspectives to the listening murīds.

The nature of ṭarīqa discipline also has impacted upon the music. During the praise of the Prophet during his mawlid, one ends the praise with distinctive phrases of recognition. Thus there is a specified Ḥarrāqiyya praise formula, while in the Tijāniyya, one finds a slightly different praise formula. The presence of distinctive recognition formulas indicates that phraseology has changed, a feature that would not be possible if the textual tradition were inured from change. Still, these barely perceptible changes indicate a mindfulness of tradition and a commitment to the norms laid down by this consequential past. Without this continuing memory, the borders between Sufi music and secular folk music might have been destroyed centuries ago. That it has not reflects the importance of remembering the past and making it present today.

Sufi Music as Traditional Entertainment

Consider these facts: the Sufi musical medium has moved away from the close confines of the zāwiya, where it once reigned supreme, to the festival. The shift is observed and commented upon by those loyal to a remembered heritage of music, to those who view it as essential to religious expression and who regard its entrance into popular culture as a mixed blessing at best. The more it becomes accepted by the population as a feature of entertainment, the more those who progressively reject its forms as part of a reformed Sufism come to dominate Sufi opinion. In the process the shift of the music is profound—toward a public expression of an Islamic nature. A considerable movement has emerged in Morocco around some aspects of this music becoming "folk." As Schuyler has noted, the Nāss el-Ghiwane and the Jīl Jilālā became the most successful of all groups in Morocco, based upon traditional songs by mystical poets.[72] The festivals indicate the public acceptance and articulation of a musical remembrance, now embraced by the public as a traditional artistic and religious form.

The late king undertook to bring Sufi art more into the public eye. He was himself a member of the ṭarīqa, and he regarded the Sufis as his ally in ruling the country. The general view was that the ṭarīqas and the king were as hand in glove. Not only did Sufism not have the character of rejecting the king's government, but it was widely believed to be the power behind the government. Generally, the king placed emphasis on those traditional arts that were amenable to his reign. A good case in point was his evenings of madīḥ, in which the best poets of the land came and performed qaṣā'id in his honor. This is modeled on the praises to the Prophet, but with the king as the recipient of the praise. The evenings usually started with madīḥ to the Prophet, and ended with praise to the king. Since the current king is not a member of the orders, the interest in this aspect of tradition has dropped in significance for the royal household.

Now that Maghribian music has hit the world music charts, the import of Sufi music to the public at large can no longer be denied. It has come out of the ṭarīqa, and is the sound relished literally by millions. It is too early to say what will become of this phenomenon, or how it will affect Sufi music in the ṭarīqa. But certainly the way it has migrated to popular entertainment means that, on at least one level, it is not dying. Some would argue that there is evidence of a local renaissance.

Thus Sufi music seems flexible enough for several kinds of messages in Morocco, and it is obvious that the spiritual realities addressed are nuanced and powerful. At the very least, this music indicates another dimension of Sufi presence in Morocco, carried by a music deemed to be a reflection of Moroccan identity.

7

THE CONTEMPORARY MUNSHID

Between Memory and Attestation

We live in your remembrance
For love of the lovers revives and moves us
Without your love within, we could not live.

Sufi chant from Abū Madyan al-Ghawthʾ (d. 1198)

I weep out of loyalty even if you do not generously grant me a love union;
Yet a dream image will satisfy and a remembrance will suffice us.

From the *Nūniyyah* of Ibn Zaydūn (d. 1071)

The Munshid as Professional

The munshid is a Sufi master . . . a master of a "power" performance. He does not understand his chanting as *just his performance.* It comes from a transcendent dimension, he believes, in that the origin of his words and music is not within himself, and the power to chant is not from him. His goal is to be part of a process of activizing memory.

Moreover, as we have seen, the words he chants are something more than mere words. The notion here is very much akin to the Hindu concept that the priests chant the words because the words have the power.[1] At one level, then, the munshid represents a professionalization of the mystical environment into a specialty of ritual reenactment.

What we wish to deal with in this section is the nature of that professionalization, in order that the full range of contribution to Sufism can be established. In chapter 4 we surveyed the repertoire of the chanter; here we want to deal with the general perspectives that inform the munshid's task. It is the principal contention of this section that the munshid's performance is judged by how well the lyrics, music, and articulation accomplish mythification,[2] that is, transform the ingredients into a seamless event of engagement with a divine Presence. This is the munshid's primary, but not only, arena of engagement. Behind this are countless small skirmishes and struggles against polemics of various sorts. Some of these have to do with Sufism in the contemporary scene, but some of them arise out of the emotional nature of the munshid's art and the very real pressure that the chanter feels.

In order to grasp these aspects of the professionalization of the chanter, we will survey the various aspects of the performance in their relative importance to the whole. This provides the framework for exploring the contemporary scene of the munshidūn in Morocco.

The first step in this exploration is reporting on the life of the leading munshid of his time, Muḥammad Bennīs, whose experience demonstrates some of the issues being explored.

Reflections of the Contemporary Munshid, Muḥammad Bennīs

In order to evaluate the situation of the contemporary munshid, I interviewed Muḥammad Bennīs, who is probably Morocco's best-known national munshid. He is also the founder of Jamʿiyyat al-Imām al-Būṣayrī liʾl-Inshād waʾl-Samāʿ, an organization committed to the preservation and development of young munshidūn. Bennīs is living in Fez.[3]

Bennīs was born in 1955 in that ancient city. His father was a craftsman who had a small home-based workshop where he made and sold silk scarves. It was not the business that interested young Muḥammad, however. His inclination to madīḥ started when he was young, helping his father, who used to chant *Bourda* and *Hamzīyya* while working in the shop. So predominant was this type of chanting in their home environment that all his brothers and sisters memorized almost all these poems and could recite them on demand.

> I have been singing in the ribāṭ for thirty-two years because I learned from my father and my grandfather. My grandfather was the muqaddam in the Tījāniyya ṭarīqa. His grandfather was also in the ṭarīqa, in the Kittāniyya, when I began my career in Sufism. My grandfather was also the leading munshid of Fez, so I am at home in the tradition of the munshidūn. Even though my father was an artisan, he spent a lot of time in the dhikr. Now, in my family, everyone knows dhikr.

Bennīs still has a soft spot in his heart for this early period of his life for he sees it as the formation of a strong trend in the family. He is particularly proud that one of his brothers, ʿAbd al-Fattāḥ, is "now a great munshid and a member of the [official] Rabat Andalusian Musical Orchestra."

Beyond that, he went to the mausoleum of Mūlay Idrīs in Fez every Friday, where many of the local munshidūn chanted the *Bourda* and *Hamzīyya,* and young Muḥammad reveled in their voices and their music. Moreover, he used to accompany his father to the Friday prayers and listen to the chanting. After the noon prayer, his father would invite these chanters to his house for dinner and an inshād session. It was the colorful group of munshidūn and Qurʾān reciters that filled the boy's mind with the great texts of the Sufi tradition. Their presence impelled Muḥammad to concentrate on the religious texts and to commit them to memory.

Bennīs memorized the Qurʾān at age eight with Shaikh Muḥammad al-Zaytūnī, a widely respected Sufi shaikh in Fez. Even at that age, Bennīs demonstrated a fine felicity for memorization, and he wanted to know more and to understand the texts in a deeper way. "Before choosing my Shaikh al-Zaytūnī, I went around to see different shaikhs to try to find out how much they knew and what they could teach me. No one else was satisfactory to me as almost all of them just memorized qaṣāʿid in a partial manner, and most of them had no knowledge of the context in which the qaṣāʿid were composed. Few of them had really mastered the techniques of samāʿ."

So he began attending the ḥaḍra of Shaikh al-Zaytūnī, who commenced instructing him in samāʿ and madīḥ. He was the youngest among fifteen or sixteen students with al-Zaytūnī, but the shaikh always gave him precedence and cherished him despite his young age. By the age of twelve, he showed extraordinary memorizing skills (he could memorize a seventy-verse qaṣīda in a single day): "This is a gift from Allah to me, along with a pleasant singing voice." Although he was the youngest of the students, his shaikh admired his talent and determined to push him toward public expression of the great texts.

> The leader of a madīḥ session is like a driver; he must have training but he must also be gifted (mawhība). I myself memorized qaṣāʿid by writing them down first, then memorizing them, and finally rewriting them again. I just didn't read them from a book.

The better he became, the more Shaikh al-Zaytūnī wanted him to be totally devoted to his study with him in his house, to the point where it interfered with his work in his father's shop.

In 1974, his love of music brought on a personal crisis. From the beginning of his singing, he had been attracted to Andalusian music, because it was the basis of samāʿ but also because, in his view, Sufi chanting could not be understood without reference to its rhythms and melodies. He became greatly attracted to inshād, delighting in the songs encompassed in all the old texts, including Andalusian love songs. If he moved in this direction, he could perform outside the ṭarīqa and receive some money for his talent.

There were two problems: First, the time and energy necessary to excel at this demanded more than his role in the family workshop would allow. Second, singing for money would cause a rift with his old shaikh, who regarded chanting anything but Sufi music a desecration of his God-given talents. He struggled with these complex issues for over a year. Finally, he left al-Zaytūnī and gravitated toward a shaikh with a broader musical repertoire. Later his old shaikh, al-Zaytūnī, would become embroiled in a political dispute with the government, and he eventually ended up dying in jail, to Bennīs's continuing sorrow.

His move toward the popular spectrum of inshād led him to a shaikh who had a strong national following as a munshid along with a reputation as a pious Tījānī adherent. This artistic (fannī) shaikh was ʿAbd al-Wahhāb Saqqāṭ. Saqqāṭ was a formidable singer whose abilities were appreciated even beyond the borders of the Sufi circle to which he belonged, and he regularly chanted for funerals and sang for weddings and circumcisions. These public-spirited performances he provided gratis, so that it could not be claimed that he had sold out for the money. The local head of the Tījāniyya, perhaps recognizing that his star could not be contained, and despite the exclusive character of the Tījāniyya, "authorized" Saqqāṭ to sing in any zāwiya or in any soirée to which he was invited. Although Saqqāṭ was illiterate, he was gifted, and he groomed Bennīs carefully. He especially imparted to him the stories and motivations behind the great poetry he was singing. He particularly trained him in the expectations the great writers had of him:

> Shaikh Saqqāṭ used to tell me that whenever I begin a madīh session, I should picture the imāms who composed the qaṣā'id, such as al-Imām al-Būṣayrī, al-Nabhānī, ʿAbd Raḥīm al-Buraʿī, Ibn al-Fāriḍ, and al-Shustarī, and try to give every one of them a "share" by singing his poems in the ḥaḍra. That way they would all remain happy and would not demand of me in the hereafter why I was not just to them.

This "bringing to life" of the famous writers through a cognitive process was further developed by Saqqāṭ's emphasis on context. This moved Bennīs to spend much more time in further study in addition to the information that was available to him within the ṭarīqa. Consequently, he began to research the background of the music, studying ancient sources to complement the shaikh's instruction. He also went deeper into the Sufi life personally. This spiritual movement had a direct effect on his performance:

> I used to sing many qaṣā'id and muwashshaḥāt, thanks to the divine gift of a sharp memory. Many of these were what the shaikh taught me, or what I found in the old texts. But I also used to receive some qaṣā'id in my dreams, and then I would sing them. I even sometimes would just find myself knowing a qaṣīda from nowhere . . . I just would be singing or meditating and it would come into my head . . . I may never have heard of it before. On any occasion in which I was singing, I would picture my shaikh standing right there in front of me and start singing like I was in his presence . . . I almost became another person because I was carried away by my shaikh's presence, and then he (the shaikh) would bring a very deep and old qaṣīda, one that was even forgotten by people, but they would recognize in me the stamp of Shaikh Saqqāṭ that they once knew.

Bennīs became so well regarded that when Saqqāṭ died, Bennīs was widely recognized as his heir, and he replaced him as the main munshid in the ṭarīqa: "When my shaikh died, I was regarded as the "depository of his merchandise" so that when I sang people would remember my shaikh and would ask Allah to bless him."

Despite this close spiritual connection to the Tījāniyya, it was obvious that Bennīs would have no career with them. The Tījāniyya were becoming increasingly resistant to any form of music among their murīdin, and Bennīs determined to continue his engagement with the great Sufi and Andalusian traditions. A local maqaddam, ʿAbd Laṭīf Ben Mansur, advised him to become a member of another ṭarīqa on the grounds that every munshid had to have a "principle" or a discipline. After much meditation and discussion—some of the best qaṣāʾid he had memorized and liked to sing belonged to those of Imām al-Ḥarrāq, the founder of the Ḥarrāqiyya—he decided to move on. He could not give up his commitment to the great traditions of vocal chanting so long part of ṭarīqa life in Morocco: "Although my father and all my ancestors have been Tijānī adherents, I joined the Ḥarrāqiyya because, for me, a munshid is like a bird who can sing in all kinds of trees."

Thus it was that, in 1990, in a gathering of the Ḥarrāqiyya at the zāwiya of Sīdī Masʿūd in Fez, Bennīs took the wird formally from Shaikh Ghālī al-Ḥarrāq and became a member of the Ḥarrāqiyya. He remains a member of the ṭarīqa, even if he now regards himself as a munshid for all ṭarīqas. He is, he says, "a member of God's ṭarīqa."

Bennīs on the Role of the Munshid

Bennīs has certain strong views about Sufi chanting. In the first place, he affirms that madīḥ and samāʿ

> originally had nothing to do with the Sufi ṭarīqa. They were (are) an art form intended mainly for entertainment (fann). In fact, samāʿ is mostly *tarbiyya* and *rafāhiya* (teaching and entertainment). What is required is for a shaikh to teach its rules and then one can complement this with special studies. Still one will always be grateful to one's first shaikh, because he learns the spiritual depths from him.

In contrast, the needs of the ṭarīqa center around dhikr and ʿamdah in each zāwiya. Thus he insisted that madīḥ and samāʿ are not associated with any specific ṭarīqa, and all the orders could draw on them if they wished. At the same time, Bennīs sees little real difference in the way the texts are chanted all over Morocco:

> Madīḥ and samāʿ are chanted virtually the same wherever you go in Morocco. They have the same ṭarīqa [here in the sense of style or manner] all over Morocco, except for a few nuances in some cities like Casablanca, because they follow the Andalusian music in both their rhythm (īqāʿ) and melody. It is necessary to distinguish madīḥ from samāʿ. Madīḥ is associated with the praise of the Prophet specifically as it is chanted in *al-Bourda* and *al-Hamzīyya* of al-Būsayrī, while samāʿ is based on poems of the Sufi shaikhs such as al-Imām al-Ḥarrāq, Ibn al-Fāriḍ, ʿAbū al-Ḥassan al-Shustarī, ʿAbd al-Ghanī an-Nabūlsy, Ibn al-ʿArabī, that is, those poems that are know as *Kalām al-Qawm*.

That his shift to the Ḥarrāqiyya was not as dramatic as it would appear on the face of it can also be gleaned from his view of the "calling" of the munshid. He is quite steadfast in his conviction that it is not the munshid that attracts people to the Sufi way. Rather, he sees the content of the poems of inshād and samāʿ as the key ingredient. These poems, if they are sound, should lead "to the way of Allah, and a munshid is like an ʿalim in admonishing people and helping them to come to Allah." While he acknowledges there are different abilities and techniques for doing this, "it is really through the content of the Sufi poems and ʿamdah that he sings" that his fame will come. Moreover, he believes it is the role of the munshid to "show the way to Allah, not just to a specific ṭarīqa."

Bennīs sees a special quality in the munshid of Morocco, based on the faithfulness to what he sees as the true text of the Sufi:

> The *Hamzīya* of Būṣayrī is the basis of inshād. This is why the operating principle of inshād in the first instance is the *Bourda* or *Hamzīyya*. This is why, when we create an ʿamdah, we create it in the name of Imām Būṣayrī. So, from the Moroccan perspective, the *Hamzīyya* and the *Bourda* are the basis of all inshād, and they should retain their place in performance. The fact is that the rhythm of inshād is beginning to disappear now, with modern singing taking its place; this is why some of us want to preserve the inshād and its basis in Imām Būṣayrī. The Moroccans, of all Muslims, are known to know and use the texts of Imām Būṣayrī. The other countries do not learn the entire texts of Imām Būṣayrī. When they perform, they try to sing either malḥūn or inshād. Not in Morocco. We chant first and foremost Imām Būṣayrī's texts. Each Friday we go to the mosque of Mūlay Idrīs to chant the *Hamzīyya* and the *Bourda*.

Bennīs attributes special powers or spiritual resistances to these texts . . . they are not just words. For example, when asked if he feels that singing is a way of escaping the influence of Satan, he said:

> My shaikh affirmed that Satan has no chance to be present in places where madīḥ and Sufi poems are sung. While there are different situations that call for different kinds of madīḥ, if the occasion is a happy one (marriage or circumcision), then happy poems should be sung. If the occasion is a sad one (that is, death) then appropriate poems will be chosen. In all cases the place where these poems are chanted, it is forbidden for Iblis to be present, because the remembrance of Allah drives Iblis away, especially if the munshid has strong faith and adopts the appropriate behavior in the presence of Allah.

Pressed on what this appropriate behavior might be, he indicated that the munshid should not be distracted from the content of what he is chanting, for the simple reason that he is performing in the presence of God.

Bennīs has a clear idea of the technique of inshād. He regards the munshid as "the shaikh of the inshād and samāᶜ sessions." He calls himself a *muᶜallim* (one who is learned), or *naffaq* (one who is an entrepreneur). As a naffaq, he chooses a theme from madīh, whether in praise of the ahl al-bayt or the Prophet, or from Sufi love poems. Once the theme is chosen, poems composed by various shaikhs but pertaining to the same theme become the basis of the whole performance. Having picked the theme, it is up to the munshid to carry on through the various texts in a smooth and convincing manner:

> The shaikh al-inshād should be able to make smooth transitions from one poem to another. He also will have to please his audience and respond to the spiritual and artistic expectations of the audience. The session should give everyone in the audience what he needs to be happy. A savvy naffaq should pay attention to the constitution of his audience and choose poems accordingly. This is so because some Sufi qaṣāᶜid are very esoteric and should be sung only to the knowledgeable people who will appreciate them. We sing them only in the zāwiya where people know their meaning. The youth nowadays do not believe in that deep sort any more and ask for only easy-to-understand qaṣāᶜid, especially now that many refute this kind of Sufism.

The mention of the youth of today brings up the issue of public taste and the training of young munshidūn. To Bennīs, all the poems are equally valuable for the process of Sufi meditation, but he himself does have preferences. For example, he prefers those compositions in the madīh of the prophet Muḥammad as compared to Sufi poems. This preference, he points out, arises out of the very process of sessions (*jalsa*—formal, legislative-type sittings): It starts with the Qurʾān, then proceeds with the poems of madīh, and then the samāᶜ. This process involves the ability to move from one kind of text to another, without breaking the mood of the session: "The transition from one kind of text to the other is left to the naffaq and his artistic ability. He must choose noghamat corresponding to the context and the occasion. Thus in maulid sessions, we choose ᶜamdah and praises of the Prophet and his family only."

Bennīs believes that his work in training youth in inshād is rooted in the ṭarīqa. Asked if there was a "school" of samāᶜ and madīh associated with him and his shaikh, Bennīs answered that he was entrusted with what he got from his shaikh and his role is to transmit it to the youth and that is why he founded many associations before and he is now directing a school and a group of munshidūn.

> I have formed an association in the mosque of Tajmuti because I have a class of students who I am teaching rather than just sending them to Sīdī Mūlay Idrīs. . . . The Mūlay Idrīs school is reputed to be the best school of inshād in Fez. All munshidūn must pass up the steps of Mūlay Idrīs in Fez. Each day I assist at the ᶜamdah and inshād and recite *Hamziȳa* and *Bourda*.

Munshid Muhammad Bennis with some pupils in his chanting school and the author (third from right), Fez, Morocco, August 8, 1995

I started when I attended the mūssem of Mūlay Idrīs at Zarhun in 1974 and found that people there were criticizing the munshidūn of Fez because they used to have special closed sessions of madīḥ in the zāwiya as-Sqalliyya and not at the mausoleum of the saint. The next year I returned to the mūssem with a group of sixteen young munshidūn. The local people greatly appreciated this practice, and I continued to take young munshidūn [to the mūssem of Mūlay Idrīs].

His work in developing young munshidūn was so successful that he founded another group each year, and then, in 1994, he decided to make it a permanent feature. He established a school in his house called al-Baraʿim (the burgeoning) from which many renowned singers "graduated," including his own brother ʿAbd al-Fattāḥ, mentioned above.

There is no doubt Bennīs applies quite different teaching techniques than even his own shaikh did with him. He places far greater emphasis on music as the background against which to understand the text. Unlike the old shaikhs, he teaches his students the basic elements of Andalusian tradition, like the *buḥūr* (modes) of the qaṣāʿid, the nagham, and the īqāʿ (the meter), and then he gives an explanation of the content of each qaṣīda and the biography of its composer. In his view this will assist them in understanding the meaning of the words, and they will come to comprehend the technicalities of samāʿ for themselves. This contrasts starkly with the old style of "mere repetitions (*muqallidūn*) of qaṣāʿid like the old shaikhs did."

Despite his attempts to develop a highly skilled corps of munshidūn, he acknowledges that it has not been easy. It is a constant struggle to get the munshidūn to go beyond a rather shallow understanding of the texts. They do not have the spiritual depth:

> There is a lack of good munshidūn in these groups who could help me go deeper and perform highly esteemed, complex poems. The youth know many popular texts. Among the things they do is each Friday morning they chant the *Bourda* at Fez and then in the afternoon they chant with the malḥūn. Young munshidūn do not want the work of memorizing these deeper poems, so when they are asked to sing, I always choose the easier qaṣīda for them. After all, the munshid's group knows these easy pieces by heart, and I do not want to embarrass my students. But . . .

He ended in a shrug.

The mention of complex texts such as served the Sufi tradition raises the issue of the criticism of these texts by those outside the mystical fold. Bennīs agrees that the criticism has impacted directly upon both his performance and what he sings. He indicated that he would only sing deeply spiritual Sufi poems when the audience is *aqṣā* (elite, or insiders; utmost) who can understand the significance and comprehend the parables of the Sufi poems. "There is little sense in talking about wine drinking among those who don't understand the context of such language."

Still, he regards his commitment to the world of samāʿ and inshād to be part of a larger educative role for Sufism. He suggests that the emphasis on education may be somewhat innovative. For example, Bennīs acknowledges that the Moroccan musical tradition is very complicated, and this has brought about one change: "Moroccan inshād is more complicated than Eastern [Egyptian/Syrian] inshād, above all in the area of rhythm. This is why the Moroccan munshid begins to perform the Eastern tawāshīḥ as a way of attracting the attention of young people who really do not understand Moroccan inshād. It's just simpler for them to relate to."[4]

He also agrees that many people want to listen to the munshid out of pleasure, rather than out of awareness of the meaning. Hence he sees the role of the munshid today as partly to educate, so that people will understand the deeper meanings of what they are hearing. The one innovation that he does support is the use of cassette tapes and videos; he believes these bring an awareness to the population that they did not have, since many of them had no connection to Sufism. Thus there is a place for tapes and videos in the education he is trying to promote in the country.

> The munshidūn should strive to conserve the Islamic patrimony and educate the audience instead of following the audience's [bad] taste that now appreciates only light and profane music. And I believe that when the munshidūn shoulder this "mission," Allah will endow them with more gifts, to aid in their

role of calling people to Allah. They will have a ṭarbiyya to attract the youth to Allah, and Allah will grant them success (*tawfīq*).

Muhammad Bennīs is a contemporary munshid of stellar proportion in Morocco, and his commitment to developing a school of young singers clearly will impact on the growth of the genre of music and its place in Moroccan culture. From his perspective the future of the munshidūn in Morocco is bright.

Principles of Contemporary Munshid Performance in Dhikr

The munshid is first and foremost a member of a socially prominent group, an order. He sees himself as the inheritor of many memories, of many important legacies. As Bennīs said, "This is part of my jihād, my inheritance. I must undertake this chanting for God."[5]

So being a munshid is often a personal jihād, a personal commitment to one's social past, to one's ancestors who were or are powerful Sufis. This notion also plays a role in the preservation and expression of pious texts. Munshidūn regard the textual and musical traditions associated with their ṭarīqa as part of their personal legacy, and handing it on as a sacred responsibility bequeathed by their family. This continues to today in the sense of maintaining family greatness. Ben Cherīfa notes:

> The family was the key element so far as Andalusian influence was concerned. Families moved from Andalus to two principal cities, Rabat and Tetuoan. A sizeable majority came to Rabat. The first part of them settled at Salé, where they were called Moriscoes. They kept the same names they had had in Andalus. The family al-ʿAzifiyūn in Subtah, near Tetouan, now under Spain's control, was an important link to the development of malḥūn singing. One family, the Goudera, or in Arabic, Kudera, still have a number of relatives in Spain; this family continues to be important to today. Francisco Goudera is a Spanish orientalist whose family has been well known in Spain since the nineteenth century. Another is Barkas, as is Karakso. Another is Rundah. The scholar Ibn al-Ibbād is from this family. He was a great Sufi. He is buried at Fez. At any rate, when the great families were expelled from Andalusia, they came here and brought their culture with them. This depth of important families and their connection to Sufism is why Moroccan and Andalusian music have become so interwoven in the zāwiya, and gives Sufism here a strong family sense.

Furthermore, the munshid's performance, like that of any theatrical performer, is not just remembering words in a literal fashion and singing them; rather, he should perform with the emotional authority embodied in the words, because it arises out of his conviction that this phrase has the appropriate power to move the dhikr beyond where it is now. Such a process is a complex task involving his own spiritual

memory, the power of the words, and his ability to engage creatively with his imagination, and to utilize the musical formulas properly. Successful preparation for his
chanting requires both learning the process sketched here and preparing his own
spiritual state so that he can read the dhikr appropriately. In fact, he regards this as
an attesting function. He is trying to get the dhikr participants to "see" what he has
seen, to know what he has known, to share what he feels. As we noted in chapter 6,
Ashhab places this seeing in another domain, quite distinctive from the ordinary one
associated with the shaikh. Thus imaginational realities play a key role in the attestation process.[7]

> Ibn al-ʿArabī regarded this ability to manipulate the imagination this way as
> "unveiling." The knowledge required in unveiling takes, according to him,
> four different forms: tasting, witnessing, opening, and insight. Chittick had
> stressed that imagination was a kind of unveiling,[8] in which the imagination
> made an individual open to spiritual forces, and then, according to Sufi theo-
> reticians, God or the spiritual realm give form and shape to those realities so
> that the seeker can relate to them. In this way, imagination serves as facilitator,
> allowing articulation to take place.

There are those who raise questions about Ibn al-ʿArabī's religious structure, and
argue that neo-Sufism has really developed annihilation in the Prophet, or in the
shaikh as an alternative to his views, so that the goals of the Sufi liturgies are really
conceived differently because of the reformist movements in Islam. Hoffman has
argued that Ibn al-ʿArabī taught the doctrine.[9] Most munshidūn in this study
regarded these nuances as pertaining to advanced theory in Sufism; they distinguished different levels of mystical achievement to be based on the level of individual accomplishment in esoteric understanding, not on doctrinal distinctions brought
on by reactions to Ibn al-ʿArabī. Some even argued that there could be no qualita-
tive difference between different types of fanāʾ experiences, because they all come
from God. My research in Morocco leaves the formal part of this issue open, but indicates that the imagination is still the tool that must be used, and it must be inspired
from above to achieve any level whatsoever.

Most performers acknowledge the crucial notion of a deep spiritual experience in
allowing them to deliver a powerful performance. Otherwise, the munshid will be
regarded as not strong, as having little depth, as just mouthing the words. Interestingly, then, the depth of personal mystical understanding has a very pragmatic side.

This poses some difficulty for the munshid. It is almost like a prophet who must
prove himself in his own country. There is, in Sufi terms, a secret to every chanter.
Some kinds of things bother him and drive him in ways that others do not. While
his hadra compatriots would not openly criticize him, since it is the shaikh who
approves the chanter, it is clear that participants favor one kind of munshid over
another, and some of this favoring has to do with the spirituality they perceive in the

munshid. One soon learns that there is a hierarchy of munshidūn in each group. Some will never become a principal munshid because they have neither the voice nor the personal brokenness regarded as essential to comprehend the spiritual life. For some, especially those who lack a sense of confidence, their performance is a secret between them and the saint, that is, they will make certain kinds of commitments to the saint in return for a good dhikr. These are spiritual negotiations that mark the development of any munshid. Sufi ritual, then, at least as far as the munshidūn are concerned, operates within a principle of reciprocal probe: "If, O God, you will grant this, then I will respond by doing that."

Both spiritual and physical maturity is a factor in munshid selection. Youths are prized for their "tender" voices, their fear of not being adequate to the ritual requirements, their terror at destroying a good ḥaḍra through their inability to "go with the flow." They are burdened by the role, suffering the constant threat of failure in order to accomplish some spiritual goal.

The experienced munshidūn, however, are seasoned in the way of the Presence, can read and deliver phrases quickly and perceptively, and have a more take-charge attitude. They are comfortable in front of the "spirit" of the dhikr and brethren; they handle the spiritual modulations with precision and firm direction. They know what phrases are likely to have the greatest impact. Even they suffer, though, because they are most often criticized for not learning new chants, for not growing with their sound. They also have a long history with many of the members, with all the potential areas of conflict that come from small-group dynamics. So they must deal with their own set of afflictions.

One would think that there would be a kind of automatic element to these performances. After all, Sufi poetry is fixed, the *Bourda* and *Hamzīyya* or the poetry of the Sufi shaikhs, all are subject to rigidity in meter and ṭurāth; there is no way to innovate. The mawwāl is the only part that can be subject to innovation. Indeed, the mawwāl has the potential to be very creative. Yet this is also rooted in the memory of Andalusian music, in terms of rhythm and words. So no one has the freedom to move beyond the boundaries of the genre and produce some really new form of meditation. None are really the creator of a kind of new song. The band of performance within which the munshidūn work is hedged about with tradition, controlled by the collective memory, and restricted by the goals and intentions of the shaikh.

And yet the experienced munshidūn find their role meaningful. That is, most do. A few do not. When I went to Meknes to met the top chanter, "Muḥammad," in the ʿAissawiyya as had been planned, he was not available, because, we were told, he had decided to move into entertainment and no longer saw himself as "only" a munshid.[10] There was some consternation at this, since the brethren regarded him as having a wonderful voice and able to chant with great conviction. Yet as Nabīl noted when indicating to me that Muḥammad was moving "outside," "If the world of the brethren no longer attracts him, then he is lost to us anyway." Somehow he had forgotten who he was and had broken ranks, even if he came back to chant on occasion. The occurrence indicates that the munshid, especially if he is good, is tempted by the money and fame attendant upon entertainers. His reluctance to even talk about his decision, though, indicates that he knew full well the sense of loss that the brethren felt. He had broken with his religious "family," not over doctrine or position but over materialism. He had lost his place in the hierarchy of the ṭarīqa. He clearly had to deal with that loss himself. Ashḥab, in commenting on this scenario, was blunt: "In this society, now, there are those who are regarded as munshidūn and maddāḥūn but who no longer have the religious experience to make it living. Once they lose it, they may as well move on into secular singing."[11]

The language of the brethren also indicated that they felt a kind of terror at this decision that they could not comprehend; sentiments such as "I hope he knows what he is doing" were common. So affliction can be of many different kinds.[12]

On the other hand, various other informants indicated that, while he appeared to have broken with the spiritual state of his ṭarīqa, many others were also doing so now because the old line of shaikh-based Sufism was losing its hold. No longer did all the piety of the ṭarīqa revolve around the norms and standards set by the shaikh. Today, many younger members are opposed to the headship of the shaikhs because the shaikhs often gain their position not by dint of spiritual insight but because of their perceived "reliability."

As a result of the new problems within the structure of the order, some munshidūn withdraw from shaikh-based dhikr because the focus has shifted from the state of heart to one of numbers and loyalty to the shaikh. This is what one said: "The objective of dhikr before, in the past, was on everyone's mind. The murīdīn, they listened with everything, heart, head, body. Now one does not find rūḥānī in the dhikr because the rhythm is what interests the people. There is no longer ilḥām in the zāwiya, just the desire to move in tandem with the beat."

One reason the role of shaikh-based ṭarīqa life is under stress arises from the way shaikhs become head of the ṭarīqas. Traditionally based on the lineage of the shaikh or by designation before the death of the old shaikh, now troubled ṭarīqas are assigned leaders based on the ability of the potential contender to demonstrate money-raising abilities. One example of this is the story of the flags.

Each ṭarīqa has a series of flags and processional banners that it uses for celebrations. One flag has Qur'ān on it, on another the emblem of the ṭarīqa. One processional flag is in yellow, another in blue. But the most important of all is the flag of the muqaddam, and it is green (the Prophet's color). When a contender for the muqaddam came before the council of ʿulamāʾ who awarded the leadership of ṭarīqas, he was told it was six thousand Moroccan dirhams. The contender said, "I'm sorry, I just don't have that kind of money."

"Fine," they said, "we won't expect any money from you for four years." The person recounting this episode noted that gifts from friends, relatives, and devotees allowed the contender to come the following year, at the time of the mūlid al-nabi, with sufficient money to pay for the position.

The storyteller gave this story as an example of how God leads some people to be heads of ṭarīqas even if they are not rich. I, however, think it also indicates how the affairs of the ṭarīqa can easily slip into pure financial manipulation, with the result that many people lose faith in the system.

According to my sources, the persons who allocate such leadership roles must judge a number of different qualities among the contenders. Yet the ability to raise funds seems to be a crucial one, which I take to be secular. A munshid who does not want his name used tells the following: "The ten judges must agree to a person being raised to a muqaddam and must sign the paper. When I was a dhikran, I was invited to Meknes to chant. I chanted a qaṣīda that only three of the judges knew. The judges were impressed and wanted me to be a muqaddam, but I refused because it is very expensive to be a muqaddam."

Another secular situation that has impacted on the munshid's repertoire relates to commercial tapes; the modern convenience of the cassette has allowed people to judge what kind of music they like from within the Sufi genre, and they are choosing the more dramatic, more "musically Morocco" stylings of the ʿAissawiyya. It is because of the cassettes that a great deal of people know something about them, where before they were such a closed group that few knew just what went on in their performances. Now Moroccans know that Sufi dhikr is the same as others, but Moroccan Sufi cassettes are more interesting from the point of view of rhythm. So musically, they are building a following. Contrarily, the dhikr of other more conservative groups is concerned with words and their meanings, and is less amenable to translation into pure entertainment. This is another dimension of what might be seen as a secularization of the dhikr.

Part of this secularization has a political basis. Since the 1970s the king has laid much greater stress upon the ṭarīqas, not necessarily for the advancement of their deeper spiritual purposes, but as a way to offset rival political factions. Where once Sufism deflected Marxist influence in Morocco, it is being used today to offset fundamentalist influence. Sensitive members find the traditional ṭarīqa culture taken over by these historical and political pressures, and they react very negatively to it. Talented young chanters can become quickly disenchanted when they see their talents being ignored or manipulated for the shaikh's benefit, or even worse, according to some political intrigue. So the ṭarīqas of the city are seeing this kind of falling away ever more evident.

A story I was told will illustrate the disillusionment. A long-time country member of a zāwiya traveled many kilometers to visit the shaikh in the town. When he sat down with the brethren, the shaikh asked who he was and what he wanted. The adept was outraged with this attitude. He retorted: "How will you recognize me and speak for me on the day of resurrection if you do not reecognize me today? How will you know me among millions if you do not know me among twenty?"

The shaikh's reply indicated that he missed the point. He said, "When we are together at the judgment, I will have special powers to recognize you." This was just not good enough. The country believer traditionally relied on a personal, conscious relationship with his shaikh, based on a common spiritual cohesion. He relied on the shaikh both to get him through this world and to guide him through the next. That dimension of Sufism is now rapidly being lost, at least in part because the shaikh is only another appointee of the government or a government-sanctioned Sufi committee, without the baraka of the great saints of the past. There is a disengagement process going on. It therefore is possible that "Muḥammad," the ʿAissawiyya chanter who left his ṭarīqa, was responding to the same kinds of pressure and used the excuse of entertainment to flee an organization that no longer seemed to represent what it once did.

There is, of course, the classic contradiction in Sufi practice now taking on a Moroccan hue. If, as is often said, Plotinus's cosmology forever sealed God in his heaven and separated Him from mundane human life, then the basic philosophical problem has to be addressed: an all-powerful God can only be reached by some kind of emanational means. The more rationalist the analysis of the Sufi relationship with God, the more necessary is an alternate means of comprehending the Presence in the ḥaḍra. That is, under the force of today's materialism and fundamentalism, the specifics of Sufi ideology are pushed ever more closely to articulating how God could be present at all. Sufis cannot resort to rationalism, so they have to articulate how a special spiritual content is present with them. Without a spiritual awareness in the adept, the case is lost, and the murīdin become conscious of a new, widespread forgetfulness.

Certainly this is forgetting of a different sort than loss of chanting skills. If, as we have indicated, the munshid's performance is a kind of forgetting, now he is confronted by alternative religio-ethical schemas. His performance refuses to address the rationalist potential of the question, opting instead to "forget" it in the light of the concreteness of the experienced Presence. Yet his friend next door may question the validity of his experience, and particularly the training that leads to its experience. The munshid must "forget" a great deal.

How, then, can a spiritually sensitive individual address what is happening? Mūlay ʿArbi al-Darqāwī gives us one possible alternative: the conception of rationality is incorrect:

Men with knowledge do not run away from things as others do, for they contemplate their Lord in everything. . . . And know that nothing prevents us from contemplating our Lord but the fact of being preoccupied with the desires of our souls. Do not say that it is existence that veils the maker of existence, for by God, it is imagination/illusion (*wahm*) alone that hides Him from us, the wahm which gives rise to ignorance. If we only knew, it would lead us to the knowledge of certainty and certainty would distract our heart and inmost consciousness from the sight of ephemeral things.[13]

In this reading, that is, that of "classical" mysticism, the Sufi does not see rationality functioning with the same meaning. Yet this shaikh-centered Sufism is just the Sufism that is somewhat suspect in contemporary Morocco, especially in the cities. There are tensions here that cloud the clear sky of mystical truth.

Clearly, the ordinary munshid is not party to the greatest secrets, so he therefore has had to construct a different scheme of things. He understands performance as having a cathartic purpose, a role that shifts him away from either trance or extinction. The munshid grounds his meaning in the "good" dhikr, in the cathartic moment in which the brethren participate in a genuine mythic event . . . the Presence in all its power. Nabīl had this to say about inspiration: "There are many kinds of *insijām*. There is insijām of the religious festival. There is the general insijām of the brethren when they are together. But the real insijām is the insijām of the dhikr when the spirit of depth in spiritual affairs envelopes the participants and a general uplifting takes place. Everyone then senses ilhām and a special kind of insijām takes place."

Clearly there are different conceptions of how this power works. One munshid was quite explicit: the power did not rest on him but on the group. He was only a tool for a process that was taking place in the hearts of the brethren to whom he sang. He explained, "We *all* feel shaṭaḥāt (tranced states) from another world, and ḥudūd (feelings of boundlessness), but the munshid exists here in this world. So ilhām rests only on the [person who is] Sufi, not on the munshid."

This is different from what is said by most other munshidūn, who recount that ilhām is part of their experience, an experience that they bring to the performing situation. While the issue does have an element of the semantic to it, it is worth noting the difference, for it suggests that the munshid's ideology may not always be expressed the same way, or be so firmly in place.

Ashḥab notes:

The ʿamdah begins at 8 P.M. and continues to 2:30 A.M. We use many different kinds of texts because each poet has his own nafas-like style, but each zāwiya has a few words and a kind of universe of performance that is distinctive to it. So the munshid feels that he is rūḥ, that he is spirit . . . but he has to conform his chanting to ṭurāth (tradition). So if one feels strongly about a text from outside, he has to change it to make it conform to the ṭurāth of the order. Then he can use his own style to get the message across. That can be a problem.

The Traditional Experiential Foundation of Performance

There is no doubt that the ṭurāth of the order rests in a value system rooted in a sense of well-being in the dhikr. The munshid has a healing role to play, to bring back a sense of balance to the adept's life: "The sickness afflicting your heart, faqīr, comes from the passions which pass through you; if you were to abandon them and concern yourself with what God ordains for you, your heart would not suffer as it now suffers. So listen to what I say and may God take you by the hand."[14]

The good munshid remembers . . . not all the words and music he has heard, but the primary events of an engagement with the shaikh. It is the power of this remembering that transmutes into a fine performance, for he sings as if to his shaikh. Every powerful munshid has an experiential narrative that forms the basis of his performance. Each of these is mythic in dimension, framing the ongoing experience he hopes to incarnate in his performances. This is Nabīl's "foundational narrative":

> Bībā Aḥmad Shawqī is my true shaikh. We have a saying that one is a shaikh who is truly a master. This man is truly a master. Even today, when I sit with him . . . his health is not too good and he seldom can come . . . Even now, my hair stands on end. When I was very small, I used to sit next to him and I listened to him throughout the year, year in, year out . . . he had me right beside him. He told the muqaddam that I had a special gift, but of course he never said that to me. Yet I know that we had a special relationship. He is my father, my grandfather in a spiritual sense. When he touched the middle of my forehead with his finger, I could feel the connection to him. I love that man a great deal.

This intimate connection fixes a spiritual agenda in the munshid's mind, and it impacts on his performance. He tries to replicate that foundational experience in each performance. The contemporary munshid, then, consciously affirms that he is an intermediary between a powerful Presence that is not yet articulated but which he must articulate in order for the ummah to grow.

Even this quality of being an intermediary, however, places him in a position of vulnerability. Since the munshid is a ritual specialist, he is required to be a kind of master of an uplifting enactment; his maneuvering through music, drumming, hand clapping, lyrics, and gesture is essential to the positive benefits of the dhikr.[15]

In addition, his performance provides an emotional cognitive map by which the adepts can find their own level of spiritual achievement in the dhikr.[16] We have seen how he constructs this map with the lyrics and the music of the ṭarīqa, yet draws from himself his own sense of spiritual need. His performance projects the spiritual map as a kind of experiential coding for the brethren. So when he and the adepts forget the world and concentrate on the visualizing process, they then bring to the dhikr the potential for this "presence," with all that it entails in terms of baraka. Thus his performance has in it a type of aesthetic, an aesthetic of spiritual well-being.

This is, itself, a very old notion. The munshid sees himself allied to the ancient poem of ladhidhʾ al-ʿasāla, the honey of life. This harks back to the tenth century and could be called the "constitution" (dustūr) of the *fuqahāʾ*, that is, "This is the wine that Ḥallāj and the Rifāʿī drank before us." That wine may be very ancient, but like popular conceptions of wine and honey, it has a therapeutic role to play in the lives of the fuqahāʾ to whom he chants. This is his true spiritually mandated performance, the result of his established Islamic identity.

Issues in Contemporary Morocco and the Social Influence of the Munshid

There are a number of issues and problems that became obvious during this research. While some only involve individual cases, such as conflicts between a new shaikh and an old munshid, there are others that relate to the larger role of Sufism and the munshid within Moroccan society. Four of these issues are particularly important: the impact of Islamism on Sufism; criticism of Sufism and ṭarīqa culture; and the use of drugs and stimulants within Sufism.

The Impact of Islamism on Sufism

In the course of my research, the Islamist reformation and its impact in Morocco was discussed at some length. I was intrigued to know whether the munshidūn were attracted by this phenomenon and how they responded to it. The conclusion was that some areas of their lives had been directly affected by the Islamist doctrine, but overall, the impact has not been all that significant. A student friend of Nabīl, Aḥmad, said: "Yes, there is an Islamist movement in Morocco. Just about all the important student-elected positions at the university have gone to the Islamists. But you can't take them too seriously. Once they get a job and get married and have responsibilities, they soon forget all this revolutionary talk. They just want a good life for themselves and their families."[17]

Most of the people with whom I discussed the problem regarded the Islamists as serious Muslims, but they rejected their views on Islam and the contemporary state. The consensus seems to be that the Islamist forces in Algeria demonstrate the violence and mayhem that lie at the root of the Islamist agenda. For most Sufis, then, the politicization of Islam has not been successful. In order to do so the Islamists must prove that they will make peoples' lives better, and they have not done that, therefore, their ideology cannot be from God. Since adopting the Islamist agenda would scuttle personal views of the interiority of Islam, they see no advantage to it for the zāwiya. Moreover, they decry the further fragmenting of the ummah around these ideologies and cannot see how this can be part of God's plan for his community.

Islamism has also affected the interchange between the orders. Thus Ashḥab notes: "The Ḥarrāqiyya accept all wird and samāʿ, but the Tijāniyya go far away from the *ghullu* (fetters, bounds). The Tijāniyya operate like a kind of fundamentalism, and they do not want to listen to other inshād. Their shaikh has laid down some principles that do not allow them to listen to others, but the Ḥarrāqiyya are much more liberal. I have often been asked to sing in many other ṭarīqas."

And the import of Islamism on critiquing the texts of the munshid has been significant. Said one munshid:

Here the shaikhs only choose the simple texts from Ibn al-ʿArabī because they do not want to get involved with the ʿulamāʾ on issues like *waḥdat al-wujūd* (unity of being). Only those poems that are not problematic are used. I know that Qayrawān University has ʿulamāʾ who make pronouncements on the validity of Ibn al-ʿArabī. Frankly, I don't know if there are some texts under interdiction. I usually don't chant them unless I'm with a select group of Sufis.

Criticism of Sufism and Ṭarīqa Culture

Asked about the modern criticisms of the ṭarīqa and the ṭāʾifa, the munshid typically shrugs and notes that just because they chant songs of great depth related to a vibrant memory of the past does not mean that they are burying their head in the sand. As Ashḥab noted:

> The shaikh often speaks in the ṭarīqa before the ḥaḍra about modern issues. We spend a great deal of time together, and we talk of many things. We are, after all, a big family. The shaikh explains what the Qurʾān says about women, and we discuss this in the zāwiya. We talk about many issues. But he is limited in what he can say and do because the people do not understand the significance of these things. After all, not very many people are educated enough to know the issues. But he tries to educate them.

Sufis are puzzled at the lack of understanding of the role that the zāwiya plays in a community. Thus, the munshid does not perform as part of a ritual priesthood that is completely cut off from the crises of the group; rather, he is party to almost all the crises facing the order. Nabīl has this to say:

> Take poverty, for example. The zāwiya is part of a much larger economic system. We have resources to help our members, and sometimes if someone comes with problems the muqaddam will help him. The other day, a man from the ṭarīqa came whose brother had died and he did not have enough to take care of expenses, and the muqaddam helped him out. But these are problems that we share with all Muslims. So we share what we have with everyone who joins with us or is connected to us in some way. That's our contribution to being Muslim.

Evidently, then, the zāwiya is a social mediator for the government in some areas of concern, and is able to provide a social safety network arising out of motivations for the betterment of the community. The munshid sees himself as part of this public outreach, and his role is an important one in maintaining the attractiveness and power of the order in Moroccan culture.

Use of Drugs and Stimulants within Sufism

If there is a truly controversial issue, it is the use of stimulants and drugs during samāʿ and ʿamdah. The meaning of drugs in Western culture has alerted Sufis to cultural differences, and they are shy to discuss the use of stimulants because of it. Ashhab was very direct: "It is better not to talk, since those who speak do not know what they are speaking about. Those who speak much do not know the subject. If you know love like I do, then you will rest without speaking. I do not want to judge another. When I talk to you about drugs, I am speaking of another poet, not myself. I do not use them, and will never do so."

Dr. ʿAbdūl Mujib ʿAbd al-Surūr related a story of a problem that Sufism experienced in the nineteenth century. Apparently the founder of the Harrāqiyya al-Darqāwiyya encouraged the use of *marffū* (something that supports, lifts up), that is, stimulants, at which time the use of drugs by highly placed munshidūn became entrenched. When they were asked to chant at prestigious parties because the people appreciated the Sufi stylings, they were supplied with helwa mixed with hashish. The fact that the use of drugs was embraced by folk singers and popular singers made it attractive to a certain class of chanters. Some of these chanters did not have the constraints of the brethren to help them as much as they should have, and they became addicted. Since Ashhab is from the Darqāwiyya, I asked him about this:[18]

> There is no doubt that drug use is present in secular malhūn performances, and often one sees the *riqa* pipe at an evening of malhūn with the *qut* drug in use. But I see little or almost none of it in my circles. We know that the entertainment-type singers of malhūn are invited to parties in Spain where drugs may be present. But using drugs is not a requisite even in these evening soirées. It is generally agreed that the Ginawa used *qif* even in their religious rituals, but if it is used at all in most Sufi circles, it is confined to a very few.[19]

Still, if there are pressures to move into entertainment-type strands of Moroccan singing, then drug use might be a factor in the attractiveness of doing so for some munshidūn. However, it does not appear that the issue is of immediate concern, apart from generating strong opinions among the munshidūn.

Moving Inshād into the Public: The Festival and Royal Initiatives

Some Sufis regard the bad press they receive to be a direct result of the dominance of a secular press corps. Therefore, for them, the national side of the tarīqas may be diminished in the press because many of the current directors and media people have been trained under the secular "lost" generation of scholars at the universities who are far more interested in Morocco's role in international affairs than in its national culture. But leaders like Shaikh al-Barrāda regard the press as a narrowing instrument in Moroccan structures of reality, that is, they reflect the same kind of homogenization that the orientalists were accused of participating in. The one thing that mediated this in Morocco was the important role the late king played in raising the Sufi agenda to contemporary national prominence, perhaps as a way of offsetting both the secularism of the press and the politicizing of the Islamists.

One way this was done was to raise the scope and importance of public festivals. The Prophet's birthday has evolved into a major festival within Morocco; scholar Faṭīma al-Yazīdi argues that the whole emphasis on this festival was to counter the influence of Christian festivals on popular life, and, while some ʿulamāʾ condemned it as contrary to Islam, the fuqahāʾ, on the other hand, agreed that, while it was *bidʿa*, it was *bidāʿ muḥassana*, that is, preferred or allowable deviation.[20] The impetus for celebrations like mūlids and mūssems also comes as a response to the need for specifically festive religious holidays that are less associated with ritual requirements than occasions such as the ʿĪd al-Aḍḥā and ʿĪd al-Fiṭr celebrations.

During Merinid times, the royal family wanted to create a celebration for the Muslims. They endowed the mūlid al-nabī, modeled on the quasi-religious holidays of Christmas. The Merinids made the holiday official in all the great cities of Morocco. These festivals incorporated the poets, the munshidūn, the *maddaḥun*, and the singers. The singers were called *muzemzemoun*, an ancient word from Merinid times that required the shaikh to direct the celebrations. In Ibn Marzūq, we have the earliest descriptions of the role of royalty in shaping Muslim festive life.[21]

The celebrations have almost always differed from one area to another, and resources for the celebrations were dependent on local authorities for their size and largess. Recently, though, the national government has supported the development of a Moroccan fete around the festivals in Salé and Rabat.

The festivities have been organized around local mythical events, like that of the candle in Salé (the fete of the candle is very ancient in Salé and perhaps was attached to the mūlid al-nabī in antiquity). Now it is a magnificent event, with lights and candles and much celebration. The festivals are great showcases for Andalusian singing and especially for samāʿ, where, of course, well-known munshidūn, including Bennīs, perform.

During our interviews, Dr. ʿAbd al-Surūr the munshid who was also a doctor said there was a distinction between madḥ and samāʿ. For him, samāʿ arises out of the zāwiya and Sufism, and exists because of that social context, while madḥ may be used in popular festivities like weddings. The latter can also be sung to Andalusian music, and thus has a far wider appeal than just music for the mystical adepts.

When we visited the festival in Tetouan, it was clear that munshidūn were there from many different places and many different ṭarīqas. This raised the question whether there was a real distinction between ʿumda (or ʿamdah) and samāʿ, since some called the festival both names. It is difficult to get practitioners within the festival to delineate the difference between them. This festival is about ten years old and was originally known as an ʿamdah. Then about four years ago the organizers added samāʿ. So the festival itself is really an amalgamation of these two genres. (Neither Ashḥab nor Bennīs distinguished between the two.)

In the festival, the munshidūn came from different towns but did not represent any zāwiya; rather in the festival they were representing their town. If a particular group was not present in the festival, either the zāwiya in the town did not have munshidūn or the shaikh forbade them from participating in these kinds of "secular" festivals.

In order to get some contemporary views on this issue, I interviewed ʿAbdul-Raḥmān al-Karumbī, director of the Salé and Rabat festivals. While the festivals have evolved into great artistic and creative events, they were first presented in their current scope only in April of 1990. Karumbī noted:

These festivals have been in place now for five years. Before that they were confined to the various regions, in the various ṭarīqas. In order to preserve and expand the ʿamdah and samāʿ and to teach the young about the Prophet, we have decided to make this a national festival. Each region has a committee composed of the minister of culture and an official of the local community who knows the ʿamdah and samāʿ and musicians. They listen to each singer and choose the best on the basis of their abilities in the several kinds of Andalusian music and their knowledge of ʿamdah and samāʿ texts. The king also invites the best singers for an evening of ʿamdah and samāʿ, based on the same formula. But in that soirée, the poetry is changed while the music remains the same, so that the king can be praised. It is part of our desire to further religious knowledge. For example, during the month leading up to the Prophet's birthday, we have a recital of the life of the Prophet. Every night we have a different aspect of his life recited. We do this to acquaint the children with the life of the Prophet and to refresh our awareness of his accomplishments. During the festival associated with mūlid al-nabī, we have three nights dedicated to the celebration, and the final night we have this national festival of ʿamdah and samāʿ. In it we begin with the Qurʾān, then proceed to the *Bourda* and *Hamzīya* of al-Būṣayrī, then we have qaṣāʿid from the great writers like Ibn al-Fāriḍ, al-Shustarī, al-Ḥarrāq, and so on. Then tilālā (four times), then Qurʾān, then we end the evening with Fātiha.

Karumbī says much of the musical character of the event derives from Shaikh Badjdūb, who, as a professor of music, has spent much of his life studying and developing this resource. According to Karumbī, Shaikh Badjdūb "cannot be called just a munshid or a malḥūn. He knows all forms of traditional music. The munshidūn tradition is linked in Morocco to the Sufi tradition and to the dhikr . . . but someone with the talent of Shaikh Badjdūb also sings for weddings, celebrations, of all kinds, and the mūlid." It is also the case that he knows the material so well that he can improvise, and he has the authority to do so. Thus, one informant commented:

He is a mujaddid. He is in charge of choosing what ʿamdah and samāʿ will be sung in the festival. He chooses the qaṣāʿid and can thus introduce new texts into the evening. By virtue of his position, these songs have to be sung, although technically he cannot bring in material from the famous writers that has never been used before. But he does it in small ways.

Karumbī noted, however, that all the munshidūn in Morocco were amateurs, and this means that locals had to have training in order to make their singing of national interest: "There are really no 'professional' munshidūn in Morocco. They all have other jobs and chant as part of their religious commitment. The training, however, is all done locally, so we have to help with this in order to develop these resources."

Still, the role of the king cannot be discounted here. Every day after prayers, one is to praise the king. (A formula well known throughout the Morocco that I toured was "Three kinds of persons should be killed: those who do not believe in God, those who do not believe in Morocco, and those who do not believe in the king.")

It was widely reported that the late king and the orders worked together "like hand in glove," as my researcher Sayyid put it. He added, "Sufism does not have the character of rejecting the king's authority in government. In fact, it is the power behind the government."

In addition, the late king established a royal formal acceptance procedure; in it each official appeared before the king and acceptance of the ʿahd (acknowledgment of loyalty) of all officials, men of state, presidents of community organizations, shaikhs of ṭarīqas and zāwiyas, heads of tribes, and so on were formally accepted by the king. Each presented a list of members of his group and indicated that all were the king's loyal subjects.

The late king deliberately embraced Sufi chanting as Islamic and traditional. There were some local views as to why he did this. For example, the music that is chanted is popular; it is favored by the people, so much emphasis is put on the zajal. These texts are preferred because the local people can understand their meanings and comprehend their language, and make connections with their everyday life. As a result, one can hear local phrases and endearment phrases like "sīdī," or "bībī," depending on the kind of malḥūn and the formality of the occasion. At official celebrations, there is still reference to the religious hierarchy, for the evening begins with the *Bourda,* then moves to madīḥ for the Prophet, then finally to the king. This is the same pattern that one sees in a mūssem. There the celebrations begin with the *Bourda,* then madīḥ to the Prophet, then to the wālī or saint, and finally to the king. Hence the people themselves have pushed the chanting away from classical forms of Arabic poetry toward the zajal of Andalusia. In addition, some hold that the zajal has an educative purpose, conveying ideas and concepts that have social impact. The best indicator of this split is in the madḥ offered to the king. Where it used to be offered in classical form, now much of the praise is couched in popular language, so the king is deemed closer to the people. An entire soirée in classical form would be difficult for people to relate to (the earliest evenings apparently were entirely in classical Arabic, much to the population's dismay), so the late king made the decision to incorporate zajal into these performances, with the result that they have been very popular.

Karumbī notes: "During the king's soirée, we follow the same procedure as followed when praising the Prophet, except we introduce modern poets praising the king utilizing music of Andalusia, just as we do during mūlid al-nabī. The difference is that we use modern writers who say things about the king parallel to the praises accorded to the Prophet."

In the mūssem sponsored by the king, the munshidūn begin with the *Bourda* of Būsayrī, and the first set focuses on the Prophet. Following a break, the poetry then moves on to the king. Hence the pattern of the zāwiya extends into the public festivities surrounding the king, since in the zāwiya one begins with the *Bourda* and then moves to the shaikh. During a mūssem in celebration of a shaikh, one begins with the *Bourda,* then moves to praise of the Prophet, then to the wālī, then to the king. If one examines the presentations before the king (see appendix), roughly the same structure is operative: Būsayrī's *Ḥamziyya* and *Bourda* predominate the opening sessions, and then the central focus of the classical Sufi shifts to national elements, including poetic offerings that reflect various areas of the state, and various kinds of praise. In effect, the program moves from the sacred to the profane, from the holy references to the Prophet to the profane eulogy of the accepted national values, reflecting the influence of the traditional structure derived from the Sufi orders.

While dhikr and inshād are not necessarily integrated in Morocco, the fact is that in some orders it is; consider the ṭarīqa of Ben Sayyid in Rabat. When I visited on April 25, 1995, the ʿamdah, held every Thursday, included what might be called an integrated program.

1. Qurʾān reciting
2. A text of Shaikh Nāṣir, recited by shaikh al-ṭarīqa
3. *Bourda*
4. Text from the same genre as *Bourda,* but sung by ʿAbdullāh Karīm bin ʿAbdullāh, muqaddam of the order
5. Text, inshād, sung by munshid
6. Change of text and change of rhythm, with three rhythm changes during performance
7. Mawwāl, and transition to new text
8. Text of duʿa, at fast rhythm, with emphasis on plea for acceptance of this offering
9. Call-response song of madḥ of Prophet
10. *Bourda*
11. Text of shaikh al-ṭarīqa finishes ḥaḍra

During my research, I arranged to meet three munshidūn who chant in their respective orders. They wished to design an evening of music that they felt represented the best in the munshid's repertoire. Ashḥab is a businessman, ʿAbdūl Wahhāb is a physician who chants in the Ḥarrāqiyya order, and Moḥammed Salāḥ is a lawyer who has four years of music training and chants in the ʿAissawiyya order. It was, in effect, a demonstration ḥadra. The structure of the evening reflected only the stylings that these three chanters held to be an ideal presentation. This is the format they chose:

1. *Bourda* in Draj, performed together by all three chanters
2. Mawwāl, featuring munshid Ashḥab
3. Meditation on the Prophet, by Dr. ʿAbdūl Wahhāb
4. Mawwāl by Moḥammed Salāḥ
3. *Hamzīya* performed by the group as a zajal
4. Meditation on the Prophet, by Ashḥab
5. Meditation, by Ashḥab
6. Meditation on the Prophet, by Ashḥab
7. Mawwāl-zajal, performed by the group
8. Faʿshiyya, performed by the group
9. Meditation on Prophet, zajal, performed by the group
10. Ending with *Bourda* and the Fātiḥa

It is interesting to note that Ḥajj Barrāda from the ʿAissawiyya in Meknes insisted that, during his ḥadras, it is not ʿamdah they sing but dhikr. "We call it d'ker in the local dialect, and the one who sings is a d'kar, the same written form but pronounced differently. Perhaps the shaikh's songs were originally in classical Arabic but they have been changed now. All songs are in brāwīl, that is, they are short texts all done in our Arabic dialect." Thus, what was performed in this impromptu setting was quite typical in one way: it was an amalgam of genres and types of music combined for a particular kind of local, informal occasion.

These notions reflect the ʿAissawiya idea that all musical forms have a zajal character but are not strictly drawn from the malḥūn. As the shaikh pointed out, "There are very few original ʿAissawiyya texts, and we have no need to depart from the wealth we have, but there are important differences between malḥūn performance and the ʿAissawiyya."

The difference between dhikr and malḥūn is evident because the rhythm is khafīf (*leger,* light), and within dhikr per se, they do not use musical instruments. In addition, the shaikh pointed out that, in the Sufi context, the awrād (spiritual disciplines) and the ḥizb (admonitions) are distinctive elements in an evening's rituals and cannot be equated to dhikr. The result is that the entire musical context is shaped by the spiritual environment. Moreover, for Shaikh Barrāda and his murīdin, there are also what is known as maqāmāt mawwāl, and these are specifically based on the power that they have to awaken the heart to God.

This introduces us to the problematic of the Moroccan tradition from a larger perspective, from that of general piety. It is the profound conviction of the Moroccan tradition that the original life created by God has a beneficence about it; furthermore, that beneficence is resident right from the moment of coming into being. There is, then, a collective awareness, a happy, positive appreciation of life, that is rooted in the foundations of human existence. This positive expectation shapes everything about living one's life. How else would we know to seek for this sense of happiness, if it were not bequeathed in some archetypal past, to become part of human collective memory? At the same time, it establishes the symbolic framework for the remembering: this is one's personal jihād, a heartfelt striving at the core of religious life. One will not grasp happiness without spiritual effort.

It is, then, not sufficient to perceive the past as golden. One must work to retrieve it into today's world. The retrieval is demanding, and the munshidūn of Morocco see it as their spiritual bequest, making sense of all the demands that are laid upon them, and inspiring them to skirt the many shoals. They can do nothing else, because they *remember*.

8

THE MUNSHIDŪN, MEMORY, AND RELIGION

From this ocean of ideas I harvest what strikes my fancy, gems of verses that I string intricately.

Nabaṭī poet ar-Ribīʿī

Dhikra al-fata ʿumrūhu al-thānī (The remembrance of youth is his second life)

Al-Mutanabbī (d. 965)

But the birds have gone and left me
They did not understand the meaning of my song.

Salāḥ Aḥmad Ibrāhīm, Sudanese poet

The Moroccan Munshid: Master of Remembrance and Memory

The munshidūn base their religious life on the notion of return—to God, to the experience of fanāʾ or passing away, to a moment of covenant with God and reality—by activating the resources of memory. Memory is seen by them to carry the freight of religious meaning. We might say that it is the religious character of memory, then, that guarantees the validity of the munshidūn's religion, just as the so-called archaic person was held to seek the authenticating moment when all began as the primal moment for all life. The munshidūn show us that the religion of the archaic person need not be understood as buried in some long-ago event in the early days of human existence, but is captured instead in a distinctive process of memory, of remembering the paradigmatic as an activating element in the human discourse of religion.

Nuances of that memory include commitment to various musical and poetic legacies in the Muslim past, reinterpreted and refocused for the believers of today. This is not a rehearsal, contrary to what Eliade was wont to stress; this is an affirmation to return to a moment of religious inspiration of the past that has become normative and mythic. Henceforth it informs and provides a character for the ideal presence of God. We would say that memory is the vehicle for clothing the experience with veracity.

Still, what is remembered is clearly distinctive for each group. Even though carrying the tradition, it nevertheless is flexible enough that individual ṭarīqas and even the individual munshid has obvious input into its reality. It is a tradition firmly rooted in the liturgically formulated dhikr. This in turn rests upon a complex understanding of memory and the role memory plays in religion. The munshid works within a religious ecology with its own coding system. This ecology emphasizes religious meaning as a process, a constant remembering of "exemplary moments" of past encounters and constituting those as the occasion par excellence of engagement with reality.

Being Muslim for the Sufi practitioner, then, becomes a process of going back to an experience of well-being and fulfilment, which itself is intimately connected to and designated as an experience of Divine Presence. Thus, with regard to comprehending Moroccan Islam, with its long, crucial relationship with Sufism, one might best speak of a particular kind of Islamization—a process that engages the social and cultural fabric in a remembering of an exemplary reality, which remembering is understood not only to be normative but also fulfilling.

The singular process essential for the remembering of the munshid is the role of scripting the mythic domain, as we have often referred to it here, through music and powerful metaphoric phrase. Each ṭarīqa fosters remembrance through these metaphors of reality, a kind of authoritative template operating in consciousness, and responsible for the patterning of remembrance. This is a conceptual formation attempting to locate the motivations and intentionalities of the spiritual world in a quasi-stable encoding system, a system, however, that has the potential for change built into it. It also has the potential to constitute the relationship with God and the spiritual world in a dynamic and vivid manner. It is a spiritual rendering of a process related to that which Sowayan identifies in the Nabatian poet:

> He works within a modular structure in which themes are components that can be augmented, truncated, added, deleted, and shifted around for artistic effect. The poet tries as skillfully as possible to relate the thematic components of his poems to each other and coordinate them gracefully in one harmonious whole. This is achieved by the intricate interlacing of themes and by the smooth transition from one theme to the next so that all converge together to form a poem that is at once traditional and original.[1]

In carrying out this process, memory operates in many ways, but for the munshid, allegiance to the enlightening experience of dhikr ritual is essential, as we have seen. This allegiance to dhikr underscores that religion cannot be understood as a fixed environment but rather is subject to a number of influences that are subject to the experiential context of the adept. Memory and remembering are endowed with a creative ability, both with regard to the data and to the enlivened encounter. No wonder Abū Madyan sang, "We live in your remembrance."

Everywhere I traveled in Morocco, I was struck by an underlying sense of the munshidūn engaging in acts of remembrance whose ends were religious in nature and had to do with achieving spiritual well-being. Remembrance delivers closeness, even a kind of dependence. One sees this exemplified at the Sufi shrines, and indeed, one could encounter a great deal of it there. When one is in the presence of a shaikh or muqaddam, there are always acts one could describe as endearing, submissive, and replete with gestures of closeness. The traditional way of understanding this is to see it as a fruit of the relationship with the marabout. Michon caught this spirit quite well:

> One must continue in the company of the shaikh and establish oneself in his presence so that he [that is, the shaikh] can give guidance [through the munshid], except when the shaikh orders him to do otherwise. Even a fleeting contact with the shaikh is indispensable, because the assistance conveyed by the master is comparable to the water flowing into the ladles of the water-wheel, or in the irrigation canal: the more prolonged the flow, the more water gushes up in abundance; but as one turns aside from the master through heedlessness so one will find his water more rarefied and it ends by drying up. . . . One drinks in proportion to one's sincerity; one is sincere in the measure of one's love; and the sign of one's love is to follow [one's master] and to venerate him.[2]

This closeness develops into a special dependence, which translates into pleas for help for a wide variety of problems, not just those related to spiritual health. Businessmen looking to close a large contract send small gifts and ask for special prayers, students faced with exams come to purchase a talismanic verse written by the shaikh's hand, expectant mothers come seeking a blessing for an easy birth . . . all these and many more can be seen regularly at the zāwiya. All these factors signal, though, that remembrance is the key to their operation, for without that specially charged memory, nothing would be effective.

The general view of religious specialists on this behavior is that these favors are based on the perceived baraka resident in the shaikh or his intercessory powers with the extrahuman powers, that is, that the shaikh has a kind of charisma that delivers this benefit to the believer. Such requests are part of the intercessory role played by the local shaikh and for which he receives small gifts and favors.[3] An intricate integration of personal desires and goals, spiritual benefits, and saintly respect between shaikh and believer results. This study suggests a more complicated relationship obtains.

So how is the tradition being modified under contemporary movements? No doubt today, this model is being refined. Memory is becoming more personally directed. The dhikr is shifting to a personal *well-being*, or a personal well-being within the embrace of the order. This shift is reflected in the munshid's character and work. What appears to be occurring is the development of a sharper awareness of the transcendent realities *individually* available and powerful. Each person is now conscious of the crucial role of dhikr to *his or her* own life. This modification brings the potential for a subtle shift: engaging with divine realities raises the possibilities of becoming a conduit for blessing without the mediatorial role of the order. The ambiguity over this shift is present in contemporary Morocco. This has important implications for the munshid and for the role of memory in religion.

This study has demonstrated that the munshid cannot be conceived as a minor official who is master of the sound and lyrics during dhikr and samāʿ. Nor is he just a ritual official who exists only for the duration of the rituals. Rather, the munshid is *the expression of a complex way of understanding the religious situation, and at the heart of a very complicated philosophy of response.* Once the chanter becomes aware of his potential within the liturgy of the adepts, he establishes a sense of his own contribution to this philosophy. It is only in that way that we can explain development of a Bennīs who sees himself as *God's munshid,* that is, set apart from any particular ṭarīqa. His awareness now is of a destiny apart from the limitations imposed by closeness to an order's definition of true piety. He sees the shift to a personal spiritual complex with the center in his past experience with the shaikh.

We are now in a better position to grasp the importance of the munshidūn within their environment. Perhaps, in and of themselves as individuals within the local zāwiya, they have neither the political nor spiritual clout that would warrant an extended study. But as figures within the long span of Moroccan Sufism, and as a cipher of a particular hold on religious reality, they are exemplary. They are the masters of an ecology of consciousness called *remembrance,* which itself is rooted in a special cognitive understanding of religious understanding—*religious memory.* Through them, access is provided to the deepest spiritual resources that Islam has to offer. They stand for a tradition that is larger than themselves, encompassing not only the brethren, but technically all believers who hold that there are spiritual means to gain God's assistance for the daily task of living. From the point of view of the munshidūn, the ecology has the following characteristics:

Return to the Exemplary.   When the munshidūn chant, presenting again a great classic from Andalusia, or a text from one of the saints, their goal is not to entertain, nor even to convince. Rather, they want to chant the group into a certain religious state. The format that is used for this process is dhikr, or samāʿ, but the participation is designed to *take the hearer back to an exemplary moment.* This is a deliberate attempt to relocate the participant, in terms of time, into another moment, one that has its mythic dimension where reality is held to exist. The goal may also be conceived of as a "multiplace," since the munshidūn are not concerned with where the hearer revisits, as long as the templatic elements of experience of fulfilment are present.

Many Islamic iconic references can be used to comprehend this exemplary moment, but some may see it as a moment of closeness to the shaikh, or a moment of visitation with the Prophet, or, among the most advanced in spiritual state, to the moment of unity with God.

Integrational Foundation.   The munshidūn chant because the words they use are rooted in a collective consciousness. Their very tone and quality create audibly conceived linkages to the foundations of Muslim awareness. Thus, chanting the *Bourda* is not to chant words written at one point in a historical continuum, but to articulate a remembered occasion each participant can visualize with the Prophet. The experience of *going back* is understood to be a transforming of the current group into a cohesive umma that stands *as if* the collective was there when the elements of the story were intoned. Still there is no conscious attempt to "make believe." This is a real going back that takes place here and now and on this occasion.

The munshidūn must also be open to that transforming capability of the words, because their correct emotional and religious state is essential for it to occur. When all the elements come into focus, and the group senses the return of that special moment, integration takes place. The individual members are aware of their singular experience of going beyond their normal selves as well as the integration taking place with a spiritual presence depicted through the efficacy of the ritual.

Master of Memory.   The munshidūn are not there to present their interpretation of texts. They are there to promote the texts so that they can produce again the inspiration that is associated with them, that is, to bring into articulation spiritual realities. This means that the munshidūn must be masters of the texts, on the one hand, to understand the potential within them to meet certain spiritual needs. At the same time, they must *read the religious barometer* of the group, and determine what level of spiritual depth they can be expected to probe, and then deliver the piece with all the inspiration available.

The memory that motivates them, however, is not the memory of their best performance, even though that has some relevance to them. Rather it is the memory of the exemplary spiritual moment that they are urgently trying to recapture. It is when they, individually, within some group, achieved that sense of unity and well-being. It is a moment they say lives in their own conscious memory bank that takes them to a time when they entered into a state of fanāʿ, a state of going beyond themselves to being at one with reality. So the moment is not an abstraction but is part of their own perception of what the ultimate experience is. In effect, they are convinced that if that moment can be recaptured in their performance, they will have an exemplary performance from the other participants' point of view. Mastering this *going-back* makes them valuable to the order as liturgical specialists, and gives them fulfilment within the framework of the encoding system.

Master of Musical Performance.   It is evident that the munshidūn understand that sounds are powerful. Chanted words are not neutral. They convey truths. They move people to inspired heights. They revitalize the brethren's souls. These effects could not be accomplished unless the munshidūn had a sense of rhythm and sound, and so any conceptual formulation of the reality they encounter must also involve a sonal dimension.

Here is where performance becomes a factor in inspiration. While the music that is chanted is formulaic, it is not created anew but relates to familiar sonal patterns. The music is not irrelevant but is an integral part of the going-back process. Whether it is the crying dhikr of the ʿAissawiyya, the Andalusian tunes among the Darqāwiyya, or the drumbeat of the Ginawa, music is the power that drives the message into the heart. It is not a matter, then, as to whether music is Islamic or not. It is rooted in the religious reality. This is a tool from God to draw humans to Himself, and this vehicle is part of the process of engagement with reality.

Anchor of Well-Being for Muslim Life.   While the individual chanter is the master of this religious going back, the role of the munshidūn as a group can be read against the larger framework of religious meaning within Morocco. Specifically, this is based on a profound sense of the fragility of human existence and the need to buttress one's life with resources from beyond for one's own repertoire of survival. We are dealing with a religious viewpoint that provides security for many Moroccans as a means to construct their lives and their society; as indicated in chapter 7, it derives from a profound sense of well-being deriving from Islamic belief. Among some munshidūn their role is to bring directly health and healing through presentation of the powerful mythic domain; among others, it is to show the way to baraka. Regardless, behind each manifestation is the return to the power that grants all life its greatness. Clearly this is a larger topic than can be summarized easily, but it is of profound importance in understanding Moroccan religion. The concept of well-being is a significant one in Moroccan culture, and it requires further study and articulation.

Confronting the Problematic of the Past.   Upon the munshidūn also hangs another legacy, that is, just what is remembered and whether remembering is valuable. The inheritance is not all glorious, and periods of colonialism have left their mark. Especially for Berbers and Africans, the Muslim past *itself* may have elements of colonialization of a different type buried within it. Then, too, with the pressure coming from across the Mediterranean for greater integration into Europe, can the remembrance of Andalus provide sufficient footing to link Muslims with with Spain and beyond?

Of even greater possible import is the impact of postcolonial ideas, especially the problematic of remembering. For in remembering, death never occurs, and meanings continue to haunt and hinder. Asking the question "How is the past remembered?" implies that the remembering is a neutral process, unaffected by religious or political or national tinges. This study shows that remembering is always contextual, freighting with it spiritual and literary legacies that may be very difficult to filter out. The remembering that nations and states embrace will inevitably have an impact on the future. As Werbner and his colleagues point out, Africa is facing a crisis of remembering that will surely have a decisive effect on cultural traditions.[4] Morocco, and most likely the entire Middle East, will not be immune to these movements. After all, the rise of Islamism is itself founded upon a certain kind of remembering.

The contemporary munshidūn are aware of these movements and have a certain angst about them. Still they continue to believe that the religious engagement with remembrance is the only really meaningful reality. The munshidūn believe that whatever political or social forces are ahead, the only way to confront them is through the convictions of Islam, that is, the Islam that is bequeathed to them from the greats of the past, and ultimately from the Prophet himself. The religious past can only be constructed meaningfully through ritual remembrance,[5] and the munshidūn view it as their prerogative to revivify Morocco in this God-given manner. Despite the fact that some of their colleagues have abandoned the way and moved to popular and secular entertainment, the continuing commitment to this way of being Muslim continues to attract and satisfy.

The Moroccan Munshid and the Western Theory of Religion

I began this study by pointing out that religious studies theory had explored the issue of memory very sparsely. However, historian of religions Mircea Eliade characterized archaic religion as determined by what happened *in illo tempore* when the gods shaped reality. He saw the process of validating that early experience as foundational for the earliest kind of religion. According to him, given the alienation of modernity in today's world, our losses have generated a nostalgia for origins. The study of munshidūn in Morocco raises basic concerns with this view.

This work argues that Eliade was correct in seeing religious man as intimately tied up with archetypal occurrences at the beginning; but where he stressed the religious meaning of the return to origins, and grounded it in a primitive religiosity, this study has stressed the mechanism for that returning: memory. Whatever the archaic person was doing, he or she was "remembering" an exemplary moment and acting accordingly. What Eliade evidently missed was that that beginning was constituted primarily by memory, and hence itself was constructed in ways peculiar to the people who held the memory. Consequently, this study has demonstrated that memory is crucial to any comprehensive idea about religious development; both what is remembered and how it is recalled are part of a complex religious act, and any attempt to construct the religious experience of the past requires the articulation of the system of remembrance.

Hence it is my contention that the munshid sheds important light on the construction of religion. By focusing on memory and remembrance, the munshid opens up the understanding of religion not as beliefs that are held or intellectually assented to, but as personal and collective memory that informs daily life. Memory from this perspective is more than an intellectual exercise; it involves both body and soul . . . the whole person remembers by moving in sync with the encoded elements that are construed as the basic movements of God's universe. Certainly some kind of belief plays a role in this, but it is the interplay between held beliefs and the spiritual clothing of them in experience that is key. In that sense, the Qurʾān's insistence that revelation is the recalling of the original message is but an affirmation of an encoded memory, which it openly and firmly holds has been in place from the beginning of time. Thus, from the Qurʾān's perspective on official "remembering' as an accepted pattern in all religious systems.

This suggests that Western theory should reorient its conception of religion around the types, descriptions, and processes by which religious memory is constructed. We may then find that the archaic person is not the only human who comes to know himself or herself through the facility of memory, but that going back is a constituent means of any attempt to integrate the person into a whole; memory itself is the subject of a dynamic process of search and embrace. Perhaps it is this process that *is* the spiritual enterprise, that becomes the foundation of one's religion. Such an approach to religion will open up new and fascinating challenges for scholarship.

This study also suggests that remembering the past in a significant way is freighted with meaning; it constructs that past upon powerful models and metaphors that *tell us only the most "important" things from the standpoint of a particular religious or theoretical viewpoint,* and not necessarily the way that all people would view them or experience the past. This is insightful, for scientific ways of acting and speaking are themselves *rememberings,* albeit rememberings that others can replicate. This assumes that only group-validated memory is efficacious. This study suggests that one's history is more related to one's *way* of remembering than to any one kind of knowing. We can see, then, that, for some, remembering religiously is remembering the way of the ancestors, or the elders, or the prophets, or the authorities—in short, the patterns as determined by those we hold up as having insight into the proper way of remembering. These authorities tell us the "myth" in the language of a particular religious discourse. These have been laid down for us, and within our own experience, we encounter them and thus determine that these exemplary memories are borne out in our own lives. In short, authoritative remembering is a particular way of expressing religiosity, which itself must be analyzed.

Eliade was perhaps correct to see archaic humans as remembering what happened in a sacred moment, another to enshrine that memory in ritual. In his construction of the archaic case, he held this memory as a return to the sacred moment. He should not have limited the going back to the mythic archaic man. Based on this study of the munshidūn, we have seen the import of an encoded experiential past that provides the patterns for reality. Clearly these are templatic, even paradigmatic, but they are more models than patterns resistant to change. They are deemed as the most basic and nuclear; they are mythic in that they cannot be proven, but are accepted as iconic and normative; they take on the color of permanence since they operate according to long-standing corporate expressions of the basic systems. Perhaps they are like scripts, which may be read with different emphases. However, they cannot easily be changed by the person or group, and it is unlikely that they could be altered if, as in the experience of the munshid, the going back is existentially visited each returning time, thus validating the mythic domain. Eliade's insight may have been better articulated that religion likely could not exist without some kind of going back through memory.

Evidently, contemporary humans have opted to modify accepted patterns of memory in terms officially unrelated to the gods or to the traditionally designated sacreds, judging by the plethora of religions available in the marketplace. Indeed, a pattern such as "hockey" in Canada can take on the elements of import along with attachment. In effect, we must now evaluate how corporate memories are constructed to determine just how these encoded systems are understood today to the Saint in Morocco, since what is "religious" today cannot be determined in relationship to the designated structures of yesteryear. Far more diverse systems of memory are tolerated and empowered. Indeed, religion from a structural point of view may now be almost always syncretic, if religion is conceived on the basis of memory construction. All of these issues have resonance in the material that we have encountered in Moroccan Islam. At the very least, the Moroccan Muslim munshidūn, masters of memory, point suggestively to other ways of conceiving religious meaning.

Finally, the munshidūn teach us that there is far more wisdom in Kipling's chained elephant than at first blush. We see that he perceives himself through an earlier, more "authentic" lens. Hence his cry "I remember what I was" is representative of the yearning for a primal wholeness, before the grime of history and profane experience clouded "reality." And for adherents of Morocco' s mystical tradition, and perhaps for all who wonder at the strange power religion has in human life, it is a plea we all are conscious of in the inner recesses of our beings.

Appendix

PROGRAM OF THE KING'S MŪSSEM

First Segment: Focus on the Prophet

1. Būṣayrī: *Hamzīya* and *Bourda*
2. Poem from Imām Hallabī
3. Recitation from Shaikh al-Ḥarrāq
4. Recitation from Būṣayrī
5. Meditation
6. Poetry by al-Jaiy ʿIdrīs al-Jaiy (deceased; had a program on poetry called *Nashyat al-Adab,* The Youth of Adab)
7. Two recitations
8. A ghazal from Andalusia
9. A meditation by Qurtūbī
10. A recitation from Buqqālī ʿAḥmed ʿAbd al-Salām al-Baqqālī, a poet and novelist from Tetouan (composed the text of the Moroccan national anthem, retired in Tetouan)
11. Meditation
12. Recitation by Nāblusī

(*A break for tea*)

Second Segment: Focus on the King

1. Poem from Ameena Mareeni (pioneer female musician; originally played in Tetouan orchestra of Andalusian music under al-Tamsamanī; still lives in Tetouan)
2. Recitation from Muḥammad Halwī (born in Fez in 1922; studied in Qarawyān Mosque; a scholar and poet of the traditional variety)
3. Recitation
4. Recitation from Nuḥ Sabaih (Moroccan; deceased)
5. Recitation from ʾAlawī
6. Recitation from Wajeeh Fahmy al-Salāh (Syrian granted rare honor of Moroccan citizenship by king; died in 1997)
7. Recitation from an Eastern writer
8. Two Moroccan recitations
9. Recitation from Ḥajj Muḥammad Bahnīniʾ (Moroccan Arabist who taught Arabic to Ḥassan II)

GLOSSARY

adhān Muslim call to prayer

ahl al-baīt (or ahl al-bayt) people belonging to the Prophet's line; symbolically or generically of the family of the Prophet

ahouach Berber term for a call-response chanted prayer prior to dancing

akbār Lit., "great"; prose opening in a qaṣīda that depicts the story's setting

āla, pl. ālāt Lit., instrument; nonsacred music of classical type; repertory of nūbat of Morocco

al-ᶜālah Basic form of Andalusian music

ᶜālam al-mithāl; ᶜālam al- rūḥ; ᶜālam al-rūḥānī Phrases used to indicate the intermediate world between the world of sensibility and the realm of the divine; spiritual domain; world of the spiritual life

Alastū bi rabbikūm "Am I not your Lord?"; covenantal declaration from God to spirits at the founding of the world; recalls God's central role in fashioning humans with His two hands, as recounted in the Qurᵓān, and breathing into them His spirit

alētheia Greek word literally meaning nonforgetfulness, truth

aliyin Instrumentalist of classical āla music in Morocco

ᵓamāna Bond of allegiance; "ties that bind"

ᶜamdah, ᶜumda Ritual "listening" session in Sufi contexts, utilizing qaṣīda, malḥūn, etc., also known as samāᶜ

amdiyya Prayer and praise segment at the beginning of dhikr session

amydaz Berber poet; rhythmic cycle or period; mode; couplet-type chant; type of chant specifically Egyptian in origin

amygdala Emotional center in the brain in contemporary psychology

aqṣa Elite; insiders; top people in a ṭarīqa

ᶜarīf A "knower"; one who comprehends inner spiritual understanding

ᶜarūbiyya Lit., women; openings of a zajal poem

ᶜasāla Authenticity; honey, thick and sweet chanting voice; descriptive term to indicate the kind of voice and demeanor a munshid brings to a performance

ᶜaṣbahān Third of the Arabic modes or ṭubūᵓ

āyat Verse in the Qurᵓān

baḥḥāth Lit., researcher; here, eminent searcher in spiritual affairs

baḥr, pl. buḥūr Lit., sea; here, prosodic meter, mode; basic mode in prosody

baḥr tawīl Major mode in Moroccan/Andalusian prosody

baitīn Transitional phrase in moving from one rhythm system to another

baitiyya Chant, large movement; second type of chant of the Andalusian nūba rhythm, first phrase/cycle of the Moroccan nūba; prosodic meter, classical type of singing with noble themes and particularly gracious virtuosity; chants of the munshid

balā   "Indeed"; response of spirits to primordial question of "Am I not your Lord?"

baraka   Charismatic power associated with founders of the orders; gifts and qualities specially given by God to saints; holiness

bard   Lit., cold; for Sufis, a state of inner awareness deficient in spiritual life; here, a state of the soul far away from the divine

barwal, pl. barāwil, brāwīl   Rhythmic chant; second series of vocal pieces from the Tunisian nūba; third movement of the Libyan nūba

barwala   Popular poems with stanzas of unequal length, sung like classical tunes

basīṭ   Large movement, chant, song; second series of vocal pieces of Andalusian nūba; in Morocco, the first rhythmic cycle of the Moroccan nūba, 6/4 in time

bayt (or baīt), pl. abyāt   "House" stanza of the muwashshaḥ; strophe; single segment of poetry in musical opening

bībī   Term of endearment; shortened form of *ḥabībī,* my beloved

bidᶜa muḥassana   "Allowable" innovation; preferred innovation

bilād al-sibat   Pejorative appellation applied to Berber lands; lit., lands of vituperation

bilād al-sūdān   Land of the Sudan

bouji   Tiny bird, regarded as the poet's muse in famous poem by the same name; often sung to reflect the baleful condition of the lover of God who searches for Him

Bourda, Burda   The Mantle Ode; the story of the Prophet's gift to Kaᶜb, who had previously lampooned him but came asking forgiveness

brūla   Distinctive munshidūn chants, close to the classical qaṣīda in form but also near to zajal of Andalusian music

bṭāyḥi, pl. bṭāyḥiyya   Rhythm; rhythmic chant cycle (the third in the Moroccan īqaᶜat), 8/4 time

ḍaᶜīf   Weak; pliant, malleable; munshidūn characteristics deemed beneficial for excellent performance

dakat   Popular term among ᶜAissawiyya for munshid

dalīᶜla   "Sweets" added to wine; symbolic wine of the spirit

dandanah   Rhythm, chant; vocal series or rhythmic cycle (the fourth in the Moroccan nūba, third in both the Tunisian and Algerian); soft humming style introduced by Abū al-Azīz al-Maghrāwī into Sufi chanting

darabukka, darabouka   Single-headed goblet-shaped drum (in Morocco called a *guellal*)

daᶜsa   Eleven-beat pattern of traditional

dawr, daur   From the word meaning "body," first musical section of the muwashshahāt; also called *badaniyyah*

derdeba   Ginawa cultic ceremony at the center of aspects of religious life

dhākir   Constant witnessing to God's message

dhikr   To remember, recollect; liturgical segment of Sufi rites; meditational liturgy; Sufism

dhᵓkara   Female munshid in the ᶜAissawiyya tradition in Meknes

diyāfa   Hospitality; central motif in the *Bourda* story

dīn   Religion; Islamic religious tradition in its entirety

draj (also drouj, derj)   Rhythm, chant, song; a vocal series or rhythmic cycles of nūba in Morocco; four iqāʿat; 4/4 time

dridka   Increasingly fast choral segment indicating end of suite

duʿa, daʿwa   Teaching; certain statements about spiritual life that the munshid weaves throughout performance

dukhūl   Entry; the opening lines of a zajal poem

dūraydika   Rapid recitation, usually at the end of a dhikr session

dustūr   Rules and regulations of the ṭarīqa; the "constitution" of the fuqahāʾ

fakhr   Boasting, pride; crucial theme in muwashshaḥāt expression

fanāʾ   Original goal of Sufi ideology, now regarded as reserved for spiritual elite; extinction (mergence) into Allah or in passing away into ecstasy; "invisible to myself"; the essence of reality within

fanāʾ fi al-nabi   Second level of spiritual achievement; extinction (mergence) in the Prophet

fanāʾ fi al-shaikh   First level of spiritual achievement; extinction (mergence) in the shaikh of the order

fann   Popular song

fannanīn   Singer; popular vocalist

fannī   Reflects popular musical form and singing

faqīh, pl. fuqahāʾ   Legist; theologian; sometimes a reciter of Qurʾān

faqīr, pl. fuqarāʾ   Lit., poor; dervishes; committed members of ṭarīqa; devotees to saints

faqirāt   Female chaters in dhikr sessions

farḍ   Obligatory rakʿah in Islamic canonical prayer

frash   Intention

ghaība   Absence, concealment; Sufi term indicating secret nature of God in the human heart; character of mystical life

ghaita, rhaita   Reed instrument, flute; hautboy

gharnāṭī   Quasi-classical form of music in Morocco, spawning a distinctive sound and form; derives from Grenada in Spain; word used primarily in Rabat

ghina   General term for music; chant; song

ghiṭaʾ   Lit., cover; alternative name for third and final section of the muwashshahāt; also, instrument called oboe

ghrybat ḥusaīn, gharībat al-ḥusaīn   Tenth mode of Moroccan nūba

ghullū   Lit., bounds, fetters; the outer borders of the order's belief

Ginawa, Gnawa   African Sufi ṭarīqa; distinctive group focusing on Black consciousness within Islam in North Africa; Moroccan healing rites associated with mystical practices

gubāhī   An assertive, authoritative tone in the munshid's chanting

hadhouj   Stringed instrument used in traditional Andalusian orchestras

ḥadīth   Traditions of the Prophet

ḥaḍra   Lit., presence; sensing of God's presence; liturgical occasion for engaging with God; name given the Sufi liturgical service

ḥaffaḍ (or ḥāfiẓ)   Qurʾān reciter; chanter in the zāwiya of Raḥmānija (Raḥmāniyya)

ḥakam   Arbitrator; wise person whose role as mediator was accepted to resolve tribal feuds

ḥāl, pl. aḥwāl   Ecstatic, mystical state; spiritual condition or position; conscious elevation into another state of consciousness; inner level of reality engaged through dhikr

ḥamās   Lit. inspiring to courage; a key theme in muwashshaḥāt

handqa   Small brass cymbals; used in zajal and malḥūn background music

haniyya   Soft, gentle, light demeanor; munshid quality of spiritual tone when performing in a splendid manner

ḥaqīqa   Cosmic reality; a neutral position beyond the separation of self from the other, which may be conceived as union with God

al-Ḥaqq   Truth; a name of God; divine principles evident in all things

ḥarba   Refrain; found at end of qsam in zajal

ḥarība   Little ḥarba; separate refrain within zajal; a strophic form

ḥasana   Beautiful act, set in opposition to *sayyiʾa*, an ugly act or sin.

hāwī   Amateur; part-time reciter

haybah   Intense awe; deep religious awareness

hefqa   ʿAissawiyya leader of the ḥaḍra chanting

hijāʿ   Satire; important theme in muwashshaḥāt

ḥijāz kabīr   Fourth Moroccan nūba; important mode in Andalusian music

ḥijāz masharqī   Second Moroccan mode, deriving from East

ḥila   Attributes; theoretical and theological concept indicating characteristics said to reside in God but not of His essence

hilāliyya   Pertaining to the Hilāl, of Sīrat Banī Hilāl fame, original people of Arabia; moon celebrations

hindī   Rhythm in Indian style in contemporary Arab music

ḥiss   Right "feel" in dhikr and samāʿ

ḥizb   Admonition; stylized entreaties and petitions

ḥizb ʿamdiyya   Formalized prayer; part of opening of Sufi litanies in Sufi meeting

ḥubb   Love; theme of lovers and their trials in muwashshaḥāt

hudhārī   Compressed style of chanting that runs words together in an ecstatic manner; effective technique of rapid chanting

ḥudūd   Boundless; extremities of emotional experience; feeling of expansiveness during performance

ḥullah   Robe of honor given by ancient ruler in exchange for particularly delightful verse of praise

ḥusainī   Melodic type in Moroccan music

ifranji   Western or French style rhythmic mode in contemporary Arab music

ʿifrīt   Pre-Islamic conception of a spiritual being, interpreted as a troublesome and mischievous spirit; a sprite

ifsād   Working in a corrupt situation; degradation

iḥsān   Lit. "to do well"; intense commitment to spiritual betterment; reformist interpretation as activism toward a truly Islamic life and society; beautiful achievement

ᶜijmāᶜ ijtihād   Interpretation of the law to allow for new directions to be taken

ilhām   Inspiration; in Sufi context, denotes spiritual inspiration from beyond one's own resources

imān   Faith; belief

in illud tempore   Sacred time before historical time, in Eliadean analysis

inshad, pl., anāshī   Song; chanted text; package of material used in dhikr or samāᶜ

insijām   Imagination; illusion

insirāf   Rhythm in 5/8 time heard at ending of gharnāṭī suite

īqāᶜ, pl. īqāᶜāt   Metric cycle; rhythmic mode in Arabic music

iqān   Certitude; inner confidence in rectitude of belief

ᶜirāq al-ᶜajam   Sixth Moroccan nūba

islah   Making wholesome; opposite of *ifsād,* working in a corrupt situation

ism al-sadr   A type of dhikr with rasping breath, banned by Khedive Ismaᶜīl in Egypt

istihlāl   Seventh Moroccan nūba

jāhiliyya   Pre-Islamic era deemed to be less moral and upright, reformed by the coming of Islam; denotes a metaphorical wilderness of the spiritual life

jalālā   Attribute of God explored in phrasing of zajal; spiritual relationship between human and divine realms

jalsah   Sitting position during the cycle of prayer; formal sitting of legislative body

jihād   Struggle or battle; the "greater jihād" of struggling with one's inner being, the focus of much Sufi meditational practice

jiwār   Protection; central motif in *Bourda* story

juzᵓ, pl. ajzaᵓ   An element of verse or chant; foot

kāhin   Soothsayer; pre-Islamic fortune teller

kamanja, kamenjah   A large violin played vertically on the knee; used in orchestras of zajal

karāmāt   Miracles; special gifts afforded to saints by God for the benefit of the people

karkorru   Berber instrument fashioned from sole of shoe

kashf   Unveiling; a type of insightful knowing having different forms of expression; knowledge of tasting, witnessing, opening, insight

khafīf, pl. khafayif   "Rhythmic mode; light rapid rhythm, fourth vocal series in the Tunisian nūba; "sung," "irregular," incorrect discourse; popular poetry or the chant that applies to the poetry; light, easy in Moroccan munshid's discourse

khal al-naᶜlain   Birth celebration of the saint

khalq, pl. akhlāq   Manners, spiritual characteristic; instilled elevation of one's personality through spiritual discipline; morality; character

khalwa   Small cell used for meditation in some Sufi zāwiyas

khānah   Lit. inn or square of chessboard; second musical section of the muwashshaḥāt

khāniqāh   Sufi retreat or location for carrying on Sufi liturgies

Khārijī   Early Muslim movement stressing the judgmental nature of God and the independence of personal piety in confessing sins

kharja   Closing section in muwashshaḥāt duplicated in the song; not found in zajal

khaṭīb   Preacher during canonical prayers on Friday; orator

khirqa   Sufi garment indicating adherence to life of piety

khitām, pl. khatām   Final rhythm in nūba

khumāra   State of consciousness likened to wine by advanced Sufis

kūmriya hilāya   Special wine of a spiritual sort beloved by Sufis

ladhīdh   Delicious; the honey of life; metaphor for pious experience of adept

laḥana   To chant, to sing; to make errors; root of word malḥūn

laḥn, pl. alḥān   Melody; music, octaval steps; musical mode; vocal music melody, music, melodic mode system, aria

laila   Evening of song and celebration; in Sufi terms an evening of samāʿ

al-Laṭīf   Special prayer, focusing on God as benevolent; crisis prayer, often used during ṣalāt al-istisqāʾ, prayer for rain

lēsmosune   Greek word meaning forgetfulness

lēthē   Greek word meaning forgetting

lifṣāla   Traditional sections or chapters in zajal poems, broken by ḥarba comprised of *aqsam* or sections

liqṣīd, liqṣīda   Poetic creation of the zajal poet; popular-language poetic form; middle segment of a zajal poem

lumʿa, pl. lumaʾ   Twinkling, flashing of stars; metaphoric representation of inspiration at heart of the munshid's spiritual life

madād   Blessing, invocation for beneficence; interjection during chant

maddāḥūn   Reciters of praise that emerged during Merinid period; precursor to munshidūn

madḥ (or madiḥa)   Segment ending a qaṣīda; a panegyric section

madīḥ al-nabi   Praise or eulogy of the Prophet

makhlaṣ   Rhythm (6/8) heard at ending of gharnāṭī suite

Malamatiyya   Sufi group deliberately violating Islamic codes to bring condemnation so that its members as a whole would be set apart from other Muslims, blame or criticism being deemed necessary for spiritual advancement

malḥūn   Popular poetry or songs, characterized by having irregular forms and discourses

maʿnān   Essence; inner reality, being; meaning or thematic intent; specific melody; contour

maqām, pl. maqāmāt   Lit., a place where one should stand, a place where people gather to listen and participate in a cause; place, memorial, construction in honor of a saint who is mystical; musical mode in Morocco and Arab East

maqāmāt mawwāl   Inspired sayings drawn from the Qurʾān and Ḥadīth, and sacred sayings such as ghaiba, sife, etc. used by munshid during performance

marffu   Uplifting stimulant used by some Sufis

maʿrifa   Gnosis; spiritual insight of a profound kind; inner knowledge; contemplative awareness

maṣmūdī   A Berber rhythm, named after a Berber tribe, that has become a recognized Arab rhythm in contemporary Morocco

matlāʿ   A praising of humans untoward in proper religious circles

mawlānā   Honorific name meaning "my master," applied to saint or other persons to whom one is devoted

mawlid, maulid, mūlūd, mūlid, moulid (or Mūssem)   A celebration of the saint's birthday; festive occasion in celebration of special day in person's life

mawwāl   Generally speaking, a quatrain with major improvisation

māya   Eleventh mode in Moroccan nūba

mazlūk   An amorous reflection; in Sufi terms, a special quality of voice that can move from gentleness to aggressiveness quickly and effectively

mergent   A quiet state of engagement with God to the point that the self disappears as a separate entity and only God is held to be present; alternative translation of *fanā*

miʿrāj   Ascension to heaven by the Prophet; metaphor for ascent of Sufi soul in mystical state

mīthāq   Covenant, believed to have taken place at the beginning of all human life, between souls and God, in which remembrance of relatedness to God was established

mīzān   Metrical pattern of a poem

mnēmosunē   Greek word meaning remembering

mṣaddar, maṣdar   Rhythm in 4/4 heard at the opening of gharnāṭī suite of music

muʿallif   Known as the Surah al-Laṭīf, in Praise of God

mudhakkirāt   Rememberers; derived from root *to remember* or *to recollect*

Mufaḍḍaliyat   Oldest of Arab poems; pre-Islamic in setting and tone

mujaddid   Official personage to choose textual side of festive chants

mujāhada   Sufi concept of battle against spiritual forces

mulay   Honorific term for spiritual authority

mūlid al-nabi   See *mawlid;* birthday celebration of the Prophet

munshid, pl. munshidūn   Chanter in dhikr and samāʿ sessions in the orders; master rememberer

muqaddam   Official in ṭarīqa; director of Sufi liturgies; spiritual leader in ṭarīqa; official below the shaikh

muqaddimāt   Distinctive openings written into the beginning of each aqsam in zajal poems, sometimes called *al-ʿarubiyya* (women)

muqallidūn   Repetitions; rote repetitions without knowledge of qaṣīda's meaning

Murābiṭūn   Garrisoned troops of early Moroccan rulers who built upon ribāṭ culture and established the Almoravid dynasty; word from which comes *marabout,* or denotation of saint

murīd, pl. murīdūn   Adept in Sufi system; committed believer in the mystical life

muṣḥaf   Official text of the Qurʾān

musamaᶜ   Meditational song and chant form sung by munshid

mūsīqa   General term for music, adapted from the West

musmiᶜin   Spiritual assistant; alternate word for munshid; technically, those who help others hear the eulogies; a kind of munshidūn dedicated to eulogies of the Prophet

mūssem   Birth celebrations of the saints; see mawlid

mutadarīk   Transitional meter after third segment and movement to final rhythmic modes

mutawwal   Old, ancient, archaic form of ghina; extended performance

Muᶜtazilī   Rationalist theological school of thinkers in early Islam

mutrib, mughānnī   Soloist; singer, poetic reciter

Muwaḥḥidūn   Contingent law; Almowahids

muwashshaḥ, pl. muwashshaḥāt   Organized on a variety of strophic forms determined by complex pattern of rhymes and meters

muwazẓafīn   Alternate word for munshidūn

muzemzemoun   Merinid terms for chanters and singers who helped institute festivals through their poetry and musical expressions

nafaqa, nafʾqa   Monetary gift; allowance; token payment of appreciation

nafas   Spirit; spiritual quality the munshid exemplifies during chanting

nafāthāt rūḥīyya   Muqaddam who sets the tone for the dhikr by instructing munshid to use a certain ṭabʾ

naffaq   Alternate name for munshid, used by Bennīs

naghma, pl. nagham   Model characteristic, musical note

naghamāt muttaᶜid   Style associated with southern chanters who ascend and descend scale quickly; melody with ascending scale

nāī, nāy   Flute; seldom used in background in Morocco, unlike Eastern music

nakhā   Flavor; character of song; texture

naqīb   Ritual official in dhikr; person in charge of spiritual progress of dhikr

nashīd   First movement of four in the Andalusian nūba; musical form chanted by munshid

nashshādin   Alternative word for munshid; one who chants inshād

nasīb   Amorous reflection in classical qaṣīda following the opening

naᶜūra, pl. nawaᶜīr   From the verb "to gush"; little strophes that sometimes accompany qsam segments

nawāfil   Those prayers regarded as supererogatory and nonobligatory but highly recommended for piety's sake

nisba   Connection, link, conformity, relationship through marriage

niyyah   Intention; intent of the heart essential for efficacious prayer; "threshold disengagement," the shift to another level of awareness needed for prayer to be effective

niẓām   Canon of songs or tunes of a ṭarīqa

nūba, nawba, pl. nūbat   Great musical composition consisting, in Andalusia, of four movements; type of North African musical expression; artistic styling in music

oud   Middle Eastern and North African lute

qadi   Judge; legal official in traditional Islam

qafala, qaflah   Lit., key or closing; the third and last *qufl* or strophe of the muwashshaḥ

qāʾm wa niṣf   Distinctive nūba in 8/4 time; performed second of the īqāʿāt

qānūn   Triangular zither with cords changed by means of a brace or clamp; used in zajal performance orchestras

qaṣīda, pl. qaṣāʾid   Middle Eastern poem with a distinctive line form with a single rhyme scheme and a single meter throughout; distinctive poetic form adaptable to many purposes

qiṭʿa, pl. qiṭaʿ   Piece, poem; popular poetic zajal

qiyām   Segment of the liturgical prayer; involves standing during prayer cycle

qsam, pl. aqsām   Lit., division; composed of qsam and ḥarba or qsam proper and a ḥarba or refrain; solo verses

qudamā   Old masters

quddām   Rhythm; last (fifth) of the īqāʿāt in popular zajal performed in 6/8 time

rabāb   Two-stringed fiddle or rebec instrument used in performance by poets and oral storytellers

Rabbānī   "My Lord"; honorific term referring to sacred or elevated personage

radm   From radama; lit., filled with earth; an ending hemistich for zajal poem

rafāhiya   Teaching and entertainment combined in munshids' repertoire

raḥīl   Journey segment in classical qaṣīda toward a vanished love

al-Raḥmān   The Merciful; a name of God, indicative of His attributes

raʿis   Head; chevalier

rakʿah, pl. rukūʿ   Bowing; segment or section of Islamic liturgical prayer

ramal māya   The first and basic form of musical expression in the modal system in Moroccan nūbat

raṣd   Fifth mode in Morocco and a nūba throughout North Africa

raṣd dhaīl   Ninth mode in Moroccan nūbat

rāwī, pl. ruwāh   Reciter and memorizer of ancient poems; sometimes another word for munshid

rāwiya   Tradition of remembering and reciting poetry

raziʾa   Warrior tradition instrumental in organized raiding parties designed to undermine stability and gain booty

ribāṭ   Inn; protective environment for traveler; later, convent for devotees of Sufism; alternative word for zāwiya

rithāʾ   Lamentation for the dead; important theme in muwashshaḥāt expression

riwāyah   Transmission of a text; variant reading of poetry

riy   Musical phrasing that munshid in Ginawa changes in order to maintain trance behavior

riyāḍa   Spiritual exercise directed toward improving character

rubāʿi, pl. rubāʿyyah   Quatrain whose length may be changed by virtue of the music

rūḥ   Spirit; spiritual dimension of human existence; spirit from God at conception

rūḥānī   World of love, especially exemplified in the life of the Prophet; the area of the heart, where encounter with God is made; spiritual quality or state

rujᶜā   Lit., return; alternative term for third and final section of muwashshaḥāt

rukūᶜ   Bow required in canonical prayer

rūmwiya   Special spiritual elixir regarded as wine of the soul

ruᵓyā   Vision of the shaikh; special spiritual visitation that confirms the realities chanted during ḥaḍra

ṣafāᵓ   Purity; cleanliness of heart

ṣāfi   Pure, a term implying a state of inner being that is free from condemnation and vanity; Sufi term indicating purity of heart

ṣāhī   Sufi wine of an advanced experience

saᶜj   Rhymed prose form of literary and linguistic expression

sākī   Spiritual wine

ṣāliḥāt   Those who perform wholesome deeds; sometimes a title of the saints; itinerants, restless travelers; in Sufism, a stage in the process of becoming a murid

ṣāliḥūn   Wholesome activity when one is doing iḥsān

sālik   One who follows the spiritual path; spiritual itenerant

samāᶜ   Lit., listening; meditative performance of sacred songs and chants for edification of tarīqa followers

sanāᶜa   Brilliance

saraba, pl. sararīb   Entrance, denoting the opening section of a zajal poem

ṣarī   Traditional suite form of five beat pattern.

sayyiᵓa   Sin, improper behavior

sayyid   Leadership position of honor and respect dating to the pre-Islamic era

selihot   Yiddish stories of the ancestors; sacred memories made tangible by the telling

shaᶜab songs   Referred to as "chaabi" in Morocco; folk and popular songs of the people, sung in everyday life

shahāda   "Lā ilāha ilāha illā-Llāh"; basic Islamic confession and affirmation

shaikh al-ḥuffāẓ   Lead chanter, denoting singer who knows material by heart

shaikh al-nushshad   Another name for munshid

shaikh al-sajjāda   Titular head of Sufi orders in Egypt

shāᶜir, pl. shuᶜarāᵓ   Arabic poet or versifier

shajarāt al-ṭubūᶜ   Tree that metaphorically represents a fundamental reality behind the material world, and constituting the same reality expressed in musical form; cf ṭabᵓ

shuqar   Highly refined spiritual wine

Sharīᶜah   Classical word in Islam for the law in its entirety

Ṣharifl   Related to the Prophet's line; sacred genealogy

shaṭaḥāt   Trance-induced state; spaced out; signs of presence in music

shiᶜr   verse; poetry

shuhūd al-ᶜiyān   Illuminative contemplation

siah   Distinctive musicians who accompany the munshid

sīdī   Honorific terms for shaikh; "sir" or "lord"

ṣife, ṣaff   Rank; level; Sufi term for place in the mystical hierarchy

simāwī   Long, involved poems chanted by munshid, with only tentative relationship to classical qaṣīda or mawwāl form, designed to pull the listener into the theme

ṣināᶜat   Collection of songs; three to four to a mizan

sinād   Profound type of chant form the munshid attempts to develop; elaborate style of singing designed to embellish the text and to take advantage of sonal characteristics of text; graceful chanting

sīra   Biography of the Prophet; life story

ṣirāf   5/8 rhythm found in qharnāṭī performance

ṣīr ezor   Jewish form of zajal; popular song-form in Jewish Andalusia and North Africa

smriti   Remembrance or memory in Sanskritic tradition

sujūd   Segment of Islamic liturgical prayer; prostration a term already indicating a doctrinal debate and affirmation

Sunna   Guidance for the community, constructed upon the community memory of the doings and sayings of the Prophet

ṣūq   Marketplace; outdoor sales pavilion

swisen   Violin-type instrument found in Moroccan orchestras

ṭabᵓ, pl. ṭubūᵓ   Encompasses modal level, as well as coherent system underlying Andalusian music; held by Guettat to be based upon psychophysical realities as expressed in the writings of the Ikhwān al-Ṣafāᵓ as well as Pythagorean harmonic principles

ṭabaqa kabīra   Large register

ṭabaqāt   Extended performance

ṭabla   Large drum

tadhkir, tazkīr   Reminding

tadhkirah   Qurᵓān's depiction of itself; reminder

taghtiya   Covering or veiling; postlude after mawwrāl mode

tadmin, talwīn   Modulation

tahlal, tahlīl   Texts used as basis for improvisation at certain moments in the dhikr by ᶜAissawiyya munshidūn, when inspired by the Presence being manifested; baiteen phase featuring transition from one rhythm system to another in dhikr

ṭāᵓifa, pl. al-tawāᵓif   Lit., faction; in Morocco, religious order or community of Muslim adepts; organized group of followers of the shaikh

takbīr   Essential statement in Islamic piety, the saying of "God is the most Great"

taqiyya   Dissimulation; outward display of compliance while secretly living according to different and contradictory principles

taqlīd   Imitator; mimic; follow a pattern of the munshid

taqmaṣ, pl. taqammuṣ   Lit., enrobed in; indication of spiritual state the munshid enters in order to chant with inspiration

taqsīm   Overture; musical interlude and introduction in Andalusian music

ṭārr   Long-bodied drum used in accompanying zajal in performance orchestra

ṭarab   Emotional response to music; aesthetic delight

ṭarbiyya   Infancy; good manners; purposive education

tāʿrīja   Tambourine; accompanying munshid during chanting

ṭarīqa, pl. ṭuruq   Lit., way or path; term designating the organization around a spiritual guide or shaikh that then becomes a social and cultural complex focusing on Islamic piety of a mystical sort; congregational aggregate of believers

Ṭarṣūn   Famous qaṣīda named after little falcon, metaphor of lover

tartīl   Chant (associated with reciting of Qurʾān)

tashbīb   Love for a special person

taslīm   Segment of liturgical prayer that involves greeting the angels guiding each side of one's body

tawāshīḥ maʿlūf   Lit., simple tawāshīḥ; predominant form of muwashshaḥāt per d'Erlanger.

tawāṣin   Creedal affirmation

tawāṣṣul   Role of supplication accorded to the Prophet

tawfīq   Success, achievement

Tawḥīd   Oneness; goal of all liturgies in Sufism, that is, to deny existence of any reality apart from God

ṭawīl   Dedication to the form and language of text in such a way as to preserve the dominance of the text over the chanting of it; correct prosodic meter; allegorical interpretation of the Qurʾān; special anthropomorphic interpretation espoused by Almohads

tayla   Connected to the "pure" line of the Prophet's family, and thus unencumbered by local cultural or Sufi heterodoxy

tayyʿ   Quality of voice that reflects a broken, humble attitude

ṭbīqa (or ṭibōq)   See ṭaboqah

telic   From Greek word *telos*, meaning goal; shaping trend within Sufi trance depicting overall bent of the trance state

timwila   Modification of mawwāl's form to conform to dhikr needs; munshid technique

ṭurāth   Tradition; normative expression resting on the way it was done in the pas

ʿulamāl   Scholars in traditional Islamic sciences

ʿushshāq   Eighth mode, called nūba of the halo

ʿusul   Lit., sources; indicating contextual material for the determination of law

waḥdat al-wujūd   Doctrine of oneness of all being held by Ibn -al ʿArabī and often represented in chant lyrics

wahm   Imagination; illusion

wajd   Trance; altered state of consciousness

wajh, wijh   First hemistich of a verse

wālī, pl. awliyāʾ   Saint; holy personage in Islamic tradition; spiritual personages in Moroccan Sufism

wārith   Inheritor; one who receives the spiritual legacy of the Prophet

waṣf   Description of nature; theme in muwashshaḥāt

wazn   Underlying poetic meter

wird, pl. awrād   Devotional and affirmative recitations within Sufi liturgical life, usually based on discipline established by the founder

wusṭā   Eight-beat pattern of traditional suite; to make wholesome

wuṣūl   Union with God; flexible notion of a progressive intimate relationship with God

zajal   Poetic genre begun in Andalusia; popular form of chant for some munshidūn, using North African dialect.

zajjāl   Zajal poet who writes poems called *liqsid*

zāwiya   A building for purposes of Sufi retreat; place for Sufi liturgies and social gatherings

zuhd   Renunciation or ascetic mode of behavior; opposition to worldliness on the part of believers

NOTES

Preface

1. Ludwig Wittgenstein, "Remarks on Frazer's *Golden Bough,*" trans. A. C. Miles and Rush Rhees, *Human World* 3 (May 1971): 36.

Chapter 1

1. Earle H. Waugh, *The Munshidīn of Egypt: Their World and Their Song* (Columbia: University of South Carolina Press, 1989). Egyptian popular Arabic tends to say munshidīn, hence the different spelling; I have retained the classical form munshidūn throughout this book.

2. As, for example, in Edouard Montet, *Les culte des saints musulmans dans Afrique du Nord et plus spécialement au Maroc* (Geneva: Librairie Georg, 1909).

3. Clifford Geertz, "Religion as a Cultural System," in *Anthropological Approaches to the Study of Religion,* ed. Michael Banton, 3:1–46, American Society of Anthropological Monographs (London: Tavistock, 1979).

4. Mircea Eliade, *The Quest: History and Meaning in Religion* (Chicago: University of Chicago Press, 1969), 76. The following exposition is based on 76–87.

5. Ibid., 76.

6. See Hans Schärer, *Ngaju Religion: The Conception of God among a South Borneo People,* trans. Rodney Needham (The Hague: Nijhoff, 1963). I became aware of the works of Danièle Hervieu-Léger and Maurice Halbwachs too late to relate them to my own thoughts here. See a recent work by Danièle Hervieu-Léger, *Religion as a Chain of Memory* (New Brunswick, N.J.: Rutgers University Press, 2000).

7. See Jonathan Z. Smith, *To Take Place: Toward Theory in Ritual* (Chicago and London: University of Chicago Press, 1987), 26.

8. John Kotre, *White Gloves: How We Create Ourselves through Memory* (New York: Free Press, 1995), 34–37, 117.

9. Daniel Goleman, *Emotional Intelligence* (New York: Bantam Books, 1995), 10–11.

10. See ibid., 20–22. Goleman's writing is based on the research of neuroscientist Joseph LeDoux, "Emotion as Memory: Anatomical Systems Underlying Indelible Neural Traces," in *The Handbook of Emotion and Memory: Research and Theory,* ed. S. Christianson, 269–88 (Hillsdale, N.J.: Lawrence Erlbaum, 1992); Joseph LeDoux, *The Emotional Brain: The Mysterious Underpinnings of Emotional Life* (New York: Simon and Schuster, 1996).

11. See Larry R. Squire, Barbara Knowlton, and Gail Musen, "The Structure and Organization of Memory," in *Human Memory: A Reader,* 153, 179–83 (London: Arnold, 1997).

12. For mood states, see K. S. Bowers, "On Being Unconsciously Influenced and Informed," in *The Unconscious Reconsidered,* ed. K. S. Bowers and D. Meichenbaum, 227–72 (New York: Wiley, 1984); for fears, phobias, and so on, see W. J. Jacobs and L. Nadel, "Stress-Induced Recovery of Fears and Phobias," *Psychological Review* 92 (1985): 512–31; for self-conceptions, see H. Markus and Z. Kunda, "Stability and Malleability of the

Self-Concept," *Journal of Personality and Social Psychology* 51 (1983): 858–66. For a fine overview of the area, see Daniel L. Schacter, "Implicit Memory: History and Current Status," *Journal of Experimental Psychology* 13 (1987): 501–18. This case, referring to an individual in Agadir, was related to me by a Moroccan professor, Muḥammed al-Nouhī, in March 1999.

13. Mahzarin R. Banaji and Curtis Hardin, "Affect and Memory in Retrospective Reports," in *Autobiographical Memory and the Validity of Retrospective Reports,* ed. Norbert Schwarz and Seymour Sudman, 86 (New York: Springer-Verlag, 1994). For research showing the relationship of implicit memory to perceptions, see Tim Curran and Daniel L. Schacter, "Implicit Memory and Perceptual Brain Mechanisms," in *Basic and Applied Memory Research Theory in Context,* ed. D. Herrmann, C. McEvoy, C. Hertzog, P. Hertel, and M. K. Johnson, 1:221–40 (Malwah, N.J.: Lawrence Erlbaum, 1996).

14. See Robert Bringhurst, *Native American Oral Literatures and the Unity of the Humanities* (Vancouver: Department of English, University of British Columbia, 1998), 14–17; Barre Toelken, "Seeing with a Native Eye: How Many Sheep Will It Hold?" in *Seeing with a Native Eye,* ed. Walter H. Capps, 11–14 (New York: Harper and Row, 1976); Mircea Eliade, *Myth and Reality* (New York: Harper and Row, 1963), 6–7; Sam Gill, *Sacred Words: A Study of Navajo Religion and Prayer* (Westport, Conn.: Greenwood Press, 1981), 50–55; Leland C. Wyman, *Blessingway: With Three Versions of the Myth Recorded and Translated from the Navajo by Father Berard Haile, OFM* (Tucson: University of Arizona Press, 1970).

15. Hesiod, *Theogony.* In *Hesiod,* trans. Richmond Lattimore (Ann Arbor: University of Michigan, 1959), lines 53–55, 103 (pages 126, 129).

16. Gregory Nagy, "The Crisis of Performance," in *The Ends of Rhetoric: History, Theory, Practice,* ed. John Bender and David E. Wellberg, 47 (Stanford, Calif.: Stanford University Press, 1990).

17. Ibid., 48–49.

18. Paul de Man, "Literary History and Literary Modernity," *Daedalus* 99 (1970): 388–89.

19. Jefferson A. Singer and Peter Salovey, *The Remembered Self: Emotion and Memory in Personality* (New York and Toronto: Free Press, 1993), 4. See also 9–46.

20. Quoted in Marvin Zonis, "Autobiography and Biography in the Middle East: A Plea for Psychohistorical Studies," in *Middle Eastern Lives: The Practice of Biography and Self-Narrative,* ed. Martin Kramer, 60 (Syracuse, N.Y.: Syracuse University Press, 1991).

21. Katherine Nelson, "The Psychological and Social Origins of Autobiographical Memory," *Psychological Science* 4 (1993): 12.

22. The mode of expressing oneself through memory is a new and promising arena of discourse; see *Interpreting the Self: Autobiography in the Arabic Literary Tradition,* ed. Dwight F. Reynolds (Berkeley and Los Angeles: University of California Press, 2001).

23. The various dimensions of time consciousness are discussed in chapter 6, "Reconstructive Memory for Time," in *Autobiographical Memory: Remembering What and Remembering When,* ed. C. P. Thompson, J. J. Skowronski, S. F. Larsen, and A. L. Betz, 101–23 (Mahwah, N.J.: Lawrence Erlbaum, 1996).

24. See Barbara D. Metcalf, "What Happened in Mecca: Mumtaz Mufti's *Labbaik,*" in *The Culture of Autobiography: Constructions of Self-Representation,* ed. Robert Folkenflik, 149–67 (Stanford, Calif.: Stanford University Press, 1993).

25. J. J. Gibson, *The Ecological Approach to Visual Perception* (Boston: Houghton Mifflin,

1979), 9. For an extended discussion, see Ulric Neisser, "Nested Structure in Autobiographical Memory," in *Autobiographical Memory,* ed. David C. Rubin, 71–81 (Cambridge: Cambridge University Press, 1986).

26. See René Girard, *Deceit, Desire, and the Novel,* trans. Yvonne Freccero (Baltimore: Johns Hopkins University Press, 1966); *Critiques dans un souterrain* (Paris: Grasset, 1976), especially "Dostoievski, du double a l'unité," 41–135; *Things Hidden since the Foundation of the World,* trans. Stephen Bann and Michael Metteer (Stanford, Calif.: Stanford University Press, 1987); *Job, the Victim of His People,* trans. Yvonne Freccero (Stanford, Calif.: Stanford University Press, 1987); "Theory and Its Terrors," in *The Limits of Theory,* ed. Thomas Kavanagh, 225–54 (Stanford, Calif.: Stanford University Press, 1989); *A Theatre of Envy: William Shakespeare* (New York: Oxford University Press, 1991). I owe my introduction to the thought of René Girard to my colleague in English, Professor Lahoucine Ouzgane, to whom I am very grateful.

27. See, for example, Michael Taussig, *Mimesis and Alterity: A Particular History of the Senses* (New York: Routledge, 1993).

28. For an examination of this notion see Paul J. Eakin, *Fictions of the Self: Studies in the Art of Self-Invention* (Princeton, N.J.: Princeton University Press, 1985).

29. For a recent study utilizing this perspective see Mondher Kilani, *La construction de la memoire: Le lineage et la sainteté dans l'oasis d'El Ksar* (Geneva: Éditions Labor et Fides, 1992).

30. Paul Connerton, *How Societies Remember* (Cambridge: Cambridge University Press, 1989), 48ff.

31. Bridget Connelly, *Arab Folk Epic and Identity* (Berkeley: University of California Press, 1986), 245.

32. Ibid., 249.

33. Heinrich Zimmer, *Philosophies of India,* ed. Joseph Campbell, 323 (Princeton, N.J.: Princeton University Press and Bollingen Foundation, 1951).

34. Printer's preface, *Selihot le-yom ha-'esrim le-Sivan* (Cracow, 1650), translated in Josef Hayim Yerushalmi, *Zakhor: Jewish History and Jewish Memory* (Seattle and London: University of Washington Press, 1982), 50–51.

35. Ibid., 51.

36. Ibid., 99.

37. Saint Augustine, *Confessions,* 9:25–26, quoted in Francis Yates, *The Art of Memory* (London: Routledge and Kegan Paul, 1966), 47.

38. Ibid., 49.

39. Ibid., 74–75.

40. Jack Finegan, *Jesus, History and You* (Richmond, Va.: John Knox Press, 1964), 14.

41. Ibid., 135.

42. Jan von Ruysbroeck, *The Adornment of the Spiritual Marriage,* quoted in Nelson Pike, "Comments," in *Art, Mind and Religion,* ed. W. H. Capitan and D. D. Merrill, 146 (Pittsburgh, Pa.: University of Pittsburgh Press, 1965). See also the discussion of the passage in Philip C. Almond, *Mystical Experience and Religious Doctrine: An Investigation of the Study of Mysticism in World Religions* (Berlin, Amsterdam, and New York: Mouton, 1982), 158–60.

43. See M. T. Cicero, *De Oratore* II, 87:357: "The keenest of all our senses is the sense of sight."

44. See von Ruysbroeck: "There (in the mystic state) all is full and overflowing, for the spirit feels itself to be one truth and one richness and one unit with God." Quoted in Pike, "Comment." See Steven Katz's discussion in "Language, Epistemology and Mysticism," in *Mysticism and Philosophical Analysis,* ed. S. Katz, 51 (London: Sheldon Press, 1978).

45. Waugh, *Munshidīn of Egypt,* 82.

46. George P. Landow, *Hypertext: The Convergence of Contemporary Critical Theory and Technology* (Baltimore: Johns Hopkins University Press, 1992).

47. According to hypertext theory, there can be no single "text" nor any objective center-ing reality in the variety of texts linked to the text at hand. See Jacques Derrida, "Structure, Sign, and Play in the Discourse of the Human Sciences," in *The Languages of Criticism and the Sciences of Man: The Structuralist Controversy,* ed. Richard Macksey and Eugenio Donato, 251 (Baltimore: Johns Hopkins University Press, 1970).

Chapter 2

1. Ibn Khaldūn, *The Muqaddimah: An Introduction to History,* trans. F. Rosenthal, 2d ed. (Princeton, N.J.: Princeton University Press, 1967), 2:430–31. One could argue that this is a distinctive contribution by Moroccans to Islam, an indication that North African Islam certainly has contributed significantly to the Islamic world, as against Brunschvig's claim that North Africa is a "poor relation" in cultural creation. Robert Brunschvig, "Dis-cussion and Comments," in *Unity and Variety in Muslim Civilization,* ed. Gustave E. von Grunebaum, 257 (Chicago: University of Chicago Press, 1956).

2. Dale F. Eickelman, "The Art of Memory: Islamic Education and Its Social Repro-duction," *Comparative Studies in Society and History* 20, no. 4 (October 1978): 485–516; see also his *Knowledge and Power in Morocco: The Education of a Twentieth-Century Notable* (Princeton, N.J.: Princeton University Press, 1985), esp. 56–68.

3. See, for example, Qur'ān 43:44, where the message is regarded as a dhikran, remembrance.

4. Qur'ān 10:47, 16:89.

5. Qur'ān 6:155.

6. As is found in Ibn Ishāq's *Sīrat Rasūl Allāh,* trans. as *The Life of Muhammad,* by A. Guillaume (Lahore: Oxford University Press, 1953), and the collections of the Ḥadīth, both of which represent the collective memory of the early Muslim community.

7. Scholars have pointed out that there are no independent sources depicting the first crucial years of the Islamic state and of the Prophet within it, so they are skeptical of the Muslim version of its history. This is an issue larger than we can deal with here. Much of it focuses upon the validity of the ḥadīth literature. I. Goldziher's *Muhammedanische Studien* (Hildesheim: Georg Olms Verlag, 1971) sets the Western tone with widespread skepticism about the veracity of many assertions that Muslims make. For one view from within Islam, see Mohammad Mustafa Azmi, *Studies in Early Hadīth Literature: With a Critical Edition of Some Early Texts* (Indianapolis, Ind.: American Trust Publications, 1978).

8. See Marshall G. S. Hodgson, *The Venture of Islam: Conscience and History in a World Civilization* (Chicago: University of Chicago Press, 1974), 1:246–47.

9. See Vernon Schubel, "The Muḥarram Majlis: The Role of a Ritual in the Preserva-tion of Shi'a Identity," in *Muslim Families in North America,* ed. Earle H. Waugh, Sharon M. Abu-Laban, and Regula B. Qureshi, 118–31 (Edmonton: University of Alberta Press, 1991).

10. See Annemarie Schimmel, *Mystical Dimensions of Islam* (Chapel Hill: University of North Carolina, 1975), 167–78; Waugh, *Munshidīn of Egypt,* 66–95; Valerie J. Hoffman, *Sufism, Saints and Mysticism in Modern Egypt* (Columbia: University of South Carolina Press, 1995), 167–78.

11. See Waugh, *Munshidīn of Egypt,* 192.

12. *Muṣḥaf al-Madīnah al-Nabawiyyah (The Holy Qurʾān: English translation of the meanings and commentary)*, rev. and ed. Presidency of Islamic Researches, IFTA, Call and Guidance, based on translation of Abdallah Yusuf ʿAlī (Medina, Saudi Arabia: King Fahd Holy Qurʾan Printing Complex, 1991).

13. Michael A. Sells, *Mystical Languages of Unsaying* (Chicago and London: University of Chicago Press, 1994), 66–68.

14. See Michael Burke, *Among the Dervishes* (London: Octagon Press, 1973), 49.

15. Schimmel, *Mystical Dimensions,* 30–31.

16. Ibid., 231–32.

17. Shaikh Sayyid Barrāda, interview by the author, Fez, May 19, 1995, tape no. 5.

18. See the review of Sufis who preached in medieval Cairo, for example, and of the effects of their preaching in Boaz Shoshan, *Popular Culture in Medieval Cairo* (Cambridge: Cambridge University Press, 1993), 12–13.

19. See Schimmel, *Mystical Dimensions,* 203–13.

20. Hodgson, *Venture of Islam,* 1:397–98.

21. Ibid., 399. I am struck by the similarity of his notion of moral consciousness to the work of Dr. R. M. Bucke, the Canadian psychiatrist who introduced the notion of "moral treatment" into North American psychiatry, the basis for which was developed in *Man's Moral Nature* (1897); Bucke went on to publish *Cosmic Consciousness: A Study of the Evolution of the Human Mind* (Philadelphia: Innes and Sons, 1901), in which he argued for three kinds of consciousness: simple, self, and cosmic. It was common knowledge among students at Chicago in the 1960s that Hodgson was a mystic and a Quaker; certainly Bucke was a mystic, but whether he had some connection to Quakerism I have not been able to confirm.

22. This position allowed him to see classical Islam as the unification of a mystic vision and a moral perspective, a point of view that provided an explanation for the essential unity of Islam across diverse peoples and its multiplicity of political forms.

23. In the literature, "mousem" is transliterated by a number of different spellings, including mussem, moussem, moulid, mouloud, and the recent form of mawlid, as in J. Knappert, "mawlid," *Encyclopaedia of Islam,* new ed., ed. E. van Donzel, B. Lewis, and Ch. Pellat (Leiden: E. J. Brill, 1978). I have retained the popular Moroccan form "mūssem." See Paul Paquignon, "Le mouloud au Maroc," *Revue du Monde Musulmane* 14, no. 4 (1911): 525–36.

24. Hilda Kuper, with Diane Weiner and Beth Rosen-Prinz, "The Power of Secrecy in the Political Process," in *Africa in World History: Old, New, Then, and Now,* ed. Michael W. Coy Jr. and Leonard Plotnicov, 80 (Pittsburgh, Pa.: Dept. of Anthropology, University of Pittsburgh, 1995).

25. The question is whether this is appreciably different from the operation of secrecy in government or crime. See James Michael, *The Politics of Secrecy* (Harmondswort: Penguin, 1982).

26. "Baraka" is a complicated term, not easily reduced to charisma or blessings as is

usually done. See Dietrich von Denffer, "Baraka as Basic Concept of Muslim Popular Belief," *Islamic Studies* 15, no. 3 (autumn 1976): 166–86.

27. The classical form, *mawlid,* can be found in H. Fuchs, *Encyclopedia of Islam,* 1st ed. (1913–36; repr., Leiden: E. J. Brill, 1987), 481–84, s.v. "Maulid." For a more recent appraisal see Pessah Shinar, "Traditional and Reformist Mawlid Celebrations in the Maghrib," in *Studies in Memory of Gaston Wiet,* ed. Myriam Rosen-Ayalon, 371–413 (Jerusalem: Institute of Asian and African Studies, Hebrew University of Jerusalem, 1977).

28. For information on the Darqāwiyya see F. de Jong, "Materials Relative to the History of the Darqāwiyya Order and Its Branches," *Arabica* 26, no. 2 (June 1979): 126–43.

29. Mehmet Ali Ainī, *Un grand saint de l'Islam, Abd-al-Kadir Guilānī, 1077–1166* (1938; repr., Paris: Paul Geuthner, 1967), 173.

30. Ibid., 201–4.

31. Ibid., 252.

32. Cf. *Saḥīḥ Muslim ibn al-Hajjaj al-Qurhayri,* trans. ʿAbdul Ḥamid Ṣiddqī (Lahore: Sh. Muhammad Ashraf, 1976), 48:2.

33. Ibn al-ʿArabī, *The Bezels of Wisdom,* trans. R. W. J. Austin (New York: Paulist Press, 1980), 280–81.

34. al-ʿArabī al-Darqāwī, *Letters of a Sufi Master,* trans. Titus Burckhardt (London: Perennial Books, 1973), 37. The quoted phrase is a saying of the Prophet.

35. It was al-Ḥārith b. Asad al-Muḥāsībī (d. 857) who stressed the importance of self-examination (*muḥāsabah*) in early Islam, establishing it as a discipline in Sufism. Intention is a complicated element, however, for self-examination immediately brings awareness of sins and deficiencies, as well as problems that may have sinful implications. This "weighing" feature of prayer's opening framework is crucial.

36. Schimmel, *Mystical Dimensions,* 152–55.

37. William Graham, *Divine Word and Prophetic Word in Early Islam* (The Hague: Mouton, 1977).

38. For an example see my "Silence and the Speech of God in the Mawlid al-Muhammadi of the Demirdashiyya," *Studies in Religion* 17, no. 1 (1988): 53–64.

39. See Judith Lynne Hanna, *To Dance Is Human: A Theory of Nonverbal Communication* (Austin: University of Texas Press, 1979), 107.

40. R. W. J. Austin, trans., *Sufis of Andalusia: The "Rūḥ al-Quds" and "al-Durrat al-Fākhirah" of Ibn ʿArabī* (London: George Allen and Unwin, 1971), 87. Austin notes the reference to body and limbs testifying for or against their owners on the Last Day (Qurʾān 24:24).

41. William S. Haas, "The Zikr of the Raḥmānija-Order in Algeria," *Moslem World* 33, no. 1 (January 1943): 18.

42. Ibid., 24.

43. E. Durkheim, *The Rules of Sociological Method* (1895; repr., London: Collier-Macmillan, 1964), 106: "Collective representations . . . are caused not by certain states of the consciousness of individuals but by the conditions in which the social group in its totality is placed."

44. A. Radcliffe-Brown, *Structure and Function in Primitive Society* (London: Cohen and West, 1952), 153–77, where social drives create the need for religion.

45. E. Evans-Pritchard, *Theories of Primitive Religion* (Oxford: Clarendon Press, 1965), 46, where ritual is "a creation of society."

46. Mary Douglas, *Natural Symbols* (London: Barrie and Rockliff, 1970), 81, that is, "the principle of symbolic replication of a social state."

47. James Kennedy, "Psychological and Social Explanations of Witchcraft," *Man* 2 (1967): 224.

48. Herman Landolt pointed out that Bayazid al-Biṣṭāmī, the great Islamic ecstatic, when asked if the human can attain God, replied with the question, "Has anybody ever attained Him?" thus indicating that the mystical experience is not a once-gained-always-attained type. Herman Landolt, "Mystical Experience in Islam," in *Personality Change and Religious Experience,* ed. Raymond Prince, 73 (Montreal: R. M. Bucke Memorial Society, 1965).

49. This is the positive position of David Hay, "Religious Experience and Its Induction," in *Advances in the Psychology of Religion,* ed. L. B. Brown, 147 (Oxford: Pergamon Press, 1985).

50. Haas, "The Zikr," 26–27.

51. Max Weber, *Economy and Society: An Outline of Interpretive Society,* ed. Guenther Roth and Claus Wittich, trans. Ephraim Fischoff (1968; repr., Berkeley: University of California Press, 1978), 535.

52. A revisionist version is available in Steven L. Carlton-Ford, *The Effects of Ritual and Charisma: The Creation of Collective Effervescence and the Support of Psychic Strength* (New York and London: Garland, 1993), which gives greater place to ritual in the definition of trance.

53. See Larry G. Peters and Douglas Price-Williams, "A Phenomenological Overview of Trance," *Transcultural Psychiatric Research Review* 20 (1983): 5–39.

54. *Religion, Altered States of Consciousness, and Social Change,* ed. Erika Bourguignon (Columbus: Ohio State University Press, 1973).

55. Mircea Eliade, *Shamanism: Archaic Techniques of Ecstasy,* trans. Willard R. Trask (New York: Bollingen Foundation, 1964), 503–6. Also see Kocku von Stuckrad, "The Formation of Shamanic Discourses in Religious Studies and Esotericism: Studies on the Interdependency of Academic Research and Religious Practice" (unpublished research project, 2000). I appreciate the author forwarding a copy of this to me.

56. See for example Felicitas D. Goodman, *Where the Spirits Ride the Wind: Trance Journeys and Other Ecstatic Experiences* (Bloomington: Indiana University Press, 1990); and Goodman, *Ecstasy, Ritual and Alternate Reality: Religion in a Pluralistic World* (Bloomington: Indiana University Press, 1988).

57. For example Goodman lists under "sojourn" everything from mild visionary experience that moves in and out of consciousness to full-blown mystical states that are completely transforming, a range too great for there to be one port of entry and one experience. Goodman, *Where the Spirits Ride,* passim.

58. Ainī, *Un grand saint,* 175.

59. See Marijan Molé, "Les danse extatique en Islam," Sources orientales no. 6, *La danses sacrées* (Paris: Seuil, 1963), 147–79.

60. See Knut S. Vikør, "Sufism and Revolt: Tijānis, Sanūsis, and Safavids" (paper presented at Middle East Studies Association conference, November 21–24, 1996); and his "*Jihād, ʿIlm* and *Taṣawwuf*—Two Justifications of Action from the Idrīsī Tradition," *Studia Islamica* 84 (2000): 153–76.

61. All three terms are used by Michael J. Apter, but the way he has utilized them does not always meet the Islamic case. I have therefore modified the understanding somewhat. I

have changed the last to reflect better the Islamic data. See Michael J. Apter, "Religious States of Mind: A Reversal Theory Interpretation," in *Advances in the Psychology of Religion,* ed. L. B. Brown, 62–75 (Oxford: Pergamon Press, 1985).

62. I met with Shaikh Boukoulousī July 14, 1995, and during the interview he confirmed this fact. Vincent Crapanzano, *The Hamadsha: A Study in Moroccan Ethnopsychiatry* (Berkeley and London: University of California Press, 1973), 229–30; Frank M. Welte, *Der Gnawa-Kult: Trancespiele, Geisterbeschwörung und Besessenheit in Marokko* (Frankfurt am Main: Peter Lang, 1990), 180–85.

63. See al-ʿArabī al-Darqāwī, *Letters of a Sufi Master,* 36. Husayn Sharif indicates he is of the genealogy of Husayn, the grandson of the Prophet; al-Siqalli was an eighteenth-century founder of a Naqshbandi-influenced Shadhdhili order who came from Sicily.

64. See Schimmel, *Mystical Dimensions,* 58, 206, 277, 283.

65. Ibn al-ʿArabī, *Bezels of Wisdom,* 27, cf. 128–44.

66. Haas, "The Zikr," 19–22.

67. al-ʿArabī al-Darqāwī, *Letters of a Sufi Master,* 38, modifying his translation somewhat.

68. See Schimmel, *Mystical Dimensions,* 86–87.

69. See references to heedlessness in Schimmel, *Mystical Dimensions,* 134, 169, 170, 175.

70. Genesis 17:3.

71. Earle H. Waugh, *Dissonant Worlds: Roger Vandersteene among the Cree* (Waterloo: Wilfrid Laurier University Press, 1989), 143–47.

72. See Gordon W. Hewes, "The Current Status of the Gestural Theory of Language Origin," in *Origins and Evolution of Language and Speech,* ed. Stevan R. Harnad, Horst D. Steklis, and Jane Lancaster, 482–504 (New York: New York Academy of Sciences, 1976), esp. 495.

73. *Connerton, How Societies Remember, 95. Cf. M. Merleau-Ponty, Phenomenology of Perception,* trans. Colin Smith (London: Routledge, 1962), 144.

74. Connerton, *How Societies Remember,* 94.

75. Roy A. Rappoport, *Ritual and Religion in the Making of Humanity* (Cambridge: Cambridge University Press, 1999), 119.

76. This makes dhikr quite different from theatrical performance, where the audience has to provide the imaginary world to make the performance meaningful. See the fine description of Euripides' play *The Trojan Women,* in *Form in Performance, Hard-Core Ethnography,* ed. Marcia Herndon and Roger Brunyate (Austin: College of Fine Arts, University of Texas, 1975), 64–65.

77. Ibn ʿAṭaʾillāh, *al-Ḥikam Ibn ʿAṭaʾillāh,* ed. ʿAbd al-Halim Maḥmūd (Cairo: Dar al-Shaʿb, 1985), translated by Victor Danner as *The Book of Wisdom: Sufi Aphorisms* (Leiden: E. J. Brill, 1973), 18n1. I have only slightly modified his text.

78. See Tetouan munshid Yussef: al-Ḥāḍra, taken as an experiential encounter is rendered as a particular type of feeling, and is conceived, at least in Ibn al-ʿArabī's system, as one of several kind of "feelings" that one can have when God takes on a "feeling" form. Thus, as Rudolph Otto noted, the Numinous is experienced as awe, or fear, or the holy, and all these words are merely ways of talking about a peculiar kind of mystical encounter. See Rudolph Otto, *The Idea of the Holy,* trans. John W. Harvey (New York: Oxford University Press, 1958). Danner notes that Ibn al-ʿArabī distinguishes between several kinds of Presence: *al-ḥaḍra,* or *ḥaḍrat qudsih* (the presence of His Holiness), *al-ḥuḍūr* (sense of the presence of God), and *al-ghayba* (nonexistence brought about by the effacement of self in the presence of God). Ibn ʿAṭaʾillāh, *Sufi Aphorisms,* 74.

79. I owe this reference to my colleague Don Kuiken in educational psychology. See J. H. Riskind, "The Mediating Mechanisms in Mood and Memory: A Cognitive Priming Formulation," in *Mood and Memory: Theory, Research and Applications,* ed. Donald Kuiken, 185–96 (Newbury Park, Calif.: Sage, 1991), and his "Nonverbal Expression and the Accessibility of Life Experience Memories," *Social Cognition* 2 (1983): 62–86.

80. I have seen trance behavior in Pentecostalism, Aboriginal traditions, and Sufism, and while they have similar features, all are group-specific in terms of the process to trance and reactions during trance. It should be noted that little study has been done on such religious scripting. However, the nature of emotional scripting is touched upon in the work of Laird and Bresler and also that of Tomkins.

81. Plotinus, *On the Nature of the Soul, Being the Fourth Ennaed,* trans. Stephen Mac-Kenna (London: The Medici Society, 1924), 4.6.1–3.

82. See William C. Chittick, *Self-Disclosure of* God, 258, from *al-Futūḥāt al-makkiyya* (Cairo: Bulaq, 1911), 2:240.32.

83. Crapanzano, *The Hamadsha,* 20, 184ff.

84. William Wordsworth, *The Prelude,* 1805 ed., 6:743–45.

85. Shaikh Maḥjūb, interview by the author, Meknes, July 5, 1995, tape no. 5.

86. See Waugh, *Munshidīn of Egypt,* 147–49.

87. See Julius Lipner, *Hindus: Their Religious Beliefs and Practices* (New York: Routledge, 1994), 25–54.

88. Gustave E. von Grunebaum spoke of the "aesthetic" qualities in Arabic literary production, noting that the imagination was considered opposed to that of "reason" in most Arabic medieval writers except the Sufis: "The Aesthetic Foundation of Arabic Literature," *Comparative Literature* 3 (1951): 323–40.

89. al-ʿArabī al-Darqāwī, *Letters of a Sufi Master,* 25.

90. Chittick, *Self-Disclosure of God,* xxii.

91. al-ʿArabī al-Darqāwī, *Letters of a Sufi Master,* 32. The term "knowledge of certainty" (*ʿilm al-yaqīn*) is one of three degrees of intuitive knowledge taught in Morocco, the others being the "eye of certainty" (*ʿayn al-yaqīn*) and "truth of certainty" (*ḥaqq al-yaqīn*). Clearly this kind of imagination cannot be the type that imagines untrue or imaginary realities.

92. See Janice Boddy, *Wombs and Alien Spirits: Women, Men, and the Zar Cult in Northern Sudan* (Madison: University of Wisconsin Press, 1989), 134f.

93. In a perceptive article James D. Laird argues against twenty-five hundred years of common sense and experimental assumption to say that emotions and cognitions are functionally the same kind of thing. He claims that this conclusion is the only way to account for new evidence. See "Mood Affects Memory Because Feelings *Are* Cognitions," in *Mood and Memory: Theory, Research and Applications,* ed. Don Kuiken, 33–38 (Newbury Park, Calif., and London: Sage Publications, 1991). I owe this point to Professor Kuiken, who brought it to my attention.

Chapter 3

1. Clifford Geertz, *Islam Observed* (New Haven, Conn.: Yale University Press, 1968), 51.

2. Daisy Hilse Dwyer, "Women, Sufism and Decision-Making," in *Women in the Muslim World,* ed. Lois Beck and Nikki Keddie, 586 (Cambridge, Mass.: Harvard University Press, 1978).

3. Ibn Khaldūn, *Al-Muqaddimah,* 1:492.

4. See Susan Slyomovics, *The Merchant of Art: An Egyptian Hilāli Oral Epic Poet in Performance* (Berkeley: University of California Press, 1987); also her "Approaches to Transcription and Translation of Oral Epic Performance (Sīrat Banī Hilāl)" (paper presented at *Colloque Internationale sur les Banu-Hilāl: Geste et Historie,* May 20–23, 1990, Centre National d'Études Historiques, Algiers); Dwight F. Reynolds, "Heroic Poets, Poetic Heroes: Composition and Performance in an Arabic Oral Epic Tradition of Northern Egypt" (Ph.D. diss., University of Pennsylvania, 1991); Paul Zumthor, *Introduction à la poésie orale* (Paris: Seuil, 1983); Fadhl ibn Ammar al-Ammary, "Application of Oral Tradition Theory on Pre-Islamic Poetry," *Journal of the College of Arts, King Saud University* 14, no. 1 (1987): 39–61.

5. M. Ben Rahhal, "À travers les Benī Snassen," *Bulletin de la Sociéte de Géographie d'Oran,* no. 9 (1889): 5–50.

6. V. Loubignac, *Étude sur le dialecte des Zaian et des Ait Sgougou* (Paris: E. LeRoux, 1924).

7. See, for example, *Colloque Internationale sur les Banu-Hilāl: Geste et Historie,* May 20–23, 1990, Centre National d'Études Historiques, Algiers.

8. Connelly, *Arab Folk Epic,* 249.

9. J. Christoph Bürgel, "Qaṣīda as Discourse on Power and Its Islamization: Some Reflections," in *Qaṣīda Poetry in Islamic Asia and Africa,* ed. Stefan Sperl and Christopher Shackle, 1:451–73 (Leiden, New York, and Cologne: E. J. Brill, 1996). Note that Stefan Sperl earlier argued for the Persian and Mesopotamian authoritative systems as the generator of early Arab panegyric: "Islamic Kingship and Arabic Panegyric Poetry in the Early 9th Century," *Journal of Arabic Literature* 8 (1977): 20–35, esp. 21.

10. Ben Cherīfa, interview by the author, Rabat, July 15, 1995.

11. Indeed, it is a simplification, according to the study by ʿAbd al-Jawād Sayyid al-Shaibānī, "al-Hijra al-hilāliyya ila Ifriqiyya al-ziridiyya wa Atharuha al-hamma" (The Hilali migration to zirid Africa and its central effects) (Ph.D. diss., Muhammad V University, Rabat, 1988).

12. Connelly, *Arab Folk Epic,* 245.

13. See John Burton, *The Collection of the Qurʾān* (Cambridge: Cambridge University Press, 1977), 119.

14. For example, in Marzuki's preface to his commentary on the Mufaḍḍaliyyāt poems, collected for the caliph al-Mahdi around 776 c.e., we read: "In Ataif there were shāʿir and rāwī, but not many," thus indicating that the distinction between them is very ancient. See *The Hudsailian Poems,* ed. (in Arabic) and trans. John G. L. Kosegarten (Hildesheim and New York: Georg Olms Verlag, 1984), 1:v in the Arabic, 6 in the translation; ʿAbd al-Raḥmān al-Abnoudy, "al-Sīra al-shaʿbiyya bayna al-shāʿir wa-l-rāwī," in Connelly, *Arab Folk Epic,* 21, 71, 148, 213, 271–72.

15. Zākī ʿAlī, interview by the author, Agadir, July 2, 1994, tape no. 1. Terri Brint Joseph, in a review of Michael Zwettler's *The Oral Tradition of Classical Arabic Poetry: Its Character and Implication* (Columbus: Ohio State University Press, 1978), states: "Lord and Parry insist so categorically on composition *in the act of performance* that they exclude from the oral poets those artists who first compose a work, memorize it, and then perform it in sequential order; for them the true oral poet must improvise while performing." *Arab Studies Quarterly* 3, no. 1 (winter 1981): 108. If we accepted this definition of performance, the munshidūn would not be included. Yet they are, since they are manipulating

parts of texts and rephrasing lines drawn from traditional sources. What they do not consider themselves doing is composing a *new* poem.

16. See A. Arazi, *Encyclopaedia of Islam,* s.v. "Shiʿr."

17. Alison Lennick, "Taghrībat Banī Hilāl al-Dayāghim: Variations in the Oral Epic Poetry of the Najd" (Ph.D. diss., Princeton University, 1984), 152.

18. Ashḥab, interview by the author, Rabat, May 20, 1995, tape no. 2.

19. Nabīl, interview by the author, Rabat, May 25, 1995, tape no. 2.

20. Ibid.

21. Ben Cherīfa, interview by the author, Rabat, May 30, 1995, tape no. 2.

22. Ḥajj Ḥusain Toulālī, interview by the author, Meknes, July 2, 1995, tape no. 5.

23. See Reynold A Nicholson, *A Literary History of the Arabs* (Cambridge: Cambridge University Press, 1954), 77–78.

24. Suzanne Stetkevych, "Pre-Islamic Panegyric and the Poetics of Redemption," in *Reorientations: Studies in Arabic and Persian Poetics,* ed. Suzanne Stetkevych , 33–34 (Bloomington: Indiana University Press, 1994). For goddesses see Miriam Robbins Dexter, *Whence the Goddesses: A Source Book* (New York: Teachers College Press, 1990), esp. chap. 2, "Goddesses of the Ancient Near East." However, Innana was not herself a mother, while retaining her role as deity of fertility. Furthermore, the goddesses of the Ancient Near East could also be associated with martial arts and achievements, see Dexter, *Whence the Goddesses,* 31.

25. In *Roles of the Northern Goddesses* (London: Routledge, 1998), 188–89, Hilda Ellis Davidson argues that goddesses cannot be limited to their "function," agreeing with David Kinsley that there are some goddesses who are not associated with fertility. Kinsley, *Hindu Goddesses* (Berkeley: University of California Press, 1986), x. For Ancient Near East goddesses and related discussions, see Raphael Patai, *The Hebrew Goddess* (New York: Avon Books, 1978); Carl Olsen, *Book of the Goddess Past and Present: An Introduction to Her Religion* (New York: Crossroads, 1983); James B. Pritchard, *Palestinian Figurines in Relation to Certain Goddesses Known through Literature,* AOS no. 24 (New Haven, Conn.: American Oriental Society, 1943); Patrick D. Miller Jr., Paul D. Hanson, and S. Dean McBride, eds., *Ancient Israelite Religion* (Philadelphia: Fortress Press, 1987); Elinor W. Gadon, *The Once and Future Goddess* (San Francisco and New York: Harper and Row, 1989).

26. I note that Jaroslav Stetkevych, in his essay "Toward an Arabic Elegiac Lexicon," in Susanne Stetkevych's *Reorientations,* uses "bliss" and associates it with an Arabian Orphic tradition (119).

27. Sayyid Barrāda, interview by the author, Fez, May 19, 1994, tape no. 1.

28. Muḥammed al-Nouhī, Agadir, personal note.

29. See Michael A. Sells, "*Banāt Suʿād:* Translation and Introduction," *Journal of Arabic Literature* 11, no. 2 (1990): 140–54.

30. Sells points out the possibly fictitious nature of the story, "*Banāt Suʿād,*" 141n2.

31. Stetkevych, *Reorientations,* 43.

32. Ibid., 20–21.

33. See Hassan Rachik, *Sacré et sacrifice dans le Haut Atlas marocain* (Casablanca: Afrique, 1990); also D. Hammoudi, *La victime et ses masques* (Paris: Seuil, 1988), translated by Paul Wissing as *The Victim and Its Masks: An Essay on Sacrifice and Masquerade in the Maghrib* (Chicago: University of Chicago Press, 1993).

34. See Stetkevych, *Reorientations,* 28.

35. See Charles James Lyall, ed. and trans., *The Mufaddaliyat: An Anthology of Ancient*

Arabian Odes Compiled by al-Mufaddal Son of Muhammad According to the Reclension and with the Commentary of Abu Muhammad al-Qasim ibn Muhammad al-Anbari, vol. 1, *Arabic Text,* vol. 2, *Translation and Notes* (Oxford: Clarendon Press, 1918).

36. Kenneth L. Brown, *People of Salé: Tradition and Change in a Moroccan City, 1830–1930* (Manchester: Manchester University Press, 1976), 91–92.

37. Ibid., 200–202.

38. Abbās Ibn ʿAbdullāh al-Jirārī, "al-Qaṣīdah" (Ph.D. diss., University of Cairo, 1970), 360.

39. For a good overview and examples, see Ahmed Salmi, "Le genres des poèmes de nativité (Maulūdiyya-s) dans le royaume de Grenade et au Maroc du XIIIe au XVIIe siècle," *Hespéris* 43 (1956): 335–435.

40. Al-Jirārī, "Qaṣīdah," 417–26.

41. Earle H. Waugh, "Religious Levitation and the Muslim Experience: A Study in the Flight Symbolism of Intermediary Figures and Other Images in Medieval Islam" (Ph.D. diss., University of Chicago, 1972), chap. 3.

42. al-Jirārī, "Qaṣīdah," 493.

43. Ibid., 453. We will explore below some aspects of contemporary secular madīḥ directed to the king. This madīḥ is usually called *madīḥ calipha* to indicate that the texts are directed to the reigning monarch.

44. See Muḥyī ad-dīn Abū Bakr Muḥammad bin ʿAlī Ibn al-ʿArabī, *al-Futūḥāt al-Makkiyyah* (Cairo: Bulaq, 1911), 1:10, where he dedicates the book to him.

45. Found in a manuscript in Damascus. See Denis Gril, "Le *Kitāb al-Inbāh ʿala Ṭarīq Allāh de ʿAbdallāh Badr al-Ḥabashī:* Un temoignage de l'enseignement spirituel de Muḥyī l-dīn Ibn ʿArabī," *Annales Islamogiques* 15 (1979): 97.

46. Ibid., 121.

47. Ibid., 107.

48. Bennīs, interview by the author, Fez, June 9, 1995, tape no. 6.

49. Ibid.

50. Ibid.

51. See Martin Lings, "Mystical Poetry," in *Abbasid belles-lettres,* ed. J. Ashtiany et al. (Cambridge: Cambridge University Press, 1990); and Annemarie Schimmel, *As Through a Veil: Mystical Poetry in Islam* (New York: Columbia University Press, 1982).

52. See Ibn al-ʿArabī, *al-Futūḥāt,* 3:88. Ibn Qisya was one Sufi who worked with rebels against the Almoravids in Algarve.

53. See Austin, *Sufis of Andalusia,* 112.

54. A. A. Afifi, introduction to *Mystical Philosophy of Muhyīd-Dīn Ibnul ʿArabī* (Cambridge: Cambridge University Press, 1939).

55. Ibn al-ʿArabī, *Bezels of Wisdom,* 19.

56. Ibn al-ʿArabī, *Al-Futūḥāt,* 1:153.

57. See Austin, *Sufis of Andalusia,* 112.

58. Ibn al-ʿArabī, *Bezels of Wisdom,* 95; recorded in ḥaḍra al-Ḥārrāqiyya, June 1995.

59. Ibn al-ʿArabī, *Al-Futūḥāt,* 3:45.

60. Michael Sells, *Mystical Languages of Unsaying* (Chicago and London: University of Chicago Press, 1994), 8–9.

61. See a good example of the mystical argument in the poem translated by Sells, *Mystical Languages,* 72.

62. Quoted in Roger Boase, foreword to *Ibn Saʿīd al-Maghribī* in *The Banners of the*

Champions: an Anthology of Medieval Arabic Poetry from Andalusia and Beyond, sel. and trans. by James A. Bellamy and Patricia Owen Steiner, xi (Madison, Wis.: Hispanic Seminary of Medieval Studies, 1989).

63. This is a *ḥadīth al-qudsī,* Bukhari, 81:38.

64. *Fuṣūṣ al-ḥikam,* 1, 70. I have utilized Sells' translation, in *Mystical Languages,* 100; cf. Austin, *Bezels of Wisdom,* 75.

65. *Fuṣūṣ al-ḥikam,* fol. 1., sec. 121. Translation from Sells, *Mystical Languages,* 97–98.

66. Sells, *Mystical Languages,* 101–2.

67. See Muḥammad Sahl ibn ʿAbdullāh al-Tustārī, *Tafsīr al-Qurʾān al-ʿAẓīm* (Cairo: Dar al-Kutub al-Gharbiyya al-Kubra, 1911), 40–41. For translations and discussion see Gerhard Bowering, *The Mystical Vision of Existence in Classical Islam: The Qurʾanic Hermenuetics of the Sufi Sahl at-Tustari, d. 283/896* (Berlin: Walter de Gruyter, 1980), 153–57.

68. See Sells, *Mystical Languages,* 63–89.

69. See Ibn al-ʿArabī, *Bezels,* 15n64.

70. *The Interpreter of Desires* was written in honor of the attractive daughter of Abū Shaja Zahīr b. Rustam, leading citizen of Mecca. He was later accused by some critics of having written sensual love poetry to his daughter. See *Tarjumān al-ashwāq* (Beirut, 1961), 7–8.

71. See Waugh, *Munshidīn of Egypt,* 153.

72. See A. L. Beeston, et. al. *Arabic Literature to the End of the Umayyad Period* (Cambridge: Cambridge University Press, 1983), 416–27.

73. Ibn Qutayba, *al-Shiʿr waʾl-shuʿarā,* ed. de Goeje, translated by A. J. Arberry as *The Mystical Poems of Ibn al-Fāriḍ* (Dublin: Emery Walker, 1956), 11–12.

74. Ibn Qutayba, *Mystical Poems,* no. 3, 36.

75. Ibid., no. 1, 23; no. 2, 29; no. 4, 41; no. 5, 46; no. 7, 60; no. 8, 79; no. 9, 75; no. 10, 81; no. 11, 90; no. 12, 95; no. 13, 102; no. 14, 117. Poem no. 6 gives special reference to memory.

76. See Sells, *Mystical Languages,* 63–89, for discussion of the Mirror in Ibn al-ʿArabī; see R. A. Nicholson, *Studies in Islamic Mysticism* (Cambridge: Cambridge University Press, 1921), 77–148.

77. See Ibn Qutayba, *Mystical Poems,* 68.

78. Ibid., 69.

Chapter 4

1. Ben Cherīfa, interview by the author, Rabat, July 20, 1995, tape no. 6.

2. Otto Zwartjes, "Berbers in al-Andalus and Andalusis in the Maghrib as Reflected in *Tawshih* Poetry," in *Orientations no. 4: Poetry, Politics and Polemics: Cultural Transfer between the Iberian Peninsula and North Africa,* ed. O. Zwartjes, Geert Jan van Gelder, and Ed de Moor, 35–55 (Amsterdam and Atlanta: Rodopi, 1996).

3. Readers will find a fine study of the genesis of this Eastern classical poetry in Alan Jones, ed. and trans., *Early Arabic Poetry,* vol. 1, *Marathī and Suʿlūk Poems* (Reading, England: Ithaca Press for Oxford University, 1992).

4. See Robert Montagne, *Les Berbères et le makhzen dans le sud du Maroc* (Paris: Alcan, 1931). Translated as *The Berbers: Their Social and Political Organisation* (London: Frank Cass, 1973), 13.

5. Doyle G. Hatt, "A Tribal Saint of the Twentieth Century," in *An African Commitment: Papers in Honour of Peter Lewis Shinnie,* ed. Judy Sterner and Peter Lewis Shinnie, 3 (Calgary: University of Calgary Press, 1992). See also his "Sainthood in Christianity and

Islam," in *Selected Proceedings,* Sixth Annual Meeting of the Canadian Ethnology Society, 1981, National Museum of Canada, Ottawa, 2–18.

6. See Robert Montagne's discussion of this period of history in *The Berbers,* 13–14.

7. F. Corriente argues that the meters of muwashshaḥ derive from adaptation of classical ʿArūd. See "The Metres of the *Muwaṣṣah,* an Andalusian Adaptation of ʿArūd (A Bridging Hypothesis)," *Journal of Arabic Literature* 13 (1982): 76–82. See also J. Derek Latham, "New Light on the Scansion of an Old Andalusian *Muwaṣṣah,"* *Journal of Semitic Studies* 27, no. 1 (spring 1982): 61–75.

8. See al-Jirārī, "Qaṣīdah," 1–3.

9. Jirārī, interview by the author, Casablanca, May 15, 1995, tape no. 4; "Qaṣīdah," 1. Cf. his article "Qaṣīdah al-Malḥūn," in *Fīʾl Ibdāʾ al-Shiʿrī* (Rabat: Islamic Education Scientific and Cultural Organization [ISESCO], 1972), 59–102.

10. Sayyid at-Takkafī, interview by the author, Rabat, July 1995, tape no. 7.

11. Sayyid at-Takkafī, interview by the author, Rabat, June 29, 1994, tape no. 1.

12. Al-Jirārī, "Qaṣīdah," 38–40, 85–90.

13. A good article on the orality of this tradition is James T. Monroe, "Which Came First, the *Zajal* or the *Muwaṣṣaha?* Some Evidence for the Oral Origins of Hispano-Arabic Strophic Poetry," *Oral Tradition* 4, no. 1–2 (1989): 38–64.

14. Al-Jirārī, "Qaṣīdah," 60.

15. The *ḥizb* is a formalized prayer, part of the opening litanies of a Sufi meeting. See Georges Drague, *Esquisse d'historie religieuse du Maroc: Confréries et Zaouias* (Paris: J. Peyronnet, n.d.), 285; Crapanzano, *The Hamadsha,* 190; and René Brunel, *Essai sur la confréries religieuses des ʿAïssouïa au Maroc* (Paris: Paul Geuthner, 1926), 57, 93–96, 102–7.

16. Shaikh Maḥjūb, interview by the author, Meknes, July 5, 1995, tape no. 5.

17. These divisions are found in al-Jirārī, "Qaṣīdah," 10–19.

18. Ibid., 17.

19. See David Gill, "The *Muwashshaḥ:* Artistic Convention or Cognitive Universal," *Israel Oriental Studies* 2 (1991): 137.

20. It is obvious that this would clash with Lord's affirmation of performer only as an initial creator: "We must eliminate from the word 'performer' any notion that he is one who merely reproduces what someone else or even he himself has composed." Albert Lord, *Singer of Tales* (Cambridge, Mass.: Harvard University Press, 1964), 13. As far as I can see, memory plays no role in his perception of performance. Others have modified this, including Michael Zwettler, *The Oral Tradition of Classical Arabic Poetry: Its Character and Implications* (Columbus: Ohio State University Press, 1978); and Dwight F. Reynolds, "Heroic Poets, Poetic Heroes: Composition and Performance in an Arabic Oral Epic Tradition of Northern Egypt" (Ph.D. diss., University of Pennsylvania, 1991).

21. Lois al-Faruqi, "Muwashshahah: A Vocal Form in Islamic Culture," *Ethnomusicology* 19, no. 1 (1972): 4.

22. Carol Card Wendt, "North Africa: An Introduction," in *The Garland Encyclopedia of World Music,* vol. 1, *Africa* (New York and London: Garland, 1998), 535.

23. Linda Fish Compton, *Andalusian Lyrical Poetry and Old Spanish Love Songs: The Muwashshahah and Its Kharja* (New York: New York University Press, 1976), xiii–xiv.

24. James L. Kugel, ed., *Poetry and Prophecy* (Ithaca, N.Y.: Cornell University Press, 1990), 100.

25. The usual diffusionist model is found in Alois R. Nykl, *Hispano-Arabic Poetry, and*

Its Relations with the Old Provençal Troubadors (Geneva: Slatkine Reprints, 1974); J. T. Monroe, "Formulaic Diction and the Common Origin of Romance Lyric Tradition," *Hispanic Review* 34 (1975): 341–50, as well as Compton, *Andalusian Lyrical Poetry.*

26. See Muhammad Ben Cheneb, *Encyclopaedia of Islam,* s.v. "Abū Nāṣr al-Fatḥ bin Ḥaqan."

27. Al-Fatḥ ibn Ḥakan, *Qalāʾid al-ʿIqyān* (Marseille: n.p., 1860). The entire selection is found in French translation in Henri Pérès, "La poésie à Fes sous les Almoravides et les Almohades," *Hespéris* 18 (1934): 13.

28. Cited in Pérès, "La poésie à Fes," 27, from Ṣafwan Ibn Idrīs, *Zad al-musāfir,* ms. 355, fol. 2b-3a, fol. 2a.

29. See *Zad al-musāfir,* ms. 355, fol. 2a–b; 356, fol. 1b; and Pérès, *La poésie* à Fes, 29–30.

30. See L. Massignon, *La passion d'al-Hosayn Ibn Mansour al-Hallaj: Martyr mystique de l'Islam* (Paris: Paul Geuthner, 1922), 1:61

31. Ibid., 1:405; 2:526, sec. 852.

32. See I. Goldziher, *Introduction au livre de Mohammed Ibn Toumert* (Algeria: P. Fontana, 1903), 11, 56.

33. Found in Ibn al-ʿArabī's *Risālat al-Mubashshirāt,* included in Yuṣuf al-Nabhānī's *Saʿdat al-Darayn fī al-Ṣalat ʿala Sayyid al-Kawnayn* (Beirut, n.d.). Translated in James Winston Morris, "Seeking God's Face: Ibn ʿArabi on Right Action and Theophanic Vision," part 2, *Journal of the Muhyiddin ibn ʿArabi Society* 17 (1995): 1.

34. Translated in Vincent J. Cornell, *The Way of Abū Madyan* (Cambridge: Islamic Texts Society, 1996).

35. Al-Fatḥ Ibn Ḥakan, *Qalāʾīd al-ʿIqyān,* 118.

36. Ibid., 196. A French translation is found in Henri Pérès, *La poésie andalouse en arabe classique* (Paris: Adrien-Maisonneuve, 1953), 63.

37. See L. Massignon, *Essai sur les origines du lexique technique de la mystique musulmane* (Paris: J. Vrin, 1922), 268.

38. See Compton, *Andalusian Lyrical Poetry,* 3, citing S. M. Stern, *Les chansons mozarabes* (Palermo: n.p., 1953), reprinted, Oxford: Oxford University Press, 1964.

39. Compton, *Andalusian Lyrical Poetry,* 129n1.

40. Al-Jirārī, "Qaṣīdah," 37n.

41. Ibid., 37.

42. Abbās al-Jirārī, *Muwashshaḥāt maghribiyya* [Moroccan muwashshaḥāt] (Casablanca: Dar an-Nashr al-Maghribiyya, 1973), 43–55.

43. Alan Jones, "Sunbeams from Cucumbers? An Arabist's Assessment of the State of *Kharja* Studies," *La Corónica* 10 (1981): 47–49. For a repudiation of some aspects of his article, see Samuel G. Armistead, "Speed or Bacon? Further Meditations on Professor Alan Jones' 'Sunbeams,'" *La Corónica* 10, no. 1 (1981): 38–53; and Samuel G. Armistead and James T. Monroe, "Beached Whales and Roaring Mice: Additional Remarks on Hispano-Arabic Strophic Poetry," *La Corónica* 13, no. 2 (1985): 206–42.

44. See Maḥmūd ʿAlī Makki, ed., *al-Muqtābas min Anbāʾi ahli l-Andalus* (Beirut: Dar al-Kitāb al-ʿArabi, 1973), 32–33. Translated in James T. Monroe, "Which Came First, the Zajal or the Muwashshaha? Some Evidence for the Oral Origins of Hispano-Arabic Strophic Poetry," in *Oral Traditions* 4, no. 1–2 (January-May 1989): 53–54.

45. David Wulstan, "The *Muwassah* and *Zagal* Revisted," *Journal of the American Oriental Society* 102, no. 2 (April–June 1982): 258.

46. Philip Daniel Schuyler, "Comments," *La Corónica* 10 (1981–82): 263.

47. Jones, "Sunbeams from Cucumbers," 38.

48. Al-Jirārī, "Qaṣīdah," 28.

49. Ibid., 39.

50. Ibid., 39.

51. Mohammed el-Fasi, "Le Tarchoun de Ben ʿAlī Cherīf," *Hespéris Tomuda* 4 (1965): 39.

52. Ashḥab, interview by the author, Rabat, May 20, 1995, tape no. 2.

53. Al-Jirārī, "Qaṣīdah," 551.

54. Ibid., 360.

55. Al-Jirārī lists the most important dates and names of poets in "Qaṣīdah," 165–80.

56. See the Nāṣiriyya poem in al-Jirārī, "Qaṣīdah," 172.

57. Al-Jirārī, interview, November 1993.

58. See Muhammad Miftāḥ's dissertation on Sufi poetry, "al-Tayyāru al-Sūfiyu wu'l-miytāmu fī-l-andalusī wa al-maghribi" (Ph.D. dissertation, Muhammad V University, Rabat, 1990).

59. Al-Jirārī says the words "function" to educate, "Qaṣīdah," 240.

60. For a list of these terms, see al-Jirārī, "Qaṣīdah," 236.

61. For his analysis of Moroccan qaṣida structure, see al-Jirārī, "Qaṣīdah," 147–64.

62. Benchekroun suggests there were reciters of Qurʾān and tawḥīd in zāwiyas, which I take to mean that they took a public role in the zāwiya culture. Mohammed B. A. Benchekroun, *La vie intellectuale marocaine sous les Merinides et les Wattasides* (Fez: Imprimérie Mohammed V, 1974), 73.

63. Ameena Mareeni was heard in the king's soirée in 1995. Several women were mentioned by passers-by.

64. Julia A. Clancy-Smith, *Rebel and Saint: Muslim Notables, Populist Protest, Colonial Encounters (Algeria and Tunisia, 1800–1904)* (Berkeley: University of California Press, 1994), 231–53.

65. Translated by Jones, "Sunbeams from Cucumbers," 40; Henri Pérès in his *La poésie andalouse*, 145.

66. See Hatt, "A Tribal Saint," 2.

67. Al-Jirārī, "Qaṣīdah," 331–40.

68. Nabīl, interview by the author, Rabat, May 19, 1995, tape no. 3.

Chapter 5

1. See Ross E. Dunn, *Resistance in the Desert: Moroccan Responses to French Imperialism, 1881–1912* (London: Croom Helm, and Madison: University of Wisconsin Press, 1977), 48.

2. Muḥammad al-Nouhī, Moroccan historian, interview by author, 1999.

3. Yuṣuf bin Yahyia al-Taḍilī, *Al-Tashawwuf ilā Rijāl al-Taṣawwuf*, ed. Aḥmed Toufīq (Rabat: Faculty of Letters, 1984); it was also edited by Adolph Faure and published by the Institut des Hautes Études Marocaines (Rabat, 1958).

4. Perhaps the use of the hands predominates as a way to keep time. Note Mohammed el-Fasi, "La musique marocaine dite 'musique andalouse,'" *Hespéris Tamuda* 5 (1966): 105.

5. Muḥammad Darīf, *Muwashsha al-sultān (al-sharīf) bi al-Maghrib* (Casablanca: Afriqiyya al-Sharq, 1965), 88, 98. Note also Brahim Boutaleb, "Comptes Rendus Bibliographiques," review of *La zoauia de Dila: Son rôle religieux, scientifique et politique,* by Mohammed Hijji, *Hespéris Tamuda* 2 (1963): 415, where the same viewpoint is expressed.

6. Darīf, *Muwashsha al-sultān,* 88.

7. Doyle G. Hatt, "Religious Institutions and Religious Establishments in a Tribal Region of Southern Morocco," in *Networks of the Past: Regional Interaction in Archaeology,* ed. Peter D. Francis, F. J. Kense, and P. G. Duke, 214–15 (Calgary: University of Calgary Archaeological Association, 1981).

8. "The Burda in Praise of the Prophet Muhammad," trans. Stephan Sperl, in *Qaṣīda Poetry in Islamic Asia and Africa,* ed. Stefan Sperl and Christopher Shackle, 2:389–411 (Leiden: E. J. Brill, 1996) (hereafter, "The Burda").

9. See "The Burda," commentary on Būṣayrī, Sperl and Shackle, *Qaṣīda Poetry,* 473.

10. Jacque Berque, "The Rural System of the Maghrib," in *State and Society in Independent North Africa,* ed. Leon Carl Brown, 194 (Washington, D.C.: Middle East Institute, 1966).

11. W. M. Watt, *Islamic Political Thought* (Edinburgh: Edinburgh University Press, 1968), 40–41.

12. See Ann K. S. Lambton, *State and Government in Medieval Islam: An Introduction to the Study of Islamic Political Theory: The Jurists* (Oxford: Oxford University Press, 1981), 23; Hamid Dabashi, *Authority in Islam* (New Brunswick, N.J.: Transaction, 1989), 121–45.

13. See, for example, H. Capitaine, "Colonies noires de Kabylie," *Revue Africaine* 4 (1859): 73–77; J. Comhaire, "Notes on Africans in Muslim History," *Muslim World* 46 (1956): 335–44.

14. See Leon Carl Brown, "Color in Northern Africa," in *Daedalus,* no. 96 (spring 1967): 464–82.

15. Viviana Pâques, "Le monde des *gnawa,"* in *L'Autre et d'ailleurs: Hommage à Roger Bastide,* ed. Jean Poirier and François Raveau, 180 (Paris: Bager-Levrault, 1976). See also Viviana Pâques, "The Gnawa of Morocco: The Derdeba Ceremony," in *The Nomadic Alternative: Modes and Models of Interaction in the African-Asian Deserts and Steppes,* ed. Wolfgang Weissleder, 319–29 (Paris / La Havre: Mouton, 1978).

16. Bilāl, interview by author, Rabat, September 8, 1995, tape no. 8.

17. Some background on this issue is to be found in Oruno D. Lara, "Esclavage et révoltes négro-africaines dans l'Empire musulman du Haut Moyen Age," *Presence Africaine* 98, no. 2 (1976): 50–103; and Maurice Delafosse, "Les debuts des troupes noires du Maroc," *Hespéris* 3 (1923): 1–11. For modern material see Daniel J. Schroter, "Slave Markets and Slavery in Moroccan Urban Society," in *The Human Commodity: Perspectives on the Trans-Sahara Slave Trade,* ed. Elizabeth Savage, 185–213 (London: Frank Cass, 1992); and Ralph A. Austen, "The Mediterranean Islamic Slave Trade Out of Africa: A Tentative Census," in *The Human Commodity,* 214–47.

18. See G. Vadja, in *Encyclopaedia of Islam,* s.v. "Ham (Cham)"; and W. ʿArafat, in *Encyclopaedia of Islam,* s.v. "Bilāl b. Rabih."

19. Mohammed Ennaji, *Soldats, domestiques et concubines: L'Esclavage au Maroc au XIXe siecle* (Casablanca: Eddif, 1994), 106–7.

20. Ibid., 16–17.

21. Ibid., 18–19.

22. Comhaire, "Notes," 341.

23. F. Stark, *The Southern Gates of Arabia* (London: Granet, 1936), 51.

24. V. Loubignac, "Un saint berbère: Moulay Bou ʿAzza," *Hespéris* 1 & 2 (1943): 24.

25. Bilāl, interview by author, Rabat, July 26, 1995, tape no. 6.

26. Ibid.

27. Ibid.

28. D. Jemma indicates that ṭbiqa comes from the root *Ṭ B Q* from which the word *ṭabaqa* comes, signifying class, or level, or grade. "Les confréries noires et le ritual de la derdeba à Marrakech," *Libyca* 19 (1971): 245. It might also mean degree.

29. Crapanzano, *The Hamadsha,* 192, 200, 204.

30. Jemma identifies two in "Les confréries," 243; the writer of "el-Qçar el-Kebir," *Archives Marocaines,* vol. 2 (Paris: Ernest Leroux, 1905), identifies groups by color and notes there are eight, 201–2.

31. Eickelman argues that the sunni—or what he designates as "orthodox"—view about possession states reflects a "great tradition" and a "little tradition" on the issue, with the urban masses little interested in the phenomenon. Still, many Ginawa are now centered in towns and cities, so a much more refined model is needed. Dale F. Eickelman, "The Islamic Attitude towards Possession States," in *Trance and Possession States,* ed. Raymond Prince (Montreal: R. M. Bucke Memorial Society, 1968), 189–92.

32. Bilāl, interview by the author, Rabat, July 26, 1995, tape no. 6.

33. Louis Blin, "Les noirs dans l'Algerie contemporaire," *Jeune Afrique* 1273 (1972): 29.

34. For a groundbreaking study on the phenomenon, see Jonathan G. Katz, *Dreams, Sufism and Sainthood: The Visionary Career of Muḥammad al-Zawawi* (Leiden, New York, and Cologne: E. J. Brill, 1996).

35. Nabīl al-Jaiy, interview by author, Rabat, June 16, 1994, tape no. 1.

36. Abdullāh Larouī has a fine statement about the power of this baraka: "The Berber saint will be, according to this theory, the inheritor of an ancient role, and by means of this same inheritance will provide the boundaries of a true Islamization. The Berber zāwiya, home of the resident saint, is a symbol of a double reality, of both an autonomous yet dependent group, concentrated totally on the sacred." *Les origines sociales et culturelles du nationalisme marocain (1830–1912)* (Paris: François Maspero, 1977), 134.

37. For a discussion of the relationship of imagination and unveiling see William C. Chittick, *The Self-Disclosure of God: Principles of Ibn al-ʿArabī's Cosmology* (Albany: State University of New York Press, 1998), xxii.

38. This notion has to be mediated by the kind of ṭarīqa one is participating in; for example, there is a great difference between the Ḥarrāqiyya and the Bu Dshishiyya with regard to the munshid's performance. It is mediated by the following factors: (1) There are no instruments in the Bu Dshishiyya; (2) there are no texts exclusive to the Bu Dshishiyya; (3) the Bu Dshishiyya do not form a circle in the ḥaḍra, but stand in rows; (4) the rhythm is kept in the Bu Dshishiyya by the feet and by hitting the chest, just as is done in the ʿAissawiyya; (5) zajal are used during the ḥaḍra; and (6) most of the murīdīn are intellectuals and professionals.

39. Philip Daniel Schuyler, "The Master Musicians of Jahjouka," *Natural History* 92 (October 1983): 60–61. Sīdī Ḥmed Shaikh came from the East to draw the people in the northwestern corner of Morocco to Islam, and he did so by his amazing baraka that even tamed a lion to pull a plow. Healing still predominates at his shrine.

Chapter 6

1. Marcia Herndon and Norma McLeod, *Music as Culture,* 2d ed. (Darby, Pa.: Norwood Editions, 1981), 119.

2. Paul Friedrich, *The Language Parallax: Linguistic Relativism and Poetic Indeterminancy* (Austin: University of Texas Press, 1986), 36.

3. David P. McAllester, *Peyote Music,* Publications in Anthropology no. 13 (New York: Viking Fund, 1949), 4. See also Philip V. Bohlman, "Ethnomusicology's Challenge to the Canon: The Canon's Challenge to Ethnomusicology," in *Disciplining Music: Musicology and Its Canons,* ed. Katherine Bergeron and Philip V. Bohlman, 118–36 (Chicago: University of Chicago Press, 1992).

4. Mahmoud Guettat, *La musique classique du Maghreb* (Paris: Sindbad, 1980), 188, following Muḥammad b. Ghāzī, *al-Rawzh al-ḥatūn fī akhbār miknasa al-zaytān* (Rabat: Royal Press, 1964).

5. See Reynold Nicholson, *The Mystics of Islam* (London: Routledge and Kegan Paul, 1966), 63–64; Abū Naṣr ʿAbdallāh ibn ʿAlī al-Ṣarrāj al-Tūsī, *Kitāb al-Lumaʿ fī l-Taṣawwuf,* ed. Reynold A. Nicholson (London: Luzac, and Leiden: E. J. Brill, 1914), 287.

6. The best sociocultural approach to music in Islam is clearly Ammon Shiloah, *Music in the World of Islam* (Detroit: Wayne State University Press, 1995). See 40–43 for his discussion of mystical music.

7. Ahmed Aydoun, "Les musiques sacrés du Maroc," *Revue Maroc Europe* 6 (1994): 146.

8. Henry G. Farmer, *Encyclopaedia of Islam,* s.v. "Ghinā<V>z."

9. See Henry G. Farmer, *A History of Arabian Music to the XIIIth Century* (London: Luzac, 1973), 110–16.

10. James T. Monroe seems to see a complex relationship between Andalusian poetry and song: "Poetic Quotation in the *Muwassaha and Its Implications: Andalusian Strophic Poetry as Song," La Corónica* 14 (1985/86): 230–50.

11. Guettat, *La musique classique,* 28n2.

12. Lois al-Faruqi, "The Nature of the Musical Art of Islamic Culture: A Theoretical and Empirical Study of Arabian Music" (Ph.D. diss., Syracuse University, 1974), 15–34.

13. See Lester P. Monts, "Conflict, Accommodation and Transformation: The Effect of Islam on Music of the Vai Secret Societies," *Cahiers d'Études Africaines* 24 (1995): 321–42.

14. The assignment of music to an inferior place in the understanding of culture likely has its roots in functionalism. The critique from an ethnomusicological standpoint is Chernoff's: "The variety and the complexity of the ways in which human societies have organized institutional life bent and twisted the functionalist interpretive scheme, loosening its hold on its terminological and empirical base and making its insights occasionally seem reductive and superficial. Attempts at further theoretical sophistication have often led to sophistry, and nowadays the assumption that any and all descriptive data are grist for the functionalist ethnological mill is no longer accepted." John M. Chernoff, "The Relevance of Ethnomusicology to Anthropology," in *African Musicology: Current Trends,* ed. Jacqueline C. Djedje and William G. Carter, 67 (Los Angeles: African Studies Center and Crossroads Press, 1989).

15. See Edouard Michaux-Bellaire, *Les confréries religieuses au Maroc* (Rabat: Protectorate de la Republique Française au Maroc, 1923), 58ff.; and his "Essai sur l'histoire des confréries marocaines," *Hespéris* 1 (2d trimester, 1921): 148.

16. Abū ʿAbdallāh Muḥammad b. ʿAbd al-Raḥman al-Jazūlī (d. 1465).

17. J. Christoph Bürgel, "Repetitive Structures in Early Arabic Prose," in *Critical Pilgrimages: Studies in the Arabic Literary Tradition,* ed. Fedwa Malti-Douglas, vol. of Literature East and West, 62 (Austin: Department of Oriental and African Languages and Literatures, University of Texas, 1989).

18. Guettat, *La musique classique,* 95–97.

19. al-Faruqi, "Nature of Musical Art," 153.

20. See Rodolphe d'Erlanger, *La musique arabe* (Paris: Paul Geuthner, 195), 6:162.

21. Guettat, *La musique classique,* 126n1. There he also indicates that there is apparently another kind of muwashshaḥ in the Yemen, but it is a poetic form based entirely on an Arab dialect.

22. See David Muddyman, "Markets, Moussems, Mosques: Music of the Kingdom of Morocco," in *World Music: The Rough Guide,* ed. Simon Broughton, Mark Ellington, David Muddyman, and Richard Tillop, 117 (London: Rough Guides, 1994).

23. al-Faruqi, "Nature of Musical Art," 155.

24. d'Erlanger, *La musique arabe,* 6:173.

25. Ulf Haxen, "Hargas in Hebrew Muwassahas," *al-Qantara: Revista de Estudios Arabes* 3 (1982): 473–82, esp. 475; G. Reese, *Music in the Middle Ages* (New York: Norton, 1968).

26. See Guettat,*La musique classique,* 223n1.

27. See Herbert Schneider, "Die Parodieverfahren Igor Stravinskis" *Acta Musicologica* 54 (1982): 285f. Ibn Khaldūn, *The Muqaddimah,* 3:391.

28. Muddyman, "Markets, Moussems, Mosques," 118.

29. Crapanzano, *The Hamadsha,* 88.

30. Ben Cherīfa, interview; Guettat, *La musique classique,* 187n1.

31. Muddyman, "Markets, Moussems, Mosques," 119.

32. Guettat, *La musique classique,* 121.

33. Ibid., 124.

34. Ibid., 124–25.

35. *Diwān Ibn al-Fāriḍ* (Cairo: Maktabāt al-Qahīra, n.d.).

36. Abū al-Laṭīf Muḥammad bin Mansoura, *Al-Kuwakba al-*Yusefiyya (Rabat: al-Amin Press, 1970).

37. The entire seventh poem (pp. 132–33) from *Diwān Ibn Al-Fāriḍ* reads thus:

> If I plead to see the truth, do allow me, and never offer "no" as an answer.
> Ah, my heart! In love, you promised . . .
> Patience!! Take care not to begrudge or grumble
> (You promised) that love was life, and
> you would die for love, without passing away.
> Say to all those (lovers) who came before me, and all those who came after
> And to those who saw my anguish
> "Take me as an example!!"
> (For) they would gossip about my young love behind my back.
> I was alone with my beloved,
> Moments more tender than a breath of air.
> My eyes caught a glimpse of hope
> Was acknowledged, and yet was denied.
> I lived in all the beauty and strength
> Compassion could articulate for me.
> In your eyes, the reflection
> The beauty shimmering above
> Could all beauty be portrayed,
> It would be filled with joy and ecstasy.

38. Section titled "Drouj nūbāt gharība al-Ḥusain," 7–9.

39. Desmond Stewart, "The Difficult Muse," *Encounter* 20 (1963): 51.

40. Muddyman, *World Music,* 120–21.

41. L. Justinard, "Notes d'histoire et de litterature berbères," *Hespéris* 5 (1925): 229.

42. Quoted in Guettat, *La musique classique,* 98.

43. A fine and judicious study of gender positioning in Islam is Sachiko Murata, The *Tao of Islam: A Sourcebook on Gender Relationships in Islamic Thought* (Albany: State University of New York Press, 1992).

44. See my examination of a female public chanter, in Waugh, *Munshidīn of Egypt,* 143–47.

45. Ashḥab, interview by the author, Rabat, May 20, 1995, tape no. 2. Much more research must be done on the role of women in the zāwiya. Women were very much in evidence all through my work, taking active part in most aspects of the social life of the orders. I am reluctant to say that they are derivative in any way just because they do not predominate in the dhikr. Pamela Johnson discusses this issue in her dissertation on an ʿAissawiyya zāwiya in Tunisia, "A Sufi Shrine in Modern Tunisia" (Ph.D. diss., University of California, Los Angeles, 1979), chap. 4.

46. Jean During, *Musique et extase* (Paris: Albin Michel, 1988), 163–66.

47. Gilbert Rouget, *Music and Trance: A Theory of the Relations between Music and Possession* (Chicago: University of Chicago Press, 1985).

48. Lester L. Monts, "Vai Women's Roles in Music, Masking, and Ritual Performance," in Djedje and Carter, *African Musicology,* 1:230.

49. Fazlur Rahman, *Islam,* 2d ed. (Chicago: University of Chicago, 1979), 126; Earle H. Waugh, "Beyond Scylla and Kharybdis: Fazlur Rahman and Islamic Identity," in *The Shaping of an American Islamic Discourse,* ed. Earle H. Waugh and Frederick M. Denny, 15–36 (Atlanta, Ga.: Scholars Press, 1998).

50. Francisco Salvador-Daniel, *Musique et instruments de musique du Maghreb* (Algeria, 1867; repr., Paris: La Boîte à Documents, 1986), 157–59.

51. See Muddyman, "Markets, Moussems, Mosques," 117.

52. Muḥammed el-Nouhī, interview by the author, Rabat, May 15, 1998, tape no. 7.

53. Crapanzano, *The Hamadsha,* 76.

54. See al-Faruqi, "Nature of Musical Art," 149.

55. Herndon and McLeod, *Music as Culture,* 119.

56. Monts, "Via Women's Roles," 230.

57. We will have occasion below to survey Ziryāb's contribution to what is known as musicotherapy, by which the "trees of mode" or "trees of temperament" express similar relationships between the body and earth/heaven as exist between physical and psychological states.

58. Waugh, *Munshidīn of Egypt,* 183–85.

59. See Wayne Slawson, *Sound Color* (Berkeley: University of California Press, 1985), and "Features, Musical Operations, and Composition: A Derivation from Ewe Drum Music," in Djedje and Carter, *African Musicology,* 1:308–11; D. Locke and G. K. Agbeli, "Drum Language in Adzogbo," *The Black Perspective in Music* 9, no. 1 (1981): 25–50.

60. See Philip Daniel Schuyler, "A Repertory of Ideas: The Music of the 'Rwais.' Berber Professional Musicians from Southwestern Morocco" (Ph.D. diss., University of Washington, 1979).

61. Jonathan D. Hill, *Keepers of the Sacred Chants: The Poetics of Ritual Power in an Amazonian Society* (Tucson and London: University of Arizona Press, 1993), 203.

62. Ashhab, interview by the author, Rabat, August 20, 1995, tape no. 6.

63. Guettat, *La musique classique,* 369.

64. James T. Koetting, "Africa/Ghana," in *Worlds of Music: An Introduction to the Music of the World's Peoples,* general ed. Jeff Todd Titon, 67–68 (New York: Schirmer Books, 1984).

65. Bin Mansour, interview by the author, Rabat, August 1995, tape no. 6.

66. Muhammad al-Turābī, interview by the author, April 28, 1995, tape no. 2.

67. Al-Jirārī, "Qasīdah," 480.

68. Guettat, *La musique classique,* 362.

69. Ibid., 195n1.

70. Muhammed al-Nouhī, interview by the author, Agadir, August 1995, tape no. 7.

71. Sometimes the results are not very flattering. Qawwali music is used as background for *Eyes Wide Shut* during the most erotic parts of the movie, a travesty as far as the original music is concerned.

72. See Philip Daniel Schuyler, "A Folk Revival in Morocco," in *Everyday Life in the Muslim Middle East,* ed. D. L. Bowen and E. A. Early, 264–65 (Bloomington: Indiana University Press, 1993).

Chapter 7

1. See Julius Lipner, *Hindus: Their Religious Beliefs and Practices* (New York: Routledge, 1994), 25–30.

2. The term "mystification" originates, I think, with Hill, *Keepers of the Sacred Chants,* 202, but he uses it to refer to "the transformation of mythic speech into relatively stable lines of chanted and sung speech." This means that the shaman/singer "knows" the mythic realities and modifies them into chant so that the ordinary person can understand them. Mutational facility is his calling. The munshid does not do that. By expressing the power phrases, the mythic appears, giving content to the Presence.

3. Based on an interview of Muhammad Bennīs by the author, Fez, July 1995, and a follow-up interview, Fez, October 2000, tape nos. 4 and 12, respectively.

4. Bennīs, interview by the author, Fez, July 1995, tape no. 4.

5. Bennīs, interview by the author, Fez, October 2000, tape no. 12.

6. Nabīl al-Jaiy, interview by the author, Rabat, June 16, 1994, tape no. 1.

7. Ben Cherīfa, interview by the author, Rabat, May 30, 1995, tape no. 2.

8. Chittick, *Self-Disclosure of God,* xxii.

9. Valerie J. Hoffman, "Annihilation in the Messenger of God: The Development of a Sufi Practice," *International Journal of Middle East Studies* 31 (1999): 351–69n12.

10. "Muhammad" is not his real name, since I was not able to confirm the scenario with him.

11. Ashhab, interview by the author, Rabat, August 20, 1995, tape no. 6.

12. There is another explanation, drawn from ethnographical material on the shaman, whose similarities are striking to the munshid: he may just not have had confidence, like Chini. See Laurel Kendall, "Chini's Ambiguous Initiation," in *Shamans and Cultures,* ed. Mihaly Hoppal and Keith D. Howard, 15–26 (Los Angeles: International Society for Trans-Oceanic Research, 1993). The principal difference is, of course, that Chini was just

being introduced to the spirit world, while Muḥammad had been a long-time practitioner. Munshidūn can be "strong," however, or "weak," depending on their perceived spiritual power, which is reminiscent of shamanism. Cf. Cora DuBois, *Wintu Ethnography,* vol. 36 of Publications in American Archeology and Ethnology (Berkeley: University of California Press, 1935).

13. al-ʿArabī al-Darqāwī, *Letters of a Sufi Master,* 32. For a discussion of "knowledge of certainty" (*ʿilm al-yaqīn*), see chapter 6, note 90.

14. al-ʿArabī al-Darqāwī, *Letters of a Sufi Master,* 9.

15. See Janice Boddy, *Wombs and Alien Spirits: Women, Men, and the Zar Cult in Northern Sudan* (Madison: University of Wisconsin Press, 1989), 134f.

16. For a discussion of the merging of emotions and the physical, see the section titled "Islamic Memory: Remembrance as a Way of Knowledge," in chapter 2 of this volume.

17. Aḥmad, interview by the author, Meknes, July 3, 1995, tape no. 6. For a different view, see Henry Munson Jr., "The Social Base of Islamic Militancy in Morocco," in *Middle East Journal* 40, no. 2 (spring 1986): 269–71.

18. Ashḥab did mention that the director of the munshidūn in the Ḥarrāqiyya dhikr was a known drinker; he was reputed to drink Scotch straight. This was regarded, however, as a peculiarity to him. Ashḥab himself never used alcohol and sought his inspiration from something different: God. He thought getting involved with these things was morally and religiously wrong.

19. Ashḥab, interview by the author, Rabat, August 20, 1995, tape no. 6.

20. Fāṭima al-Yazīdī, "Kitābu al-durr al-munaddam fī maulidī al-nabiyi al-Aʿdami, al-Sīdī (533–557h)" (Masters thesis, Muhammad V University, 1990–91).

21. Ibn Marzūq, *al-Masnad al-ṣaḥīḥ al-ḥasan fī māʾāthīr mawlānā Abi al-Ḥasan (al-sultān)* (Madrid: Instituto Hispana Arabe de Cultura, 1977).

Chapter 8

1. Saad Abdullah Sowayan, *Nabati Poetry: The Oral Poetry of Arabia* (Berkeley, Los Angeles, and London: University of California Press, 1985), 95.

2. J.-L. Michon, "L'Autobiographie (*Fahrasa*) du Soufi marocain Ahmad Ibn ʿAïba (1747–1809)," *Arabica* 16, no. 3 (June 1969): 124–25. He calls these attitudes an interior *adab*.

3. The issue of intercession is a favorite challenge by the Islamists. For an interesting analysis of Ibn Taymiyya and the Egyptian debate over intercession, see Julian Johansen, *Sufism and Islamic Reform in Egypt* (Oxford: Clarendon Press, 1996), 104–14.

4. Richard Werbner, ed., *Memory and the Postcolony: African Anthropology and the Critique of Power* (London and New York: Zed Books, 1998). This collection includes articles by Brigit Meyer and Rijk van Dijk, among others, that point out the difficulties of coming to terms with the remembered religious past.

5. For a very recent study that draws somewhat the same conclusion but from a ritual perspective, see Paulo Pinto, "Mystical Bodies: Ritual, Experience and the Embodiment of Sufis in Syria" (Ph.D. diss., Boston University, 2002). I wish to thank one of my reviewers for bringing this study to my attention.

SELECTED BIBLIOGRAPHY

Abun-Nasr, Jamil M. *The Tijaniyya: A Sufi Order in the Modern World.* Oxford: Oxford University Press, 1965.

Afifi, A. E. *The Mystical Philosophy of Muhyid Dīn-Ibnul ʿArabi.* Cambridge: Cambridge University Press, 1939.

Ainī, Mehmet Ali. *Un grand saint de l'Islam, Abd-al-Kadir Guilānī, 1077–1166.* 1938; Paris: Paul Geuthner, 1967.

Almond, Philip C. *Mystical Experience and Religious Doctrine: An Investigation of the Study of Mysticism in World Religions.* Berlin, New York, and Amsterdam: Mouton, 1982.

al-Ammary, Fadhl ibn Ammar. "Application of Oral Tradition Theory on Pre-Islamic Poetry." *Journal of the College of Arts, King Saud University* 14, no. 1 (1987): 39–61.

Amrous, M. "Les confréries religieuses et l'Islamisme au Maroc au XIX et XXc." Doctoral diss., University of Nanterre, 1986.

Antoun, Richard. "On the Modesty of Women in Arab Villages: A Study in the Accommodation of Traditions." *American Anthropologist* 70, no. 4 (1968): 671–97.

Apter, Michael J. "Religious States of Mind: A Reversal Theory Interpretation." In *Advances in the Psychology of Religion,* edited by L. B. Brown, 62–75. Oxford: Pergamon Press, 1985.

al-ʿArabī al-Darqāwī. *Letters of a Sufi Master.* Translated by Titus Burckhardt. London: Perennial Books, 1973.

ʿArafat, W. *Encyclopaedia of Islam,* s.v. "Bilāl b. Rabih."

Arazi, A. *Encyclopaedia of Islam,* s.v. "Shīʿr."

Armistead, Samuel G. "Speed or Bacon? Further Meditations on Professor Alan Jones' 'Sunbeams.'" *La Corónica* 10, no. 1 (1981): 38–53.

Armistead, Samuel G., and James T. Monroe. "Beached Whales and Roaring Mice: Additional Remarks on Hispano-Arabic Strophic Poetry." *La Corónica* 13, no. 2 (1985): 206–42.

Augustine, Saint. *Confessions and Enchiridion.* Edited and translated by Albert C. Outler. Philadelphia: Westminster Press, 1955.

Austen, Ralph A. "The Mediterranean Islamic Slave Trade Out of Africa: A Tentative Census." In *The Human Commodity: Perspectives on the Trans-Saharan Slave Trade,* edited by Elizabeth Savage, 214–47. London: Frank Cass, 1992.

Austin, R. W. J., trans. *Sufis of Andalusia: The "Rūḥ al-Quds" and "al-Durrat al-Fākhirah" of Ibn ʿArabī.* London: George Allen and Unwin, 1971.

Aydoun, Ahmed. *Musiques du Maroc.* Casablanca: Eddif, 1993.

———. "Les musiques sacrées du Maroc." *Revue Maroc Europe* 6 (1994): 145–50.

Azmi, Mohammad Mustafa. *Studies in Early Hadīth Literature: With a Critical Edition of Some Early Texts.* Indianapolis, Ind.: American Trust Publications, 1978.

Banaji, Mahzarin R., and Curtis Hardin. "Affect and Memory in Retrospective Reports."

In *Autobiographical Memory and the Validity of Retrospective Reports,* edited by Norbert Schwarz and Seymour Sudman, 71–86. New York: Springer-Verlag, 1994.

Beeston, A. L., et. al. *Arabic Literature to the End of the Umayyad Period.* Cambridge: Cambridge University Press, 1983.

Bel, A. *La religion musulmane en Berbèrie.* Paris: Paul Geuthner, 1938.

Benchekroun, Mohammed B. A. *La vie intellectuale marocaine sous les Merinides et les Wattasides.* Fez: Imprimerie Mohammed V, 1974.

ben Cheneb, Muhammad. *Encyclopedia of Islam,* s.v. "Abū Nāsr al-Fath bin-Hagan."

Bennani-Chraibi, Mounia. *Soumis et rebelles: Les jeunes au Maroc.* Paris: CNRS Éditions, 1994.

Bennigsen, Alexandre. "Official Islam and Sufi Brotherhoods in the Soviet Union Today." In *Islam and Power,* edited by Alexander S. Cudsi and Ali E. Hillal Dessouki, 95–106. London: Croom Helm, 1981.

Berque, Jacque. "De nouveau sur les Bani Hilal?" *Studia Islamica* 56 (1972): 7–11.

———. "The Rural System of the Maghrib." In *State and Society in Independent North Africa,* edited by Leon Carl Brown, 170–94. Washington, D.C.: Middle East Institute, 1966.

Blau, J. "Le rôle des cheikhs Naqshbandi dans le mouvement national kurde." In *Naqshbandis,* edited by M. Gaborieau, A. Popovic, and T. Zarcone, 371–77. Istanbul: Institut Français d'Études Anatoliennes, and Paris: Institut Français de Recherches en Iran, 1990.

Blin, Louis. "Les noirs dans l'Algérie contemporaire," *Jeune Afrique* 1273 (1972): 22–31.

Boase, Roger. Foreword to *Ibn Saᶜid al-Maghribī,* in *The Banners of the Champions: an Anthology of Medieval Arabic Poetry from Andalusia and Beyond,* sel. and trans. James A. Bellamy and Patricia Owen Steiner. Madison: Hispanic Seminary of Medieval Studies, 1989.

Boddy, Janice. *Wombs and Alien Spirits: Women, Men, and the Zar Cult in Northern Sudan.* Madison: University of Wisconsin Press, 1989.

Bodin, Marcel. "La Zouia de Tamegrout." *Les Archives Berbères* 3 (1918): 259–93.

Bohlman, Philip V. "Ethnomusicology's Challenge to the Canon: The Canon's Challenge to Ethnomusicology." In *Disciplining Music: Musicology and Its Canons,* edited by Katherine Bergeron and Philip V. Bohlman, 118–36. Chicago: University of Chicago Press, 1992.

Bourguignon, Erika, ed. *Religion, Altered States of Consciousness, and Social Change.* Columbus: Ohio State University Press, 1973.

Boutaleb, Brahim. "Comptes rendus bibliographiques." Review of *La Zoauia de Dila: Son rôle religieux, scientifique et politique,* by Mohammed Hijji. *Hespéris Tamuda* 2 (1963): 415–17.

Bowering, Gerhard. *The Mystical Vision of Existence in Classical Islam: The Qurʾānic Hermeneutics of the Sūfi Sahl at-Tūstarī, d. 283/896.* Berlin: Walter de Gruyter, 1980.

Bowers, K. S. "On Being Unconsciously Influenced and Informed." In *The Unconscious Reconsidered, edited* by K. S. Bowers and D. Meichenbaum, 227–72. New York: Wiley, 1984.

Bringhurst, Robert. *Native American Oral Literatures and the Unity of the Humanities.* Vancouver: Department of English, University of British Columbia, 1998.

Brown, Kenneth L. *People of Salé: Tradition and Change in a Moroccan City, 1830–1930.* Manchester: Manchester University Press, 1976.

Brown, Leon Carl. "Color in Northern Africa." *Daedalus* 96 (spring 1967): 464–82.

———, ed. *State and Society in Independent North Africa.* Washington, D.C.: Middle East Institute, 1966.

Brunel, René. *Essai sur les confréries religieuses des ʿAïssouïa au Maroc.* Paris: Paul Geuthner, 1926.

Brunschvig, Robert. "Discussion and Comments." In *Unity and Variety in Muslim Civilization,* edited by Gustave E. von Grunebaum, 254–59. Chicago: University of Chicago Press, 1956.

Bucke, R. M. *Cosmic Consciousness: A Study of the Evolution of the Human Mind.* Philadelphia: Innes and Sons, 1901.

———. *Man's Moral Nature.* Toronto: Willing and Williamson, 1897.

Bürgel, J. Christoph. "Qasida as Discourse on Power and Its Islamization: Some Reflections." In *Qasida Poetry in Islamic Asia and Africa,* edited by Stefan Sperl and Christopher Shackle, 1:451–73. Leiden, New York, and Cologne: E. J. Brill, 1996.

———. "Repetitive Structures in Early Arabic Prose." In *Critical Pilgrimages: Studies in the Arabic Literary Tradition,* ed. Fedwa Malti-Douglas, vol. of Literature East and West, 49–64. Austin: University of Texas, Department of Oriental and African Languages, 1989.

Burke, Michael. *Among the Dervishes.* London: Octagon Press, 1973.

Burton, John. *The Collection of the Qurʾān.* Cambridge: Cambridge University Press, 1977.

Calvert, John. "The Individual and the Nation in Twentieth-Century Egyptian Autobiography: Sayyid Qutb's *Tifl min al-qarya* (A child from the village)." *Muslim World* 90, nos. 1 & 2 (spring 2000): 107–32.

Capitaine, H. "Colonies noires de Kabylie." *Revue Africaine* 4 (1859): 73–77.

Carlton-Ford, Steven L. *The Effects of Ritual and Charisma: The Creation of Collective Effervescence and the Support of Psychic Strength.* New York and London: Garland Publishing, 1993.

Chelhod, Jacques. "La baraka chez les Arabes ou l'influence bienfaisante du sacré." *Revue de l'Historie des Religions* 148 (1955): 68–88.

Chernoff, John M. "The Relevance of Ethnomusicology to Anthropology." In *African Musicology: Current Trends,* edited by Jacqueline Cogdell Djedje and William G. Carter, 59–92. Los Angeles: African Studies Center and Crossroads Press, 1989.

Chittick, William C. "Between Cairo and the Algerian Kabylia: The Rahmaniyya *Tariqa,* 1715–1800." In *Muslim Travellers: Pilgrimage, Migration, and the Religious Imagination,* edited by Dale F. Eickelman and James Piscatori, 200–215. Berkeley: University of California Press, 1990.

———. *The Self-Disclosure of God: Principles of Ibn al-ʿArabī's Cosmology.* Albany: State University of New York Press, 1998.

———. "The Theological Roots of Peace and War According to Islam." *Islamic Quarterly* 33, no. 1 (1989): 145–63.

Clancy-Smith, Julia A. *Rebel and Saint: Muslim Notables, Populist Protest, Colonial Encounters: Algeria and Tunisia, 1800–1904.* Berkeley: University of California Press, 1994.

Comhaire, J. "Notes on Africans in Muslim History." *Muslim World* 45 (1956): 335–44.

Compton, Linda Fish. *Andalusian Lyrical Poetry and Old Spanish Love Songs: The Muwashshahah and Its Kharja.* New York: New York University Press, 1976.

Connelly, Bridget. *Arab Folk Epic and Identity.* Berkeley: University of California Press, 1986.

Connerton, Paul. *How Societies Remember.* Cambridge: Cambridge University Press, 1989.

Cornell, Vincent J. *The Way of Abū Madyan.* Cambridge: Islamic Texts Society, 1996.

Corriente, F. "The Metres of the *Muwaṣṣaḥ,* an Andalusian Adaptation of ʿArūd (a Bridging Hypothesis)." *Journal of Arabic Literature* 13 (1982): 76–82.

Coward, Harold, and David Goa. *Mantra: Hearing the Divine in India.* Chambersburg, Pa.: Amina Books, 1991.

Craib, Ian. *Experiencing Identity.* London: Sage Publications, 1998.

Crapanzano, Vincent. *The Hamadsha: A Study in Moroccan Ethnopsychiatry.* Berkeley and London: University of California Press, 1973.

Curran, Tim, and Daniel L. Schacter. "Implicit Memory and Perceptual Brain Mechanisms." In *Basic and Applied Memory Research Theory in Context,* edited by D. Herrmann, C. McEvoy, C. Hertzog, P. Hertel, and M. K. Johnson, 1:221–40. Mahwah, N.J.: Lawrence Erlbaum, 1996.

Dabashi, Hamid. *Authority in Islam.* New Brunswick, N.J.: Transaction Publishers, 1989.

Darīf, Muḥammad. *Muwashshaḥ al-sultān (al-sharīf) biʾl-maghrib.* Casablanca: Afriqiyya al-Sharq, 1965.

Davidson, Hilda Ellis. *Roles of the Northern Goddesses.* London: Routledge, 1998.

de Jong, Frederick. "Materials Relative to the History of the Darqāwiyya Order and Its Branches." *Arabica* 26, no. 2 (June 1979): 126–43.

———. *Turuq and Turuq-Linked Institutions in Nineteenth-Century Egypt.* Leiden: E. J. Brill, 1978.

Delafosse, Maurice. "Les debuts des troupes noires du Maroc." *Hespéris* 3 (1923): 1–11.

de Man, Paul. "Literary History and Literary Modernity," *Daedalus* 99 (1970): 38.

Dermenghem, Emile. *L'Éloge du vin: Poem mystique de ʿOmar ibn al-Faridh.* Paris: Véga, 1931.

Derrida, Jacques. "Structure, Sign, and Play in the Discourse of the Human Sciences." In *The Languages of Criticism and the Sciences of Man: The Structuralist Controversy,* edited by Richard Macksey and Eugenio Donato, 247–72. Baltimore: Johns Hopkins University Press, 1970.

Dexter, Miriam Robbins. *Whence the Goddesses: A Source Book.* New York: Teachers College Press, 1990.

Diwān Ibn al-Fāriḍ. Cairo: Maktabat al-Qāhira, n.d.

Douglas, Mary. *Natural Symbols.* London: Barrie and Rockliff, 1970.

Drague, Georges. *Esquisse d'histoire religieuse du Maroc: Confréries et Zaouias.* Cahiers de l'Afrique et l'Asie, vol. 2. Paris: J. Peyronnet, n.d.

DuBois, Cora. *Wintu Ethnography.* Publications in American Archeology and Ethnology. Berkeley: University of California Press, 1935.

Dunn, Ross E. *Resistance in the Desert: Moroccan Responses to French Imperialism, 1881–1912.* London: Croom Helm, and Madison: University of Wisconsin Press, 1977.

During, Jean. *Musique et extase.* Paris: Albin Michel, 1988.

Durkheim, E. *The Rules of Sociological Method.* 1895. London: Collier-Macmillan, 1964.

Dwyer, Daisy Hilse. "Women, Sufism and Decision-Making." In *Women in the Muslim World,* edited by Lois Beck and Nikki Keddie, 586–98. Cambridge, Mass.: Harvard University Press, 1978.

Eakin, Paul J. *Fictions of the Self: Studies in the Art of Self-Invention*. Princeton, N.J.: Princeton University Press, 1985.

Eickelman, Dale F. "The Art of Memory: Islamic Education and Its Social Reproduction." *Comparative Studies in Society and History* 20, no. 4 (Oct. 1978): 485–516.

————. "The Islamic Attitude towards Possession States." In *Trance and Possession States*, edited by Raymond Prince, 189–92. Montreal: R. M. Bucke Memorial Society, 1968.

————. *Knowledge and Power in Morocco: The Education of a Twentieth-Century Notable*. Princeton, N.J.: Princeton University Press, 1985.

————. *Moroccan Islam: Tradition and Society in a Pilgrimage Center*. Austin: University of Texas Press, 1976.

Eickelman, Dale F., and James Piscatori, eds. *Muslim Travellers: Pilgrimage, Migration, and the Religious Imagination*. Berkeley and Los Angeles: University of California Press, 1990.

Eliade, Mircea. *Myth and Reality*. New York: Harper and Row, 1963.

————. *The Quest: History and Meaning in Religion*. Chicago: University of Chicago Press, 1969.

————. *Shamanism: Archaic Techniques of Ecstasy*. Translated by Willard R. Trask. New York: Bollingen Foundation, 1964.

Ennaji, Mohammed. *Soldats, domestiques et concubines: L'Esclavage au Maroc au XIXe siècle*. Casablanca: Eddif, 1994.

d'Erlanger, Rodolphe. *La musique arabe*. 6 vols. Paris: Paul Geuthner, 1959.

Evans-Pritchard, E. *Theories of Primitive Religion*. Oxford: Clarendon Press, 1965.

Farmer, Henry George. S.v. "Ghinā'." In *Encyclopaedia of Islam*, vol. 2, new edition. Edited by E. van Donzel, B. Lewis, and Ch. Pellat, 1072–75. Leiden: E. J. Brill, 1978.

————. *A History of Arabian Music to the XIIIth Century*. 1929. Reprint, London: Luzac, 1973.

al-Faruqi, Lois. "Music, Musicians and Muslim Law." *Asian Music* 17, no. 1 (1985): 3–36.

————. "Muwashshaḥāh: A Vocal Form in Islamic Culture." *Ethnomusicology* 19, no. 1 (1975): 1–29.

————. "The Nature of the Musical Art of Islamic Culture: A Theoretical and Empirical Study of Arabian Music." Ph.D. diss., Syracuse University, 1974.

el-Fasi, Mohammed. "La musique marocaine dite 'musique andalouse.'" *Hespéris Tamuda* 5 (1966): 79–106.

————. "Le tarchoun de Ben ʿAlī Cherīf." *Hespéris Tamuda* 4 (1965): 39–45.

Finegan, Jack. *Jesus, History and You*. Richmond, Va.: John Knox Press, 1964.

Fletcher, Madeleine de Gogorza. "Poetry and Music of Muslim Spain: *Zegels, Muwashshahs,* and *Cantigas*." *La Corónica* 10 (1981–82): 254–67.

Friedrich, Paul. *The Language Parallax: Linguistic Relativism and Poetic Indeterminacy*. Austin: University of Texas Press, 1986.

Gadon, Elinor W. *The Once and Future Goddess*. San Francisco and New York: Harper and Row, 1989.

Geertz, Clifford. *The Interpretation of Cultures*. New York: Basic Books, 1973.

————. *Islam Observed*. New Haven, Conn.: Yale University Press, 1968.

————. "Religion as a Cultural System." In *Anthropological Approaches to the Study of Religion*, edited by Michael Banton, 3:1–46. American Society of Anthropology Monographs. London: Tavistock, 1979.

Gellner, Ernest. *Muslim Society.* Cambridge: Cambridge University Press, 1981.

———. *Saints of the Atlas.* London and Chicago: Weidenfeld and Nicolson, 1969.

al-Ghazālī, Abū-Ḥamid Muḥammad. *Iḥyaᶜulum al-dīn* [*Revival of the Religious Sciences*]. Translated by Fazul-ul-Karim. Lahore: Sind Sagar Academy, 1971.

Ghazi, Muhammad b. *Al-Rawzh al-ḥatun fi akhbār miknasa al-zaytān.* Rabat: Royal Press, 1964.

Gibson, J. J. *The Ecological Approach to Visual Perception.* Boston: Houghton Mifflin, 1979.

Gill, David. "The *Muwashshaḥ*: Artistic Convention or Cognitive Universal." *Israel Oriental Studies* 2 (1991): 137–59.

Gill, Sam. *Sacred Words: A Study of Navajo Religion and Prayer.* Westport, Conn.: Greenwood Press, 1981.

Girard, René. *Critiques dans un souterrain.* Paris: Grasset, 1976.

———. *Deceit, Desire, and the Novel.* Translated by Yvonne Freccero. Baltimore: Johns Hopkins University Press, 1966.

———. *Job, the Victim of His People.* Translated by Yvonne Freccero. Stanford, Calif.: Stanford University Press, 1987.

———. *A Theater of Envy: William Shakespeare.* New York: Oxford University Press, 1991.

———. "Theory and Its Terrors." In *The Limits of Theory,* edited by Thomas Kavanagh, 225–54. Stanford, Calif.: Stanford University Press, 1989.

———. *Things Hidden since the Foundation of the World.* Translated by Stephen Bann and Michael Metteer. Stanford, Calif.: Stanford University Press, 1987.

Goldziher, Ignace. *Introduction au livre de Mohammed Ibn Toumert.* Algeria: P. Fontana, 1903.

———. *Muhammedanische Studien.* 1850–1921; Hildesheim: Georg Olms Verlag, 1971.

Goleman, Daniel. *Emotional Intelligence.* New York: Bantam Books, 1995.

Goodman, Felicitas D. *Ecstasy, Ritual and Alternate Reality: Religion in a Pluralistic World.* Bloomington: Indiana University Press, 1988.

———. *Where the Spirits Ride the Wind: Trance Journeys and Other Ecstatic Experiences.* Bloomington: Indiana University Press, 1990.

Gouilly, Alphonse. *Islam dans l'A.O.F.* Paris: Larose, 1952.

Graham, William. *Divine Word and Prophetic Word in Early Islam.* The Hague: Mouton, 1977.

Grandguillaume, Gilbert. "Islam et politique au Maghreb." In *L'Islam et l'état,* edited by Olivier Carré, 45–64. Paris: Presses Universitaires de France, 1982.

Gril, Denis. "Le *Kitab al-inbahᶜala Ṭarīq Allāh* de ᶜAbdallāh Badr al-Ḥabāshi: un temoignage de l'enseignment spirituel de Muḥyīd-d-din Ibn ᶜArabī." *Annales Islamologiques* 15 (1979): 97–148.

Guettat, Mahmoud. *La musique classique du Maghreb.* Paris: Sindbad, 1980.

Haas, William S. "The Zikr of the Raḥmānija-Order in Algeria." *Moslem World* 33, no. 1 (January 1943): 16–28.

al-Ḥabasi, Badr. "Un temoignage de l'enseignment spirituel de Muhyi l-din Ibn ᶜArabi." *Annales Islamogiques* 15 (1972): 437–72.

Hagopian, C. E. "The Status and Role of the Marabout in Pre-Protectorate Morocco." *Ethnology* 3 (1964): 42–52.

Hammoudi, D. *La victime et ses masques.* Paris: Levil, 1988. Translated by Paula Wissing as *The Victim and Its Masks: An Essay on Sacrifice and Masquerade in the Maghreb.* Chicago: University of Chicago Press, 1993.

Hanna, Judith Lynne. *To Dance Is Human: A Theory of Nonverbal Communication.* Austin: University of Texas Press, 1979.

Harris, W. B. *The Morocco That Was.* Edinburgh: Edinburgh University Press, 1921. Reprint, London: Eland, 1983.

Hatt, Doyle G. "Establishing 'Tradition': The Development of Chiefly Authority in the Western High Atlas Mountains of Morocco." *Journal of Legal Pluralism and Unofficial Law* 37–38 (1996): 123–53.

————. "Religious Institutions and Religious Establishments in a Tribal Region of Southern Morocco." In *Networks of the Past: Regional Interaction in Archeology,* edited by Peter D. Francis, F. J. Kense, and P. G. Duke, 213–18. Calgary: University of Calgary Archeological Association, 1981.

————. "Sainthood in Christianity and Islam." Selected Proceedings, Sixth Annual Meeting of the Canadian Ethnology Society, 2–18. National Museum of Canada, Ottawa, 1981.

————. "A Tribal Saint of the Twentieth Century." In *An African Commitment: Papers in Honour of Peter Lewis Shinnie,* edited by Judy Sterner and Peter Lewis Shinnie, 3–30. Calgary: University of Calgary Press, 1992.

Haxen, Ulf. "Hargas in Hebrew Muwassahas." *Al-Qantara: Revista de Estudios Arabes* 3 (1982): 473–82.

Hay, David. "Religious Experience and Its Induction." In *Advances in the Psychology of Religion,* edited by L. B. Brown, 147. Oxford: Pergamon Press, 1985.

Herndon, Marcia, and Norma McLeod. *Music as Culture.* 2d ed. Darby, Pa.: Norwood Editions, 1981.

Herndon, Marcia, and Roger Brunyate, eds. *Proceedings on Form in Performance, Hard-Core Ethnography.* Austin: College of Fine Arts, University of Texas, 1975.

Hervieu-Léger, Danièle. *Religion as a Chain of Memory.* Translated by Simon Lee. New Brunswick, N.J.: Rutgers University Press, 2000.

Hesiod. *Theogony.* In *Hesiod.* Translated by Richmond Lattimore. Ann Arbor: University of Michigan Press, 1959.

Hewes, Gordon W. "The Current Status of the Gestural Theory of Language Origin." In *Origins and Evolution of Language and Speech,* edited by Stevan R. Harnad, Horst D. Steklis, and Jane Lancaster, 482–504. New York: New York Academy of Sciences, 1976.

Hill, Jonathan D. *Keepers of the Sacred Chants: The Poetics of Ritual Power in an Amazonian Society.* Tucson and London: University of Arizona Press, 1993.

Hodgson, Marshall G. S. *The Venture of Islam: Conscience and History in a World Civilization.* 3 vols. Chicago: University of Chicago Press, 1974.

Hoffman, Valerie J. "Annihilation in the Messenger of God: The Development of a Sufi Practice." *International Journal of Middle East Studies* 31 (1999): 351–69.

————. *Sufism, Saints and Mysticism in Modern Egypt.* Columbia: University of South Carolina Press, 1995.

The Hudsailian Poems. Contained in the Manuscript of Leyden. Edited in Arabic and translated with annotation by John Godfrey Lewis Kosegarten. 2 vols. 1854. Reprint, Hildesheim: Georg Olms Verlag, 1984.

Ibn al-ʿArabī, Muḥyi ad-dīn Abū Bakr Muḥammad bin ʿAlī. *The Bezels of Wisdom* (Fuṣūṣ al-ḥikam). Translated by R. W. J. Austin. New York: Paulist Press, 1980.

———. *Al-Futūḥāt al-Makkiyyah*. 4 vols. Cairo: Bulaq, 1911.

Ibn ʿAtaʾillāh. *Al-Ḥikam Ibn ʿAṭāʾillāh*. Edited by ʿAbd al-Halim Mahmud. Translated by Victor Danner as *The Book of Wisdom: Sufi Aphorisms*. Leiden: E. J. Brill, 1973.

Ibn Ḥakan, al-Fath. *Qalāʾid al-ʿIqyān*. Marseille: n.p., 1860.

Ibn Isḥāq. *Sīrat Rasūl Allāh*. *Translated* by A. Guillaume as *The Life of Muhammad*. Lahore: Oxford University Press, 1953.

Ibn Khaldūn, ʿAbd ar-Raḥman. *Al-Muqaddimah*. Translated by Franz Rosenthal as *The Muqaddimah: An Introduction to History*. 3 vols. 2:430–31. Princeton, N.J.: Princeton University Press, 1967.

Ibn Marzuq. *Al-Musnad al-saḥiḥ al-hasān fī maʿathir mawlanā ʿabi al-Ḥasan (al-sultān)*. Madrid: Instituto Hispaña Arabe de Cultura, 1977.

Ibn Qutayba. *Al-Shiʿr waʾl-shuʿarā*. Edited by de Goeje. Translated and annotated by A. J. Arberry as *The Mystical Poems of Ibn al-Fāriḍ*. Dublin: Emery Walker, 1956.

Idris, H. R. *Encyclopaedia of Islam*, s.v. "Hilāl."

Jacobs, W. J., and L. Nadel. "Stress-Induced Recovery of Fears and Phobias." *Psychological Review* 92 (1985): 512–31.

Jemma, D. "Les confréries noires et le ritual de la derdeba á Marrakech." *Libyca* 19 (1971): 243–50.

al-Jirārī, Abbās Ibn ʿAbdullāh. *Muwashshaḥāt maghribiyya* [Moroccan muwashshaḥāt]. Casablanca: Dar an-Nashr al-Maghribiyya, 1973.

———. "Al-Qaṣīdah." Ph.D. diss., University of Cairo, 1970.

———. "Qaṣīda al-Malḥūn." In *Fiʾl Ibdā al-Shiʿri*. Rabat: Islamic Education Scientific and Cultural Organization, 1972, 59–102.

Johnson, Julian. *Sufism and Islamic Reform in Egypt*. Oxford: Clarendon Press, 1996.

Johnson, Pamela. "A Sufi Shrine in Modern Tunisia." Ph.D. diss., University of California, Los Angeles, 1979.

Jones, Alan. "Sunbeams from Cucumbers? An Arabist's Assessment of the State of *Kharja* Studies." *La Corónica* 10 (1981): 38–53.

———, ed. and trans. *Early Arabic Poetry*. Reading, England: Ithaca Press for Oxford University, 1992.

Joseph, Terri Brint. Review of *The Oral Tradition of Classical Arabic Poetry: Its Character and Implication*, by Michael Zwettler. *Arab Studies Quarterly* 3, no. 1 (winter 1981): 106–9.

Justinard, L. "Notes d'histoire et de litterature berbères." *Hespéris* 5 (1925): 227–38.

Katz, Jonathan G. *Dreams, Sufism and Sainthood: The Visionary Career of Muhammad al-Zawawi*. Leiden, New York, and Cologne: E. J. Brill, 1996.

Katz, Steven. "Language, Epistemology and Mysticism." In *Mysticism and Philosophical Analysis,* edited by S. Katz, 22–74. London: Sheldon Press, 1978.

Kauffman, Robert. "African Rhythm: A Reassessment." *Ethnomusicology* 24, no. 3 (September 1980): 393–415.

Kendall, Laurel. "Chini's Ambiguous Initiation." In *Shamans and Cultures,* edited by Mihaly Hoppal and Keith D. Howard, 15–26. Los Angeles: International Society for Trans-Oceanic Research, 1993.

Kennedy, James. "Psychological and Social Explanations of Witchcraft." *Man* 2 (1967): 216–25.

Kilani, Mondher. *La construction de la memoire: Le lineage et la saintéte dans l'oasis d'El Ksar.* Geneva: Éditions Labor et Fides, 1992.

Kinsley, David. *Hindu Goddesses.* Berkeley: University of California Press, 1986.

Knappert, J. *Encyclopaedia of Islam,* 2d ed., s.v. "Mawlid."

Koetting, James T. "Africa/Ghana." In *Worlds of Music: An Introduction to the Music of the World's Peoples,* general editor Jeff Todd Titon, 67–68. New York: Schirmer Books, 1984.

Kotre, John. *White Gloves: How We Create Ourselves through Memory.* New York: Free Press, 1995.

Kugel, James L., ed. *Poetry and Prophecy.* Ithaca, N.Y.: Cornell University Press, 1990.

Kuper, Hilda, with Diane Weiner and Beth Rosen-Prinz. "The Power of Secrecy in the Political Process." In *Africa in World History: Old, New, Then, and Now,* edited by Michael W. Coy Jr. and Leonard Plotnicov, 79–91. Pittsburgh, Pa.: Dept. of Anthropology, University of Pittsburgh, 1995.

Laird, James D. "Mood Affects Memory Because Feelings *Are* Cognitions." *Mood and Memory: Theory, Research, and Applications,* edited by Don Kuiken, 33–38. Newbury Park, Calif., and London: Sage Publications, 1991.

Lambton, Ann K. S. *State and Government in Medieval Islam: An Introduction to the Study of Islamic Political Theory: The Jurists.* Oxford: Oxford University Press, 1981.

Landolt, Herman. "Mystical Experience in Islam." In *Personality Change and Religious Experience,* edited by Raymond Prince. 70–76. Montreal: R. M. Bucke Memorial Society for the Study of Religious Experience, 1965.

———. *Encyclopaedia of Islam,* s.v. "Khalwa."

Landow, George P. *Hypertext: The Convergence of Contemporary Critical Theory and Technology.* Baltimore: Johns Hopkins University Press, 1992.

Lara, Oruno D. "Esclavage et révoltes négro-africaines dans l'Empire musulman du Haut Moyen Age." *Presence Africaine* 98, no. 2 (1976): 50–103.

Larouī, Abdullāh. *Les origines sociales et culturelles du nationalisme marocain (1830–1912).* Paris: François Maspero, 1977.

Latham, J. Derek. "New Light on the Scansion of an Old Andalusian *Muwaṣṣah.*" *Journal of Semitic Studies* 27, no. 1 (spring 1982): 61–75.

LeDoux, Joseph. *The Emotional Brain: The Mysterious Underpinnings of Emotional Life.* New York: Simon and Schuster, 1996.

———. "Emotion as Memory: Anatomical Systems Underlying Indelible Neural Traces." In *The Handbook of Emotion and Memory: Research and Theory,* edited by S. Christianson, 269–88. Hillsdale, N.J.: Lawrence Erlbaum, 1992.

Lennick, Alison. "Taghribat Banī Hilāl al-Dayaghim: Variations in the Oral Epic Poetry of the Najd." Ph.D. diss., Princeton University, 1984.

Lings, Martin. "Mystical Poetry." In *Abbasid Belles-lettres,* edited by J. Ashtiany et al. Cambridge: Cambridge University Press, 1990.

———. *A Sufi Saint of the Twentieth Century.* 1961. Berkeley: University of California Press, 1973.

Lipner, Julius. *Hindus: Their Religious Beliefs and Practices.* New York: Routledge, 1994.

Locke, D., and G. K. Agbeli. "Drum Language in Adzogbo." *Black Perspective in Music* 9, no. 1 (1981): 25–50.

Lord, Albert. *Singer of Tales.* Cambridge, Mass.: Harvard University Press, 1964.

Loubignac, V. *Étude sur le dialecte des Zaian et des Ait Sgougou.* Paris: E. LeRoux, 1924.

———. "Un saint berbère: Moulay Bou ʿAzza." *Hespéris* 3 (1923): 15–34.

Luizard, Pierre-Jean. "Le rôle des confréries soufies dans le système politique égyptien." *Monde Arabe Maghreb Machrek* 131 (January-March 1991): 26–48.

Lyall, Charles James, ed. and trans. *The Mufaddaliyat: An Anthology of Ancient Arabian Odes Compiled by al-Mufaddal Son of Muhammad according to the reclension and with the Commentary of Abu Muhammad al-Qasim ibn Muhammad al-Anbari.* Vol. 1, *Arabic Text.* Vol. 2, *Translation and Notes.* Oxford: Clarendon Press, 1918–21.

al-Maghribi, Ibn Saʿid. *The Banners of the Champions: An Anthology of Medieval Arabic Poetry from Andalusia and Beyond.* Selected and translated by James A. Bellamy and Patricia Owen Steiner. Madison: University of Wisconsin, 1989.

Makki, Mahmud ʿAli. *Al-Muqtābas min Anbāʾi ahli-l-Andalus.* Beirut: Dar al-Kitāb al-ʿArabi, 1973.

Marcais, Georges. *La berbérie musulmane et l'orient au moyen age.* Casablanca: Afrique Orient, 1918.

Markus, H., and Z. Kunda. "Stability and Malleability of the Self-Concept." *Journal of Personality and Social Psychology* 51 (1983): 858–66.

Massignon, L. *Essai sur les origines du lexique technique de la mystique musulmane.* Paris: J. Vrin, 1922.

———. *La passion d'al-Hosayn Ibn Mansour al-Hallaj: Martyr mystique de l'Islam.* 3 vols. Paris: Paul Geuthner, 1922.

McAllester, David P. *Peyote Music.* Publications in Anthropology, no. 13. New York: Viking Fund, 1949.

Mercier, L. "Note sur la mentalité religieuse dans la région de Rabat et de Salé." *Archives Marocaines* 6 (1906): 423–35.

Merleau-Ponty, M. *Phenomenology of Perception.* Translated by Colin Smith. London: Routledge, 1962.

Metcalf, Barbara D. "What Happened in Mecca: Mumtaz Mufti's *Labbaik.*" In The *Culture of Autobiography: Constructions of Self-Representation,* edited by Robert Folkenflik, 149–67. Stanford, Calif.: Stanford University Press, 1993.

Michael, James. *The Politics of Secrecy.* Harmondsworth, England: Penguin, 1982.

Michaux-Bellaire, Edouard. *Les confréries religieuses au Maroc.* Rabat: Protectorate de la Republique Française au Maroc, 1923.

———. "Essai sur l'histoire des confréries marocaines." *Hespéris* 1 (2d trimester 1921): 141–59.

Michon, J.-L. "L'Autobiographie (*Fahrasa*) du Soufi marocain Ahmad Ibn ʿAïba (1747–1809)." *Arabica* 16, no. 3 (1969): 129–46.

Miftāḥ, Muhammad. "Al-Tayyāru al-Sūfiyu wuʾl-miytamāu fi-l-andalusī wa al-maghribi." Ph.D. diss., Muhammad V University, Rabat, 1990.

Miller, Patrick D., Jr., Paul D. Hanson, and S. Dean McBride, eds. *Ancient Israelite Religion.* Philadelphia: Fortress Press, 1987.

Molé, Marijan. "La danse extatique en Islam." In *La danses sacrées,* Sources Orientales 6. 147–79. Paris: Seuil, 1963.

Monroe, James T. "Formulaic Diction and the Common Origin of Romance Lyric Tradition." *Hispanic Review* 34 (1975): 341–50.

———. "Poetic Quotation in the *Muwassaha* and Its Implications: Andalusian Strophic Poetry as Song." *La Corónica* 14 (1985/86): 230–50.

————. "Which Came First, the *Zajal* or the *Muwaṣṣaha?* Some Evidence for the Oral Origins of Hispano-Arabic Strophic Poetry." *Oral Tradition* 4, nos. 1–2 (1989): 38–64.

Montagne, Robert. *Les Berbères et le makhzen dans le sud du Maroc.* Paris: Alcan, 1931. Translated by David Seddon as *The Berbers: Their Social and Political Organisation.* London: Frank Cass, 1973.

Monteil, Vincent. *Islam noir.* Paris: Seuil, 1964.

Montet, Edouard. *Les cultes des saints musulmans dans Afrique du Nord et plus spécialement au Maroc.* Geneva: Librairie Georg, 1909.

Monts, Lester L. "Conflict, Accommodation and Transformation: The Effect of Islam on Music of the Vai Secret Societies." *Cahiers d'Études Africaines* 24 (1995): 321–42.

————. "Vai Women's Roles in Music, Masking, and Ritual Performance." *African Musicology: Current Trends,* edited by Jacqueline Cogdell Djedje and William G. Carter, 1:219–35. Los Angeles: African Studies Center and African Arts Magazine, 1989.

Morris, James Winston. "Seeking God's Face: Ibn ʿArabi on Right Action and Theophanic Vision." Part 2. *Journal of the Muhyiddin ibn ʿArabi Society* 17 (1995): 1–39.

Morsy, Mogali. *Les Ahansala: Examen du rôle historique d'une famille maraboutique de l'Atlas marocain.* Paris: Mouton, 1972.

El-Moudden, Abderrahmane. "The Ambivalence of *Rihla*: Community Integration and Self-Definition in Moroccan Travel Accounts, 1300–1800." In *Muslim Travellers: Pilgrimage, Migration, and the Religious Imagination,* edited by Dale F. Eickelman and James Piscatori, 69–84. Berkeley: University of California Press, 1990.

Muddyman, David. "Markets, Moussems, Mosques: Music of the Kingdom of Morocco." In *World Music: The Rough Guide,* edited by Simon Broughton, Mark Ellington, David Muddyman, and Richard Tillop, 115–23. London: Rough Guides, 1994.

Murata, Sachiko. *The Tao of Islam: A Sourcebook on Gender Relationships in Islamic Thought.* Albany: State University of New York Press, 1992.

*Muṣḥaf al-Madīnah al-*Nabawiyyah (*The Holy Qurʾān: English Translation of the Meanings and Commentary*). Revised and edited by the Presidency of Islamic Researches, IFTA, Call and Guidance, based on translation of Abdallāh Yusuf ʿAlī. Medina, Saudi Arabia: King Fahd Holy Qurʾān Printing Complex, 1991.

Muslim, Ibn al-Hajjaj al-Qurhayrī. *Saḥīḥ Muslim.* Translated by ʿAbdul Hamīd Ṣiddīqī. 4 vols. Lehore: Sh. Muhammad Ashraf, 1976.

Nagy, Gregory. "The Crisis of Performance." In *The Ends of Rhetoric: History, Theory, Practice,* edited by John Bender and David E. Wellberg. 43–49. Stanford, Calif.: Stanford University Press, 1990.

Neisser, Ulric. "Nested Structure in Autobiographical Memory." In *Autobiographical Memory,* edited by David C. Rubin, 71–81. Cambridge: Cambridge University Press, 1986.

Nelson, Katherine. "The Psychological and Social Origins of Autobiographical Memory." *Psychological Science* 4 (1993): 7–14.

Nelson, Kristina. *The Art of Reciting the Qurʾān.* Austin: University of Texas Press, 1985.

Nicholson, Reynold A. *A Literary History of the Arabs.* Cambridge: Cambridge University Press, 1954.

————. *The Mystics of Islam.* London: Routledge and Kegan Paul, 1966.

————. *Studies in Islamic Mysticism.* Cambridge: Cambridge University Press, 1921.

Nykl, Alois R. *Hispano-Arabic Poetry, and Its Relations with the Old Provençal Troubadors.* Geneva: Slatkine Reprints, 1974.

Olsen, Carl. *Book of the Goddess Past and Present: An Introduction to Her Religion.* New York: Crossroads, 1983.

Otto, Rudolph. *The Idea of the Holy.* Translated by John W. Harvey. New York: Oxford University Press, 1958.

Pâques, Viviana. "The Gnawa of Morocco: The Derbeba Ceremony." In *The Nomadic Alternative: Modes and Models of Interaction in the African-Asian Deserts and Steppes,* edited by Wolfgang Weissleder, 319–29. The Hague: Mouton, 1978.

———. "Le monde des *gnawa.*" In *L'Autre et l'ailleurs: Hommage á Roger Bastide,* edited by Jean Poirier and François Raveau, 169–82. Paris: Bager-Levrault, 1976.

Paquignon, Paul. "Le mouloud au Maroc." *Revue du Monde Musulmane* 14, no. 4 (1911): 525–36.

Patai, Raphael. *The Hebrew Goddess.* New York: Avon Books, 1978.

Pérès, Henri. *Esplendor de al-Andalus.* Translated from the French by Mercedes Garcia-Arenal. 1937. Madrid: Libros Hiperion, 1953.

———. "La poésie á Fes sous les Almoravides et les Almohades." *Hespéris* 18 (1934): 9–40.

Peters, Larry G., and Douglas Price-Williams. "A Phenomenological Overview of Trance." *Transcultural Psychiatric Research Review* 20 (1983): 5–39.

Pike, Nelson. "Comments." In *Art, Mind and Religion,* edited by W. H. Capitan and D. D. Merrill, 144–50. Proceedings of the Sixth Oberlin Colloquium in Philosophy, 1965. Pittsburgh, Pa.: University of Pittsburgh Press, 1967.

Pinto, Paulo. "Mystical Bodies: Ritual, Experience and the Embodiment of Sufism in Syria." Ph.D. diss., Boston University, 2002.

Plotinus. *On the Nature of the Soul, Being the Fourth Ennaed.* Translated by Stephen MacKenna. London: The Medici Society, 1924.

Pritchard, James B. *Palestinian Figurines in Relation to Certain Goddesses Known through Literature.* AOS no. 24. New Haven, Conn.: American Oriental Society, 1943.

Rachik, Hassan. *Sacré et sacrifice dans le Haut Atlas marocain.* Casablanca: Afrique, 1990.

Radcliffe-Brown, A. *Structure and Function in Primitive Society.* London: Cohen and West, 1952.

Rahhal, M. Ben. "À travers les Beni Snassen." *Bulletin de la Sociéte de Geographie d'Oran,* no. 9 (1889): 5–50.

Rahman, Fazlur. *Islam.* 2d ed. Chicago: University of Chicago Press, 1979.

Rappoport, Roy A. *Ritual and Religion in the Making of Humanity.* Cambridge: Cambridge University Press, 1999.

———. *Pigs for the Ancestors.* New Haven, Conn.: Yale University Press, 1968.

Reese, Gustave. *Music in the Middle Ages.* New York: Norton, 1968.

Reynolds, Dwight F. "Heroic Poets, Poetic Heroes: Composition and Performance in an Arabic Oral Epic Tradition of Northern Egypt." Ph.D. diss., University of Pennsylvania, 1991.

———. "Sīrat Banī Hilāl: Introduction and Notes to an Arab Oral Epic Tradition." *Oral Tradition* 4, nos. 1–2 (1989): 80–100.

———, ed. *Interpreting the Self: Autobiography in the Arabic Literary Tradition.* Berkeley and Los Angeles: University of California Press, 2001.

Riskind, J. H. "The Mediating Mechanisms in Mood and Memory: A Cognitive Priming Formulation." In *Mood and Memory: Theory, Research and Applications,* edited by Donald Kuiken, 185–96. Newbury Park, Calif.: Sage, 1991.

————. "Nonverbal Expression and the Accessibility of Life Experience Memories." *Social Cognition* 2 (1983): 62–86.

Rouget, Gilbert. *Music and Trance: A Theory of the Relations between Music and Possession.* Chicago: University of Chicago Press, 1985.

Rubin, David C., ed. *Autobiographical Memory.* Cambridge: Cambridge University Press, 1986.

al-Ṣarrāj al-Tūsī, Abū Naṣr ʿAbdallāh ibn ʿAli. *Kitāb al-Lumaʿ fīʾl-Taṣawwuf.* Edited by Reynold A. Nicholson. London and Leiden: Luzac, E. J. Brill, 1914.

Salmi, Ahmed. "Le genre des poèmes de nativité (Maulūdiyya-s) dans le royaume de Grenade et au Maroc du XIIIe au XVIIe siècle." *Hespéris* 43 (1956): 335–435.

Salvador-Daniel, Francisco. *Musique et instruments de musique du Maghreb.* Algeria, 1867. Paris: La Boîte à Documents, 1986.

Savage, Elizabeth. *A Gateway to Hell, a Gateway to Paradise: The North African Response to the Arab Conquest.* Princeton, N.J.: Darwin Press, 1997.

Schacter, Daniel L. "Implicit Memory: History and Current Status." *Journal of Experimental Psychology* 13 (1987): 501–18.

Schärer, Hans. *Ngaju Religion: The Conception of God among a South Borneo People.* Translated by Rodney Needham. The Hague: Nijhoff, 1963.

Schimmel, Annemarie. *As Through a Veil: Mystical Poetry in Islam.* New York: Columbia University Press, 1982.

————. *Mystical Dimensions of Islam.* Chapel Hill: University of North Carolina, 1975.

————. "Understanding *JIHAD*: Definition and Methodology." *Islamic Quarterly* 27, no. 2 (1983): 118–31.

Schroter, Daniel J. "Slave Markets and Slavery in Moroccan Urban Society." In *The Human Commodity: Perspectives on the Trans-Saharan Slave Trade,* 185–213. London: Frank Cass, 1992.

Schubel, Vernon. "The Muharram Majlis: The Role of a Ritual in the Preservation of Shiʿa Identity." In *Muslim Families in North America,* edited by Earle H. Waugh, Sharon M. Abu-Laban, and Regula B. Qureshi, 118–31. Edmonton: University of Alberta Press, 1991.

Schuyler, Philip Daniel. "Comments." *La Corónica* 10 (1981–82): 263.

————. "A Folk Revival in Morocco." *Everyday Life in the Muslim Middle East,* edited by D. L. Bowen and E. A. Early, 264–70. Bloomington: Indiana University Press, 1993.

————. "The Master Musicians of Jahjouka." *Natural History* 92 (October 1983): 60–69.

————. "Music and Tradition in Yemen." *Asian Music,* 1990–91, 51–69.

————. "A Repertory of Ideas: The Music of the 'Rwais.' Berber Professional Musicians from Southwestern Morocco." Ph.D diss., University of Washington, 1979.

Sells, Michael A. "*Banat Suʿad:* Translation and Introduction." *Journal of Arabic Literature* 11, no. 2 (1990): 140–54.

————. *Mystical Languages of Unsaying.* Chicago and London: University of Chicago Press, 1994.

Shahīd, Irfan. *Byzantium and the Arabs in the Fifth Century.* Washington, D.C.: Dumbarton Oaks Research Library and Collection, 1989.

al-Shaibānī, ʿAbd al-Jawad Sayyid. "al-Hijra al-hilāliyya ila Ifriqiyya al-ziridiyya wa Atharuha al-hamma" (The Hilali migration to zirid Africa and its central effects) Ph.D. diss., Muhammad V University, Rabat, 1988.

Shiloah, Ammon. *Music in the World of Islam.* Detroit: Wayne State University Press, 1995.

Shinar, Pessah. "Traditional and Reformist Mawlid Celebrations in the Maghrib." In *Studies in Memory of Gaston Wiet,* edited by Myriam Rosen-Ayalon, 371–413. Jerusalem: Institute of Asian and African Studies, Hebrew University of Jerusalem, 1977.

Shorter Encyclopaedia of Islam. Edited by H. A. R. Gibb and J. H. Kramers. Ithaca, N.Y.: Cornell University Press, 1953.

Shoshan, Boaz. *Popular Culture in Medieval Cairo.* Cambridge: Cambridge University Press, 1993.

Sicard, F. "L'Amour dans la *risalat al-qiyan.* Essai sur les esclaves-chanteuse-de Gahiz." *Arabica* 34 (1987): 326–38.

Singer, Jefferson A., and Peter Salovey. *The Remembered Self: Emotion and Memory in Personality.* New York and Toronto: Free Press, 1993.

Slawson, Wayne. "Features, Musical Operations, and Composition: A Derivation from Ewe Drum Music." In *African Musicology: Current Trends,* edited by Jacqueline Cogdell Djedje and William G. Carter, 1:308–11. Los Angeles: African Studies Center and African Arts Magazine, 1989.

———. *Sound Color.* Berkeley: University of California Press, 1985.

Slobin, Mark. *Music in the Culture of Northern Afghanistan.* Tucson: University of Tucson Press, 1976.

Slyomovics, Susan. "Approaches to Transcription and Translation of Oral Epic Performance (Sīrat Banī Hilāl)." Paper presented at *Colloque Internationale sur les Banu-Hilal: Geste et Historie,* May 20–23, 1990, Centre National d'Études historiques, Algiers, Algeria.

———. *The Merchant of Art: An Egyptian Hilali Oral Epic Poet in Performance.* Berkeley: University of California Press, 1987.

Smith, Jonathan Z. *To Take Place: Toward Theory in Ritual.* Chicago and London: University of Chicago Press, 1987.

Sowayan, Saad Abdullah. *Nabati Poetry: The Oral Poetry of Arabia.* Berkeley, Los Angeles, and London: University of California Press, 1985.

Sperl, Stefan. "Islamic Kingship and Arabic Panegyric Poetry in the Early 9th Century." *Journal of Arabic Literature* 8 (1977): 20–35.

———, trans. "The Burda in Praise of the Prophet Muhammad." In *Qasida Poetry in Islamic Asia and Africa,* edited by Stefan Sperl and Christopher Shackle, 2:389–411. Leiden: E. J. Brill, 1996.

Squire, Larry R., Barbara Knowlton, and Gail Musen. "The Structure and Organization of Memory." In *Human Memory: A Reader,* edited by David R. Shanks, 153–83. London: Arnold, 1997.

Stark, F. *The Southern Gates of Arabia.* London: Granet, 1936.

Stern, S. M. *Les chansons mozarabes.* Palermo, 1953. Reprint, Oxford: Oxford University Press, 1964.

Stetkevych, Jaroslav. "Toward an Arabic Elegiac Lexicon." In *Reorientations: Arabic and Persian Poetry,* edited by Suzanne Stetkevych, 58–129. Bloomington: Indiana University Press, 1994.

Stetkevych, Suzanne P. *The Mute Immortals Speak: Pre-Islamic Poetry and the Poetics of Ritual.* Ithaca, N.Y., and London: Cornell University Press, 1993.

———, ed. *Reorientations: Studies in Arabic and Persian Poetics.* Bloomington: Indiana University Press, 1994.

Stewart, Desmond. "The Difficult Muse." *Encounter* 20 (1963): 46–51.

Stokes, Martin. *The Arabesk Debate: Music and Musicians in Modern Turkey.* Oxford: Oxford University Press, 1992.

al-Taḍilī, Yuṣuf bin Yahyia. *Al-Tashawwuf ilā Rijāl al-Taṣawwuf,* edited by Aḥmed Toufīq. Rabat: Faculty of Letters, 1984. Also edited by Adolph Faure. Rabat: Institut des Hautes Études Marocaines, 1958.

Taussig, Michael. *Mimesis and Alterity: A Particular History of the Senses.* New York: Routledge, 1993.

Terrasse, Henri. *Histoire du Maroc des origines à l'établissement du protectorat français.* 2 vols. Casablanca: Atlantides, 1952.

Thompson, C. P., J. J. Skowronski, S. F. Larsen, and A. L. Betz. "Reconstructive Memory for Time." In *Autobiographical Memory: Remembering What and Remembering When,* edited by Thompson, Skowronski, Larsen, and Betz, 101–23. Mahwah, N.J.: Lawrence Erlbaum, 1996.

Toelken, Barre. "Seeing with a Native Eye: How Many Sheep Will It Hold?" In *Seeing with a Native Eye,* edited by Walter H. Capps, 11–14. New York: Harper and Row, 1976.

Touma, Habib Hassan. "The *Maqam* Phenomenon: An Improvisation Technique in the Music of the Middle East." *Ethnomusicology* 15, no. 1 (January 1971): 38–48.

Turner, Victor. "Social Dramas and Stories about Them." *Critical Inquiry* 7, no. 1 (autumn 1980): 141–68.

al-Tustārī, Muḥammad Sahl ibn ʿabdullāh. *Tafsīr al-Qurʾān al-ʿAzīm.* Cairo: Dar al-Kūtūb al-Gharbiyya al-Kubra, 1911.

Vadja, G. *Encyclopaedia of Islam,* s.v. "Ham (Cham)."

Vikør, Knut S. "*Jihād, ʿIlm* and *Taṣawwuf*—Two Justifications of Action from the Idrīsī Tradition." *Studia Islamica* 84 (2000): 153–76.

———. *Sufi and Scholar on the Desert Edge: Muḥammad b. ʿAlī al-Sanūsī and His Brotherhood.* Evanston, Ill., and London: Northwestern University Press, 1995.

———. "Sufism and Revolt: Tijānis, Sanūsis, and Safavids." Paper presented at Middle East Studies Association conference, November 21–24, 1996.

von Denffer, Deitrich. "Baraka as Basic Concept of Muslim Popular Belief." *Islamic Studies* 15, no. 3 (autumn 1976): 167–86.

von Grunebaum, Gustave E. "The Aesthetic Foundation of Arabic Literature." *Comparative Literature* 3 (1951): 323–40.

von Stuckrad, Kocku. "The Formation of Shamanic Discourses in Religious Studies and Esotericism: Studies on the Interdependency of Academic Research and Religious Practice." Unpublished research project, 2000.

Watt, W. M. *Islamic Political Thought.* Edinburgh: Edinburgh University Press, 1968.

Waugh, Earle H. "Beyond Scylla and Kharybdis: Fazlur Rahman and Islamic Identity." In *The Shaping of an American Islamic Discourse,* edited by Earle H. Waugh and Frederick M. Denny, 15–36. Atlanta, Ga.: Scholars Press, 1998.

———. *Dissonant Worlds: Roger Vandersteene among the Cree.* Waterloo: Wilfrid Laurier University Press, 1989.

———. *The Munshidīn of Egypt: Their World and Their Song.* Columbia: University of South Carolina Press, 1989.

———. "Religious Levitation and the Muslim Experience: A Study in the Flight

Symbolism of Intermediary Figures and Other Images in Medieval Islam." Ph.D. diss., University of Chicago, 1972.

———. "Silence and the Speech of God in the Mawlid al-Muhammadi of the Demirdashiyya." *Studies in Religion* 17, no. 1 (1988): 53–64.

Weber, Max. *Economy and Society: An Outline of Interpretive Sociology.* Edited by Guenther Roth and Claus Wittich. Translated by Ephraim Fischoff. 1968. Berkeley: University of California Press, 1978.

Welte, Frank M. *Der Gnawa-Kult: Trancespiele, Geisterbeschwörung und Besessenheit in Marokko.* Frankfurt am Main: Peter Lang, 1990.

Wendt, Carol Card. "North Africa: An Introduction." In *The Garland Encyclopedia of World Music: Africa.* New York and London: Garland, 1998.

Werbner, Richard, ed. *Memory and the Postcolony: African Anthropology and the Critique of Power.* London and New York: Zed Books, 1998.

Westermarck, Edward. *Pagan Survivals in Mohammedan Civilisation.* 1933. Amsterdam: Philo Press, 1973.

———. *Ritual and Belief in Morocco.* 2 vols. London: Macmillan, 1926.

Wittgenstein, Ludwig. "Remarks on Frazer's *Golden Bough.*" Translated by A. C. Miles and Rush Rhees. *Human World,* no. 3 (May 1971): 36.

Wulstan, David. "The *Muwassah* and *Zagal* Revisted." *Journal of the American Oriental Society* 102, no. 2 (April-June 1982): 247–64.

Wyman, Leland C. *Blessingway: With Three Versions of the Myth Recorded and Translated from the Navajo by Father Berard Haile, OFM.* Tucson: University of Arizona Press, 1970.

Yates, Francis A. *The Art of Memory.* London: Routledge and Kegan Paul, 1966.

al-Yazīdī, Faṭīma. *Kitābu al-duʿa al-muʿazzami fī maulidī al-nabiyyi al-Mūʿazzami al-Sīdī (533–557h).* M.A. thesis, Muhammad V University, Rabat, 1990–91.

Yerushalmi, Josef Hayim. *Zakhor: Jewish History and Jewish Memory.* Seattle and London: University of Washington Press, 1982.

al-Yunus, ʿAbd al-Ḥamid. *Al-Hilāliyya fīʾl-taʿrikh wa-l-ādāb al-shaʿabi.* 2d ed. Cairo: Dar al-Māʿrifa, 1968.

Zimmer, Heinrich. *Philosophies of India.* Edited by Joseph Campbell. Princeton, N.J.: Princeton University Press and Bollingen Foundation, 1951.

Zonis, Marvin. "Autobiography and Biography in the Middle East: A Plea for Psychohistorical Studies." In *Middle Eastern Lives: The Practice of Biography and Self-Narrative,* edited by Martin Kramer. Syracuse, N.Y.: Syracuse University Press, 1991.

Zumthor, Paul. *Introduction à la poésie orale.* Paris: Seuil, 1983.

Zwartjes, Otto. "Berbers in al-Andalus and Andalusis in the Maghrib as Reflected in *Tawshīḥ* Poetry." Orientations no. 4: *Poetry, Politics and Polemics: Cultural Transfer between the Iberian Peninsula and North Africa,* edited by O. Zwartjes, Geert Jan van Gelder, and Ed de Moor, 35–55. Amsterdam and Atlanta, Ga.: Rodopi, 1996.

Zwettler, Michael. "A Mantic Manifesto: The Sura of 'The Poets' and the Qurʿanic Foundations of Prophetic Authority." In *Poetry and Prophecy,* edited by James L. Kugel, 75–119. Ithaca, N.Y.: Cornell University Press, 1990.

———. *The Oral Tradition of Classical Arabic Poetry: Its Character and Implications.* Columbus: Ohio State University Press, 1978.

INDEX